AMSTERDAM

1ST EDITION

Where to Stay and Eat
for All Budgets

Must-See Sights
and Local Secrets

Ratings You Can Trust

Portions of this book appear in *Fodor's Holland*

Fodor's Travel Publications   New York, Toronto, London, Sydney, Auckland
www.fodors.com

FODOR'S AMSTERDAM

Editor: Robert I. C. Fisher

Editorial Production: Tom Holton
Editorial Contributors: Steve Korver, Jonette Stabbert, Charlotte Vaudrey
Maps: David Lindroth, Inc., Ed Jacobus, *cartographers;* Rebecca Baer and Robert Blake, *map editors*
Design: Fabrizio La Rocca, *creative director;* Guido Caroti, *art director;* Melanie Marin, *senior picture editor*
Production/Manufacturing: Colleen Ziemba
Cover Photo (café sign, Amsterdam): Kindra Clineff/Index Stock

COPYRIGHT

Copyright © 2004 by Fodors LLC

Fodor's is a registered trademark of Random House, Inc.

All rights reserved under International and Pan-American Copyright Conventions. Published in the United States by Fodor's Travel Publications, a unit of Fodors LLC, a subsidiary of Random House, Inc., and simultaneously in Canada by Random House of Canada Limited, Toronto. Distributed by Random House, Inc., New York.

No *maps, illustrations, or other portions of this book may be reproduced in any form without written permission from the publisher.*

First Edition

ISBN 1–4000–1337–2

ISSN 1548–1751

SPECIAL SALES

This book is available for special discounts for bulk purchases for sales promotions or premiums. Special editions, including personalized covers, excerpts of existing books, and corporate imprints can be created in large quantities for special needs. For more information, write to Special Markets/Premium Sales, 1745 Broadway, MD 6-2, New York, New York 10019 or e-mail specialmarkets@ randomhouse.com. Inquiries from Canada should be directed to your local Canadian bookseller or sent to Random House of Canada, Ltd., Marketing Department, 2775 Matheson Boulevard East, Mississauga, Ontario L4W 4P7. Inquiries from the United Kingdom should be sent to Fodor's Travel Publications, 20 Vauxhall Bridge Road, London SW1V 2SA, England.

AN IMPORTANT TIP & AN INVITATION

Although all prices, opening times, and other details in this book are based on information supplied to us at press time, changes occur all the time in the travel world, and Fodor's cannot accept responsibility for facts that become outdated or for inadvertent errors or omissions. So **always confirm information when it matters,** especially if you're making a detour to visit a specific place. Your experiences—positive and negative—matter to us. If we have missed or misstated something, **please write to us.** We follow up on all suggestions. Contact the Amsterdam editor at editors@fodors.com or c/o Fodor's at 1745 Broadway, New York, New York 10019.

PRINTED IN THE UNITED STATES OF AMERICA

10 9 8 7 6 5 4 3 2 1

DESTINATION: AMSTERDAM

erhaps Amsterdam's greatest charm is also its greatest enigma: How can such a gracious cultural center with an incomparable romance also multitask as the most offbeat metropolis in the world? Built on a latticework of concentric canals like an aquatic rainbow, this remains the City of Canals, a place you have to get to know from the water to be properly introduced. But Amsterdam is no Venice, content to live on moonlight serenades and former glory. Old and new often sit side by side. Crannies where time seems to be holding its breath are found around the corner from neon-lighted Kalverstraat; Red Light ladies strut by the city's most time-burnished church. Whether calling on Rembrandt's house or the Vincent Van Gogh Museum, you'll realize that Amsterdam is custom-made for sightseeing. One almost gets the impression that Amsterdam is a museum in itself, so packed is it with monuments, statues, museums, and fine architecture. Most gloriously, the city's 17th-century Golden Age left behind it a tidemark of magnificent buildings and great art—a heritage that continues to color Amsterdam's go-with-the-flow streets.

Karen Cure, Editorial Director

CONTENTS

Maps

CloseUps

ABOUT THIS BOOK

There's no doubt that the best source for travel advice is a like-minded friend who's just been where you're headed. But with or without that friend, you'll have a better trip with a Fodor's guide in hand. Once you've learned to find your way around its pages, you'll be in great shape to find your way around your destination.

SELECTION

Our goal is to cover the best properties, sights, and activities in their category, as well as the most interesting communities to visit. We make a point of including local food-lovers' hot spots as well as neighborhood options, and we avoid all that's touristy unless it's really worth your time. You can go on the assumption that everything you read about in this book is recommended wholeheartedly by our writers and editors. It goes without saying that no property mentioned in the book has paid to be included.

RATINGS

Orange stars ★ denote sights and properties that our editors and writers consider the very best in the area covered by the entire book. Many of these, the best of the best, are listed in the Fodor's Choice section in the front of the book. Black stars ★ highlight the sights and properties we deem Highly Recommended, the don't-miss sights, restaurants, hotels, and other discoveries. Fodor's Choice and Highly Recommended options are listed on the title page of each chapter. Use the index to find complete descriptions.

SPECIAL SPOTS

Pleasures & Pastimes focuses on types of experiences that reveal the spirit of the destination. Watch for Off the Beaten Path sights. Some are out of the way, some are quirky, and all are worth your while. If the munchies hit while you're exploring, look for Need a Break? suggestions.

TIME IT RIGHT

Wondering when to go? Check On the Calendar up front and chapters' Timing sections for weather and crowd overviews and best days and times to visit.

SEE IT ALL

Use Fodor's exclusive Great Itineraries, found in this chapter, as a model for your trip. For in-depth sightseeing, check out the spectacular walking tours found in the Exploring Amsterdam chapter. These Good Walks guide you to all the important sights in each neighborhood, plus any number of other fascinating spots; ⌐ indicates the starting points of walks and itineraries in the text and on the map.

BUDGET WELL

Hotel and restaurant price categories from ¢ to $$$$ are defined in the opening pages of each chapter—expect to find a balanced selection for every budget, from amazing bargains to luxurious blowouts. For attractions, we always give standard adult admission fees; reductions are usually available for children, students, and senior citizens.

BASIC INFO

Smart Travel Tips lists travel essentials for the entire area covered by the book. To find the best way to get around, see the Transportation Within Amsterdam section for all the details.

ON THE MAPS

Maps throughout the book show you what's where and help you find your way around. Black and orange numbered bullets ❶ ① in the text correlate to bullets on maps.

BACKGROUND

In general, we give background information within the chapters in the course of explaining sights as well as in CloseUp boxes and in Understanding Amsterdam at the end of the book. To get in the mood, review the suggestions in Books & Movies. The glossary can be invaluable.

DON'T FORGET

Restaurants are open for lunch and dinner daily unless we state otherwise; we mention dress only when there's a specific requirement and reservations only when they're essential or not accepted—it's always best to book ahead. Unless we note otherwise, most hotels have private baths, phones, TVs, and air-conditioning and operate on the European Plan (a.k.a. EP, meaning without meals). We always list facilities but not whether you'll be charged extra to use them, so when pricing accommodations, find out what's included.

SYMBOLS

Many Listings

★ Fodor's Choice
★ Highly recommended
⊠ Physical address
✛ Directions
⌖ Mailing address
☎ Telephone
🖷 Fax
⊕ On the Web
✉ E-mail
🎫 Admission fee
🕓 Open/closed times
▶ Start of walk/itinerary
Ⓜ Metro stations
☰ Credit cards

Hotels & Restaurants

🏠 Hotel
🛏 Number of rooms
♨ Facilities
🍴 Meal plans
✕ Restaurant
⬧ Reservations
🏛 Dress code
↘ Smoking
🍷 BYOB
✕🏠 Hotel with restaurant that warrants a visit

Other

☕ Family-friendly
🛈 Contact information
⇨ See also
⊠ Branch address
☞ Take note

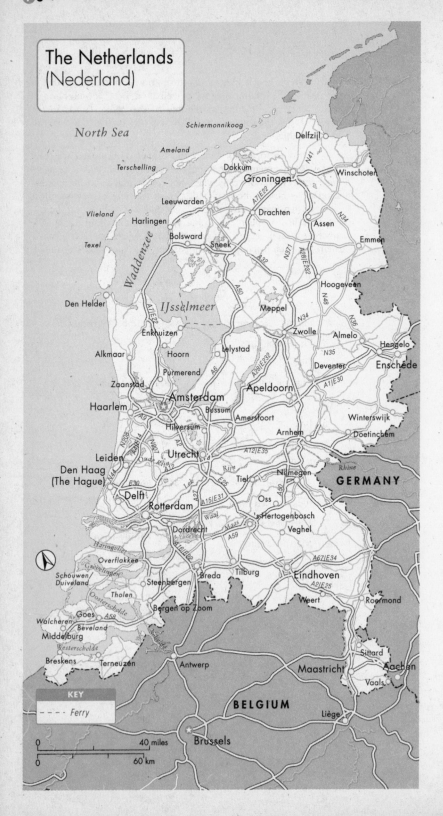

The Netherlands
(Nederland)

North Sea

Schiermonnikoog

Ameland

Delfzijl

Terschelling

Dokkum

Winschoten

Leeuwarden

Groningen

Vlieland

Drachten

Assen

N34

Harlingen

Bolsward

Emmen

Texel

Sneek

Waddenzee

Hoogeveen

Den Helder

IJsselmeer

Meppel

Enkhuizen

Zwolle

Almelo

Hengelo

Alkmaar

Hoorn

Lelystad

Deventer

Enschede

Purmerend

N35

Zaanstad

Apeldoorn

Amsterdam

Haarlem

Bussum

Amersfoort

Winterswijk

Hilversum

Arnhem

Doetinchem

Leiden

Utrecht

Rhine

GERMANY

Den Haag
(The Hague)

Tiel

Nijmegen

Delft

Oss

Rotterdam

's-Hertogenbosch

Dordrecht

Veghel

Haringvliet

Overflakkee

Goeree

Steenbergen

Breda

Tilburg

Eindhoven

*Schouwen/
Duiveland*

Tholen

Weert

Roermond

Oosterschelde

Goes

Bergen op Zoom

Walcheren

Beveland

Middelburg

Westerschelde

Sittard

Breskens

Terneuzen

Antwerp

Maastricht

Aachen

Vaals

BELGIUM

Liège

KEY
- - - *Ferry*

0   40 miles

0   60 km

Brussels

A trip takes you out of yourself. Concerns of life at home completely disappear, driven away by more immediate thoughts—about, say, what marvels will beguile the next day, or where you'll have dinner. That's where Fodor's comes in. We make sure that you know all your options, so that you don't miss something that's around the next bend just because you didn't know it was there. Because the best memories of your trip might well have nothing to do with what you came to Amsterdam to see, we guide you to sights large and small all over the city. You might set out to enjoy the famous 17th-century "Golden Age" landscape paintings in the Rijksmuseum, but back at home you find yourself unable to forget exploring the nearby Vondelpark, luminous as a Ruisdael canvas after a wintry storm. With Fodor's at your side, serendipitous discoveries are never far away.

Our success in showing you every corner of Amsterdam is a credit to our extraordinary writers. Although there's no substitute for travel advice from a good friend who knows your style, our contributors are the next best thing—the kind of people you would poll for travel advice if you knew them.

After years of travel subsidized by carpentry, set design, and B-movie acting, Steve Korver came to Amsterdam to reverse the journey his Dutch parents had made as immigrants to Canada. A decade later, he is established as a lover of raw herring and an obsessive expert on all things Amsterdam, as readers will see once they open his chapter on that amazing city. In between his bouts of Fodorifying Holland, he has written articles on film, books, art, food, and media for such publications as *Time Out, Globe & Mail* and *Condé Nast Traveler*. And when the Dutch metropolis starts feeling too cute and claustrophobic, he goes to Russia in search of Yuri Gagarin, the first man in space (a book on which should appear by the author in 2004) or to the former-Yugoslavia to find the perfect plum brandy. He is also working on a book, based on years' worth of columns and essays, that will be a relentless attempt to spicily reinterpret Amsterdam's past, present, and mythical realities. He divides his writing time between the streets of Amsterdam and the trees of his brother's farm in Ontario. For this edition, Steve wrote the complete Exploring Amsterdam, Where to Eat, Nightlife & the Arts, and Sports & the Outdoors chapters, along with the "Going Dutch" essay in our Understanding Amsterdam chapter.

From the moment she first smelled Dutch cocoa wafting on the breeze, confirmed chocoholic Jonette Stabbert knew she was here to stay in Holland. After all, breathing chocolate is only second best to eating it, but since becoming acclimated, she regularly makes the rounds of *chocolateries*. A native New Yorker—Brooklyn! (to use Breukelen's American spelling)—Jonette traded New for Old Amsterdam in 1970 and is still in love with the Dutch city. Researching this guide was like a vacation encompassing her favorite activities—she got to visit cutting-edge boutiques, frozen-in-amber museums, and enjoyed heavenly day trips, such as the Bollenstreek Bulb Route. Theories abound that living close to water is conducive to creativity. Opting for total immersion, Jonette is a writer, artist, and designer, and also teaches corporate creativity seminars and art and writing workshops. As a writer whose short stories are regularly published, she sometimes acts as a "media escort," guiding visiting novelists and journalists around town. A "people person," networking through numerous professional organizations has brought her in contact with "everybody," which has gained her access to the newest information. The Fodor's reader is the clear winner. For this edition, she researched and wrote the Where to Stay, Shopping, Side Trips from Amsterdam (The Bulb Fields and Folkloric Holland), and Smart Travel Tips chapters.

Originally writing much of this edition's Side Trips from Amsterdam chapter for the Randstat chapter in *Fodor's Holland*, Charlotte Vaudrey is a regular contributor for *Roundabout, Rush on Amsterdam,* and various *WHERE* publications.

WHAT'S WHERE

Traveling to Amsterdam, most visitors betray an appreciation of variety being the spice of life. As they often discover upon arriving, variety is often literally just around the corner. Reflecting its often turbulent history, Amsterdam's famous neighborhoods betray a certain contrariness to each other that does much to reflect the inherent contrariness of this fine city. The posh Grachtengordel sits side by side with the funky Jordaan, the tranquil Plantage is just a street market away from the vibrant Oude Zijde. These and other neighborhoods are held together by the linchpins of Amsterdam's great public squares—the Dam, the Rembrandtplein, the Munt, and the Leidseplein. The Dam, an open square overlooked by the Royal Dam Palace, is a godsend to visitors as a landmark, for even the worst student of foreign languages can easily obtain help if lost by asking for the "Dam."

But, otherwise, when it comes to getting your bearings, Amsterdam can prove a challenge. The city's shape and distinctive canal ring often remind first-time visitors of the wrinkles on their furrowed brows as they come to grip with the city's somewhat confusing layout. If you take an overview of the entire city from the sky, first imagine a horizontal line with a dip in the middle. This dip marks the point at which an artificial island was built to receive the Centraal Station (1889). The medieval core of Amsterdam, marked by a confusion of waterways that have since been partially filled in (Damrak and Rokin were once canals), is directly below this dip and thus within a few minutes' walk of the station itself. Around this core you'll notice four semicircular rings of canals—famously called the *Grachtengordel* (girdle, or ring of canals)—with two more at a somewhat greater distance. Everything within the Lijnbaansgracht, or outermost canal, is called the Centrum; everything beyond belongs to the modern development of Amsterdam and is subdivided into West, *Zuid* (south), and *Oost* (east). With this noted, we seriously advise you to do your exploring with map in hand. The concentrically circular nature of the city's layout makes it terribly easy to unwittingly walk in exactly the opposite direction from the one you thought you were heading.

The Centrum—or inner Old Center—is handily sliced in half into a westerly Nieuwe Zijde (New Side) and an easterly Oude Zijde (Old Side, including the former Jewish Quarter). It is here, within the encircling Golden Age–built canals, and the Museum District (on this horseshoe's southerly hump), that you'll find most of the famous attractions of Amsterdam. To most short-term visitors, the Museum District and Vondelpark are the city's farthest frontier, but on either side of these are two of the city's more vibrant neighborhoods: the still staunchly individualistic Jordaan to the west and the ultimately multicultural De Pijp to the east. Note that the Nieuwe Zijde and the Oude Zijde are also colloquially referred to by the local citizenry as the New and Old "Zijds" (Sides), with the final "s" referring to the areas around the districts' main streets (such as Nieuwezijds Voorburgwal). This book uses both forms of these terms.

Oude Zijde (The Old Side)
The sector you first see upon leaving the storybook gates of Amsterdam's Centraal Station, the eastern half of the Centrum (or Old Center) literally drips with history—a history where sex and religion are equally represented. It all began here almost a thousand years ago when a fishing village hanging on to the blubbery shores of the Ams-

tel River made its first unsteady but seaworthy steps in the 13th century. Ramshackle shacks slowly gave way to 17th-century epic churches and convents before many of these gave way to the warehouses of trade and industry, which in turn later almost succumbed to the oldest industry of them all: prostitution. But the Red Light District—sometimes referred to as the *Rosse Buurt* and other times called *De Walletjes* ("the little walls")—remains reined in (and surprisingly safe) and goes almost as far as to gel seamlessly with the city's oldest church, the Oude Kerk, itself now a venue for modern art exhibitions. Once the earliest core of Amsterdam, Oude Zijde has grown and expanded over time into the area east of the Oude Kerk and the street of Oudezijds Voorburgwal and south to the mighty expanse of the Amstel river. All in all, top sights of the Oude Zijde include the medieval square of **Nieuwmarkt** (now festooned with Chinese restaurants), which is landmarked by the great Waag weigh house; the 17th-century **Trippenhuis** mansion; the grand museum of Golden Age Amsterdam known as **Amstelkring** (with its hidden "Our Lord in the Attic" church), replete with sumptuous period rooms; the **Allard Pierson Museum**; the jazzy clubs and the hipster lounges along Zeedijk; and the last-but-not-least **Red Light District**, itself studded with historic jewels like the half-timbered house called "In the Monkeys." Here, too, by the waterfront area, is the **Schrierstoren**—the Wailing Tower—where Henry Hudson set off to discover a passage to the Far East (but then stumbled over Manhattan as a slight recompense). In short: everything that makes Amsterdam familiar to the global imagination.

Nieuwe Zijde (The New Side)

The New Side of the Old Center is really just as ancient—relatively speaking—as the Old Side, which sits just to the east of the Oude Zijde, separated by the Oudezijds Voorburgwal street. But if you ignore the city's focal square, the always bustling **Dam**, with its remarkable royal palace, the **Het Koninklijk Paleis** and **Nieuwe Kerk** (the "New Church" which like the Old Church, has become a religious institution prone to hosting some of the best of major art exhibits), it is of a much kinder and gentler nature. Although the major newspapers have long fled this area in favor of the suburbs, a more bookish and intellectual heart can be enjoyed around the Spui square, which also gently leads you to the **Amsterdam Historisch Museum**. A visit to this history museum will ensure that any further wanderings of the city will be amplified by what you witnessed and absorbed there. Here, too, is the classic modernist architecture of the **Beurs van Berlage** and the *gezellig* (cozy and congenial) and centuries-old **Beginhof**, one of the city's most famous inner courtyards. If they don't want to stay out of touch too long with the present, nocturnal imbibers will want to repair to the bars and cafés in and around the hipster strip of Nieuwzijdsvoorburgwal. The main thoroughfare of the area is Amsterdam's main (but far from its fanciest) shopping street, the Kalverstraat.

The Eastern Canal Ring: Beyond the "Golden Bend"

Set to the west and south of the city center is the famous Grachtengordel, or Canal Ring. Call it a "belt" or a "girdle," but the Golden Age product consisting of the three main encircling canals—**Prinsengracht** (Princes' Canal), **Keizersgracht** (Emperors' Canal), and **Herengracht** (Gentlemen's Canal)—form a ring of unparalleled historical beauty. These canals became the premier addresses—the Fifth Avenues, the Avenue Fochs, the Park Lanes—of 17th-century Amsterdam when wealthy bankers and famous merchants (even a slave trader or two) ordered homes built in the latest fashionable Neoclassical style introduced from France. The point where these canals intersected with Nieuwe Spiegelstraat became known as the Golden Bend—the **Gouden Bocht**—since houses here were occupied by the richest families of Amsterdam. Heading a few blocks over to what is called the Eastern Canal Ring you'll find assorted treasures, including Baroque-era interiors on view at the magnificent 17th-century **Willet-Holthuysen Museum**; the scenic **Munt Toren** tower; the period-room-rich **Museum van Loon**; the noted **Magere Brug** bridge; and even a stretch or two of canal benches (fairly rare, in fact) to help drink in the canal views. To the north of the Golden Bend is the western half of the Grachtengordel (i.e., west of the arterial Leidsestraat and heading up to to the magnificent reinvented warehouses of Brouwersgracht). This was the first canal sector to be built and harbors not only miles of gabled residences that reflect most sweetly and surreally in the canal waters below but also intersecting streets that harbor a plethora of high-quality/quirky shopping and eating (especially on the **"Nine Streets"**).

The Western Canal Ring & The Jordaan

The northern sectors of the Grachtengordel center around Amsterdam's beloved Jordaan (probably derived from the French for garden, *jardin*). Although this cozy, scenic, and singular neighborhood's working-class roots have long sprouted branches of gentrification, it remains a wanderers' paradise where you can take in leafy canals, funky galleries, yet funkier shops, hidden courtyards *(hofjes)* and cafés/bars/restaurants of both the posh and charmingly local persuasion—the latter often involving a terrace with a view and an interior with massive nicotine staining that color-codes nicely with a congenial sense of warmth and humor. This area—bound by Brouwersgracht, Elandsgracht, Lijnbaansgracht, and Prinsengracht—is also the setting of some of Amsterdam's most memorable sights. The most famous is the **Anne Frankhuis**, home to the fabled author of *The Diary of Anne Frank*. Nearby is the **Nederlands Theatermuseum**, housed in the fabulous Bartolotti Huis, a spectacular 17th-century Dutch Renaissance residence. Not far away are the reputed final resting place of Rembrandt in the **Westerkerk**, the docking space of the **Woonboatmuseum** (just across from the barge that is home to a whole gaggle of cats), and the fast-paced rummaging options of the Monday Morning **Noordermarkt** (Northern Market). Just put on those walking—nay, dancing—shoes and "ooh" and "aah" your day away, finding a hidden treasure around every corner. At the northern border of the Jordaan, you'll find **Brouwersgracht** (Brewers' Canal), which some believe to be the most beautiful canal in Amsterdam. Back when, traders and artisans built their homes here, prizing the canal's long, sunny vistas almost as much as today's travelers do.

De Pijp

De Pijp, although not as charmingly ancient as the Jordaan, does come up trumps as an utterly pleasant and street-oriented post–working-class neighborhood. And the street that forms its pumping heart is the **Albert Cuypmarkt**, the largest outdoor market in the country. The key words here are "multiculti" (since a more globe-embracing neighborhood complete with economically priced ethnic eats is hard to imagine) and "studeny" (since it is rich in hip but rarely rarefied beer-quaffing hangouts). A top sight hereabouts is the **Heineken Brouwerij,** the historic brewery. But with the green **Sarphatipark** and the grand Amstel River always on standby, one can always quickly opt for more introspective surroundings.

The Museum District & Amsterdam South

In short, the history of art is here at your fingertips (not to mention, your potentially blistered toetips), as Rembrandts, Van Goghs, and Bill Violas are all on evocative display in the city's three main art museums: the **Rijksmuseum** (sadly going through a massive rebuilding over the next many years, so call/surf ahead for their varying hours and exhibition locations), the **Rijksmuseum Vincent Van Gogh,** and the **Stedelijk Museum** of modern art (who should also be called since they are also due to close for a massive refurbishment). Set near the southern end of the city, this neighborhood also harbors the more posh residences, not to mention the most elitist shopping options along the country's most famous fashion strip, **P. C. Hooftstraat.** But what saves this neighborhood from drowning in its own rarified air is the not-to-be-missed people's park and city's lung, **Vondelpark,** where you can neutralize your art-soaked eyes with the restful greens of grasses and trees while sipping on a beverage or scoffing down a picnic. To the south of the park rests the poshest residential quarters of Amsterdam, known commonly as **Amsterdam Zuid** (Amsterdam South) and broken into two sectors: the Oud Zuid, near Vondelpark, and the Nieuw Zuid, around the Apollolaan avenue.

East of the Amstel: The Jewish Quarter to the Plantage

To the east of the center-city Oude Zijds and the city's aorta, the wide Amstel river, lies the extension of the Old Jewish Neighborhood known as the stately and serene Plantage ("plantation"). It was on the eastern bank of the Amstel in the 17th century that Jewish refugees from Portugal quickly colonized the area, now known as the historic **Joodse Buurt** (Jewish Quarter), located east of the Zwanenburgwal, as their own. And it was here, not far from today's glitteringly modern **Stadhuis-Muziektheater** (or "Stopera") opera and concert house, that Rembrandt set up shop in one of Amsterdam's grandest houses. The former home of Rembrandt, the **Museum het Rembrandthuis,** tops the bill of fare hereabouts, but there are many other destinations, including such 17th-century treasures as the **Pintohuis** mansion; the grand **Zuiderkerk** church; the renowned **Joods Historisch Museum,** and the old-world knickknack marketeering of the **Waterlooplein** flea market. In this sector of the city, wide 19th-century boulevards are dotted with trees, cafés, and historical treasures, such as the **Verzetsmuseum** (Resistance Museum), the **Tropenmuseum** (Museum of the Tropics), and those more biological diamonds such as the **Artis Zoo** and **Hortus Botanicus** gardens. Scenic landmarks include the **Montelbaantoren,** a tower that Rembrandt loved. If you are ever finding the hustle and bustle of dense city living a bit too much, there is much to find here in the mellow refuge department.

Although it is far from the size of metropolises such as Paris and Rome, Amsterdam manages to pack within its borders as many pleasures and treasures as cities five times its size. But in a city with as many richly stocked museums and matchless marvels, you risk seeing half of everything and all of nothing. So use the efficient itineraries below as models to keep you on track as you explore both the famous sights and those off the beaten path.

The city's "musts" include the **Het Koninklijk Paleis** (Royal Dam Palace); the **Schreierstoren** ("Weeping Tower"), from which Henry Hudson set sail in the *Half Moon* in 1609 to ultimately discover New York; **Museum het Rembrandthuis** (Rembrandt's House); the fascinating **Museum Amstelkring** (with its "attic" church); the **Begijnhof** (Beguine Court), the most peaceful courtyard in the city; the **Gouden Bocht** (Golden Bend), replete with stately burghers' mansions bearing stepped gables and Daniel Marot doorways; the **Anne Frankhuis** (Anne Frank House), that wrenching reminder of the horrors of war; and, of course, the incomparable **Rijksmuseum** (State Museum) and the world's largest collection of paintings by the legendary artist, the **Rijksmuseum Vincent Van Gogh**. With 22 Rembrandts, including the great *Night Watch,* and more than 200 Van Goghs, Amsterdam is a prime art repository. Diamonds galore fill the shops and factories of the historic **Joodse Buurt** (Jewish Quarter) east of the Zwanenburgwal.

But remember in addition to all the must-dos, Amsterdam is a great walking city because so many of its real treasures are untouted details: tiny alleyways barely visible on the map, hidden garden courtyards, shop windows, sudden vistas of church spires and gabled roofs. Also remember that Amsterdam can be rather damp. With the obvious precautions of comfortable, weatherproof shoes and an umbrella, walking might well become your favorite pastime.

If You Have 1 Day

So, you want to taste Amsterdam, gaze at its beauty, and inhale its special flair, all in one breathtaking (literally) day? Although you will never get into the casual groove of the city in a whirlwind visit, it's actually a super way to make notes as you go along to compile a Sinter Klaas (or Santa Claus) list for a plan of action for your more leisurely return trip. Still, one day can give you a real taste of the city. Leaving the main rail terminus, Centraal Station, head toward the right and the sector known as the Nieuwe Zijde ("New Side")—the westerly portion of Amsterdam's inner city, the Centrum. If it is your wont, you could head left into the Oude Zijde ("Old Side"), but hereabouts is the Red Light District—even though traditional gables vie with equally traditional leisure industries here, this sector is best left for night. So, from Centraal Station head south along the (unfortunately, tacky) Damrak street, turning right on Oudebrugsteeg for several blocks until you get to the Museum Amstelkring (at Oudezijds Voorburgwal 40), where you'll get a full blast of Golden Age splendor, thanks to spectacular period rooms and the famous "Our Lord in the Attic" church. After this dip into Vermeer's day, backtrack to the Damrak, turn left, and continue south—noting the famous Beurs van Berlage stock exchange along the way—until you reach the seething hub of the Dam, the broadest square in the old section of town. Landmarked by the Nieuwe Kerk—site of all Dutch coronations—it is also home to the magical 17th-century Het Koninklijk Paleis, which fills the western side of the square. Its richly decorated marble interiors are open to the public when the queen is not in residence. From the Dam, follow the busy pedestrian shopping street, Kalverstraat, south to the entrance to the Amsterdams Historisch Museum. Here you can get an enjoyable, easily digestible lesson on the city's past, including its freely accessible Schutters Gallery with its massive Golden Age group portraits.

Passing through the painting gallery of the Historisch Museum brings you to the entrance of the Begijnhof, a blissfully peaceful courtyard oasis. Behind the Begijnhof you come to an open square, the Spui, lined with popular sidewalk cafés, and to the Singel, the innermost of Amsterdam's concentric canals. Cut through the canals by way of the romantic Heisteeg alley and its continuation, the Wijde Heisteeg, turning left down the Herengracht to the corner of Leidsegracht. This is part of the prestigious Gouden Bocht, the grandest stretch of canal in town.

Continue down the Herengracht to the Vijzelstraat and turn right to the next canal, the Keizersgracht. Cross the Keizersgracht and turn left to find the Museum van Loon, an atmospheric canal house, still occupied by the family that has owned it for centuries but open to the public. Turn back down Keizersgracht until you reach the very posh Nieuwe Spiegelstraat; take another right and walk toward Museumplein. Rising up in front of you is the redbrick, neo-Gothic splendor of the Rijksmuseum, housing the world's greatest collection of Dutch art, or, for now, at least its "Best of the Golden Age" selection (with its world-famed Rembrandts and Vermeers) found in the only wing not undergoing massive renovation in the coming years. When you leave the Rijksmuseum, walk through the covered gallery under the building. Directly ahead is Museumplein itself; to your right is Paulus Potterstraat (look for the diamond factory on the far corner), where you'll find the Van Gogh Museum, which contains a unique collection of that tortured artist's work.

Continuing along Paulus Potterstraat, at the corner of Van Baerlestraat, you reach the Stedelijk Museum, where you can see modern art from Picasso to the present. Just around the corner, facing the back of the Rijksmuseum across Museumplein, is the magnificent 19th-century concert hall, the Concertgebouw. A short walk back up along Van Baerlestraat will bring you to the Vondelpark—acre after acre of parkland alive with people in summer.

If You Have 3 Days

Everyone's dream of Amsterdam is the grand, crescent-shape waterways of the *Grachtengordel* (girdle or ring of canals), lined with splendid buildings and pretty, gabled houses. On your second day, take full advantage of these delights—wander off the main thoroughfares, saunter along the smaller canals that crisscross them, and sample the charms of such historic city neighborhoods as the Jordaan. Begin at busy Dam Square and circle around behind the royal palace to follow the tram tracks into the wide and busy Raadhuisstraat. Once you cross the Herengracht, turn right along the canal, and at the bend in the first block you will see the Nederlands Theatermuseum, which occupies two gorgeous 17th-century houses. Return to the Raadhuisstraat and turn right, following it to the Westermarkt. Stop for a fish snack at the stall under the shadow of the tower of the Westerkerk, on the right, facing the next canal. This landmark is Rembrandt's burial place. Make a right past the church and follow the Prinsengracht canal to the Anne Frank House, where you can visit the attic hideaway in which Anne Frank wrote her diary.

The neighborhood to your left, across the canal, is the Jordaan, full of curious alleys and pretty canals, intriguing shops and cafés. At the intersection of the Prinsengracht and Brouwersgracht, discover the

Brouwersgracht, one of the most picturesque canals in Amsterdam. Oozing with ancient charm, the Jordaan's higgledy-piggledy streets and arterial canals will offer a good setting for a digestive wander, with its local brown cafés, stained brown from chainsmoking regulars and stocked with every imaginable other digestive aid. Then enhance the romance factor by finding your way back to your hotel via the wonderfully lighted canal rings.

On your third day, start by exploring "Rembrandt's neighborhood," Amsterdam's historic Jewish Quarter. Begin at its heart, Waterlooplein. Today the square is dominated by the imposing modern Muziektheater/Stadhuis (Music Theater/Town Hall), which is surrounded by a large and lively flea market. East of Waterlooplein, on Jonas Daniël Meijerplein, is the Joods Historisch Museum, skillfully converted from a number of old synagogues. Just to the east of that, on the corner of Mr. Visserplein and Jonas Daniël Meijerplein is the stately Portugees Israelitische Synagoge. Its interior is simple but awe-inspiring because of its vast size and floods of natural light.

Venturing over to the sylvan Plantage neighborhood, you'll find that the varied flora cultivated in the greenhouses of the Hortus Botanicus is just across the canal. Then you might want to make a short diversion to the Verzetsmuseum, which explains the Dutch resistance to the occupying forces, passive and active, during the Second World War. But for something more lighthearted, especially if you have children in tow, proceed to the Artis Zoo (which was attractively laid out in parklike surroundings in the 19th century and has a well-stocked aquarium). Time permitting, take Tram 9 or 14 farther east along Plantage Middenlaan, to the Tropenmuseum, which has riveting displays on tropical cultures and a special children's section.

Alternatively, you can walk from the synagogue up Jodenbreestraat, where—in the second house from the corner by the Zwanenburgwal—you'll find the Museum het Rembrandthuis, the mansion where Rembrandt lived at the height of his prosperity, which now houses a large collection of his etchings. Cross the bridge to St. Antoniesbreestraat and follow it to the Zuiderkerk, whose rather Asian spire is the neighborhood's chief landmark. Take St. Antoniesbreestraat north to Nieuwmarkt. Take Koningsstraat to the Kromboomssloot and turn left, then right at Rechtboomssloot (both pretty, leafy canals), and follow it through this homey neighborhood, the oldest in Amsterdam, to Montelbaanstraat; turn left and cut through to the broad Oude Waal canal. Follow it right to the Montelbaanstoren, a tower that dates back to the 16th century and was often sketched by Rembrandt. Up Kalkmarkt from the tower is Prins Hendrikkade, which runs along the eastern docks.

Following Prins Hendrikkade east you enter the modern world with a bang at the NEMO Science & Technology Center. A little farther on is the Nederlands Scheepvaartmuseum, where there is a fascinating replica of an old Dutch East India ship. Across the bridge on Hoogte Kadijk is the Museumwerf 't Kromhout, where wooden sailing boats are still restored and repaired. If, on the other hand, you go west along Prins Hendrikkade to Gelderskade, you can see the Schreierstoren, the tower where legend has it that women used to stand weeping and waiting for their men to return from sea. Here, Henry Hudson set sail for America in the 16th century, making for a fitting farewell finale for your third day.

If You Have 5 Days

A more extended stay can mean three things: stretching the above recommendations into a five-day period, going efficiently local by renting
a bicycle, and having the time to choose from the mass of international
concerts (perhaps there are still tickets left for a jazz legend at the
Bimhuis, your favorite conductor at the Concertgebouw, or any manner of musical acts at the former church Paradiso or the former milk
factory Melkweg). More time also means more flexibility in dealing with
Amsterdam's propensity toward sudden bursts of rain. Besides equipping yourself with an umbrella, you can decide when it looks like there
is to be a stretch of sun, the better to explore the Old Center or the Western Canal Ring and the Jordaan. A cloudy day should inspire a more
lingering exploration of the Museum District or the Jewish District, both
of which are rich with cultural refugees from rain. Of course, sunny late
afternoons and evenings should be spent on a sunny terrace or in Vondelpark, whose light at this time gives off a similar glow as you may
have witnessed earlier in a Golden Age painting at the Rijksmuseum.
At least one of your dinners should be spent indulging in either a cheese
fondue or a full-blown Indonesian rice table. Dessert, of course, will be
a walk along a canal, or even better, an evening canal cruise that will
have you admiring the city from its most complementary of vantage points.

Also to be considered is taking perhaps a full day to wander the harbor
front from the evocatively ancient and nautical Westelijke Eilanden to
the boardwalk arising beside Oostelijke Handelskade to the stunning
residential architecture of the Java and KNSM islands and the Borneo
and Sporenburg peninsulas. A pretty day can even inspire you to point
your bike farther afield—say, up the Amstel river toward Oude Kerk (a
favored route of Rembrandt) or north along the IJsselmeer to the fishing village of Marken. More time also means that you may have by now
stumbled across a friendly brown café where you feel comfortable in
establishing yourself as a temporary "regular." After all, Amsterdam by
day offers such a multitude of globally statured cultural offerings, you
may want to spend your nights taking advantage of the city's more "vil-
lagey," socially cozy aspects.

WHEN TO GO

The Netherlands is at its best when the temperatures climb and cafés and restaurants spill across sidewalks to lure happy groups to dine on canal boats moored alongside. Unfortunately, because such weather is so transient, you could find yourself sharing your sun-dappled experience with too many others for comfort. Because the famous tulip fields bloom during April and May, this is perhaps the best time to visit Holland. Spring is also the driest time of the year. Rain, however, can arrive year-round to dampen your sightseeing so, like the locals, always have an umbrella at the ready as sunny afternoons are often preceded by stormy mornings.

From tulip time (mid-April to mid-May) onward, it becomes increasingly difficult to obtain accommodation reservations. In addition, with the approach of summer, museums, galleries, and tourist sights heave with visitors. Some say that if you are making an extended tour of Europe, you should consider scheduling Holland for the beginning or end of your itinerary, saving July and August for exploring less crowded countries.

But if you have to visit in high summer, be sure to take a vacation from your Amsterdam vacation and take some side trips to discover the cities that have that quaint Dutch beauty (not to mention cultural and social happenings plus historical interest), all without the crush. Optimum times to visit are May through June and September through October. Swimming is possible from May or June onward but is reserved for the hardy. The main cultural calendar runs from September through June, but happily there are so many festivals and open-air events scheduled during the summer that no one really notices.

Climate

Weather-wise, the best months for sightseeing are April, May, June, September, and October, when the days are long and the summer crowds have not yet filled the beaches and the museums to capacity. The maritime climate of The Netherlands is very changeable, though, and during these months expect weather ranging from cool to pleasant to wet and windy to hot and surprisingly humid. Eastern and southeastern provinces edge toward a more Continental climate, with warmer summers and colder winters than along the North Sea coast, which can itself be very cold from December through February and March.

Forecasts **Weather Channel Connection** ☎ 900/932-8437, 95¢ per minute from a Touch-Tone phone ⊕ www.weather.com.

AMSTERDAM

Jan.	40F	4C	May	61F	16C	Sept.	65F	18C
	34	1		50	10		56	13
Feb.	41F	5C	June	65F	18C	Oct.	56	13C
	34	1		56	13		49	9
Mar.	47F	8C	July	70F	21C	Nov.	47F	8C
	38	3		59	15		41	5
Apr.	52F	11C	Aug.	68F	20C	Dec.	41F	5C
	43	6		59	15		36	2

ON THE CALENDAR

The top seasonal events in Amsterdam (and some beyond—after all, it only takes a hour or two to venture to Holland's farthest realms by train) are listed below, and any one of them could provide the stuff of lasting memories. The Netherlands are at their most beautiful in spring. The bulb fields southwest of Amsterdam burst out in vast blocks of bright color, parks and gardens all over the country display brilliant spreads of blossoms, and there's a flower parade through the town of Lisse in early April to mark the opening of the flower exhibition season at Keukenhof gardens. Summertime in The Netherlands is festival time. The Holland Festival in Amsterdam in June attracts a glittering array of international stars in the fields of music, opera, theater, and dance. In early September there is a massive Flower Parade from Aalsmeer to Amsterdam. In Amsterdam, check the listings in local newspapers and at the VVV tourist offices to find out all the special events on the city's packed cultural calendar.

WINTER

Jan.–Feb.

If it gets really frigid—sometimes twenty years go by before the weather is deemed cold enough—the northern province of Freisland hosts its famous Elfstedentocht, a one-day, 11-city ice-skating race through some of Holland's prettiest medieval towns. There is no set day but when usually happens sometime in January or February. Thousands of participants don garb to honor the glowing hues of the House of Orange and set out to Hans Brinker their way from Leeuwarden, capital of Friesland, through the circuit towns of Sneek, IJlst, Sloten, Stavoren, Hindeloopen, Workum, Bolsward, Harlingen, Franeker, and Dokkum. All of Holland watches the race on T.V.

Mar.

The Stille Omgang (Silent Procession) (☎ 023/524–6229) has local Amsterdam Catholics processing through the streets on the Saturday night after March 10 to commemorate the 1345 Miracle of Amsterdam, when a man vomited up the host he had ingested, after which both the man and the host were found in pristine condition.

At the very southern border of Holland lies the sophisticated and ritzy city of Maastricht, which draws the high-rollers this time of year to its MECC Congress and Exhibition Hall for the European Fine Art Fair (✒ European Fine Art Foundation, Box 1035, 5200 BA, 's-Hertogenbosch ☎ 073/614–5165 ⊕ www.tefaf.com). This panoply of Old Master paintings attracts the one of the fanciest crowds of collectors from around the world for ten days beginning every mid-March. A fabled team of experts examines items to weed out any pieces of dubious authenticity—of those items that pass the test, the best known and most sought after are probably the paintings of the Renaissance to Baroque eras.

SPRING

Apr.

During the last Saturday in April, the *Bloemen Corso,* or Bulb District Flower Parade (☎ 0252/434–710) passes through Lisse to open the National Floral Exhibition (☎ 0252/465–555) at Keukenhof gardens, heralding the peak days for visiting the famous tulip fields. The 20-mile route runs from Noordwijk to Haarlem. National

Museum Weekend opens 450 museums across the country to visitors free or at a discount. April 30 is the unforgettable Queen's Day, the Dutch monarch's official birthday, when Amsterdam erupts with a citywide, all-day street party and the queen makes a more sedate official visit to a selected town in the provinces. This is actually the birthdate of Queen Juliana, but her daughter Queen Beatrix now celebrates her B-day all the same. Due to a one-day, "free-license" law, thousands of Amsterdammers mount a gigantic "yard-sale" by lining the streets with stalls filled with their attic bric-a-brac. April 29 sees an all-night party in some cities, with Utrecht being a center for the party-hearty crowd.

| May | May 4 and 5 are Remembrance and Liberation Day respectively and are marked by solemnity on the former and huge frolicsome music festivals throughout the country on the latter. Every imaginable art form is represented at the annual arts fair in Amsterdam's southern suburb RAI convention center, KunstRAI (☎ 020/549–1212), usually beginning near the end of the month. National Bicycle Day (May 8) has both professionals and novices racing through The Netherlands. Usually the second Saturday in May, Nationale Molendag is Holland's National Windmill Day, when more than half of the nation's 1,000 windmills are in action and open for visits by the public. In May, the Asparagus Season is upon kitchens across the land as chefs make hay to create concoctions with Holland's fabled bumper crop of "white gold." |

SUMMER

| June | Green-thumbers and lovers of luxury will love the Open Garden Days (☎ 020/320–3660), sponsored by Stichting De Amsterdamse Grachtentuin, when private houses along the posh Herengracht, Keizersgracht, and Prinsengracht open their private gardens and salons for several days in mid-June. Over a period of 10 days, Amsterdam Roots Festival (☎ 0900/0191) brings together the best global acts in the city's best venues. Holland Festival of the Performing Arts (☎ 020/530–7110) captures Amsterdam, spilling over to The Hague, Rotterdam, and Utrecht, making this the biggest national fête for the performing arts. Parkpop (☎ 070/361–8888), a pop music festival, livens up The Hague. To enjoy open-air concerts and theater, check out the Vondelpark Theater (☎ 020/673–1499) and its summer calendar, running from June through August. |

| July | Rotterdam's Metropolis Pop Festival hosts national and international performances in three stages in the Zuiderpark on the first Sunday of July. The Hague hosts the North Sea Jazz Festival (☎ 015/214–8900). The International Organ Competition (☎ 023/511–5733) brings musicians to Haarlem in even-number years. |

| Aug. | The Amsterdam Canal Festival brings flotillas of boats for classical music performances on a floating stage on the canal. For two weeks Parade (☎ 033/465–4577) re-creates and updates a Breughel painting by bringing together absurd theatrics in Martin Luther Park. The Gay Pride Boat Parade (☎ 020/620–8807) fills the canals with over-the-top spectacle and the canal sides with as many as a quarter million spectators on the first Saturday in August. |

FALL	
Sept.	The Bloemen Corso Floral Parade (early Sept. ☎ 0297/325–100) makes a daylong procession of floats from Aalsmeer to Amsterdam; Gaudeamus International Music Week (☎ 020/694–7349) honors contemporary classical music and its young composers in Amsterdam. During the first Saturday in September, Open Monumentendag means that you can enter many historic buildings normally closed to the public. The famous collection of historic windmills in Zaandam takes center stage every September 30 during Zaanse Windmill Day in the Zaanse Schans area, just to the north of Amsterdam.
Sept.	The Bloemencorso Floral Parade (early Sept. ☎ 0297/325–100) makes a daylong procession of floats from Aalsmeer to Amsterdam; Gaudeamus International Music Week (☎ 020/694–7349) honors contemporary classical music and its young composers in Amsterdam; and the Opening of Parliament (☎ 070/356–4000) takes place in The Hague on the third Tuesday—the queen arrives in her golden coach.
Oct.	The Holland Dance Festival (☎ 0900/340–3505) brings ballet and other dance companies to The Hague. After a few years in Amsterdam, Crossing Border (☎ www.crossingborder.nl) has returned to The Hague to continue its good work as a "literary festival that rocks."
Nov.–Dec.	With the St. Nicolaas Parade (☎ 0900/400–4040) in Amsterdam on November 18 and in cities throughout the country, the arrival of Sinter Klaas launches the Christmas season. Indeed, the American Santa Claus is a holiday descendant of the Dutch saint, who, with little padding (wouldn't you know, the jolly fat Santa is an American invention) arrives then to dispense ginger cookies. The biggest day is Sinterklaasvond, December 5. People offers poems heralding their friends and many towns host St. Nicholas, who gallops from house to house, leaving gag presents behind. In Amsterdam, Santa arrives by barge near Sint Nicholasskerk, along with his "Moorish" helper, Zwarte Piet (Black Peter). Real presents are often saved for the more commercial festivities on December 25. Amsterdam's Christmas Market in the Museumplein square is held December 7–24. Unfortunately, due to global warming, the canals of Amsterdam freeze up more and more infrequently, but when a frigid cold wave moves in from the North Sea, the city hopes the locals will permit skating on the canals, often under the stars. Of a much more adult nature, High Times Cannabis Cup (☎ 020/624–1777) employs the Melkweg to celebrate harvest season with five days of wastedness punctuated with bands, banquets, and much-coveted awards for farming abilities. The perhaps more noble and certainly more globally prestigious International Documentary Film Festival (☎ 020/626–1939) is centered around Leidseplein and attracts tens of thousands to its hundreds of screenings.

Amsterdam on Wheels

As soon as you step out of the train and leave Centraal Station, you are confronted with a great chaos of parked and moving bikes. When in Rome, you do as the Romans, so in Amsterdam you should rent a bike. It can make all the difference to your stay here and offer you an insider's perspective on this compact city. Taking the necessary care to watch for other traffic and pedestrians, you can get around on two wheels at a pace that still allows you to take in your surroundings. Most rental bikes are fitted with pedal brakes, rather than hand brakes. To stop, you pedal backward, which can take awhile to grow accustomed to. Rental bikes are usually one-speed, but this is sufficient for the flat city. Because Amsterdammers got on their bikes as soon as they were weaned, cycling lessons are anathema. If you are out of practice, wheel your bike to the Vondelpark, the city's "green lung," and start out on the grass for a soft landing without scrapes. Make sure you lock the frame of your bike to something fixed, such as a bike rack or railing, even when leaving it unattended for the shortest time.

One essential thing you should be aware of while exploring Amsterdam is that the usually friendly local folks (whose uncanny English can be exploited whenever you find yourself forever looping about) can suddenly turn ugly when confronted while bicycling along the easily identifiable bike paths with a tourist checking a map—or, heaven forbid, a guidebook. So be warned or be prepared to have the fear of the God-like stature of the Dutch bicyclist drummed into you. You can breed sensitivity by renting a bicycle by yourself and attempting to find a Zen peace within the psychotically pedaling throngs.

Nowadays the Vondelpark is also the place for a leisurely in-line skate, though there are also the hip-and-trendy practicing their pirouettes. During the summer you can rent skates and protective knee, elbow, and wrist pads from a booth at the southern end of the park. For the inexperienced it is certainly worth having a lesson with a friendly instructor, which adds only a little to the overall rental costs. Weather permitting, you can join the Friday Night Skate (⊕ www.fridaynightskate.nl), an initiative copied from the massively popular event in Paris. Here in Amsterdam, hundreds of skaters tour the streets of the city with guides and qualified first-aid officers on hand for any unlucky bumps. Join them at 8 PM outside the Nederlands Filmmuseum (Netherlands Film Museum; ⊠ Vondelpark 3, Museum District and Vondelpark) at the northeastern end of the Vondelpark.

Amsterdam's Hofjes—the Historic Almshouses

Hidden behind innocent-looking gateways throughout the city center, most notably along the main ring of canals and in the Jordaan neighborhood, are some of its most charming houses. There are about 30 *hofjes* (almshouses), mainly dating back to the 18th century, when the city's flourishing merchants established hospices for the old and needy—pensions and social security were unheard of then. Their philanthropy was supposed to be rewarded by a place in heaven. But be warned (and be prepared for disappointment): residents of these hofjes like their peace and quiet, and are often prone to locking their entrances to visitors in the name of maintaining that peace and quiet.

Most famous is the Begijnhof, and others such as the Suyckerhofje, Van Brienen-hofje, and De Zon are included in the Exploring Amsterdam walking tours. Yet others include the Sint Andrieshofje (✉ Egelantiersgracht 107–114, Jordaan); founded in 1615, it is the second-oldest almshouse in Amsterdam. Notice the fine gables, including a step gable in the style of Hendrick de Keyser. The Claes Claeszhofje (✉ junction of Egelantiersstraat, Eerste Ege-lantiersdwarsstraat, and Tuinstraat, Jordaan) was established in 1626 by a Mennonite textile trader. The Zevenkeurvorstenhofje (✉ Tuinstraat 197–223) was founded around 1645, though the houses standing today are 18th cen-tury. The Karthuizerhof (✉ Karthuizerstraat 21–131, Jordaan) was founded in 1650 and now accommodates young people around a courtyard with two 17th-century pumps.

The New Amsterdam

With Amsterdam obsessively reinventing itself as the business "Gateway to Europe," both residents and visitors are con-stantly finding themselves having to circumnavigate construction projects in the inner city. However, there are also mass concentrations of new archi-tecture arising in the city's outer limits. Historically, whenever the city ex-perienced economic and population booms, it would stretch outward: razing the shantytowns of the poor that formed outside the city walls and replac-ing them with, for instance, a new ring of canals with posh residences. And such an approach is at work today as well. The once economically weaker Bijlmer area in South-East Amsterdam has been revitalized with more mid-dle-range housing, the Arena stadium, shopping centers, film complexes, and the Heineken Music Hall. And along the harbor front, the squatters who had built up huge cultural complexes in the old warehouses that featured artists' studios, restaurants, galleries, and general event spaces have been pushed to seek space farther afield to make room for a boardwalk that is hoped to be as image enhancing as Sydney's in Australia. Already along the Eastern Docklands along the Oostelijke Handelskade, there is a luxury cruise ship terminal, a warehouse that is now a showcase for Europe's top interior designers, and the trendy and chic Panama restaurant and night-club. Soon these will be joined by many other cultural, dining, and enter-tainment spaces, including a floating cinema showing art-house films and, by mid-2004, the Muziekgebouw ("Music Building") that will be the new location for the Bimhuis and the Ijsbreker. The enjoining islands of Borneo Eiland, Sporenburg, KNSM Eiland, and Java Eiland are already pilgrimage sites for modern residential architecture buffs. However, these are already old news with the current construction of Amsterdam's most ambitious—and hence, controversial—project arising to the east: Ijburg. Over the next decade, this series of seven artificial islands will become the home to 18,000 new buildings and 45,000 residents. But meanwhile, these expanses of sand are being used as the "beach-to-be-at."

It is hoped that Ijburg will become the crowning achievement and ultimate showcase for the very much in vogue concepts of Dutch architecture as prop-agated by such pundits as Rem Koolhaas. Whereas most of the world is just now generally dealing with limits of space, the Dutch have always had to deal with this problem. In a country where almost everything is essentially artificial, the local architecture has long been fused with other disciplines such as city planning and landscape architecture. The "Dutch Big Mac" by architect bureau MVRDV that was on display at Hanover's World Expo 2000—with its dunes on the first floor, a forest on the third, windmills on the roof, and shopping, living, and recreating spaces woven in between—is probably the most visual example of this multidisciplinary approach. And indeed, Ijburg promises to be a singular community that has been obsessively planned to be, it is hoped, both futuristic and intrinsically human. Before going to check the state of progress yourself, visit the Zuider Kerk in Amsterdam's center city for further information and to see the models.

Rooms of Rembrandts

An actual trip to Holland is not necessary to savor this unique country; a short visit to any major museum in countries around the world will probably just as effectively transport the viewer—by way of the paintings of Rembrandt, Hals, Vermeer, De Hootch, Terborch, Ruysdael, Hobbema, and Van Gogh—to its legendary landscapes, city scenes, and domestic interiors. Few other countries can boast of having fathered so many great artists, but then again, Holland seems almost expressly composed for the artist by nature; Its peaceful dells, canal scenes, and verdant mantles of foliage seem so alluring they practically demand the artist pick up brush and palette. During Holland's Golden Age of the 17th century, an estimated 20 million paintings were executed and every native seemed to have an oil painting tacked on the wall. Happily, many of the masterpieces left by the greatest painters of the day virtually wallpaper the rooms of the Rijksmuseum along with other Amsterdam museums. Even better, if you browse through a book of Dutch art before you come to Holland, study the paintings of church interiors by Saenredam and De Witte, the Old Testament portraits painted by Rembrandt in Amsterdam's Jewish Quarter, the street scenes immortalized by the School of Haarlem artists, and the genre scenes perfected by Vermeer. Store them away in your mind's eye, visit the actual paintings on view in Amsterdam, and, sure enough, as you look across a market square from a certain angle, turn a corner of a canal, or wander through a church, you'll feel as if the real world appears to dissolve and, just for a moment, you have the sensation of stepping into a 17th-century painting.

Way of All Flesh: The Red Light District

The great French writer and philosopher Albert Camus probably described Amsterdam best when he observed that the city's concentric rings of canals dauntingly resembled the circles of hell. If we follow this logic, it is indeed a strong coincidence that the Red Light District would then be the central cauldron of damnation. And the fact that the rookie visitor often finds himself forever looping back to this area as if under the rigid control of some strange gravity just adds to the eeriness. However, one can hypothesize that this was a geographical trick fine-tuned through the centuries to keep that ever-arriving influx of sailors compartmentalized, thereby leaving the rest of the city to the residents—and the more savvy traveler. This theory may also help account for the endless press depicting Amsterdam as a capital of sin and depravity.

But no two ways about it, sex is a big business in Amsterdam—it is also a centuries-long saga in the making, for the history of prostitution in Amsterdam, with its successful harbor, is almost as long as the history of the city. Men who were seeking companionship and comfort have been regular visitors since the Middle Ages. In the 16th century, the city's sheriff and his enforcement officials actually ran the brothels. When prostitution was outlawed, these government officials required significant raises in their salaries because of the loss of income. In the 17th century, window prostitutes were working out of their own homes. Others solicited on the streets or in taverns along the Zeedijk, but prostitution was limited to certain sections of the city. "Honest" labor for women was poorly paid, and, therefore, many women—particularly seamen's wives—supplemented their earnings with prostitution.

The 19th century saw a dramatic rise in the urban poor and a razing of slum areas. Newly built dwellings were too expensive for craftsmen and artisans to maintain, so people started renting rooms to prostitutes and students to supplement their income. The often-privileged students, prostitutes, and artists coming together in the neighborhood stimulated a carefree and fun atmosphere that still dominates in today's Red Light District. Prostitution in Amsterdam has been appreciatively and informatively portrayed in John Irving's book *A Widow for One Year.*

Dutch pragmatism is evident in the city government's approach to the unsavory aspects of life: the goal is to control and maintain public order and safety through tolerance of existing activities. There are three official locations for window prostitution: the infamous and central Red Light District 9 in Dutch referred to as the Rosse Buurt or De Walletjes); along part of the Spuistraat on the Nieuwe Zijde; and on the Ruysdaelkade on the periphery of de Pijp. As of 2000, the permit/license system introduced in the 1990s, primarily to prevent the spread of sexually transmitted diseases by targeting the prostitutes with information and help, was extended to brothels. The women now have legal recourse should the brothel not meet the standards the license demands.

The Red Light District is active day and night. Most of the women (men's forays into the window trade have always met with failure) are scantily dressed and dance or bounce their breasts in windows and doors surrounded with red and blue fluorescent light to highlight their costumes. Prostitutes come in all sizes, shapes, and nationalities and a rainbow of color. The narrowness of the streets, with windows on both sides, has an "in your face" boldness, and the new visitor will certainly feel confronted. When visiting the Red Light District, make your first stop the Prostitute Information Center, or PIC, which is also Dutch slang for "penis" (Enge Kerksteeg 3, ☎ 020/420–7328). Founded and staffed by former prostitutes, the center provides information to prostitutes, customers, and tourists on the new laws, codes of behavior, and the neighborhood in general. For those who feel more comfortable in groups, PIC recommends tours organized by Lindbergh Excursions (✉ 26 Damrak, Nieuwe Zijde ☎ 020/622-2766).

FODOR'S CHOICE

The sights, restaurants, hotels, and other travel experiences listed below are our editors' top picks—the crème de la crème chosen from the lists of Fodor's Choices found on the opening pages of the chapters in this book. They're the best of their type in the area covered by the book. In addition, the list incorporates some of the highly recommended restaurants and hotels our reviewers have come to treasure. In the chapters that follow, you will find all the details.

LODGING

$$$$ **Amstel Inter-Continental, The Plantage.** Elegant enough to please Audrey Hepburn, extroverted enough to welcome Madonna, this grand dowager has wowed all onlookers since it opened its doors in 1867. You'll feel like a visiting V.I.P. yourself when entering the magnificent lobby, a soaring salon covered with wedding-cake stucco trim and replete with a grand double staircase that demands you glide, not walk, up it.

$$$$ **Grand Sofitel Demeure, Oude Zijde.** Once a *Prinsenhof* (Prince's Courtyard) that welcomed such illustrious guests as William of Orange and Maria de Medici, this grandly renovated hostelry now has a guest book littered with names like Mick Jagger and President Chirac of France. Café Roux opens out onto a glorious courtyard for the enjoyment of afternoon tea.

$$$$ **Hotel de l'Europe, Oude Zijde.** Owned by Freddy Heineken's daughter, this hotel is one of the comeliest tulips in Amsterdam, thanks to its storybook facade and that ruby-and-tangerine gilded lobby, a top spot to perfect the art of high tea.

$$$$ **Seven One Seven, Western Canal Ring.** Suavely fusing grandeur with tasteful glamour, the guest rooms here are minimuseums, replete with classical antiquities, framed art, flowers, and objets and candles on tables and fireplace mantels. The plush library is a setting designed after Sherlock Holmes's own heart.

$$$–$$$$ **Dikker and Thijs Fenice, Leidseplein.** "Lavish," "classical," and "cozy" are some of the adjectives typically used to describe this hotel, which has a regal address on the Prinsengracht canal.

$$–$$$ **Ambassade, Western Canal Ring.** Ten 17th- and 18th-century houses have been folded into this hotel on the Herengracht, now home-away-from-home for such literati as Lessing, Le Carré, Eco, and Rushdie.

$$–$$$ **Het Canal House, Western Canal Ring.** The owners have put a lot of love and style into this 17th-century (1640) canal-house hotel. It's a beautiful old home with high plaster ceilings, antique furniture, old paintings, and a backyard garden bursting with plants and flowers.

$$–$$$ **Seven Bridges, Rembrandtplein.** Set in an 18th-century house in the heart of "Golden Bend" country, this hotel offers uniquely stylish guest rooms and one of the more famous canal sights in Amsterdam, the lineup of seven consecutive bridges that can be seen gracing Reguliersgracht.

$$–$$$	**Toren, Jordaan.** The historic setting for the founding of the Free University in the 17th century, this is a perfect example of a canal-side hotel. Occupying two buildings from 1638, the Toren has an evocative garden and is in the shadow of the Westerkerk *toren* (Western Church tower).
$$	**Prinsen, Vondelpark.** Architect of the Rijksmuseum and Centraal Station, P. H. H. Cuijpers created several of the city's stateliest landmarks, but he rarely came up with such an adorable edifice as this one, built around 1870. Not to get you stuck in a time warp, the interior rooms are modern.
$–$$	**Piet Hein, Vondelpark.** Not all chocolates have a gooey center. When in 2003 it came time to refurbish this ornate brick Vondelpark mansion, the owners decided to go for the modern, the light, the airy, the less-is-not-a-bore, and they have gorgeously succeeded. And making this place even more popular with the *Wallpaper* crowd are the relatively gentle room rates.

BUDGET LODGING

$	**Acacia, Jordaan** In Amsterdam's friendliest neighborhood, the small family-run Acacia is a good ambassador for the nabe, thanks to its welcoming vibe, oh-so-cozy rooms, and those charming *gezelligheid* cafés and shops just outside the door.
$	**Quentin England, Vondelpark.** Both a budgeteer's and a connoisseur's delight. this place is set in a series of adjoining buildings dating from 1884, each built in an architectural style of the country whose name it bears. Adorned with a Tudor gable and five-step gable, the Quentin delightfully occupies the England and Netherlands buildings.

DINING

$$$$	**Excelsior, Oude Zijde.** For when only the classically elegant will do, take your primped-up selves here. Solicitous waiters, knowledgeable sommeliers, and towering dessert trolleys all waltz together in a setting of towering palms, tall candelabras, and shimmering chandeliers. Even more more delicious is the mouthwatering view of the Amstel River.
$$$$	**La Rive, East of Amstel.** One of the jewels of the sumptuous Amstel Inter-Continental hotel, this culinary temple is now presided over by chef Edwin Kats, whose haute nouvelle creations will delight chubby-walleted epicureans everywhere.
$$$$	**Supper Club, Nieuwe Zijde.** Simple, artful, white, and sleek, this spot offers up endless courses of food (and drink . . .) marked by irreverent flavor combinations. DJs, VJs, and live performances enhance the clublike, relentlessly hip vibe.
$$$$	**Vermeer, Oude Zijde.** Replete with Delft plates and Stern Old Dutch chandeliers, this stately place conjures up the amber canvases of the great Johannes—if he ever did the decor for a fancy hotel chain, that is. The kitchen here is one of the city's best and young chef Pascal Jalaij offers creations that are cosmic in the way they balance

texture and contrast. A poached Anjou dove with juniper berry sauce and a crunchy potato pie, anyone?

$$$–$$$$	**Breitner, Amsterdam.** With a formal interior of rich red carpeting and muted pastel colors, a grand vista over the City Hall complex, and fabulous food, it's no wonder the patrons do their share to show respect for Breitner by dressing smartly.
$$$–$$$$	**D' Vijff Vlieghen, Nieuwe Zijde.** The "Five Flies" is a rambling dining institution that takes up five adjoining Golden Age houses, all givin off a densely evocative Golden Age vibe, complete with bona fide Rembrandt etchings, wooden *jenever* (Dutch gin) barrels, crystal and armor collections, and an endless array of old-school bric-a-brac. The ambience is probably more delicious than the food.
$$–$$$	**Blue Pepper, Leidseplein.** One of the more widely acclaimed of recent newcomers in town, this blue-toned Indonesian spot features the inspired cooking of an award-winning chef. Bliss may be your dessert.
$$–$$$	**Kantjil en de Tijger, Nieuwe Zijde.** No folkloric shadow puppets adorn the walls at this unusually large and spacious Indonesian restaurant: the interior is serenely Jugendstil (a sort of Austrian Art Nouveau), which provides a refreshing surprise. Although you can order à la carte, the menu is based on three different–and delicious—*rijsttafel* (rice tables).
$$	**Haesje Claes, Oude Zijde.** Groaning with pewter tankards, stained glass, leaded windows, rich historic paneling, Indonesian paisley *fabriks,* and betasseled Victorian lamps, this is a restaurant after any Meinherr Van Tassel's heart.

BUDGET DINING

$	**Café Bern, Nieuwe Zijde.** This dark and woody café, as evocative as a Jan Steen 17th-century interior, has been serving the same cheese fondue for decades and for good reason: it's just about perfect.
¢	**Keuken van 1870, Nieuwe Zijde.** This former soup kitchen, where sharing tables is still the norm, is as reassuring as a Dutch grandmother, thanks to its warming singularities as *hutspot* (a hotchpotch of potatoes, carrots, and onions), its more free-ranging variant *stamppot* (a stew of potatoes, greens, and chunks of cured sausage), and *erwtensoep* (a sausage-fortified pea soup so thick you could eat it with a toothpick).
¢–$	**'t Smalle, Jordaan.** Set with Golden Age chandeliers, leaded-glass windows, and the patina of centuries, this gloriously charming canal-side landmark is one of Amsterdam's most delightful *bruine kroeg.* (brown cafés)

QUINTESSENTIAL HOLLAND

	Amsterdam canals at night. Walking along the canals of Amsterdam after dark is one of the simplest, cheapest, and most memorable experiences that Holland has to offer. Pedestrians (and cyclists) rule over traffic, the most beautiful gables are subtly lit up, and the pretty humpbacked bridges are festooned with lights. Alternatively,

get up early and stroll out before the city is awake as the mist gently rises off the water.

Begijnhof, Amsterdam. Feel the gentle breeze of history in the solitude of a serene courtyard that has hardly changed since the Pilgrim Fathers worshiped here centuries ago.

Bikes on dikes (most anywhere). Trundling along the top of a dike on a sit-up-and-beg Dutch bicycle, with the sea to one side of you, wetlands (alive with bird life) on the other, and the wind in your hair, is transporting in more ways than one. Enhance the delight by stopping over at one of myriad waterside cafés or charming villages as you explore the historic folkloric towns like Water-in-Broderland just to the north of Amsterdam.

Prinsenhof, Delft. How can you not take a day trip to Vermeer's hometown? Sit quietly in this courtyard garden, and then explore the atmospheric 15th-century convent before strolling off along what is probably the oldest canal in The Netherlands. At times it seems that you are stepping right into Vermeer's *View of Delft*.

WHERE ART COMES FIRST

Museum het Rembrandthuis, Jewish Quarter. Once fitted out with the ultimate in fashionable 17th-century furnishings, this former home of the great Rembrandt today casts but a dim shadow of its glory days. However, the many engravings and prints on view by the master are spectacular enough.

Museum Willet-Holthuysen, Eastern Canal Ring. Amsterdam's 17th-century Golden Age comes to life at this elegant Neoclassical mansion, brimming with sumptous damasks, Old Master paintings, French chandeliers, and a full blast of Grachtengordel (Canal Ring) luxury.

Rijksmuseum, Museum District. As if the best collection of Dutch Golden Age art in the world were not enough, "the Rijks" also offers a cornucopia of other aesthetic delights. The collection of applied arts is especially comprehensive, from early Oriental Buddhas to 17th-century four-poster beds swathed in tapestry. Rembrandt's enormous *Night Watch* is a hot contender for the title of "the world's most famous painting."

Rijksmuseum Vincent Van Gogh, Museum District It is difficult to pick a favorite from the more than 200 paintings by this great artist on view here, but *Sunflowers* is among the top choices. None of the versions you may have seen in reproduction can match the luster of the original, where brilliant blues appear unexpectedly between the bright yellows and greens.

SMART TRAVEL TIPS

Half the fun of traveling is looking forward to your trip—but when you look forward, don't just daydream. There are plans to be made, things to learn about, serious work to be done. The following chapter will give you helpful pointers on many of the questions that arise when planning your trip and also when you are on the road. Finding out about your destination before you leave home means you won't squander time organizing everyday minutiae once you've arrived. You'll be more streetwise when you hit the ground as well, better prepared to explore the aspects of Amsterdam that drew you here in the first place. The organizations in this section can provide information to supplement this guide; contact them for up-to-the-minute details. Many trips begin by contacting The Netherlands tourist bureau: consult their listings under Visitor Information, below. Happy landings!

ADDRESSES

Welkom in Amsterdam—welcome to Amsterdam! Fittingly, for a country with a history as venerable as Holland's, the country's *straten,* or streets (and other places) are often named after its famous sons and daughters. In Amsterdam, for one example, Hugo de Grootstraat is named in honor of Delft's noted lawyer-philosopher (*straat* is "street"). In addition, you get all the variations: Hugo de Grootkade (*kade* is the name of a street running parallel to a canal), Hugo de Grootplein (*plein* is "square"), ad infinitum. In Amsterdam, there's even an Eerste, Tweede, and Derde (first, second, and third) Hugo de Grootstraat. Of course, kings and queens feature: Wilhelminastraat is named after Queen Wilhelmina, the grandmother of the current queen, Beatrix. In Amsterdam, the Vondelpark is named after Holland's most celebrated poet, Joost van den Vondel, and Rembrandtplein is a touristy square, named after the artist who had a studio just across the canals.

Other geographical terms to keep in mind are a *dwarsstraat,* or street that runs perpendicular to a street or canal, such as the Leidsestraat and the Leidsedwarsstraat. A *straatje* is a small street; a *weg* is a road; a *gracht* is a canal; a *steeg* is a very small street; a *laan* is a lane. *Baan* is another name for a road, not quite a highway, but busier than an average street. Note that in The Netherlands, the house number always comes after the street name on addresses.

The Dutch have an infinite range of names for bodies of water, from *gracht* to *singel* to *kanaal* (all roughly equating to "canal"). A singel is similar to a gracht (two terraces facing each other over a canal). The difference between a singel and a gracht is hard to define, even for a Dutch person. In fact, the names can be confusing because sometimes there is *no* water at all—many grachten have been filled in by developers to make room for houses, roads, and so on.

Amsterdam streets radiate outward from Centraal Station; in general, street numbers go up in numerical sequence as you move in a direction away from Centraal Station. Don't let common address abbreviations confuse you. BG stands for *Begane Grond* (ground floor); SOUT for *Soutterrain* (sub-level/basement apartment); HS for *Huis* (a ground-floor apartment or main entry). Some common geographical abbreviations are *str.* for *straat* (street); *gr.* for *gracht* (canal); and *pl.* for *plein* (square). For example: Leidsestr., Herengr., or Koningspl.

AIR TRAVEL

BOOKING

When you book **look for nonstop flights** and **remember that "direct" flights stop at least once.** Try to avoid connecting flights, which require a change of plane. Two airlines may operate a connecting flight jointly, so ask if your airline operates every segment of the trip; you may find that the carrier you prefer flies you only part of the way. For more booking tips and to check prices and make on-line flight reservations, log on to www.fodors.com.

CARRIERS

When flying internationally to The Netherlands, you usually choose between a domestic carrier, the national flag carrier of the country, and a foreign carrier from a third country. You may, for example, choose to fly KLM Royal Dutch Airlines to The Netherlands for the basic reason that, as the national flag carrier, it has the greatest number of nonstop flights. Domestic carriers offer connections to smaller destinations. Third-party carriers may have a price advantage.

KLM and its global alliance partner Northwest—together with their regional partner airlines—fly from Amsterdam's Schiphol Airport to more than 400 destinations in more than 80 countries worldwide. Nearly 100 of those are European destinations, with three to four daily flights to most airports and up to 17 flights a day to London alone. Northwest Airlines now handles all reservations and ticket office activities on behalf of KLM in the United States and Canada, with KLM's biggest North American hubs in Detroit and Minneapolis, as well as Memphis, New York, and Washington among its gateways. KLM's direct flights connect Amsterdam to Atlanta, Los Angeles, and Miami, and numerous others. Including connections via KLM's hubs, the airline flies to more than 100 destinations in the United States from Amsterdam. In Canada, KLM/Northwest serves Montreal, Toronto, and Vancouver. For more information, contact the airline at one of the reservation numbers below. For further information about schedules and special fare promotions, go to KLM/Northwest's Web site.

Other international carriers include American Airlines, Continental Airlines, Delta Airlines, United Airlines, and US Airways, but none of these carriers makes a transatlantic flight to any of The Netherlands' regional airports. MartinAir Holland, however, along with Dutch Bird and other charters, does make transatlantic flights from some of the regional terminals. If your carrier offers Rotterdam as a final destination, you fly into Amsterdam then transfer. KLM Cityhopper and KLM Excel offer a varied schedule of flights connecting Amsterdam with the smaller regional airports, and British Airways provides a number of domestic flights; between them, the whole country is covered. Transavia Airlines flies from Amsterdam and Rotterdam to a number of European destinations, and many other carriers link European capitals with Amsterdam. For instance, Air France offers a direct route between Amsterdam and Paris. Check with your travel agent for details.

Ask your airline if it offers e-ticketing (electronic ticketing), which eliminates all paperwork: there's no ticket to pick up or misplace. You go directly to the gate and give the agent your ticket number instead of waiting in line at the counter while minutes tick by.

To & from the Netherlands **KLM Royal Dutch Airlines** ☎ 300/303-747 in Australia, 020/474-7747 in The Netherlands, 09/309-1782 in New Zealand, 0870/243-0541 in U.K. ☎ 800/447-4747 for Northwest/KLM sales office in U.S. and Canada ⊕ www.klm.com. **American Airlines** ☎ 800/433-7300 ⊕ www.aa.com. **British Airways** ☎ 0870/850-9850 in U.K., 020/346-9559 in The Netherlands ⊕ www.britishairways.com. **British Midland** ☎ 0870/607-0555 ⊕ www.flybml.com. **Continental Airlines** ☎ 800/231-0856 ⊕ www.continental.com. **Delta Air Lines** ☎ 800/241-4141 ⊕ www.delta.com. **Dutch Bird** ☎ 020/605-5800 ⊕ www.dutchbird.com. **MartinAir Holland** ☎ 020/601-1767 ⊕ www.martinair.com. **Transavia Airlines** ☎ 020/406-0406 in The Netherlands ⊕ www.transavia.nl/home. **United Airlines** ☎ 800/538-2929 ⊕ www.ual.com. **US Airways** ☎ 800/428-4322 ⊕ www.usairways.com.

Around the Netherlands **KLM** ☎ 300/303-747 in Australia, 020/474-7747 in The Netherlands, 09/309-1782 in New Zealand, 0870/243-0541 in U.K. ☎ 800/447-4747 for Northwest/KLM sales office in U.K. and Canada ⊕ www.klm.com. **British Airways** ☎ 0870/850-9850 in U.K., 020/346-9559 in The Netherlands ⊕ www.britishairways.com.

CHECK-IN & BOARDING

Always ask your carrier about its check-in policy. Plan to arrive at the airport about 2 hours before your scheduled departure time for domestic flights and 2½ to 3 hours before international flights.

Assuming that not everyone with a ticket will show up, airlines routinely overbook planes. When everyone does, airlines ask for volunteers to give up their seats. In return, these volunteers usually get a certificate for a free flight and are rebooked on the next flight out. If there are not enough volunteers, the airline must choose who will be denied boarding. The first to get bumped are passengers who checked in late and those flying on discounted tickets, so **get to the gate and check in as early as possible,** especially during peak periods.

Always **bring a government-issued photo ID to the airport;** even when it's not required, a passport is best.

CUTTING COSTS

The least expensive airfares to The Netherlands are priced for round-trip travel and must usually be purchased in advance. Airlines generally allow you to change your return date for a fee;

most-low fare tickets, however, are nonrefundable. It's smart to **call a number of airlines,** and when you are quoted a good price, **book it on the spot**—the same fare may not be available the next day. Always **check different routings** and look into using alternate airports. Also, price off-peak flights, which may be significantly less expensive than others. Lower-priced charter flights to a range of Dutch destinations are available throughout the year. Travel agents, especially low-fare specialists (⇨ Discounts & Deals), are helpful.

Consolidators are another good source. They buy tickets for scheduled international flights at reduced rates from the airlines, then sell them at prices that beat the best fare available directly from the airlines. Sometimes you can even get your money back if you need to return the ticket. Carefully read the fine print detailing penalties for changes and cancellations, purchase the ticket with a credit card, and **confirm your consolidator reservation with the airline.**

When you **fly as a courier,** you trade your checked-luggage space for a ticket deeply subsidized by a courier service. There are restrictions on when you can book and how long you can stay. Some courier companies list with membership organizations, such as the Air Courier Association and the International Association of Air Travel Couriers; these require you to become a member before you can book a flight.

Many airlines, singly or in collaboration, offer discount air passes that allow foreigners to travel economically in a particular country or region. These visitor passes usually must be reserved and purchased before you leave home. Information about passes can be difficult to track down on airline Web sites, which tend to be geared to travelers departing from a given carrier's country rather than to those intending to visit that country. Try typing the name of the pass into a search engine, or search for "pass" within the carrier's Web site.

EasyJet has low fares to Amsterdam flying in from Barcelona, Belfast, Edinburgh, Geneva, Glasgow, Liverpool, London (Gatwick and Luton), and Nice. BasiqAir flies to Amsterdam and Rotterdam from Barcelona and Nice.

Consolidators & Low-cost Airlines **BasiqAir** ☎ 0900/0737 in The Netherlands. **Cheap Tickets**

☎ 888/922-8849 ⊕ www.cheaptickets.com. **Easy-Jet** ☎ 023/568-4880 in The Netherlands ⊕ www.easyjet.com. **Global Travel** ☎ 416/516-1113 in Canada. **Now Voyager Travel** ✉ 315 W. 49th St. Plaza Arcade, New York, NY 10019 ☎ 212/459-1616 ☎ 212/262-7407 ⊕ www.nowvoyagertravel.com. **World Courier of Canada** ☎ 905/678-6007. ⤢ Discount Passes **FlightPass** EuropebyAir ☎ 888/3321-4737 ⊕ www.europebyair.com. **SAS Air Passes** Scandinavian Airlines ☎ 800/221-2350 ⊕ www.scandinavian.net.

ENJOYING THE FLIGHT

All flights within The Netherlands are no-smoking. Smoking is allowed on an increasingly limited number of international flights; **contact your carrier about its smoking policy. State your seat preference** when purchasing your ticket, and then repeat it when you confirm and when you check in. For more legroom, you can request one of the few emergency-aisle seats at check-in, if you are capable of lifting at least 50 pounds—a Federal Aviation Administration requirement of passengers in these seats. Seats behind a bulkhead also offer more legroom, but they don't have under-seat storage. Don't sit in the row in front of the emergency aisle or in front of a bulkhead, where seats may not recline.

If you have dietary concerns, **ask for special meals when booking.** These can be vegetarian, low-cholesterol, or kosher, for example. It's a good idea to pack some healthful snacks and a small bottle (plastic) of water in your carry-on bag. On long flights, try to maintain a normal routine to help fight jet lag. At night, **get some sleep.** By day, **eat light meals, drink water** (not alcohol), and **move around the cabin** to stretch your legs. For additional jet-lag tips consult *Fodor's FYI: Travel Fit & Healthy* (available at bookstores everywhere).

FLYING TIMES

Flying time to Amsterdam is 21½ hours from Auckland; 1 hour from London; 10½ hours from Los Angeles; 7 hours from New York; 20 hours from Sydney; and 8 hours from Toronto.

HOW TO COMPLAIN

If your baggage goes astray or your flight goes awry, complain right away. Most carriers require that you **file a claim immediately.** The Aviation Consumer Protection Division of the Department of Transportation publishes *Fly-Rights,* which discusses airlines and consumer issues and is available on-line. One good Web site that address many of these concerns can be found at http://airconsumer. ost.dot.gov/problems.htm. ⤢ Airline Complaints **Aviation Consumer Protection Division** ✉ U.S. Department of Transportation, C-75, 400 Seventh Street, S.W., Washington, DC 20590 ☎ 202/366-2220 ⊕ www.dot.gov/airconsumer. **Federal Aviation Administration Consumer Hotline** ☎ 800/322-7873.

RECONFIRMING

Check the status of your flight before you leave for the airport. You can do this on your carrier's Web site, by linking to a flight-status checker (many Web booking services offer these), or by calling your carrier or travel agent. Always confirm international flights at least 72 hours ahead of the scheduled departure time.

AIRPORTS

Located 17 km (11 mi) southeast of Amsterdam, **Luchthaven Schiphol** (pronounced "Shh-kip-hole") is the main passenger airport for Holland. With the annual number of passengers using Schiphol approaching 40 million, it is ranked among the world's top five best-connected airports. A hotel, a service to aid passengers with disabilities, parking lots, and a main office of The Netherlands tourist board (in Schiphol Plaza and known as "HTi"—Holland Tourist Information) can prove most useful. The comprehensive Schiphol telephone service, charged at €.10 per minute, provides information about flight arrivals and departures as well as all transport and parking facilities. ⤢ Airport Information **Amsterdam Luchthaven (Airport) Schiphol** ✈ 17 km (11 mi) southwest of Amsterdam ☎ 0900/0141 ⊕ www.schiphol.nl.

AIRPORT TRANSFER

The Schiphol Rail Link operates between the airport and the city 24 hours a day, with service to Centraal Station—Amsterdam's central railway station—or to stations in the south of the city. From 6:30 AM to 12:30 AM, a train departs from or arrives at Schiphol every 15 minutes; other hours, there is one train every hour. The trip takes about 15 minutes and costs €3. Trains leave from the platforms of Schiphol Station, found beneath Schiphol

Plaza. They head into the city using one of three routes. The most popular is the NS Schiphollijn, which runs to Centraal Station (with two stops in west Amsterdam). Another route heads to the Amsterdam Zuid/WTC (South/World Trade Center) station in south Amsterdam, and another line heads to the RAI section, near the big convention center. From these south Amsterdam stations, Tram 5 goes to Leidseplein and the Museum Quarter; from RAI, Tram 4 goes to Rembrandtplein. Keep in mind that Schiphol Station is one of Holland's busiest—make sure you catch the shuttle to Amsterdam and not a train heading to The Hague! As always, when arriving at Amsterdam's Centraal Station, keep an eye out for any stray pickpocketers. Other than taxis, you may wish to hop aboard a tram or bus to get to your hotel, so go to one of the **Gemeentevervoerbedrijf (GVB) Amsterdam Municipal Transport** booths found in front of the Centraal Station. Here you can find directions, fare information, and schedules.

KLM Shuttle operates a shuttle bus service between Amsterdam Schiphol Airport and 16 of the city's major hotels (among them, the Krasnapolsky and the Toren), along with stops that are convenient to many other hotels in the city. The trip takes about half an hour and costs €10.50 one-way. Hours for this bus shuttle are 7 AM to 6 PM, every half hour; between 6 PM and 9 PM, departures are every hour.

Finally, there is a taxi stand directly in front of the arrival hall at Amsterdam Schiphol Airport. A service charge is included, but small additional tips are not unwelcome. New laws determine that taxi fares are now fixed from Schiphol to Amsterdam; depending on the neighborhood, a trip will cost between €25 and €30. When you're returning home, a ride to Schiphol from Amsterdam center city area, the Centrum, will cost €22. A new service that might be convenient for budget travelers who count every euro is the Schiphol Travel Taxi. The taxi needs to be booked at least 48 hours in advance and rides are shared, so the trip will take a bit longer as the taxi stops to pick up passengers.

🚕 Taxis & Shuttles **KLM Shuttle** ☎ 020/653-4975. **Schiphol Rail Link** ☎ 0900/9292. **Schiphol Travel Taxi** ☎ 020/0900-8876.

DUTY-FREE SHOPPING

Although the European Union eliminated duty-free shopping in airports in The Netherlands and in Europe, Schiphol's tax-free shopping center, See-Buy-Fly, maintains its ability to sell cheaper goods thanks to a subsidy from the airport; you can also make in-flight duty-free purchases.

AMSTERDAM PASS

The recently introduced electronic Amsterdam Culture Pass provides free and discount admissions to many of the city's top museums, plus a free canal round-trip, free use of public transport, and a 25% discount on various attractions and restaurants; savings can amount to more than €100. A one-day pass costs €26, two days costs €36 and three days costs €46. The pass comes with a booklet in Dutch, English, French, and German. It can be purchased at branches of the VVV (Netherlands Board of Tourism), the GVB (City Transport Company), both at Centraal Station, and through some hotels and museums.

AMSTERDAM TOURS

BICYCLE TOURS

From April through October, guided 1½- to 3-hour bike trips through the central area of the city are available through Yellow Bike. Let's Go tours (contact the VVV for further details) takes you out of the city center by train before introducing you to the safer cycling of the surrounding countryside. Its tours include Edam and Volendam, Naarden and Muiden, and, in season, a Tulip Tour.

🚴 Fees & Schedules **Let's Go** ✉ VVV Netherlands Board of Tourism, Centraal Station, Centrum ⊕ www.letsgo-amsterdam.com. **Yellow Bike** ✉ Nieuwezijds Kolk 29, Centrum ☎ 020/620-6940 ⊕ www.yellowbike.nl.

BOAT TOURS

The quickest, easiest, and (frankly) most delightful way to get your bearings in Amsterdam is to take a canal-boat cruise. Trips last from 1 to 1½ hours and cover the harbor as well as the main canal district; there is a taped or live commentary available in four languages. Excursion boats leave from *rondvaart* (excursion piers) in various locations in the city every 15 minutes from March to October, and every 30 minutes in winter. Departures are frequent from Prins Hendrikkade near the Centraal Station, along the Damrak, and along the Rokin (near Muntplein), at Leidseplein, and Stadhouderskade (near the Rijksmuseum). For a tour lasting about an hour, the cost is around €8.50, but the student guides expect a small tip for their multilingual commentary. For a truly romantic view of Amsterdam, opt for one of the special dinner and candlelight cruises offered by some companies, notably Holland International. A candlelight dinner cruise costs upward of €24. Trips for all boat tours can also be booked through the tourist office.

Operators of canal cruises include Holland International, Meyers Rondvaarten, Rederij D'Amstel, Rederij Lovers, Rederij P. Kooij, Rederij Noord/Zuid, and Rederij Plas.

Several boat trips to museums are also available: Canalbus, which makes six stops along two different routes between Centraal Station and the Rijksmuseum, costs €15, including tickets and/or reductions for museums. Following a longer route is Museumboot Rederij Lovers, which makes seven stops near 20 different museums. The cost is €13.25 for a day ticket that entitles you to a 50% discount on admission to the museums. At Canal-Bike, a pedal boat for four costs €28 per hour.

The Canal Bike *Waterfiets* is a peddle-powered boat that seats up to four. You can tour the Grachtengordel ring of canals at your own pace. For one or two people, the hourly fee is €8 per person, and for three to four persons, it costs €7 per person, per hour. Rental hours are between 10 and 6:30 daily. There are five landing stages throughout the city, with two of the most popular ones located across from the Rijksmuseum and across from the Westerkerk.

Fees & Schedules Canal bus ⊠ Nieuwe Weteringschans 24, Leidseplein ☎ 020/623-9886 🌐 www.canal.nl. **Holland International** ⊠ Prins Hendrikkade, opposite Centraal Station, Centrum ☎ 020/622-7788. **Meyers Rondvaarten** ⊠ Damrak 4, Dam ☎ 020/623-4208. **Museumboot Rederij Lovers** ⊠ Stationsplein 8, Centrum ☎ 020/530-1090. **Amsterdam Canal Cruises** ⊠ Nicolaas Witsenkade, opposite the Heineken Brewery, De Pijp ☎ 020/626-5636. **Rederij Lovers** ⊠ Prins Hendrikkade 26 a, opposite Centraal Station, Centrum ☎ 020/530-1090. **Rederij P. Kooij** ⊠ Rokin, near

Spui, Centrum ☎ 020/623-3810. **Rederij Noord/Zuid** ⊠ Stadhouderskade 25, opposite Parkhotel, Leidseplein ☎ 020/679-1370. **Rederij Plas** ⊠ Damrak, quays 1-3, Dam ☎ 020/624-5406.

BUS TOURS

Afternoon bus tours of the city operate daily. Itineraries vary, and prices range from €15 to €30. A 2½-hour city tour that includes a drive through the suburbs is offered by Key Tours. However, it must be said that this city of narrow alleys and canals is not best appreciated from the window of a coach. Also, a number of visitors feel unhappy that part of some tours involves a visit to a diamond factory, where they feel pressured into listening to a sales pitch. The same bus companies operate scenic trips to attractions outside the city.
Fees & Schedules Key Tours ⊠ Dam 19, Dam ☎ 020/623-5051. **Lindbergh Excursions** ⊠ Damrak 26, Dam ☎ 020/622-2766.

WALKING TOURS

The Amsterdam Tourist Board (VVV) maintains lists of personal guides and guided walking and cycling tours for groups in and around Amsterdam and can advise you on making arrangements. You can also contact Guidor–Nederlandse Gidsen Organisatie (Dutch Guides Organization). The costs are from €143 for a half day to €234 for a full day. The tourist office also sells brochures outlining easy-to-follow self-guided theme tours through the central part of the city. Among them are "A Journey of Discovery Through Maritime Amsterdam," "A Walk Through the Jordaan," "Jewish Amsterdam," and "Rembrandt and Amsterdam."

Walking tours focusing on art and architecture are organized by Artifex, Stichting Arttra, and Archivisie. For walking tours of the Jewish Quarter, contact Joods Historisch Museum. Yellow Bike Tours organizes two-hour walking tours of the Jordaan and the Red Light District.

Probably the best deal in town is Mee in Mokum, which offers walking tours led by retired longtime residents. For a mere €2.50, you are given an entertaining three-hour educational tour of the inner city or the Jordaan, focusing on architecture and surprising facts. These tours are also popular with Amsterdammers who wish to discover new things about their city. The admission fee entitles you to reduced fees to a choice of museums and a reduction in the price of a pancake at a nearby restaurant. Tours are held daily and start promptly at 11 AM. You must reserve at least a day in advance. Tours are limited to eight people; private arrangements can also be made for other times of the day.

F Fees & Schedules **Archivisie** 📞 Postbus 14603, 1001 LC ☎ 020/625-8908. **Artifex** ✉ Herengracht 342, 1016 CG, Grachtengordel ☎ 020/620-8112. **Arttra Cultureel Orgburo** ✉ Staalstraat 28, 1011 JM, De Wallen ☎ 020/625-9303 🌐 www.arttra.com. **Guidor–Nederlandse Gidsen Organisatie** ✉ Hemsbrugstraat 11 ☎ 020/624-6072 or 020/627-0006. **Joods Historisch Museum** ✉ Jonas Daniel Meyerplein 2-4, Postbus 16737, 1001 RE, Plantage ☎ 020/626-9945 🖨 020/624-1721. **Mee in Mokum** ✉ Hartenstraat 18, Jordaan ☎ 020/625-1390, call between 1 and 4. **Yellow Bike** ✉ Nieuwezijds Kolk 29, Centrum ☎ 020/620-6940 🌐 www.yellowbike.nl.

BIKE TRAVEL

BIKES IN FLIGHT

Most airlines accommodate bikes as luggage, provided they are dismantled and boxed; check with individual airlines about packing requirements. Airlines sell bike boxes, which are often free at bike shops, for about $15 (bike bags start at $100). International travelers often can substitute a bike for a piece of checked luggage at no charge; otherwise, the cost is about $100. Domestic and Canadian airlines charge $40–$80 each way. A handy Web site that addresses many biking questions is www.bikeaccess.net/bikeboxs_db.cfm.

GETTING AROUND BY BIKE

Bicycling is the most convenient way to see Amsterdam. There are bike lanes on all major streets, bike racks in key locations, and special bike parking indentations in the pavement. To rent a bicycle, you'll pay from €6.50 per day, plus a deposit of about €50 per bike, and need a passport or other identification. The more days you rent, the cheaper the price, and rates by the week are even more competitive. Bikes can be rented at outlets near railway stations or by contacting rental centers. MacBike—the most popular rental firm in town—has various rental points around the city center; Bike City is near the Anne Frank House; Damstraat Rent-a-Bike is near the Dam Square.

Never leave your bike unlocked: there is a rapid turnover of stolen bikes no matter what quality or condition. Use a "D" lock, which can't be cut with the average thieves' tools, and lock your bike's frame to something that can't be shifted, such as a railing. Never buy a bicycle from someone on the street; it has probably just been stolen.

Nearly every Amsterdam resident has a bike; don't be surprised to see entire families cycling, from toddlers to octogenarians, with special seats for infants and bike baskets for dogs. As a cyclist, you'll notice that most fellow cyclers don't really observe the traffic signs and rules, nor do they stay in the bicycle lanes marked out for them, unless the road has particularly heavy traffic. However, as a result of accidents caused by aggressive cyclists, fines and other penalties are being rigorously imposed (you can also be fined for riding at night with no lights, and for drunken cycling). Cars that are turning across your path are supposed to stop for you, but it is wise to watch out. Another danger is getting your wheel stuck in tram rails; a nasty fall could result, especially since protective headgear is not legally required. Maps and route guides for Amsterdam and side trips are available at larger bookstores such as Scheltema on the Koningsplein and from the ANWB (Royal Dutch Touring Club) or the VVV (Netherlands Board of Tourism information offices), although bicycle tracks between towns are so well signposted that you do not have to rely on a map.

In this flat country, with its 19,000 km (10,000 mi) of *fietspaden* (cycle paths) in and between cities, a bicycle is an ideal means of getting around. A fietspad might easily be mistaken for a pedestrian path. If you see a circular sign, with a bicycle ringed in blue, then only bikes can use the fietspad. If, however, there is also a *bromfiets* (moped) on the sign, then mopeds can use these paths. The youngsters riding them tend to drive exceptionally fast, so beware of the potential hazards of meandering across a seemingly quiet fietspad.

F Bike Rentals **Bike City** ✉ Bloemgracht 70 ☎ 020/626-3721. **Damstraat Rent-a-Bike** ✉ Damstraat 22 ☎ 020/625-5029. **MacBike** ✉ Mr. Visserplein 2 ☎ 020/620-0985 ✉ Marnixstraat 220 ☎ 020/626-6964 ✉ Stationsplein 12 ☎ 020/624-8391.

BOAT & FERRY TRAVEL

ARRIVING & DEPARTING BY BOAT & FERRY

Traveling from the United Kingdom, there is a DFDS Seaways overnight crossing from Newcastle to IJmuiden, in Amsterdam, taking 15 hours.

DFDS Seaways ✉ Sluisplein 33, 1975 AG IJmuiden ☎ 0255/546-666 📠 0255/546-655 🌐 www.scansea.com arranges crossings from the United Kingdom to Amsterdam.

BUSINESS HOURS

BANKS & OFFICES

Banks are open weekdays 9:30 to 4 or 5, with some extending their business hours to coordinate with late-night shopping. Some banks are closed Monday mornings.

The main post office is open weekdays, 9 to 6, Saturday 10 to 1:30. In every post office you'll also find the Postbank, a money-changing facility, which has the same opening hours.

BARS & RESTAURANTS

As a general guide, bars in Amsterdam open at various times during the day and close at 1 AM throughout the week, at 2 or 3 AM on Friday and Saturday. Restaurants are open evenings 5–11, (with a few open until early morning), although some kitchens close as early as 9, and many are closed on Sunday and Monday.

MUSEUMS & SIGHTS

Major sights, such as Amsterdam's Koninklijk Paleis (Royal Dam Palace) have summer opening hours; churches and cathedrals are open 9–3; parks are open dawn to dusk; the scenic courtyard *hofjes* (almshouses) are usually open at the discretion of the inhabitants. Museum hours vary; to give some instances, the city's famous Van Gogh museum is open 10–6, and the Anne Frank House is open 9–7 and until 9 in summer.

Note that when this book refers to summer hours, it means approximately Easter to October; winter hours run from November to Easter.

SHOPS

Most shops are open from 1 to 6 on Monday, 9 to 6 Tuesday through Saturday. Hairdressers are generally closed Sunday and Monday. If you really need a haircut on those days, try a salon at one of the larger hotels. Thursday is a designated late-night shopping night—"Koopavond" (buying evenings)—with stores staying open until 9. *Markts* (markets) selling fruit, flowers, and other wares run from 10 to 4 or sometimes 5. Small *avondwinkels* (late-night shops) selling food, wine, and toiletries, are open from afternoon till midnight or later. Supermarkets are open weekdays until 8 or 10 PM and Saturday until 5 or 8 PM, with some (such as Albert Heijn on the Leidsestraat, Dam, and Museumplein) open on Sundays from 11 to 7.

BUS TRAVEL IN THE NETHERLANDS

ARRIVING & DEPARTING BY COACH

Connexxion is a company providing bus links between Amsterdam and outside towns and cities.

Eurolines run a coach service, which is essentially a well-equipped bus, to transfer passengers between countries but not between cities in the same country. You can travel from London, crossing via the Channel Tunnel or by ferry, or from Brussels to Amsterdam, but the journeys are exhaustively long. With the advent of EasyJet, it is worth looking into noncommuter time flights that beat the price of even a Euroline ticket.

Bus Information/Europe-wide Travel Connexxion ✉ Cateringweg 12, Luchthaven Schiphol, Amsterdam 1118AN. **Eurolines In The Netherlands** ✉ Rokin 10, Amsterdam ☎ 020/421-7951 🌐 www.eurolines.nl ✉ In England ✉ 4 Cardiff Rd., Luton, Bedfordshire, LU1 1PP England ☎ 0870/514-3219 in U.K., 845/228-0145 in U.S.

Transit Information Information on public transportation, including schedules, fares for **trains, buses, trams, and ferries,** to and from and within Amsterdam ☎ 0900/9292. Lost and found ☎ 020/460-5858.

CUTTING COSTS

Paying the full travel fare, without using a pass or reduction card, means that toddlers under 3 travel for free; children from 4 to 11 have an automatic 40% reduction, and children from 12 to adults are charged the full fare. If you plan to use buses, trams, and metros more often than four days a week, it is more economical for you to buy a weekly pass. Ask about all reduction cards and passes by ringing the public transport information line or asking at the local transport window in railway stations or by dropping in to the nearest VVV (tourist office).

CAMERAS & PHOTOGRAPHY

For an invaluable guide to shooting great travel pictures, go to Fodor's Web site, where nearly 100 easy-to-follow photography tips have been integrated into the on-line Smart Travel Tips section. Take a look at the sections; then click on the topics that interest you. Our tips for taking travel pictures like a pro will open up in a separate browser window.

The *Kodak Guide to Shooting Great Travel Pictures* (available at bookstores everywhere) is loaded with tips.
🖪 Photo Help **Kodak Information Center** ☎ 800/242-2424 ⊕ www.kodak.com.

EQUIPMENT PRECAUTIONS

Don't pack film and equipment in checked luggage, where it is much more susceptible to damage. X-ray machines used to view checked luggage are becoming much more powerful and therefore are much more likely to ruin your film. Try to **ask for hand inspection of film,** which becomes clouded after repeated exposure to airport X-ray machines, and **keep videotapes and computer disks away from metal detectors.** Always **keep film, tape, and computer disks out of the sun.** Carry an extra supply of batteries, and **be prepared to turn on your camera, camcorder, or laptop** to prove to airport security personnel that the device is real.

VIDEOS

The local standard for videotape is PAL.

CAR RENTAL

The major car rental firms have convenient booths at Schiphol Airport, but the airport charges rental companies a fee that is passed on to customers, so you'll get a better deal at downtown locations.

Rates in Amsterdam vary from company to company; daily rates start at approximately $50 for a one-day rental, $140 for a three-day rental, and $300 for a week's rental. This does not include collision insurance or airport fee. Tax is included and weekly rates often include unlimited

mileage. As standard, cars in Europe are stick shift. An automatic transmission will cost a little extra.
🖪 Major Agencies **Alamo** ☎ 800/462-5266, 0208/750-2800 in U.K. ⊕ www.alamo.com. **Avis** ☎ 800/230-4898, 800/272-5871 in Canada, 02/9353-9000 in Australia, 0800/655-111 in New Zealand, 0870/606-0100 in U.K. ⊕ www.avis.com. **Budget** ☎ 0144/227-6266 in the U.K. **Dollar** ☎ 800/800-3665, 800/800-6000 in U.K., where it's affiliated with Sixt, 649/255-0620 in New Zealand ⊕ www.dollar.com. **Hertz** ☎ 800/654-3001, 800/263-0600 in Canada, 0870/844-8844 in U.K., 03/9698-2555 in Australia, 0800/654-321 in New Zealand ⊕ www.hertz.com. **National Car Rental** ☎ 800/227-7368, 020/8745-2800 in U.K. ⊕ www.nationalcar.com.
🖪 Local Agencies **Avis** ⊠ Nassaukade 380, Oud West ☎ 020/683-6061. **Budget** ⊠ Overtoom 121, Vondelpark ☎ 020/604-1349 ⊕ www.budget.com. **Hertz** ⊠ Overtoom 333, Vondelpark ☎ 020/612-2441.

CUTTING COSTS

Most major American rental-car companies have offices or affiliates in The Netherlands, but the rates are generally better if you make a reservation from abroad rather than from within Holland.

For a good deal, **book through a travel agent, who will shop around.**

Do **look into wholesalers,** companies that do not own fleets but rent in bulk from those that do and often offer better rates than traditional car-rental operations. Prices are best during off-peak periods. Rentals booked through wholesalers often must be paid for before you leave home.
🖪 Wholesalers **Auto Europe** ☎ 207/842-2000 or 888/223-5555 🖷 207/842-2222 ⊕ www.autoeurope.com. **Destination Europe Resources (DER)** ⊠ 9501 W. Devon Ave., Rosemont, IL 60018 ☎ 800/782-2424 🖷 800/282-747 ⊕ www.dertravel.com. **Europe by Car** ☎ 212/581-3040 or 800/223-1516 🖷 212/246-1458 ⊕ www.europebycar.com. **Kemwel** ☎ 800/678-0678 or 207/842-2285 🖷 207/842-2286 ⊕ www.kemwel.com.

INSURANCE

When driving a rented car you are generally responsible for any damage to or loss of the vehicle. Collision policies that car-rental companies sell for European rentals typically do not cover stolen vehicles. Before you rent—and purchase collision or theft coverage—see what coverage you already have under the terms of your personal auto-insurance policy and credit cards.

SURCHARGES

Before you pick up a car in one city and leave it in another, **ask about drop-off charges or one-way service fees,** which can be substantial. Note, too, that some rental agencies charge extra if you return the car before the time specified in your contract. To avoid a hefty refueling fee, **fill the tank just before you turn in the car,** but be aware that gas stations near the rental outlet may overcharge. It's almost never a deal to buy the tank of gas in the car when you rent it; the understanding is that you'll return it empty, but some fuel usually remains.

CAR TRAVEL

A network of well-maintained superhighways and other roads covers The Netherlands, making car travel convenient. Major European highways leading into Amsterdam from the borders are E19 from western Belgium; E25 from eastern Belgium; and E22, E30, and E35 from Germany. Follow the signs for *Centrum* to reach the center of the city. At rush hour, traffic is dense but not so dense as to become stationary.

Your driver's license may not be recognized outside your home country. International Driver's Permits (IDPs) are available from the American and Canadian automobile associations and, in the United Kingdom, from the Automobile Association and Royal Automobile Club. These international permits, valid only in conjunction with your regular driver's license, are universally recognized; having one may save you a problem with local authorities.

FROM THE U.K.

From Calais (north coast of France), you can drive along the coast in the direction of Ghent, Antwerp (both in Belgium) to Amsterdam.

EMERGENCY SERVICES

If you haven't joined a motoring organization, the **ANWB** (Royal Dutch Touring Club) charges €100 for 24-hour road assistance. If you aren't a member, you can call the ANWB after breaking down, but you must pay a €78 on-the-spot membership charge. Emergency crews may not accept credit cards or checks when they pick you up.

To call for assistance push the help button on any yellow ANWB phone located every kilometer (½ mi) on highways, and a dispatch operator immediately figures out where you are. Alternatively, ring their 24-hour emergency line or their information number for details about their road rescue service.

ANWB (Royal Dutch Touring Club), ☎ 0800/0888 emergency number, 070/314-7147 office number ⊕ www.anwb.nl.

GASOLINE

Gas stations are generally open Monday–Saturday 6 or 7 AM–10 or noon. All stations have self-service pumps. Gas stations on the motorways are open 24 hours. Unleaded regular costs about €1.30 per liter.

PARKING

Parking space is at a premium in Amsterdam as in most towns, but especially in the Centrum (historic town center), which has narrow, one-way streets with large areas given over to pedestrians. Most neighborhoods are metered from 9 AM to 7 PM, so it is a good idea (if not the only option) to **leave your car only in designated parking areas.** *Parkeren* (parking lots) are indicated by a white P in a blue square. Illegally parked cars get clamped by the **Dienst Parkheerbeheer** (Parking Authority) and, after 24 hours, if you haven't paid for the clamp to be removed, towed. You'll be towed immediately in some areas of the city. If you get clamped, a sticker on the windshield indicates where you should go to pay the fine (from €63 to more than €100).

ROAD MAPS

Free city maps are generally available at VVV (tourist offices), and more detailed city maps can be bought at bookstores or large gas stations.

RULES OF THE ROAD

Driving is on the right, and regulations are largely as in Britain and the United States. Speed limits are 120 kph (75 mph) on superhighways, 100 kph (62 mph) on urban area highways, and 50 kph (30 mph) on suburban roads.

For safe driving, go with the flow, stay in the slow lane unless you want to pass, and make way for faster cars wanting to pass you. In cities and towns, approach crossings with care; local drivers may exercise the principle of priority for traffic from the right with some abandon. Although the majority of cyclists observe the stoplights and general road signs, many do not aggressively expect you, even as a driver, to give way. The latest ruling states that unless otherwise marked, all traffic coming from the right has priority, even bicycles. The driver and front seat passenger are required to wear seat belts, and other passengers are required to wear available seat belts. Fines for driving after drinking are heavy, including the suspension of license and the additional possibility of six months' imprisonment.

CHILDREN IN AMSTERDAM

Be sure to plan ahead and involve your youngsters as you outline your trip. When packing, include things to keep them busy en route. On sightseeing days, try to schedule activities of special interest to your children. If you are renting a car, don't forget to **arrange for a car seat** when you reserve.

Discounts are prevalent, so always ask about a child's discount before purchasing tickets. Children under four ride free on buses and trams. Children under 18 are sometimes admitted free or have a lowered rate on entry to museums and galleries. For general advice about traveling with children, consult *Fodor's FYI: Travel with Your Baby* (available in bookstores everywhere).

FLYING

If your children are two or older, **ask about children's airfares.** As a general rule, infants under two not occupying a seat fly at greatly reduced fares or even for free. When booking, **confirm carry-on allowances** if you're traveling with infants. In general, for babies charged 10% of the adult fare you are allowed one carry-on bag and a collapsible stroller; if the flight is full, the stroller may have to be checked or you may be limited to less.

Experts agree that it's a good idea to use safety seats aloft for children weighing less than 40 pounds. Airlines set their own policies: U.S. carriers usually require that the child be ticketed, even if he or she is young enough to ride free, since the seats must be strapped into regular seats. Do

check your airline's policy about using safety seats during takeoff and landing. Safety seats are not allowed everywhere in the plane, so get your seat assignments as early as possible.

When reserving, **request children's meals or a freestanding bassinet** (not available at all airlines) if you need them. But note that bulkhead seats, where you must sit to use the bassinet, may lack an overhead bin or storage space on the floor.

SIGHTS & ATTRACTIONS

Places that are especially appealing to children are indicated by a rubber-duckie icon (🐤) in the margin.

CUSTOMS & DUTIES

When shopping abroad, **keep receipts** for all purchases. Upon reentering the country, **be ready to show customs officials what you've bought.** If you feel a duty is incorrect, appeal the assessment. If you object to the way your clearance was handled, note the inspector's badge number. In either case, first ask to see a supervisor. If the problem isn't resolved, write to the appropriate authorities, beginning with the port director at your point of entry.

IN AUSTRALIA

Australian residents who are 18 or older may bring home A$400 worth of souvenirs and gifts (including jewelry), 250 cigarettes or 250 grams of tobacco, and 1,125 ml of alcohol (including wine, beer, and spirits). Residents under 18 may bring back A$200 worth of goods. Prohibited items include meat products. Seeds, plants, and fruits need to be declared upon arrival.

🏢 **Australian Customs Service** 🏤 Regional Director, GPO 8, Sydney, NSW 2000 ☎ 02/9213-2000 📠 02/9213-4043 🌐 www.customs.gov.au.

IN CANADA

Canadian residents who have been out of Canada for at least seven days may bring in C$750 worth of goods duty-free. If you've been away fewer than seven days but more than 48 hours, the duty-free allowance drops to C$200; if your trip lasts 24 to 48 hours, the allowance is C$50. You may not pool allowances with family members. Goods claimed under the C$750 exemption may follow you by mail; those claimed under the lesser exemptions must accompany you. Alcohol and tobacco products may be included in the seven-day and 48-hour exemptions but not in the 24-hour exemption. If you meet the age requirements of the province or territory through which you reenter Canada, you may bring in, duty-free, 1.5 liters of wine *or* 1.14 liters (40 imperial ounces) of liquor *or* 24 12-ounce cans or bottles of beer or ale. If you are 19 or older you may bring in, duty-free, 200 cigarettes and 50 cigars. Check ahead of time with the Canada Customs and Revenue Agency or the Department of Agriculture for policies regarding meat products, seeds, plants, and fruits.

You may send an unlimited number of gifts (only one gift per recipient, however) worth up to C$60 each duty-free to Canada. Label the package UNSOLICITED GIFT—VALUE UNDER $60. Alcohol and tobacco are excluded.

🔲 **Canada Customs and Revenue Agency** ✉ 2265 St. Laurent Blvd. S, Ottawa, Ontario K1G 4K3 ☎ 204/983-3500 or 506/636-5064 or 800/461-9999 (toll-free) in Canada ⊕ www.ccra-adrc.gc.ca.

IN NEW ZEALAND

All homeward-bound residents may bring back NZ$700 worth of souvenirs and gifts; passengers may not pool their allowances, and children can claim only the concession on goods intended for their own use. For those 17 or older, the duty-free allowance also includes 4.5 liters of wine or beer; one 1,125-ml bottle of spirits; and either 200 cigarettes, 250 grams of tobacco, 50 cigars, *or* a combination of the three up to 250 grams. Meat products, seeds, plants, and fruits must be declared upon arrival to the Agricultural Services Department.

🔲 **New Zealand Customs** ✉ Head Office, The Customhouse, 17-21 Whitmore St., Box 2218, Wellington ☎ 04/473-6099 ⊕ www.customs.govt.nz.

IN THE U.K.

If you are a U.K. resident and your journey was wholly within the European Union, you probably won't have to pass through customs when you return to the United Kingdom. If you plan to bring back large quantities of alcohol or tobacco, check EU limits beforehand. In most cases, if you plan to bring back more than 200 cigars, 3,200 cigarettes, 10 liters of spirits, and/or 90 liters of wine, you will have to declare the goods upon return.

🔲 **HM Customs and Excise** ✉ New King's Beam House, 22 Upper Ground London, SE1 9PJ ☎ 020/620-1313 ⊕ www.hmce.gov.uk.

IN THE U.S.

U.S. residents who have been out of the country for at least 48 hours (and who have not used the $400 allowance or any part of it in the past 30 days) may bring home $400 worth of foreign goods duty-free; the duty-free allowance drops to $200 for fewer than 48 hours.

U.S. residents 21 and older may bring back 1 liter of alcohol duty-free. In addition, regardless of your age, you are allowed 200 cigarettes and 100 non-Cuban cigars. Antiques, which the U.S. Bureau of Customs and Border Protection defines as objects more than 100 years old, enter duty-free, as do original works of art done entirely by hand, including paintings, drawings, and sculptures. You may also send packages home duty-free, with a limit of one parcel per addressee per day (except alcohol or tobacco products or perfume worth more than $5). You can mail up to $200 worth of goods for personal use; label the package PERSONAL USE and attach a list of its contents and their retail value. If the package contains your used personal belongings, mark it PERSONAL GOODS RETURNED to avoid paying duties. You may send up to $100 worth of goods as a gift; mark the package UNSOLICITED GIFT. Mailed items do not affect your duty-free allowance on your return.

🔲 **U.S. Bureau of Customs and Border Protection** inquiries ✉ 1300 Pennsylvania Ave. NW, Washington, DC 20229 ☎ 202/354-1000 ⊕ www.customs.gov ✉ complaints ✉ Customer Satisfaction Unit, 1300 Pennsylvania Ave. NW, Room 5.5A, Washington, DC 20229 ✉ registration of equipment ✉ Office of Passenger Programs, 1300 Pennsylvania Ave. NW, Room 5.4D, Washington, DC 20229 ☎ 202/927-0530.

WHERE TO EAT

For information on Dutch cuisine, mealtimes, reservations, what to wear, specific restaurants and the price chart, please consult Chapter 2. The restaurants we list are the cream of the crop in each price category.

DISABILITIES & ACCESSIBILITY

Although it is said that The Netherlands is a world leader in providing facilities for people with disabilities, the most obvious difficulty that people with disabilities face in Amsterdam is negotiating the cobbled streets of the older town center. Businesses in the tourism and leisure industry are, however, making their premises more easily accessible, and when they are found to be independently accessible for wheelchair users, the International Accessibility Symbol (IAS) is awarded. For information on accessibility nationwide, relevant to travelers with disabilities, contact Vakantie Informatie Punt (Holiday Information Center) or the NIZW (Nederlands Instituut voor Zorg en Welzijn, or National Institute for Care and Welfare).

Some cinemas and theaters have a forward-looking approach and are accessible. Train and bus stations are equipped with special telephones, elevators, and toilets in larger stations, and the metro is accessible to users of specific wheelchairs. Most trams, however, have high steps, making them inaccessible to wheelchair users, although the newer trams have low-mount doors. Visitors can obtain special passes to **ensure free escort travel on Dutch trains**—for general assistance contact the Nederlandse Spoorwegen (or NS, the Dutch Rail Service) before 2 PM at least one day in advance, or by 2 PM Friday for travel on Saturday, Sunday, or Monday, or public holidays, using the number below. For information on tours and exchanges for travelers with disabilities, contact Vakantie Informatie Punt (Holiday Information Center), whose bank of information is partly sourced from Mobility International.

Local Resources **Access Wise** ☎ 026/370-6161 ⎙ 026/377-6420. **Nederlandse Spoorwegen** (Netherlands Railways) ☎ 030/230-5566. **NIZW** (National Institute of Care and Welfare) ✑ Postbus 19152, 3501 DD Utrecht ☎ 030/230-6311. **Wheelchair Hire** ✉ Haarlemmermeerstraat 49–53, 1058 JP Amsterdam ☎ 020/615-7188, €20 per week, with a security deposit of €200.

ELECTRICITY

To use electric-powered equipment purchased in the United States or Canada, **bring a converter and adapter.**

The electrical current in The Netherlands is 220 volts, 50 cycles alternating current (AC); wall outlets take Continental-type plugs, with two round prongs.

If your appliances are dual-voltage, you'll need only an adapter. Don't use 110-volt outlets marked FOR SHAVERS ONLY for high-wattage appliances such as blow-dryers. Most laptops operate equally well on 110 and 220 volts and so require only an adapter.

EMBASSIES

Australia **Australian Embassy** ✉ Carnegielaan 4, The Hague ☎ 070/310-8200.
Canada **Canadian Embassy** ✉ Sophialaan 7, The Hague ☎ 070/311-1600.
New Zealand **New Zealand Embassy** ✉ Carnegielaan 10, The Hague ☎ 070/346-9324.
United Kingdom **British Embassy** ✉ Lange Voorhout 10, The Hague ☎ 070/427-0427.
United States **U.S. Embassy** ✉ Lange Voorhout 102, The Hague ☎ 070/310-9209. There is a **U.S. Consulate's Office** in Amsterdam at ✉ Museumplein 19 ☎ 020/575-5309.

EMERGENCIES

Police, ambulance, and fire (☎ 112 toll-free 24-hour switchboard for emergencies). The 24-hour help-line service **Afdeling Inlichtingen Apotheken** (☎ 020/694-8709) (*apotheken* means "pharmacy") can direct you to your nearest open pharmacy; there is a rotating schedule to cover evenings, nights, and weekends—details are also posted at your local *apotheken*, and in the city newspapers. The **Centraal Doktorsdienst/Atacom** (Medical Center; ☎ 020/592-3434) offers a 24-hour English-speaking help line providing advice about medical symptoms. In the case of minor accidents, phone **directory inquiries** (☎ 0900/8008) to get the number for the outpatients' department at your nearest *ziekenhuis* (hospital). **TBB** (☎ 020/570-9595 or 0900/821-2230) is a 24-hour dental service that refers callers to a dentist (or *tandarts*). Operators can also give details of pharmacies open outside normal hours.

For less urgent police matters, call the **central number** (☎ 0900/8844). The city's **police headquarters** is at the crossing Marnixstraat/Elandsgracht and can be reached with tram lines 3, 7, 12, or 17. For car breakdowns and other car-related emergencies call the big automobile agency in The Netherlands, the ANWB (⇨ Car Travel, Emergency Services).

ENGLISH- & DUTCH-LANGUAGE MEDIA

The *International Herald Tribune,* an English-language newspaper with general world news, is available daily in The Netherlands from many newsagents, and the *Financieele Dagblad* has a daily page devoted to English. Hip and happening, *Shark,* a low-budget fortnightly, is found in bars and clubs, with movie and music reviews, and its supplement, *Queer Fish,* lists gay and lesbian events. New on the scene is *Amsterdam D-Voice,* a free monthly newspaper featuring a few fun articles and mainly free classified ads. Two English-language newspapers, *Amsterdam Weekly* and *Amsterdam Times* are planning to launch their first issues in early 2004. Daily English-language newspapers are available at bigger newsstands, but they are quite expensive, running €3–€5. Sunday papers have never taken off, but larger railway stations and Sunday-opening bookstores have international Sunday papers.

BOOKS

Most bookstores in Amsterdam carry English-language books, and even the average tobacconist stocks English-language magazines. **Waterstone's Booksellers** (✉ Kalverstraat 152, just off Spui ☎ 020/638–3821) carries a large assortment of books and magazines, with the emphasis on U.K. publishers. The **American Book Center** (✉ Kalverstraat 185 ☎ 020/625–5537) has three floors of books and many magazines; they stock the largest selection of science fiction on the continent. For a literary selection, try **The English Bookshop** (✉ Lauriergracht 71, ☎ 020/626–4230).

DUTCH-LANGUAGE NEWSPAPERS & MAGAZINES

The leading newspapers *NRC Handelsblad* and *De Volkskrant* are both considered a serious read, with the politically more right-wing *NRC* priced a little above the left-wing *Volkskrant. Algemeen Dagblaad* is popular with sports fans, and *De Telegraaf* is the closest thing Holland has to a tabloid press. *Het Parool* is particularly popular with Amsterdammers. Early commuters pick up a copy of *Metro* or

Spits, the free dailies distributed on weekdays in all public transport stations. In addition to containing national and international news, *Metro* has a good guide to the day's events, and *Spits,* which shares its publisher with the *Telegraaf,* has a high human-interest gossip content.

Chic Dutch style magazines are glossy and thick and make great coffee-table accessories. *Residence* leads the pack and is mostlydevoted to antiques, antique dealers, and beautiful homes. *Elegance* embraces an upmarket lifestyle, with attention to fashion and home decor. The focus of *Avenue* is wide, including stylish homes, fashion, and interviews with stylish celebrities. Sometimes compared to the English magazine *The Face, BLVD* is among the hippest magazines and has been called a cyberglossy. It deals with the "now" in art, culture, and fashion and is produced and aimed at twenty-somethings. The *Gay Krant* is a biweekly Dutch-language newspaper aimed at the gay community and covers cultural happenings, legal and health issues and any news relevant to lesbians and gay men. For fashion, most turn to a Dutch-language, Holland-centric version of *Elle.*

Amsterdam publishes the *Uitkrant* ("Going Out"), a free monthly detailing events in the city, which can be picked up at theaters, bookstores, and tourist information centers. Published in Dutch, the listings are nonetheless a useful guide. You can also pick up folders about current cultural events at the Amsterdam Uitburo ("Going Out in Amsterdam"), a centralized bureau for cultural events. They have information on a wide array of theater, dance, film, and other events, will make reservations for a small service charge, and monitor an office at the corner of Leidseplein, under the Stadsschouwburg (the city municipal theater), to answer questions.

RADIO & TELEVISION

All daily papers contain TV and radio programming listings, and you can also buy weekly guides. Amsterdam has access to more than 30 channels, which the local council selects. This includes three Dutch channels (news, weather, soaps; fairly mundane); six commercial Dutch channels (including SBS6 and Yorin); and regional channels, such as AT5, which is for Amsterdam viewers only. You can also tune in to TMF (The Music Factory), a Dutch take on MTV, as well as National Geographic, CNN, and British state-funded channels BBC1 and BBC2; there's also TV5, the French channel, as well as German, Italian, and Arabic channels. As with foreign films screened in The Netherlands, all channels are subtitled, not dubbed, into Dutch. Late-night ads on Dutch commercial channels often feature pornographic content that may offend you; take this into consideration when channel-surfing.

GAY & LESBIAN TRAVEL

Whether or not Amsterdam is the "Gay Capital of Europe," its reputation as being more tolerant of gays and lesbians than most other major world cities makes it a very popular mecca for both the gay and lesbian traveler. The Netherlands originally decriminalized homosexuality in 1811, the age of consent was lowered to 16 back in 1971, and there are stringent antidiscrimination laws. Legislation passed in April 2001 granted same-sex couples the right to marry, when previously gay and lesbian couples could just register as partners. It's illegal for hotels to refuse accommodation to gays and lesbians, but there are details available of those specifically gay-owned. The Gay & Lesbian Switchboard can provide information on hotels that are gay- and lesbian-friendly.

Local Contacts Helpful gay and lesbian organizations include **COC National** ✉ Rozenstraat 8, ☎ 020/623-4596. COC's head office deals with all matters relating to gays and lesbians. The **local branch** ✉ Rozenstraat 14, ☎ 020/626-3087 is a busy meeting place, dealing with the social side, and has an info-coffee shop. Well-informed members of the **Gay & Lesbian Switchboard** ☎ 020/623-6565 dispense information and advice, and staff at **SAD Schorerstichting** ✉ P. C. Hooftstraat 5, ☎ 020/662-4206 provide STD tests as well as general information and HIV advice.

Gay- & Lesbian-Friendly Travel Agencies **Kennedy Travel** ✉ 130 W. 42nd St., Suite 401, New York, NY 10036 ☎ 212/840-8659 or 800/237-7433 ☏ 212/730-2269 ⊕ www.kennedytravel.com. **Now Voyager** ✉ 4406 18th St., San Francisco, CA 94114 ☎ 415/626-1169 or 800/255-6951 ☏ 415/626-8626 ⊕ www.nowvoyager.com. **Skylink Travel and Tour** ✉ 1455 North Dutton Ave., Santa Rosa, CA 95401 ☎ 707/546-9888 or 800/225-5759 ☏ 707/636-0951, serving lesbian travelers.

HEALTH

Drogists (drugstores) sell toiletries and nonprescription drugs (*see also* Emergencies). For prescription drugs go to an *apotheek* (pharmacy). While you are traveling in The Netherlands, the Centers for Disease Control and Prevention (CDC) in Atlanta recommends that you observe health precautions similar to those that would apply while traveling in the United States. The main Dutch health bureau is the GGD, which stands for Gemeentelijke Gezondheidsdienst (Communal Medical Health Service).

Medical Care For inquiries about medical care: **GGD** ✉ Nieuwe Achtergracht 100 ☎ 0900/9594.

Hospitals For emergency treatment, the **AMC** and **Sint Lucas** hospitals have first-aid departments. The largest, most modern hospital serving Amsterdam and surroundings is the **AMC (Academisch Medisch Centrum)** ✉ Meibergdreef 9, 1105 AZ, Amsterdam Zuidoost ☎ 020/566-9111. It's outside the city proper, in the Holendrecht area. **OLV (Onze Lieve Vrouwengasthuis)/Prinsengracht** ✉ Prinsengracht 769, 1017 JZ, Amsterdam ☎ 020/599-2323 is just off Leidsestraat. **OLV (Onze Lieve Vrouwengasthuis)/Oosterpark** ✉ Eerste Oosterparkstraat 279, 1091 HA, Amsterdam ☎ 020/599-9111 is in Oost. The **Sint Lucas Ziekenhuis** ✉ Jan Tooropstraat 164, 1061 AE, Amsterdam ☎ 020/510-8911 is in the western part of the city, in Geuzenveld. **Slotervaart Ziekenhuis** ✉ Louwesweg 6, 1066 EC, Amsterdam ☎ 020/512-9333 is in the southwestern part of the city. The **VU Medisch Centrum** ✉ De Boelelaan 1117, 1081 HV, Amsterdam ☎ 020/444-4444 is a university teaching hospital in the Buitenveldert area.

HOLIDAYS

Nationale feestdagen (national holidays) are New Year's Day (January 1); Good Friday (April 9 in 2004, March 25 in 2005); Easter Sunday and Monday (April 11 and 12 in 2004, March 27 and 28 in 2005); Koninginnedag (Queen's Day, April 30); Remembrance Day (May 4); Liberation Day (May 5); Ascension Day (May 20 in 2004, May 5 in 2005); Whitsunday (Pentecost) and Monday (May 30 and 31 in 2004, May 15 and 16 in 2005); and Christmas (December 25 and 26). During these holidays, banks and schools are closed; many shops, restaurants, and museums are closed. Some businesses close for May 4, Remembrance Day. Throughout the Netherlands, there is a two-minute silent pause from 8–8:02 pm, and even traffic stops. Take note and please respect this custom. For information on these and other holidays, *see also* "On the Calendar" in the Destination chapter in the front of this book.

LANGUAGE

There are two official Dutch languages: Dutch, used across the country, and Friese, used in the north. In Amsterdam, as in all the other major cities and towns, English is widely spoken. State schools teach English to pupils as young as eight, and with English TV, youngsters often have a smattering of authentic-sounding vocabulary before they even get into learning English at school. Not only is it the country's strong second language, but the general public is very happy to help English-speaking visitors, to the extent that even if you ask in Dutch they answer cheerfully in English. Signs and notices often have duplicated information in English, if not more languages.

LODGING

Accommodations in Amsterdam are at a premium, so **you should book well in advance.** Should you arrive without a hotel room, head for one of the city's four VVV (Netherlands Board of Tourism) offices, which have a same-day hotel booking service and can help you find a room. Assume that hotels operate on the European Plan (EP, with no meals) unless we specify that they use the Continental Plan (CP, with a full breakfast). Meal plan symbols appear at the end of a hotel review in this book. In general, properties are assigned price categories based on the range from their least-expensive standard double room at high season (excluding holidays) to the most expensive.

HOTELS

In line with the international system, Dutch hotels are awarded stars (one to five) by a governmental agency based on their facilities and services. Those with three or more stars feature en-suite bathrooms where a shower is standard, whereas a tub is a four-star standard. Rooms in lodgings listed in this guide have a shower unless otherwise indicated. One Dutch peculiarity to watch out for is having twin beds pushed together instead of having one double. If you want a double

bed (or *tweepersoonsbed*), you may have to pay more. Keep in mind that the star ratings are general indications and that a charming three-star might make for a better stay than a more expensive four-star. During low season, usually November to March (excluding Christmas and the New Year) when a hotel is not full, it is sometimes possible to negotiate a discounted rate, if one is not already offered. Prices in Amsterdam are higher over the peak summer period. Room rates for deluxe and four-star rooms are on a par with those in other European cities, so in these categories, ask for one of the better rooms, since less desirable rooms—and there occasionally are some—don't measure up to what you are paying for.

Check out your hotel's location, and **ask your hotelier about availability of a room with a view,** if you're not worried about the extra expense: hotels in the historic center with a pretty canal view are highly sought after. **Always ask if there is an elevator** (called a "lift") or whether guests need to climb any stairs. Even if you are fairly fit, you may find traditional Dutch staircases intimidating and difficult to negotiate. It's worth considering if you plan to stay in a listed monument, such as a historic canal-side town house. The alternative is to request a ground-floor room. In older hotels, the quality of the rooms may vary; if you don't like the room you're given, request another. This applies to noise, too. Front rooms may be larger or have a view, but they may also have a lot of street noise—so if you're a light sleeper, **request a quiet room when making reservations.** Remember to **specify whether you care to have a bath or shower,** since many bathrooms do not have tubs. It is always a good idea to have your reservation, dates, and rate confirmed by fax.

Aside from going directly to the hotels or booking a travel and hotel package with your travel agent, there are several ways of making reservations. The **Nederlands Reserverings Centrum** (the Dutch hoteliers' reservation service) handles bookings for the whole of The Netherlands on its Web site for cancellations and reservations; bookings are made on-line. The VVV (Netherlands Board of Tourism) offer the same services; branches of the VVV can be found in Schiphol Airport, Amsterdam Centraal Station, and at Leidseplein.

Contact the VVV's office, or go to their Web site ⊕ (⇨ Web Sites). Most agencies charge a booking fee, which starts at €9 per person.

A pleasant alternative to getting accommodations in a hotel is to stay at a bed-and-breakfast (B&B). The best way to track down B&Bs is through either creative city accommodations specialist City Mundo or Holiday Link, both of which deal with private houses and longer stays.

🎫 Local Contacts **City Mundo** ✉ Schinkelkade 47 II, 1075 VK Amsterdam ☎ 020/676–5270 ⊕ www. citymundo.com. **Holiday Link** ✉ Postbus 70-155, 9704 AD Groningen ☎ 050/313–2424. **Nederlands Reserverings Centrum** (Dutch hoteliers' reservation service) ☎ 0299/689144 ⊕ www.hotelres.nl. **VVV Netherlands Board of Tourism Switchboard** ☎ 0900/400–4040, calls cost 55¢ per minute ✉ Schipol Airport, Amsterdam ☎ 0900/400–4040 ✉ Centraal Station ☎ 0900/400–4040 ✉ Leidseplein ☎ 0900/400–4040.

MAIL & SHIPPING

For mail destined for outside the local area, use the *overige bestemmingen* slot in mailboxes. The national postal service's logo is PTT POST (white letters on a red oblong). The Dutch mail system can be slower than you'd expect, so allow about 10 days for mail to and from the United States and Canada and up to a week to and from the United Kingdom. For postal information within The Netherlands call ☎ 0800/0417.

POSTAL RATES

Airmail letters to the United States and Canada cost €.75 for the first 20 grams and €1.50 up to 50 grams. Always make sure that your stamps have a blue "priority" sign on them, or **write "priority"** in big, clear letters to the side of the address. Postcards cost a universal €.54, no matter where they are destined to go. Letters (for the first 20 grams) to the United Kingdom, as well as to any other EU country, cost €.59. Letters sent within The Netherlands cost €.39 for the first 20 grams. You can buy *postzegels* (stamps) with postcards from tobacconists, the post office, the VVV, and souvenir shops.

RECEIVING MAIL

Correspondence can be addressed to you care of the Dutch post office. Letters should be addressed to your name, fol-

lowed by "Poste Restante" on the next line, then the address of the main post office or the one nearest you in Amsterdam. The main office is (✉ Postkantoor, Oosterdokskd 3, 1011AD Amsterdam), near Centraal Station. You can collect it from the post office by showing your passport or photo-bearing ID. American Express also has a general delivery service. There is no charge for cardholders, holders of American Express traveler's checks, or for those who booked the vacation with American Express.

MONEY MATTERS

The price tags in Amsterdam are considered reasonable in comparison with those in main cities in neighboring countries. Good value for money can still be had in many places, and as a tourist in this Anglophile country you are a lot less likely to get ripped off in The Netherlands than in countries where English is less-widely embraced.

Here are some sample prices: admission to the Rijksmuseum is €9 cheapest seats at the Stadsschouwbourg theater run €12 for plays, €20 for opera; €6.50–€ 9.50 for a ticket at a movie theater (depending on time of show). Going to a nightclub might set you back €5–€20. A daily English-language newspaper is €3–€5. A taxi ride (1⅓ km, or 1½ mi) costs about €4.55. An inexpensive hotel room for two, including breakfast, is about €65–€125, an inexpensive dinner is €20–€35 for two, and a half-liter carafe of house wine is €11. A simple sandwich item on the menu runs to about €2.50, a cup of coffee €2. A Coke is €1.40, and a half liter of beer is €2.95.

Prices throughout this guide are given for adults. Substantially reduced fees are almost always available for children, students, and senior citizens. For information on taxes, *see* Taxes.

ATMS

The Dutch word for ATM is *Pin Automaat*; many locals call the machines simply "pin."

CREDIT CARDS

Throughout this guide, the following abbreviations are used: **AE**, American Express; **DC**, Diners Club; **MC**, MasterCard; and **V**, Visa.

🎫 Reporting Lost Cards **American Express** ☎ 800/554-2639, Global Assist, 020/504-8666 in

The Netherlands. **Diners Club** ☎ 800/234-6377. **MasterCard** ☎ 0800/022-5821 in The Netherlands. **Visa** ☎ 0800/022-3110 in The Netherlands.

CURRENCY

The single European Union (EU) currency, the euro, is now the official currency of the 11 countries participating in the European Monetary Union (with the notable exceptions of Great Britain, Denmark, Sweden, and Greece).

On the other hand, the U.S. dollar (and all other currencies that are not part of the EU community) and the euro are in direct competition. In fact, this is the reason why the euro was created in the first place, so it could box with the big boys. The result is that the gloves are off—you do have to pay close attention to where you change your money (that is, dollars into euros), thus following the old guidelines for exchanging currencies—**shop around for the best exchange rates (and also check the rates before leaving home) when it comes to non-EU currencies, such as the U.S dollar, the Japanese yen, and the British pound.**

With the advent of the euro, the days are gone when a day trip to Germany meant changing money into yet another currency and paying whatever supplementary commission thereon. Before, a trip to Europe meant carting home a small plastic bag of faded notes in all colors of the rainbow and hundreds of coins you had to examine carefully to find the origin. Now, with the euro, crossing borders is that much easier: first, you won't have to take all that time and energy following your trusty guidebook's expert advice on the best exchange locations; second, there won't be that awkward moment when you find you don't have enough local currency to buy a piece of gum; and third, you won't have to do all that math (hooray!). Unfortunately, although the euro was created as a direct competitor with the U.S. dollar, exchange rates in 2003 have seen the euro soar and the dollar take a hit. At press time (winter 2003), one euro equals US$1.14.

The euro system is classic; there are eight coins: 1 and 2 euros, plus 1, 2, 5, 10, 20, and 50 centimes, or cents, of the euro. All coins have one side that has the value of the euro on it and the other side with each country's own, unique national symbol.

There are seven colorful notes: 5, 10, 20, 50, 100, 200, and 500 euros. Notes have the principal architectural styles from antiquity onward on one side and the map and the flag of Europe on the other and are the same for all countries.

CURRENCY EXCHANGE

These days, the **easiest way to get euros is through ATMs.** An ATM is called *pin automaat,* and you can find them in airports, train stations, and throughout the city. ATM rates are excellent because they are based on wholesale rates offered only by major banks. It's a good idea, however, to bring some euros with you from home and always to have some cash and traveler's checks as backup. For the best deal when exchanging currencies not within the Monetary Union purview (the U.S. dollar, the yen, and the English pound are examples), compare rates at banks (which usually have the most favorable rates) and booths and look for exchange booths that clearly state "no commission." At exchange booths always confirm the rate with the teller before exchanging money. You won't do as well at exchange booths in Schipol or rail and bus stations, in hotels, in restaurants, or in stores. To avoid lines at airport exchange booths, **get some euros before you leave home.**

GWK/Grenswisselkantoren is a nationwide financial organization specializing in foreign currencies, where travelers can exchange cash and traveler's checks, receive cash against major credit cards, and receive Western Union money transfers. Many of the same services are available at banks, and cash can be exchanged at any post office.

📋 Exchange Services **International Currency Express** ☎ 888/278-6628 for orders ⊕ www. foreignmoney.com. **GWK (bureau de change)** branches are located near railway stations throughout the country; ☎ 0900/0566. There's an office at **Amsterdam Schiphol Airport** ☎ 020/653-5121. You can find a **GWK** branch in the hall at **Centraal Station** ☎ 020/627-2731.

TRAVELER'S CHECKS

Do you need traveler's checks? With the easy availability of euros from ATM machines, they are hardly the convenience they used to be. If you are going that route, traveler's checks are best used in Amsterdam and the cities of the Randstad region, not in rural areas and villages (where they may be hard to cash; in fact, you'll want to have cash handy, as even ATMs may be hard to find). Of course, lost or stolen checks can usually be replaced within 24 hours; to ensure a speedy refund, buy your own traveler's checks—don't let someone else pay for them, as irregularities like this can cause delays. The person who bought the checks should make the call to request a refund.

PACKING

When coming to The Netherlands, be flexible: pack an umbrella (or two—the topography results in a blustery wind, which makes short work of a lightweight frame); bring a raincoat, with a thick liner in winter; and always have a sweater or jacket handy. For daytime wear and casual evenings, turtlenecks and thicker shirts are ideal for winter, under a sweater. Unpredictable summer weather means that a long-sleeved cotton shirt and jacket could be perfect one day, whereas the next, a T-shirt or vest top is as much as you can wear, making it hard to pack lightly. Bring a little something for all eventualities and you shouldn't get stuck.

Essentially, laid-back is the norm. Stylewise, anything goes. Men aren't required to wear ties or jackets anywhere, except in some smarter hotels and exclusive restaurants; jeans are very popular and worn to the office. Cobblestone streets make walking in high heels perilous—you don't want a wrenched ankle—and white sneakers are a dead giveaway that you are an American tourist; a better choice is a pair of dark-color, comfortable walking shoes.

In your carry-on luggage, **pack an extra pair of eyeglasses or contact lenses and enough of any medication** you take to last the entire trip. You may also ask your doctor to write a spare prescription using the drug's generic name, since brand names may vary from country to country. In luggage to be checked, **never pack prescription drugs or valuables.** And don't forget to carry with you the addresses of offices that handle refunds of lost traveler's checks. Check *Fodor's How to Pack* (available in bookstores everywhere) for more tips.

To avoid customs and security delays, carry medications in their original packaging; don't pack any sharp objects, including knives of any size or material, scissors, manicure tools, corkscrews, or anything else that might arouse suspicion. If you need such objects on your trip, consider shipping them to your destination or buying them there.

CHECKING LUGGAGE

You are allowed one carry-on bag and one personal article, such as a purse or a laptop computer. Make sure that everything you carry aboard will fit under the seat or in the overhead bin. Get to the gate early, so you can board as soon as possible.

Airline liability for baggage is limited to $2,500 per person on flights within the United States. On international flights it amounts to $9.07 per pound or $20 per kilogram for checked baggage (roughly $635 per 70-pound bag) and $400 per passenger for unchecked baggage. You can buy additional coverage at check-in for about $10 per $1,000 of coverage, but it excludes a rather extensive list of items, shown on your airline ticket.

PASSPORTS & VISAS

When traveling internationally, **carry your passport** even if you don't need one (it's always the best form of ID) and **make two photocopies of the data page** (one for someone at home and another for you, carried separately from your passport). If you lose your passport, promptly call the nearest embassy or consulate and the local police.

U.S. passport applications for children under age 14 require consent from both parents or legal guardians; both parents must appear together to sign the application. If only one parent appears, he or she must submit a written statement from the other parent authorizing passport issuance for the child. A parent with sole authority must present evidence of it when applying; acceptable documentation includes the child's certified birth certificate listing only the applying parent, a court order specifically permitting this parent's travel with the child, or a death certificate for the nonapplying parent. Application forms and instructions are available on the Web site of the **U.S. State Department's Bureau of Consular Affairs** (⊕ www.travel.state.gov).

ENTERING THE NETHERLANDS

All U.S., Canadian, and U.K. citizens, even infants, need only a valid passport to enter The Netherlands for stays of up to 90 days.

PASSPORT OFFICES

The best time to apply for a passport or to renew is in fall and winter. Before any trip, check your passport's expiration date, and, if necessary, renew it as soon as possible.

🗂 Australian Citizens **Australian State Passport Office** ☎ 131-232 ⊕ www.passports.gov.au.

🗂 Canadian Citizens **Passport Office** ☎ 819/994-3500, 800/567-6868 in Canada ⊕ www.ppt.gc.ca.

🗂 New Zealand Citizens **New Zealand Passport Office** ☎ 0800/225-050 or 04/474-8100 from overseas ⊕ www.passports.govt.nz.

🗂 U.K. Citizens **London Passport Office** ☎ 0870/521-0410 ⊕ www.ukpa.gov.uk for application procedures and to request an emergency passport.

🗂 U.S. Citizens **National Passport Information Center** ☎ 202/647-4000, hot line for American Travelers 202/647-5225 ⊕ www.travel.state.gov.

SAFETY

Amsterdam is unlike any other modern metropolis: although it has had certain problems with crime, and with abuse of legalized prostitution and soft drugs, the serious crime rate is exceptionally low, so having your bike stolen is the worst thing most likely to happen to you. Still, in crowded intersections and dark alleys, it is always best to be streetwise and take double safety precautions; it may be best to keep your money in a money belt and not flaunt your expensive camera. Be especially wary of pickpockets in crowds and while riding the tram. Although it is easy to lose yourself in a romantic 18th-century haze taking a midnight stroll along the canals in Amsterdam, remember that muggings can occur. Late at night, it may be best to keep to the main throughfares and not venture down deserted streets.

SENIOR-CITIZEN TRAVEL

To qualify for age-related discounts, **mention your senior-citizen status up front** when booking hotel reservations (not when checking out) and before you're seated in restaurants (not when paying the bill). Be sure to have identification on hand. When renting a car, ask about promotional car-rental discounts, which can be cheaper than senior-citizen rates.

🗂 Educational Programs **Elderhostel** ✉ 11 Ave. de Lafayette, Boston, MA 02111-1746 ☎ 877/426-8056 🖷 877/426-2166 ⊕ www.elderhostel.org.

STUDENTS IN AMSTERDAM

Amsterdam is a popular student destination, and there are lots of facilities geared toward students' needs (housing, information, etc.). Students with identification cards (such as an ISIC card) are usually entitled to discounts in shops, clubs, museums, galleries, cinemas, and entertainment venues. The main division of the Universiteit van Amsterdam (UvA) can be found in historic buildings stretching from Spui to Kloveniersburgwal. The Vrije Universiteit (VU) is about half the size of UvA and is housed in one big building in the south of Amsterdam.

LOCAL RESOURCES

The **Foreign Student Service** (FSS; ⇨ IDs and Services, *below*) promotes the well-being of foreign students, providing personal assistance and general information on studying in The Netherlands. It also runs the International Student Insurance Service (ISIS) and organizes social activities. Accommodation agencies can help with finding a room, and for a small fee you can take part in accommodation agency lotteries, usually held daily. Each university has a service and information center; UvA's center (⇨ IDs & Services) offers personal advice on studying and student life; contact individual universities for information about their accommodation agencies and services, help lines, libraries, summer courses, student unions, and student welfare.

STUDENT ACCOMMODATIONS

In addition to the YHA hostels, young visitors to Amsterdam can stay at a youth hotel, or "sleep-in," which provides basic, inexpensive accommodations for young people. A list of these is available from the **NBT** (☎ 212/370–7360 in New York).

TRAVEL AGENCIES

To save money, **look into deals available through student-oriented travel agencies.** To qualify you'll need a bona fide student

ID card. Members of international student groups are also eligible.

F IDs & Services **British Council Education Centre** ✉ Weteringschans 85a 1017 RZ Amsterdam ☎ 020/524-7676. **Foreign Student Service** ✉ Oranje Nassaulaan 5, Amsterdam ☎ 020/671-5915. **STA Travel** (CIEE) ✉ 205 E. 42nd St., 15th floor, New York, NY 10017 ☎ 212/822-2700 or outside North America, call collect: 972/699-0200 🖷 212/822-2699 ⊕ www.statravel.com. **Travel Cuts** ✉ 187 College St., Toronto, Ontario M5T 1P7, Canada ☎ 416/979-2406, 866/246-9762 in Canada 🖷 416/979-8167 ⊕ www.travelcuts.com. **Universiteit van Amsterdam** ✉ Spui 21 ☎ 020/525-9111. **UvA Service and Information Center** ✉ Binnengasthuisstraat 9, Amsterdam ☎ 020/525-8080.

TAXES

HOTEL

The service charge and the 6% VAT (Value-Added Tax), or BTW, are almost always included in the rate. Tourist tax is never included and is 5% extra. Always inquire when booking.

RESTAURANT

In a restaurant you pay 5% service charge, 6% VAT on food items, and 19% VAT on all beverages, all of which are included in the menu prices.

VALUE-ADDED TAX

Value-Added Tax (VAT or BTW) is 19% on clothes and luxury goods, 6% on basic goods. On most consumer goods, it is already included in the amount on the price tag, so you can't actually see what percentage you're paying.

To **get a BTW refund,** you need to reside outside the European Union (EU) and you need to have spent €136 or more in the same shop on the same day (this is including tax). Provided that you personally carry the goods out of the country within 30 days, you may claim a refund at your point of departure from the EU. The simplest system is to **look for stores displaying Tax-Free Shopping,** or Global Refund signs, like those at the Bijenkorf. Although Global Refund is the largest VAT refund service, note that there are also other private companies, such as CashBack, which help facilitate these transactions for a fee. Once you have made your purchases, go to their customer service department and **ask for a VAT or Tax-Free form.** Normally you receive 15% back, but these refund service agents charge 5% commission. You then have these tax-refund forms stamped at customs at the airport where you depart from the European Union. It doesn't matter if you travel on from The Netherlands, and are leaving from Paris or Berlin—customs wants to check the total amount of your purchases. It's also a good idea to carry your purchases in your hand luggage, in case customs wants to physically check what you've bought. Once stamped, the forms can be cashed at any bank in the airport, or you can opt to have the refund credited to your bank account.

F VAT Refunds **Global Refund** ✉ 99 Main St., Suite 307, Nyack, NY 10960 ☎ 800/566-9828 🖷 845/348-1549 ⊕ www.globalrefund.com.

TELEPHONES

AREA & COUNTRY CODES

The country code for The Netherlands is 31. The area code for Amsterdam is 020. To call an Amsterdam number within Amsterdam, you don't need the city code: just dial the seven-digit number. To call Amsterdam from elsewhere in The Netherlands, dial 020 at the start of the number. In addition to the standard city codes, there are three other prefixes used: public information numbers starting with 0800 are free phone numbers, but the information lines with the prefix 0900 are charged at premium rates (35¢ a minute or more), and 06 numbers indicate mobile (cell) phones.

When dialing a Dutch number from abroad, you drop the initial zero from the local area code, so someone calling from New York, for example, to Amsterdam would dial 011 + 31 + 20 + the seven-digit phone number. From the United Kingdom, dial 00 + 31 + 20 + phone number. When you are dialing from The Netherlands overseas, the country code is 00–1 for the United States and Canada, 00–61 for Australia, 00–64 for New Zealand, and 00–44 for the United Kingdom. All mobile and land-line phones in Holland are 10 digits long (some help lines and information centers, like the rail inquiry line, have only 8 digits), with most area codes 3 digits and phone numbers 7 digits. Generally, Amsterdam phone numbers are composed of a three-digit area code and a seven-digit phone number. Venturing out into Holland, you'll find most phone numbers in the provinces comprise a four-digit area code and a six-digit phone number.

DIRECTORY & OPERATOR ASSISTANCE

To ask directory assistance for telephone numbers outside The Netherlands, dial 0900/8418 (calls are charged at €1.15 an inquiry). For numbers within The Netherlands, dial 0900/8008 (calls are charged at €1.15).

To reach an international operator, make a collect call, or dial toll-free to a number outside The Netherlands, dial 0800/0410; to speak to a local operator, or make a collect call within The Netherlands, dial 0800/0101.

LONG-DISTANCE SERVICES

AT&T, MCI, and Sprint access codes make calling long-distance relatively convenient, but you may find the local access number blocked in many hotel rooms. First ask the hotel operator to connect you. If the hotel operator balks, ask for an international operator, or dial the international operator yourself. One way to improve your odds of getting connected to your long-distance carrier is to travel with more than one company's calling card (a hotel may block Sprint, for example, but not MCI). If all else fails, call from a pay phone.

Access Codes AT&T Direct ☎ 0800/022-9111. MCI WorldPhone ☎ 0800/022-9122. Sprint International Access ☎ 0800/022-9119.

PUBLIC PHONES

Since hotels tend to overcharge for international calls, it is best to use a prepaid telephone card, or *telekaart*, in a public phone. When making a call, listen for the dial tone (a low-pitched hum), insert a phone card or credit card, then dial the number. Phone cards work only in booths affiliated with the card's company, so Telfort cards work only in orange Telfort booths, found on station platforms, and within towns; KPN cards can be used only in KPN booths, screened by green-edged glass.

Since the increase in cellular phones, the number of phone cells, or phone booths, is decreasing. At every railway station there are pay phones, either in the ticket hall or on the platforms. There are clusters of pay phones around pedestrian squares, but the railway station phones are all Libertel, and you can use only a Libertel card or coins, whereas the pay phones out on the street are KPN Telecom, where you need to use another card. Awkward, yes—and the reason is that the stations are the property of the NS (Nederlandse Spoorweg, or Dutch Train System), and so they have their own contract with Libertel, whereas public ground is owned by the government, which has a contract with former state firm KPN. The newest KPN phone booths also accept credit cards.

To make a call, lift the receiver, wait until you hear a dial tone, a low-pitched constant hum, then insert the appropriate card or coins. Dial the number, and as soon as your correspondent picks up the receiver, you are connected. To make an international call, dial 00, followed by the country code, then drop the first 0 of the area code (see Area and Country codes, above).

Telfort phone booths and public phones found in bars and cafés accept coins from €.10 to €2.

Off-peak rates apply Monday–Friday 8 PM–8 AM and all weekend. Phone cards in increments of €5, €8, and €10 (approximately) can be bought from VVVs (local branches of the Netherlands Board of Tourism), post offices, train stations, newsstands, and tobacconists.

TIME

The Netherlands is one hour ahead of Greenwich Mean Time (GMT). Daylight saving time begins on the last Sunday in March, when clocks are set forward one hour; on the last Sunday in October, clocks are set back one hour. All clocks on Central European Time (CET) go forward and back on the same spring and autumn dates as GMT. The Netherlands operate on a 24-hour clock, so AM hours are listed as in the United States and Britain, but PM hours continue through the cycle (1 PM is 13:00, 2 PM is 14:00, etc.). When it's 3 PM in Amsterdam, it is 2 PM in London, 9 AM in New York City, and 6 AM in Los Angeles. A telephone call will get you the **speaking clock** (☎ 0900/8002) in Dutch.

TIPPING

The following guidelines apply in Amsterdam, but the Dutch tip smaller amounts in smaller cities and towns. In restaurants a service charge of about 6% is included in menu prices. Tip 10% extra if you've really enjoyed the meal and you got good service, and **leave the tip as change rather than putting it on your credit card.** If you're not satisfied, don't leave anything. Though a service charge is also included in hotel, taxi, bar, and café bills, the Dutch mostly round up the change to the nearest two euros for large bills and to the nearest euro for smaller ones. In taxis, round up the fare to 10% extra. Rest room attendants expect only change, €.25, and a cloakroom attendant in an average bar expects €.50 per coat (more in expensive hotels and restaurants).

TOURS & PACKAGES

Because everything is prearranged on a prepackaged tour or independent vacation, you spend less time planning—and often get it all at a good price.

BOOKING WITH AN AGENT

Travel agents are excellent resources. But it's a good idea to collect brochures from several agencies, as some agents' suggestions may be influenced by relationships with tour and package firms that reward them for volume sales. If you have a special interest, **find an agent with expertise in that area**; the American Society of Travel Agents (ASTA; ⇨ Travel Agencies) has a database of specialists worldwide.

Make sure your travel agent knows the accommodations and other services of the place being recommended. Ask about the hotel's location, room size, beds, and whether it has a pool, room service, or programs for children, if you care about these. Has your agent been there in person or sent others whom you can contact?

Do some homework on your own, too: local tourism boards can provide information about lesser-known and small-niche operators, some of which may sell only direct.

BUYER BEWARE

Each year consumers are stranded or lose their money when tour operators—even large ones with excellent reputations—go out of business. So **check out the operator.** Ask several travel agents about its reputation, and try to **book with a company that has a consumer-protection program.** (Look for information in the company's

brochure.) In the United States, members of the National Tour Association and the United States Tour Operators Association are required to set aside funds to cover your payments and travel arrangements in the event that the company defaults. It's also a good idea to choose a company that participates in the American Society of Travel Agents' Tour Operator Program (TOP); ASTA will act as mediator in any disputes between you and your tour operator.

Remember that the more your package or tour includes the better you can predict the ultimate cost of your vacation. Make sure you know exactly what is covered, and **beware of hidden costs.** Are taxes, tips, and transfers included? Entertainment and excursions? These can add up.

F Tour-Operator Recommendations **American Society of Travel Agents** (⇨ Travel Agencies). **National Tour Association (NTA)** ✉ 546 E. Main St., Lexington, KY 40508 ☎ 859/226-4444 or 800/682-8886 🖷 859/226-4404 ⊕ www.ntaonline.com. **United States Tour Operators Association (USTOA)** ✉ 275 Madison Ave., Suite 2014, New York, NY 10016 ☎ 212/599-6599 or 800/468-7862 🖷 212/599-6744 ⊕ www.ustoa.com.

TRAIN TRAVEL IN THE NETHERLANDS

The Netherlands has a compact network; the trains are among the most modern in Europe and are the quickest way to travel between city centers. Services are relatively frequent, with a minimum of two departures per hour for each route. The carriages are modern and clean, and although many Dutch people complain about delays, the trains usually run exactly on time.

On the train you have the choice of *roken* (smoking) or *niet roken* (no-smoking), and first or second class, indicated with a large 1 or 2 painted on the outside of the train, for your reference as you get on, and at the end of each aisle. First-class travel costs about 40% more, which on local trains gives you a slightly larger seat in a compartment that is less likely to be full. At peak travel times, first-class train travel is worth the difference. Note that in 2003 there was talk of eliminating all class divisions on trains, but it hasn't been officially decided as of press time.

Intercity trains are novel in that they can come double-decker; they travel only within the country. *Sneltreins* (express trains) also have two decks but take in more stops, so they are a little slower. *Stoptreins* (local trains) are the slowest.

If you have a reduction pass (⇨ Cutting Costs), you are restricted from using it before 9 AM; further, as all trains serve commuters, you most likely won't get a seat if you travel during rush hour, which makes later travel doubly appealing.

To avoid long lines at station ticket windows when you're in a hurry, **buy tickets in advance.** Train tickets for travel within the country can be purchased at the last minute. Normal tickets are either *enkele reis* (one-way) or *retour* (round-trip). Round-trip tickets cost approximately 74% of two single tickets. They are valid only on the day you buy them, unless you ask specifically for a ticket with a different date, or not dated. If you buy a nondated ticket, **you must stamp the date on your ticket before you board the train** on your day of travel. Use one of the small yellow machines near the tracks. Just hold the ticket flat and slide it in the gap until you hear a short ring. Once stamped, your ticket is valid for the rest of the day. You can get on and off at will at stops in between your destinations until midnight.

Most main-line rail ticket windows are open Monday–Thursday 6 AM–11 PM, Friday 6 AM–11:45 PM, Saturday 7 AM–11:45 PM, and Sunday 7 AM–11 PM, and no credit cards, debit cards, or traveler's checks are valid for payment. If you don't have euros, bureau de change GWK has a branch at Centraal Station.

If you forget to stamp your ticket in the machine, or you didn't make it in time to buy a ticket, you could actively seek out an inspector and pay the on-board fare, a stinging 70% more expensive than at the railway station counter. As in a tram or metro, you often travel in a train without anyone asking to check your ticket. If you wait for the inspector to find out that you don't have a valid ticket, he or she will insist you buy a ticket at the higher rate— but there is no lesser penalty for owning up before being found out (in fact, you may also need to pay a hefty fine).

Apart from using the ticket window in a station, you can **buy tickets at the yellow ticket machines** in the main hall of the railway station, or on the platforms. These machines accept cash and cards, if you have a four-digit PIN code. Each city is allocated a number (which is also the city's postal code), which you select from the list on the machine. For example, Amsterdam is 1000, Delft is 2600. Key this in, and then choose which of the following you want as flashing lights highlight each pair of options: first or second class; full fare or with a reduction; same-day travel or without a date stamp; and, finally, one-way or round-trip.

Note that in some Dutch cities (including Amsterdam, The Hague, and Delft) there are two or more stations, although one is the principal station, and is called the Centraal. **Be sure of the exact name of the station** from which your train will depart, and at which you wish to get out. Described in more detail below, train stations in Amsterdam (all preceded by the name Amsterdam) are Centraal, Sloterdijk, Muiderpoort, Amstel, Lelylaan, Zuid WTC (World Trade Center), Rai, Bijlmer, and Duivendrecht. There are about nine train stations in the center city, but only a few are of interest to visitors. All trains for national or international destinations depart from Centraal Station. Business travelers go to Station Rai for the RAI congress center and Station Zuid WTC (World Trade Center). There is a refreshment service on intercity trains, with roller carts or a cafeteria or dining car.

🚉 In The Netherlands **NS–Nederlandse Spoorwegen/Dutch Railways** ☎ 0900/9292, €.50 per minute, door-to-door travel advice. ⊕ www.ns.nl.

CUTTING COSTS

English-language folders with information about special-rate day-trip train journeys to various destinations in Holland are available through the VVV (tourist information board) and from the information center at Centraal Station.

Once in Holland, **inquire about the Voordeel-urenkaart,** a reduction card available for all ages. It costs €49 and entitles the holder to a 40% discount on all first- and second-class tickets, when traveling after 9 AM. You need a residential address to apply for this card, as well as correct ID. The card proper will take between four and six weeks to be processed and arrive on your doorstep, but you are issued a valid card for the interim time. When you plan a day trip, inquire about special offers for cardholders for an all-in-one deal that gets you to a destination and includes the admission fee to one or more of the local sights.

Train Information Holland-wide **Public Transport Information** ☏ 0900/9292 information officer, including schedules and fares. For **lost and found** ☏ 030/235-3923 hold the line for an operator on train lines and in stations, ask for a form at the nearest station. **Nederlandse Spoorwegen** (Dutch Rail) ☏ 0900/202-1163, calls cost 10¢ per minute customer service.

TRANSPORTATION WITHIN AMSTERDAM

Everyone's dream of touring Amsterdam is to take a scenic hop on the Canal Bus, or go the two-wheel route with a bike, or just hoof it, as an eager army of bipeds does every year. Indeed, Amsterdam is relatively small as metropolises go and you can virtually connect all the main sites in a five-hour stroll. Happily, however, Amsterdam also has a full-scale bus and tram system—the GVB (city transport company)—that can whisk you from sector to sector, and attraction to attraction, throughout the city. Buses and trams run frequently; schedules and routes are posted at stops. In addition, somewhat surprisingly for this water-bound and centuries-old city, Amsterdam also has a subway, referred to as the metro, with lines running southeast and southwest. Once you understand the fanlike pattern of Amsterdam's geography, you will have an easier time getting around; most trams and buses begin and end their journeys at Centraal Station, sightseeing and shopping are focused at Dam Square and Museumplein, and the arts and nightlife are centered in the areas of Leidseplein, Rembrandtplein, and Waterlooplein. There are usually maps of Amsterdam's full transport network in individual shelters, and diagrams of routes are found on board.

The transit map published by GVB (Gemeentelijk Vervoer Bedrijf/City transport company) is very useful. It's available at the GVB ticket office across from the central railway station or at the VVV tourist information offices next door. It is also reprinted as the center spread in *Day by Day in Amsterdam*, the monthly guide to activities and shopping published by the tourist office. The map shows the locations of all major museums, monuments, theaters, and markets, and it tells you which trams to take to reach them. The GVB also has a very **useful site with transportation information** in English with route maps ⊕ www.gvb.nl. In addition, they publish folders in just about every language (including Japanese, Chinese, and Arabic) that explains everything about using public transport.

At every bus and tram stop there is a time schedule. Although the bus or tram may not arrive at the exact time listed, the time between arrivals is fairly accurate. You can also discover if the stop is on the route of a night bus. Note that all public transport is smoke-free.

The GVB telephone number listed below supplies information for public transport for all of Holland. Calling this number will get you door-to-door travel information via public transport for anywhere within The Netherlands. They'll even estimate walking time between your address and the transport, or between the bus station and the ferry depot.

METRO

Amsterdam has a full-fleged subway system, called the metro, but travelers will usually find trams and buses more convenient for getting around, as most metro stops are geared for city residents traveling to the outer suburbs. However, the Amsterdam metro can get you from point A to point C in a quantum leap—for instance, from Centraal Station (at the northern harbor edge of the city) to Amstel Station (a train station at the southeastern area of the city, with connections to many buses and trams)—much faster than a tram, which makes many stops along the way. A strippenkaart is used the same way as for other public transport.

Four metro lines, including the express tram (*sneltram*), serve Amsterdam and the surrounding suburbs. While many stops on the metro will not be of use to the tourist, several stops can prove handy. Nieuwmarkt lets you off near the Red Light District and is near the famous sights of the Oude Zijde area. Waterlooplein is near the eastern edge of the Oude Zijde, stopping at the square where the Stadhuis-Muziektheater is located and offers access to sights of the Jewish Quarter and the Plantage; a walk several blocks to the south leads you to the Eastern Canal Ring and its many historic houses. Wibautstraat is not too far from the Amstel River and provides access to the southern sectors of the city, including De Pijp. Amstel Station is a train station near the Amstel River in the southeastern area of the city, with connections to many buses and trams. Amsterdam Zuid/WTC (South/World Trade Center) is at the southern edge of Amsterdam Zuid (South), and rarely used by any tourists. VU (Vrije Universiteit) is in the suburb of Buitenveldert. It's possible to transfer from the metro to trains at several shared stops, either by crossing the platform or merely going outside to an adjacent train station. Line 50 (Ringlijn) travels from Isolaterweg in the northeastern part of the city to Gein, a southeastern suburb. Lines 51, 53, and 54 all start at Centraal Station and follow the same routes until they head into the suburbs. They ride as a subway from Centraal Station to Amstel Station, then whiz along the rest of the routes above ground, parting ways at Spaklerweg. The No. 51 passes through Buitenveldert, stopping at the VU (Vrij Universiteit) and continuing south into Amstelveen. The 53 passes Diemen and ends up southeast in Gaasperplas. The 54 also travels southeast and shares the rest of its route with the 50, passing through Holendrecht and ending at Gein.

A major new route is being constructed for a fifth metro line, the *Noord/Zuidlijn* (North/South Line) which is expected to be completed in 2011. The new line will be a subway traveling from Amsterdam North, under the IJ and Centraal Station, following major stops in the center of the city and into Amsterdam South. By using an underground system of tunnels, no buildings have to be demolished.

TAXIS

Vacant taxis on the move through the streets are often on call to their dispatcher. Occasionally, if you get lucky, they'll stop for you if you hail them but the regular practice is to wait by a taxi stand or phone them. Taxi stands are at the major squares and in front of the large hotels. You can also call Taxicentrale, the main dispatching office. Fares are €2.90, plus €1.80 per kilometer (half mile). A 5-km (3-mi) ride will cost about €12. A new initiative in the city is the *Wieler Taxi* (bike taxi), which resembles a larger version of a child's pedal-car and isn't very practical in the rain.

A water taxi provides a novel, if pricey, means of getting about. Water taxis can be hailed anytime you see one cruising the canals of the city, or called by telephone. The boats are miniature versions of the large sightseeing canal boats, and each carries up to eight passengers. The cost is €75 for a half hour, including pick-up charge, with a charge of €60 each half-hour period thereafter. The rate is per ride, regardless of the number of passengers.

⊞ Taxi Companies **Taxicentrale** ☎ 020/677-7777. **Wielertaxi** ☎ 020/672-1149. **Water Taxi** ☎ 020/535-6363 ⊕ www.water-taxi.nl.

TRAMS & BUSES

Many tram and bus routes start from the hub at Centraal Station. A large bus depot is located on the Marnixstraat, across from the main police station, and there's another one at Harlemmermeer station in the Overtoomseveld neighborhood of western Amsterdam. Trams and buses run from about 6 AM to midnight daily. The tram routes, with a network of 130 km (80 mi) of track, make this characteristic form of transport more useful than the bus for most tourists. Night owls can make use of the hourly night-bus services, with double frequency on Friday and Saturday night, but routes are restricted.

Between stops, trams brake only when absolutely necessary, so listen for warning bells if you are walking or cycling near tram lines. Taxis use tram lines, but other cars are allowed to venture onto them only when turning right. The newer fleets of buses are cleaner, and therefore nicer to use, and bus lanes (shared only with taxis) remain uncongested, ensuring that you travel more swiftly than the rest of the traffic in rush hour. If the bus is very crowded, you may have to stand, so hold on to a handrail, as the buses can travel quite fast; to **avoid rush hour,** don't travel between 8 and 9 in the morning or between 4:30 and 5:30 in the afternoon. As with all urban systems of transportation, keep an eye out for pickpockets.

In each tram, there is a clear diagram that depicts the route and the stops, including where you can transfer to other lines. There are never that many stops on a tram route, maybe twenty in total (if that many). If you ask the conductor, he will announce your stop. Alas, the colorful, decorated theme trams that were mobile "works of art" have ceased to be. The newest trams are sleek and modern, with large windows, more comfortable seating, and plasma screens that entertain passengers with ads and news reports. The entrance for new trams is wheelchair accessible, but the tram may be too crowded to board with a wheelchair. A digital display of the time and the next stop is highly visible, and above some windows, there's an additional digital display of the route, which is also announced over the sound system. You enter the tram in the middle section where the *conducteur* (ticket controller) stamps your strippenkaart. Older trams (recognizable by their small windows) are being phased out, but they still operate. For these, you need to enter at the back of the tram and either have your ticket stamped by the conductor in the booth or stamp it manually in the yellow ticket machine.

There are 16 tram lines servicing the city. Trams 1, 2, 4, 5, 9, 13, 16, 17, 24, and 25 all start and end their routes at Centraal Station. The most frequently used trams by visitors are the 1, 2, and 5 which stop at the big central Dam square and, along with 6, 7 and 10, also stop at Leidseplein square. The numbers 2, 3, 5, and 12 will get you to Museumplein and the Museum District. Trams 5, 16, 24, and 25 travel through Amsterdam's chic Zuid district. The No. 4 tram stops at the RAI convention center and the No. 5 will take you to Station Zuid WTC (World Trade Center). The remaining lines pass through East and West Amsterdam and take you farther outside the center city Centrum to areas generally more off the beaten track for tourists.

Over 30 GVB buses cover all the city's neighborhoods, and are a good way to get closer to specific addresses. The Conexxion bus company operates about 50 different buses that will take you from Amsterdam to all areas of Holland. Most of these depart from Centraal Station. Buses 110 to 117 travel to the "folkloric" area of Noord-Holland, just to the north of the city, where favorite tourist destinations include Volendam, Marken, Edam, Hoorn, and Broek in Waterland.

DE OPSTAPPER

A great new public transport option is the *Opstapper,* a transit van that traverses the elegant Prinsengracht—heart of the historic canal sector—between Centraal Station and the Music Theater. For a one-zone stamp on your strippenkaart, you can get on or off anywhere along the Prinsengracht. You can hail it on the street, or get on at its starting point in front of Centraal Station. There are no fixed stops. It passes within walking distance of the Anne Frank House, the Leidseplein, and maybe even your hotel. The buses run every ten minutes from 7:30 AM to 6:30 PM. There are eight seats and room for an additional eight standing passengers.

FERRIES

Four ferry lines leave from Centraal Station, but only one is of any interest to tourists. The Buiksloterwegveer leaves from Pier 7 behind Centraal Station every 8 to 15 minutes, day and night. The ferry transports pedestrians, cyclists, and motorcyclists across the IJ channel to North Amsterdam. There is no fee for the service. North Amsterdam may prove to be less interesting than the refreshing trip, which takes about five minutes.

TICKETS & STRIPPENKAART

The same ticket can be used in buses, trams, and metros throughout Holland. *Enkele Reis* (single-ride tickets) are valid for one hour only and can be purchased from tram and bus drivers for €1.60. However, it is far more practical to buy a *strippenkaart* (strip ticket) that includes 2 to 45 "strips," or ticket units. The best buy for most visitors is the 15-strip ticket for €6.20. A 45-strip ticket costs €18.30. Although newer trams have ticket control booths, by tradition, Dutch trams and buses work on the honor system: upon boarding, punch your ticket at one of the machines in the rear or center section of the tram or bus. The city is divided into zones, which are indicated on the transit map, and it is important to punch the correct number of zones on your ticket (one for the basic tariff and one for each zone traveled).

When it comes to strippenkaarts, a two- or three-strip ticket can be bought directly from the bus driver. They remain valid until there are no more strips left, or for one year from the first stamp. If you buy a ticket in advance, this works out to be much cheaper per journey. You can buy these at railway stations, from post offices, and many bookstores and cigarette kiosks, in Amsterdam at the public transport (GVB) ticket office in the plaza in front of the central railway station, and at many newsagents. A *dagkaart,* a travel-anywhere ticket (€5.50 for one day; €8.80 for two days; €11.30 for three days three days), covers all urban bus and streetcar routes. Fares are often reduced for children ages 4 to 11 and for people who are 65 years or older.

The All Amsterdam Transport Pass costs €19 and entitles you to a day of unlimited travel on tram, bus, metro and Canal Bus plus coupons worth about € 133 for major attractions, snacks, etc. This pass can be purchased at the GVB ticket office in front of Centraal Station and at the main Canal Bus office at Prins Hendrikkade. The recently introduced electronic Amsterdam Culture Pass provides free and discount admissions to many of the city's top museums, plus a free canal round-trip, free use of public transport, and a 25% discount on various attractions and restaurants; savings can amount to more than €100. A one-day pass costs €26, two days costs €36 and three days costs €46. The pass comes with a booklet in Dutch, English, French, and German. It can be purchased at branches of the VVV (Netherlands Board of Tourism), the GVB (City Transport Company), both at Centraal Station, and through some hotels and museums.

Amsterdam is divided into zones, and the fare you pay depends on the number of zones you travel through. You can easily travel within one zone (two strips), but to travel across Amsterdam takes you through four (five strips) zones. These zones are displayed on transport maps. Each journey you make costs one strip plus the number of zones you travel through. When you get on a bus, you show the driver your strippenkaart and simply say where your final destination is, or the number of zones you plan to travel through, and let him or her stamp the strips.

In a metro you have to stamp your ticket yourself in the small yellow machines found near the doors, and you can often do this in a tram. Count the number of strips you need, fold your ticket at the bottom of the last strip required, and stamp the final strip in the machine. A stamp on a strip uses that, and the strips above it. This may seem confusing, but it needn't be. Always count one more "strip" than the number of zones through which you pass. If you're staying within the center city Centrum, it's always two zones, so stamp three strips. If unsure, ask a fellow passenger, the ticket controller or the driver. Two or more people can travel on the same strippenkaart, but the appropriate number of units must be stamped for each person.

The newest trams in Amsterdam (recognizable by their extra-large windows) have ticket control booths in the center of the tram. You may board the tram only there, unless you already have a valid stamp on your ticket, in which case you may board at the front and show your ticket to the driver. On older trams, you can usually board only at the rear, where you will encounter either a ticket controller (*conducteur*) or a stamping machine. This makes for a lot of confusion, as you need to be in the right place when the tram arrives. Follow the lead of other passengers to be sure you don't miss getting on.

The stamp indicates the zone where the journey started, and the time, and remains valid for one hour, so you can travel within the zones you have stamped until the hour is up. If you make a mistake and stamp too many strips, tell the driver and he or she will put a sticker over the incorrect stamp.

Teams of ticket inspectors occasionally make spot checks. This doesn't happen often, but if you are checked and you don't have a stamped strippenkaart, you face a €29.40 fine.

🚋 **GVB** ✉ Prins Hendrikkade 108–114, Centrum
☎ 0900/9292 ⊕ www.gvb.nl.

TRAVEL AGENCIES

A good travel agent puts your needs first. Look for an agency that has been in business at least five years, emphasizes customer service, and has someone on staff who specializes in your destination. In addition, **make sure the agency belongs to a professional trade organization.** The American Society of Travel Agents (ASTA)—the largest and most influential in the field with more than 20,000 members in some 140 countries—maintains and enforces a strict code of ethics and will step in to help mediate any agent-client disputes involving ASTA members if necessary. ASTA (whose motto is "Without a travel agent, you're on your own") also maintains a Web site that includes a directory of agents. (If a travel agency is also acting as your tour operator, *see* Buyer Beware *in* Tours & Packages.)

Local Agent Referrals American Society of Travel Agents (ASTA) ✉ 1101 King St., Suite 200, Alexandria, VA 22314 ☎ 703/739-2782 📠 703/684-8319 ⊕ www.astanet.com. **Association of British Travel Agents** ✉ 68-71 Newman St., London W1T 3AH, U.K. ☎ 020/7637-2444 📠 020/7637-0713 ⊕ www.abtanet.com. **Association of Canadian Travel Agents** ✉ 5025 Orbitor Drive, Bldg. 6, Suite 103, Mississauga, Ontario L4W 4Y5 ☎ 905/282-9294 📠 905/282-9826 ⊕ www.acta.net. **Australian Federation of Travel Agents** ✉ Level 3, 309 Pitt St., Sydney NSW 2000, Australia ☎ 02/9264-3299 or 1300/363-416 📠 02/9264-1085 ⊕ www.afta.com. au. **Travel Agents' Association of New Zealand** ✉ Tourism and Travel House, 79 Boulcott St. Box 1888, Wellington 10033, New Zealand ☎ 04/499-0104 📠 04/499-0786 ⊕ www.taanz.org.nz.

International Agents, Approved by The Netherlands Board of Tourism American Express Travel ✉ 200 Vesey St., Lobby Level, 3 World Financial Center, New York, NY 10285 ☎ 212/640-5130 📠 212/640-9365. **Connoisseur Travel** ✉ 13315 W. Washington Blvd., Los Angeles, CA 90066 ☎ 310/306-6050 📠 310/578-1860. **Priority Travel** ✉ 35 E. Wacker Dr., Chicago, IL 60601 ☎ 312/782-7340 📠 312/558-9167. British Agents: **Supranational Hotel Reservations** ☎ 0500/303-030. Canadian agents: **Canada 3000 Tickets** ✉ TD Centre, 1201 Pender St. W, Vancouver, BC V6E 2V2 ☎ 604/609-3000. **Exclusive Tours (Merit Travel Group Inc.)** ✉ 145 King St. W, Toronto, M5H 1J8 Ontario ☎ 416/368-8332.

VISITOR INFORMATION

The VVV (Netherlands Board of Tourism) has several offices around Amsterdam. The office in Centraal Station is open daily 8-8; the one on Stationsplein, opposite Centraal Station, is open daily 9-5; on Leidseplein, daily 9-5; and at Schiphol Airport, daily 7-10.

Amsterdam Tourist Information VVV–Netherlands Board of Tourism ⊕ www.holland.com/amsterdam ✉ Spoor 2/Platform 2, Centraal Station, Centrum ✉ Stationsplein 10, Central Station ✉ Leidseplein 1, corner Leidsestraat, Leidseplein ✉ Schiphol Airport, Badhoevedorp ☎ 0900/400-4040 €.55 per minute weekdays 9-5. Outside office hours, this line has an extensive voice-response program.

Tourist Offices in the U.S. Netherlands Board of Tourism ✉ 355 Lexington Ave., 21st floor, New York, NY 10017 ☎ 888/464-6552 or 212/370-7360 📠 212/370-9507 ⊕ www.holland.com ✉ c/o Northwest Airlines, 11101 Aviation Blvd., Suite 200, Los Angeles, CA 90045 ☎ 310/348-9339 📠 310/348-9344. **Tourist Office in the U.K.** 📪 Box 30783, London WC2B 6DH, England ☎ 0207/539-7950 📠 0207/539-7953 ⊕ www.holland.com. **Tourist Office in Canada** ✉ 31 Adelaide St. E, Toronto, M5C 2KS Ontario ☎ 416/363-1577 📠 416/363-1470 ⊕ www.holland.com. **Tourist Office in Australia Dutch Consulate General** 📪 Box 261, Bondi Junction, NSW 1355, Australia ☎ 029/387-6644 📠 029/387-3962 ⊕ www.holland.com. **Tourist Office in New Zealand** 📪 Box 3816, Auckland 1, New Zealand ☎ 09/379-5399 📠 09/379-5807 ⊕ www.holland.com. **Tourist Office in The Netherlands Netherlands Board of Tourism** ☎ 070/370-5705 nationwide information ⊕ www.holland.com/amsterdam. **VVV** ✉ Stationsplein 10, 1012 AB, Amsterdam ☎ 0900/400-4040 regional specialists ✉ Koningen Julianaplein 30, 2595 AA, The Hague ☎ 0900/340-3505 regional specialists ✉ Coolsingel 67, 3012 AC, Rotterdam ☎ 0900/403-4065 regional specialists. Information lines cost €.70 per minute.

WEB SITES

Do check out the World Wide Web when planning your trip. You'll find everything from weather forecasts to virtual tours of famous cities. Be sure to **visit Fodors.com** (⊕ www.fodors.com), a complete travel-planning site. You can research prices and book plane tickets, hotel rooms, rental cars, vacation packages, and more. In addition, you can post your pressing questions in the Travel Talk section. Other planning tools include a currency converter and weather reports, and there are loads of links to travel resources.

Suggested Web Sites The official site for The Netherlands' Tourist Board is ⊕ www.holland.com. The official Amsterdam site is ⊕ www.amsterdam.nl. More information is found at ⊕ www.visitamsterdam.nl. A Holland-wide site is ⊕ www.visiteurope.com/holland. For Amsterdam maps, check out ⊕ hip-planet.com/amsterdam/maps.htm. Other general sites are ⊕ www.visitholland.com and ⊕ www.amsterdamhotspots.nl. ⊕ www.channels.nl is a Web site that guides you through the city with the help of many colorful photographs. For more information on The Netherlands, visit ⊕ www.goholland.com. Go on a virtual tour of Dutch museums at ⊕ www.tribute.nl/hollandmuseums. The American Society of Travel

Agents is at ⊕ www.astanet.com. For rail information and schedules, go to ⊕ www.ns.nl. For airport information, go to ⊕ www.schiphol.nl. For information about the national carrier go to ⊕ www.klm.com for KLM/Northwest flight information and reservations; check out the low tariffs on ⊕ www.easyjet.com/en and, for budget travelers, ⊕ www.airfair.nl.

The English-language Dutch magazine *Expats Magazine* has on-line articles about news and current cultural events at ⊕ www.expatsonline.nl. One of the most informative English-language Web sites about the Netherlands is at ⊕ www.expatica.com. *Shark* is a free newspaper with alternative listings; their site is at ⊕ www.underwateramsterdam.com. Go to ⊕ www.citymundo.com to view City Mundo's creative city-specialist directory of accommodations. Make bookings on-line with Nederlands Reserverings Centrum (the Dutch hoteliers' reservation service) at ⊕ www.hotelres.nl. For budget accommodations, try ⊕ www.stayokay.com, which provides comprehensive information for The Netherlands—just click on "English" to access all information. Hostelling International has a site for worldwide reservations at ⊕ www.iyhf.org. For information on car-breakdown rescue service, camping, biking, hiking, and water sports, go to ⊕ www.anwb.nl, the Dutch Touring Club. Go to ⊕ www.raileurope.com for pan-Europe ticket sales, for U.S. residents, which also has links to sites for Australian, Canadian, New Zealand, and British residents. You'll find these at the top of the screen. At ⊕ www.weer.nl you can find out the weather forecasts for The Netherlands (in Dutch but with figures and visuals so it's accessible). For a fun site where you can learn a bit of Dutch, go to ⊕ www.learndutch.org.

EXPLORING AMSTERDAM

1

FODOR'S CHOICE

Amsterdam Historisch Museum, *a grand introduction*

Anne Frankhuis, *birthplace of* The Diary of Anne Frank

The Begijnhof, *so picturesque it will click your camera for you*

Brouwersgracht, *a canal laced with storybook bridges*

The Jordaan, *Amsterdam's most distinctive "village"*

The Gouden Bocht, *home to the 17th-century rich and famous*

Het Koninklijk Paleis, *the grandest palace in Holland*

Magere Brug, *a storybook lift-bridge over the Amstel*

Museum Amstelkring, *with its "Our Lord in the Attic" church*

Museum het Rembrandthuis, *the immortal artist lived here*

Museum Willet-Holthuysen, *for its Golden Age elegance*

Nederlands Theatermuseum, *set in the lavish Bartolotti Huis*

Rijksmuseum, *home to Rembrandt's* Night Watch

Rijksmuseum Vincent Van Gogh, *a crescendo of color*

HIGHLY RECOMMENDED

CHURCHES   Westerkerk, *with the tallest church tower in town*

Zuiderkerk, *jewel of the Nieuwmarkt district*

MUSEUMS   Nederlands Filmmuseum, *calling all movie-lovers*

Stedelijk Museum, *from Picasso to Pop*

VISTAS   Bloemgracht, *the most beautiful canal of the Jordaan*

Montelbaanstoren, *a tower loved by Golden Age painters*

Many other great sights enliven Amsterdam. For other favorites, look for the black stars as you read this chapter.

By Steve
Korver

AMSTERDAM HAS AS MANY FACETS AS A 40-CARAT DIAMOND polished by one of the city's gem cutters: the capital, and spiritual "downtown," of a nation ingrained with the principles of tolerance; a veritable Babylon of old-world charm; a font for home-grown geniuses such as Rembrandt and Van Gogh; a cornucopia bursting with parrot tulips and other greener—more potent—blooms; and a unified social zone that takes in cozy bars, archetypal "brown" cafés, and outdoor markets. While impressive gabled houses bear witness to the Golden Age of the 17th century, their upside-down images reflected in the waters of the city's canals symbolize and magnify the contradictions within the broader Dutch society. With a mere 730,000 friendly souls and with almost everything a scant 10-minute bike ride away, Amsterdam is actually like a village—albeit a largish global one—but one that happens to pack the cultural wallop of a megalopolis. A wry bit of self-criticism has the city of Rotterdam making the money, the bureaucratic Hague figuring out what to do with the money, and Amsterdam spending the money.

However, this kind of thinking is fast losing ground as Amsterdam reinvents itself as the business "Gateway to Europe." Hundreds of foreign companies have established headquarters here to take advantage of Amsterdam's central position within the European Union. One result of this windfall is that the city is hastening to upgrade its infrastructure and to create new cityscapes that will, it is hoped, lure photographers away from the diversions of the Red Light District. Within a few years, the Eastern Docklands—once a bastion for squatters attracted to its abandoned warehouses—will be transformed into a new hub of cultural and nightlife, with a boardwalk planned to be as image enhancing as Sydney's in Australia. Could this be the birth of a new "Golden Age"?

Still, it will take time to fully erase more than eight centuries of erratic history, much of which was of a spicy nature: Anabaptists running naked in the name of religious fervor in 1535; a go-go bar claiming tax-exempt status as representing the Church of Satan; mass suicides after the 1730s crash of the tulip bulb market; riots galore, from the Eel Riot of the 1880s to the squatter riots a hundred years later; famed trumpeter-turned-junkie Chet Baker's swan-song leap from a hotel window; the 1960s proto-hippie Provos playing mind games with city officials; the festival of Queen's Day, whereby the city transforms itself into a remarkably credible depiction of the Fall of Rome; and the endless debates—about sin, students, gayness, sex and drugs, even, yes, about coffee shops.

Rembrandt to Rock 'n' Roll

We tend to take stereotypes with a grain of salt, but, in the case of Amsterdam, go ahead and believe them. At the same time, we need to remember that there's so much more. To find the "more," one must be deliberate in planning explorations; otherwise some visitors may find themselves looping back—as have sailors for centuries—to the city's gravitational center, the Red Light District. After all, it is hoped that as a visitor, you are here, at least partly, to unburden yourself of some misconceptions. Certainly this town is endearing because of its kinder, gentler nature—a reputation for championing Sex, Drugs, and Rock 'n' Roll cannot alone account for Amsterdam's being the fourth most popular travelers' destination in Europe (after London, Paris, and Rome). Carrying far greater weight—cultural, moral, social—is the fact that within a single square mile the city is home to some of the greatest achievements in Western art. Is there a conscious inmate of our planet who doesn't revere Rembrandt, who doesn't love Van Gogh? The French writer J-K Huysmans called Amsterdam "a dream, an orgy of houses and water." So true: the city of Amsterdam, when compared with other major European cities, is uniquely defined by houses, not palaces, estates, and other aristocratic folderol. With 7,000 registered monuments, most of which began as residences and warehouses of humble merchants, set on 160 man-made canals (stretching 75 km [50 mi]), Amsterdam has the largest historical inner city in Europe.

The city's advancement to the Golden Age of the 17th century actually began some time before the 13th century. A local legend has Amsterdam discovered by two fishermen who, while lost at sea with their dog, vowed to found a town on any bit of land that offered them safety—foreshadowing Amsterdam's future as a place of refuge. When they finally landed on terra firma, their dog was quick to baptize the spot with some "regurgitation"—and before you knew it, a little fishing hamlet rose on the boggy estuary at the mouth of the Amstel River. To keep the sea at bay, the plucky but essentially leaderless inhabitants were forced to join together in the building of dikes, creating a proto-democracy of sorts in the process. But Amsterdam's official voyage toward global domination began only in 1275, when it attracted members of the aristocracy: Floris V, count of Holland, decreed that the little settlement would be exempt from paying tolls. Consequently, this settlement of Aemstelredamme was soon taking in tons of beer from Hamburg, along with a lot of thirsty settlers. Following the dictum that it takes money to make money, beer profits opened up other fields of endeavor, and by the 17th century, Amsterdam had become the richest and most powerful city in the world.

But to truly understand Amsterdam is not merely to look at its vertical time line. Like the canals' waters, the city's historical evolution follows a cyclical pattern of both down spins and upswings. Today's influx of multinationals, to name but one example, makes sense in a town that produced the world's first-ever multinational: the East India Company (VOC). The merchant traders of the day realized they could lose everything with the sinking of a single ship, so they cleverly banded together to buy shares in what was now their collective of sailing ships, thereby each losing only a percentage if a ship was lost. In short order, the VOC made trade with Asia efficient, and its massive profits led directly to Amsterdam's Golden Age, when it was called, in Voltaire's words, "the storage depot of the world."

Naturally, there was a downfall: unprecedented wealth led to cockiness, which in turn led to corruption, which in turn led—so the Calvinists believed—to the arrival of Napoléon. Although many factors led to the decline of the Golden Age—chief among them increasing competition from other colonial powers—there is no doubt that its "embarrassment of riches" did affect local character. With no king or monarch, the people of Amsterdam have always behaved in a progressive manner, indulging in their freedom to do their own thing. While the rest of Europe still felt it necessary to uphold the medieval tags of "honor" and "heroism," Amsterdam had the luxury of focusing just on money—and the means to make it. And with money came confidence and liberty. French historian Henri Mechoulan said, "all the people of the 17th-century say Amsterdam is a . . . 'Temple of Trade' but primarily Amsterdam must be regarded as the cradle of freedom." Certainly it's no coincidence that Amsterdam was the place where the noted 16th-century political thinker John Locke wrote his *Epistula de Tolerantia*, that a 17th-century scientist like Jan Swammerdam could lay the basis for entomology, that philosophers like Spinoza and Descartes could propound controversial world views, or that architects like Hendrick de Keyser, Joseph van

Campen, and Daniel Stalpaert could pursue their own visions of the ideal. The Enlightenment was in fact ushered in by books, including those by Voltaire, that were not allowed to be published anywhere else but here. Even the United States Declaration of Independence's statement of freedom and equality was based on a manifesto written here in 1581 by Dutch rebels engaged in setting up a republic after freeing themselves from the rule of Phillip II.

A New Golden Age?

Amsterdam's arms, indeed, were spread wide to all rebels with a cause. But pragmatic motives were often behind such a welcoming posture. Consummate masters at "clinching the deal," Amsterdammers were known for a pragmatic approach to business, and this, in turn, led to a broad tolerance for people of diverse cultures and religions. Such an attitude drew not only oppressed Jews, perhaps from Portugal and Eastern Europe, but also every other stripe of political or economic refugee, and from the whole continent. So, not merely "modern," Amsterdam has historically been "multicultural" *avant la lettre*. The onset of a second goldenish age in the late 19th century, through an escalation of Indonesian profits, the discovery of diamonds in South Africa, and the opening of the North Sea Channel, resulted in a doubling of the population. Then, with the post–World War II boom, another wave of immigrants, now from the former colonies of Indonesia, Suriname, and the Antilles as well as "guest workers" from Morocco and Turkey, thronged in. Today, as the "Gateway to Europe," Amsterdam finds itself scrambling to provide housing to employees of multinational companies from across Europe, North America, and the world at large.

The pragmatic laws of supply and demand also account for Amsterdam's eminence as a city of the arts. The iconic heroes of the first Golden Age—from Rembrandt to Steen—were basically commercial artists supplying services to a population with money to burn. If Van Gogh had not been distracted by personal problems, he might have been free to better exploit—as did many of his contemporaries—the favorable economic climate, and both to revolutionize art and make a viable living while doing so. In contrast to the art of the past, which was driven by inspiration, today's Dutch artistic revolutions are taking place more under the guise of "design," with many of the city's visually inclined professionals achieving instant acclaim for their dazzling configurations on the graphical "canvas" of the Internet. Because there is no going back, it makes sense that a tiny town, where space must be obsessively organized, should be at the precipice of this new virtual world.

Similarly, Amsterdam is enjoying a renaissance as a showcase for the newly voguish concepts of Dutch architecture (best represented by ambitious building projects like those along the Eastern Docklands and Ijburg). These may yet prove to be as enduring, influential, and image defining as were the canal-side gabled houses and the Amsterdam School of past boom years. However, visual smartness is not much in evidence in such inner-city areas as the Wallen, Damrak, Nieuwendijk, and Rembrandtplein, which at present reflect an area heading straight for Disneyification. But for now, let us leave the complaining to the locals. Your assignment, while visiting this endlessly fascinating city, is strictly to enjoy yourself. It's remarkably easy to do: just take on the characteristics of the local waterways and go with the flow.

Getting Your Bearings

This chapter divides Amsterdam into seven fascinating explorations. Heading out from Amsterdam's Centraal Station, the main transport hub, you first discover the Nieuwe Zijde—the "New Side," comprising the western half of the Centrum (city center). You then head westward to the Grachtengordel West, or Western Canal Ring, and its fascinating and funky Jordaan neighborhood. This section deposits you at the next sector, which begins at the northwest end of Grachtengordel Oost, or the Eastern Canal Ring, famed for its 17th-century Golden Bend area. Continuing south, you head past Leidseplein square to Amsterdam's famous Museum District and, just beyond, De Pijp, the colorful district that sits shoulder to shoulder with Amsterdam Zuid, today, the poshest residential sector of Amsterdam (sorry, it has no historic sites). The chapter then heads back up north to cover the eastern half of Amsterdam, beginning again at Centraal Station and taking in the historic Oude Zijde—the "Old Side," comprising the eastern half of the Centrum. You then move south to cover two memorable neighborhoods, the Jewish Quarter—immortalized by Rembrandt—and the Plantage. Finally, you conclude with a tour of the sights of the city's waterfront and shipping district.

For a detailed and geographic overview of these neighborhoods, consult the "What's Where" section near the front of this book. And when it comes to street terms, a few helpful rules are in order. There are a number of address endings that indicate the form of thoroughfare: a *straat* is a street; a *laan* is a lane; a *gracht* or *sloot* is a canal, though some of these have been filled in to accommodate more road traffic; a *kade* is a canal-side quay; and a *dijk* is a dike, though in the urban environment this is not always obvious. House numbers are counted from nearest the center of the city, with the Dam as epicenter. Unfortunately, postal codes do not adhere to a system that will help you navigate from one neighborhood to another.

THE NIEUWE ZIJDE: THE WESTERN HALF OF THE CENTRUM

A city with a split personality, Amsterdam is both a historic marvel and one of the most youthful metropolises in the world—and you'll get complete servings of both sides of the euro coin in this first, introductory tour. In fact, a full blast of its two-faced persona will be yours simply by walking into Amsterdam's heart (if not soul): the Dam. For, as the very center of the *Centrum,* or center city, this gigantic square has hosted many singular sights: Anabaptists running nude in the name of religious freedom, the coronation of kings and queens, stoned hippies camping out under the shadow of its surrealistically phallic National Monument. The Dam is just one showpiece of the western side of the historic center, known as the Nieuwe Zijde (New Side), a neighborhood just west of the Oude Zijde sector and taking up the area between Damrak (and its Rokin extension) and the Singel canal.

The terms "Old Side" and "New Side" came into being when an expanding Amsterdam was split into two parochials: one around the then more conservative Oude Kerk and the other around Nieuwe Kerk, which attracted the rising merchant class. Although the Old Side always had the highest density of monasteries and nunneries, one event occurred on the New Side's Kalverstraat that made Amsterdam a major pilgrimage site for more than two centuries—the economic windfall that was fundamental to Amsterdam's rapid growth toward its 17th-century Golden Age. "The Miracle of Amsterdam" occurred on March 15, 1345, when a dying man coughed up the host he had just swallowed during communion. A maid cleaned up the effluence and threw it into

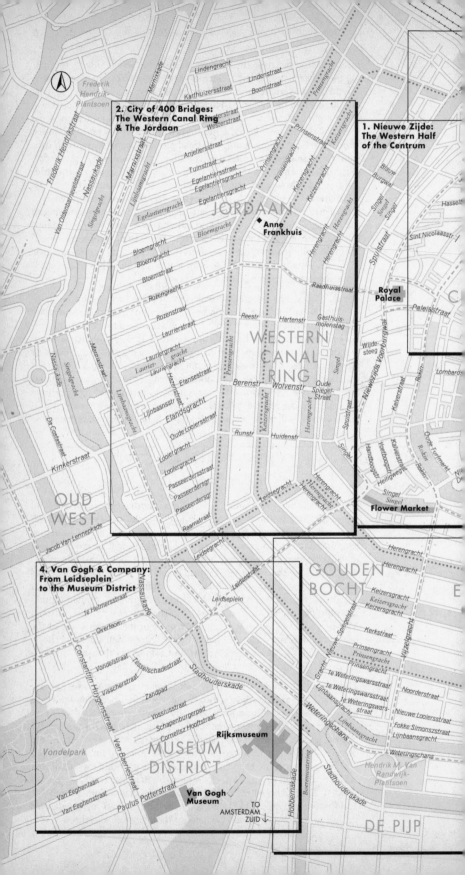

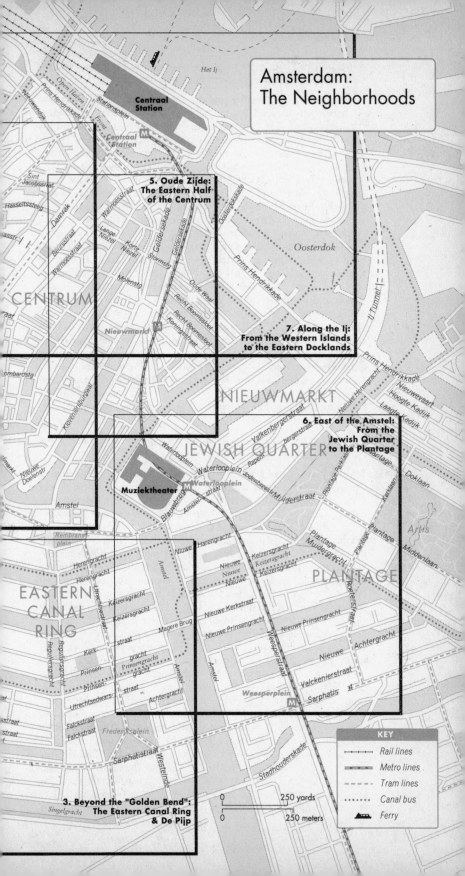

Amsterdam: The Neighborhoods

Centraal Station

Het Ij

Open Haven

Prins Hendrikkade

Nieuwendijk

Sint Jacobsstraat

Hasseltssteeg

Stationsplein

Centraal Station

assstr

Damrak

Beurssstraat

Warmoesstraat

CENTRUM

**5. Oude Zijde:
The Eastern Half
of the Centrum**

Warmoesstraat

Lange Niezel

Korte Niezel

Stormsteeg

Geldersekade

Geldersekade

Molensteeg

Oude Waal

Recht Boomssloot

Krom Boomssloot

Koningsstraat

Nieuwmarkt

Oosterdokskade

Prins Hendrikkade

Oosterdok

**7. Along the Ij:
From the Western Islands
to the Eastern Docklands**

Ij Tunnel

Prins Hendrikkade

Nieuwevaart

Hoogte Kadijk

Laagte Kadijk

ombardstg

Kloveniersburgwal

NIEUWMARKT

Nieuwe Herengracht

Dolaan

Nieuwe
Doelenstr

JEWISH QUARTER

Valkenbergerstraat

Rapenburgerstraat

Jodenbreestraat

**6. East of the Amstel:
From the
Jewish Quarter
to the Plantage**

Nieuwmarkt

Muziektheater

Waterlooplein

Waterlooplein

Waterlooplein

Muiderstraat

Plantage

Plantage Parklaan

Kerkstraat

Amstel

Blauwbrug

Amstelstraat

Plantage Muidergracht

Plantage

Artis

Rembrandt
plein

Herengracht

Herengracht

Nieuwe Herengracht

Keizersgracht

Keizersgracht

Keizersgracht

PLANTAGE

Plantage
Middenlaan

EASTERN
CANAL
RING

Keizersgracht

Amstel

Nieuwe
Nieuwe

Nieuwe

Plantage

Utrechtsestraat

Keizersgracht

Magere Brug

Nieuwe Kerkstraat

Roetersstraat

Nieuwe Achtergracht

Kerk

straat

gracht

Prinsengracht

Prinsen-

Prinsen-

straat

Achtergracht

Amstel

Nieuwe Prinsengracht

Nieuwe Prinsengracht

Nieuwe
Achtergracht

Reguliersgracht

Amstel

Weesperstraat

Valckenierstraat

Weesperplein

Sarphatis

Falckstraat

Falckstraat

Frederiksplein

Utrechtsedwars

Sarphatistraat

Westeinde

KEY

Stadhouderskade

Singelgracht

sstraat

straat

**3. Beyond the "Golden Bend":
The Eastern Canal Ring
& De Pijp**

╾┼┼╾	*Rail lines*
▭▭▭	*Metro lines*
─ ─ ─	*Tram lines*
· · · ·	*Canal bus*
⛴	*Ferry*

0   250 yards

0   250 meters

a fire, only to discover the next day in the midst of the ashes that the host was still in pristine and overly gracious condition.

As this centuries-old history reveals, the "new side" is far from new. Archaeologists have uncovered buildings that date from the dawn of the 13th century. The New Side's structure and evolution has directly mirrored the Old Side ever since the city's soggy beginnings as two boggy strips on either side of the Amstel River. The Old Side's Oudezijds Voorburgwal ("Old Side's Front of the City Wall") and Oudezijds Achterburgwal ("Old Side's Back of the City Wall"), and the New Side's now paved-over Nieuwezijds Voorburgwal ("New Side") and the Nieuwezijds Achterburgwal (now called Spuistraat), used to be the moats on the inside and outside of the medieval city's wall fortifications. At the center of all is the Dam square, or *de Plaets* ("the place"), as this space was originally called. Before Centraal Station was built, the Damrak port was essentially the Amstel River, where ships could sail clear up to the Dam area (which then bore a dam across the river) to unload their products and have them weighed before being sent to market. Today, the Damrak has shrunk to toy-size dimensions and is most popular now as the launching pad for glass-roof boats that tour the city canals. But although you'll want to be sure to take one of those tours—this is a city you have to get to know from the water to become properly acquainted—the New Side is a fine sector in which to ease into Amsterdam. The more sedate New Side—particularly around Spui—has a reputation for being the intellectual heart of the city, since it was where until recently most of the newspapers were based and where still the cafés ring with talk that is often more ambitious than that heard elsewhere in the city.

Numbers in the text correspond to numbers in the margin and on the Nieuwe Zijde & Western Canal Ring map.

a good walk

Beginning at **Centraal Station** ① ⌐, wander straight up the once-watery **Damrak** ② while erasing with your mind's eye all the tourist tack and neon that disgrace the formerly epic buildings on the right. No such technique is required at the first prominent building on the left: the former stock exchange, **Beurs van Berlage** ③, considered the most important piece of Dutch architecture from the 20th century. Once you have entered the **Dam** ④, you will be quick to realize that this freshly scrubbed square—with its centerpiece, the National Monument (which has long attracted the backpacking community to sit beneath its granite shadow)—has been the city's center for centuries. On the right lies the square's most imposing building in both stature and history: the monumental **Het Koninklijk Paleis te Amsterdam** ⑤ (Royal Palace), which is flanked to the right by the **Nieuwe Kerk** ⑥—the certainly not new "New Church." Less ancient features of the square are **Madame Tussaud Scenerama** ⑦ wax museum, the huge and bustling department store Bijenkorf (which appropriately means "beehive"), and the famous diamond outlet Cassans. Ignore the middle-of-the-road walking-and-shopping streets that come out in front of the Royal Palace—the Kalverstraat to the left and its slightly more lowbrow Nieuwendijk to the right—to take the Mozes en Aäronstraat, which runs on the palace's right side. The Neo-Gothic Magna Plaza—the former post office, which has been transformed into a specialty shopping plaza—will force you to take a left. Take the second right, Paleisstraat, but not before admiring the massive load that Atlas is carrying on the top of the Royal Palace's rear, and then perhaps glancing down the Nieuwezijds Voorburgwal, once the country's Fleet Street but whose current bars and cafés form a magnet to the arty, hip drinking scene.

Then take the first left to walk down Spuistraat. If you see a huge build-ing on the right with a huge punk-rocky mural on its facade, you are on the right track: this is the squat Vrankrijk, which has been the focal point of radical politics, music, and cheap beer for decades. Keep going until you get to Rosmarijnsteeg on the left. Proceeding down here and crossing Nieuwezijds Voorburgwal will drop you at the front door of the **Amsterdams Historisch Museum** ❽—certainly one of the city's best mu-seums. If you choose to save it for later, take the alley, Sint Luciensteeg, to its left. Walking onward will connect you to the busiest shopping street of The Netherlands, the previously mentioned Kalverstraat (Calf Street), named after its former function as a cattle market. Turn right into the mass of shopping sheep and walk a minute until you get to No. 92, where you can enter the Amsterdams Historisch Museum's courtyard café, the David & Goliath, with its central lime tree, planted for Queen Wil-helmina's coronation. In an adjacent passage across the courtyard is a grand enfilade of 17th-century civic guard portraits, on display here be-cause some were too big to fit into the museum proper.

The next goal is to enter Amsterdam's largest and most ancient *hofje* (almshouse): the tree-filled **Begijnhof** ❾. Although this painfully pic-turesque courtyard with its encircling houses and their pert little gar-dens is no longer home to nuns, its still entirely female residents do enjoy their quiet, and therefore the two entranceways regularly alternate their opening hours, to confuse the merely casual. (But be warned: the hours are getting more and more irregular as some of the residents are bat-tling to close the doors completely—as of press time, the doors were open only between 8 and 11 AM daily until local courts resolve the issue.) If the entrance on the right along the Schutters Gallery's street extension, Gedempte Begijnensloot, is closed, head straight to the **Spui** ❿ square, following the wall on the right to get to the other arched entranceway. This route was once impossible when this street and square were moats protecting the honor of the Begijnhof's holy residents.

Once you are able to pull yourself away from this delightful part of Am-sterdam, exit Spui to the southeast down Voetboogsteeg, whose entrance is immediately recognizable by the Arts and Crafts extravagances grac-ing the Art Nouveau Helios building (which won its architect, G. A. van Arkel, a bronze medal at the 1900 Paris World Fair) on the left and the more restrained grandeur of the University of Amsterdam's Maagden-huis on the right (its name, Virgin House, refers to the orphans who lived here between 1629 and 1953).

Voetboogsteeg (Foot Restraint Alley) will connect you with Heiligeweg (Holy Road), the tiny remains of the Miracle of Amsterdam pilgrim-age route that used to follow Leidsestraat and Overtoom out of the city and into Europe. A rather nasty dominatrix type greets you over an arched entranceway whose inscription translates as "wild beasts must be tamed." And indeed, this once led into the Rasphuis (Shaving House) prison, which was quite the tourist attraction in its Golden Age hey-day, when folks came to watch the prisoners shaving Brazilian hard-wood for the use in paint. Nowadays, tourists might just want to pop through here to enjoy the view from the top of the Kalvertoren shop-ping complex.

Head south down Heiligeweg toward Koningsplein, an innocent-enough-looking square of sorts that has the sporadic habit of breaking out in riot: once in 1696 to protest the taxing of funerals and once in 1876 when the annual circus was canceled (Amsterdammers sure know how to fight for their rights). Turn left down the far side of the Singel to browse through the floating and fragrant **Bloemenmarkt** ⓫ flower market.

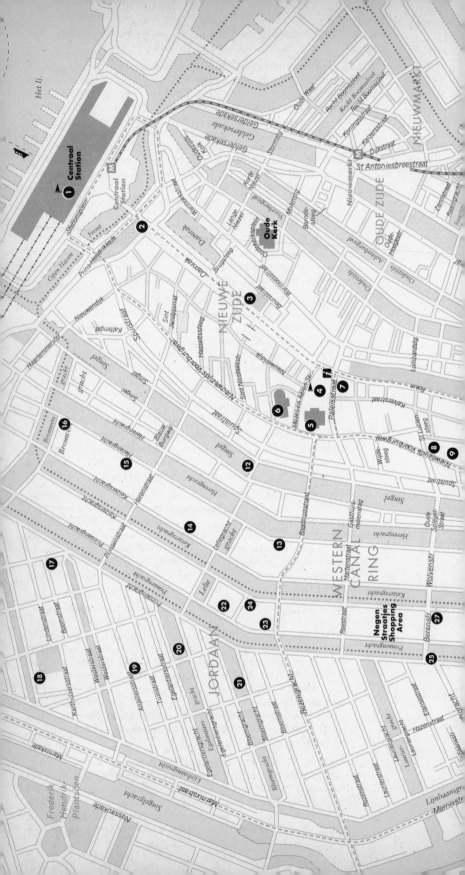

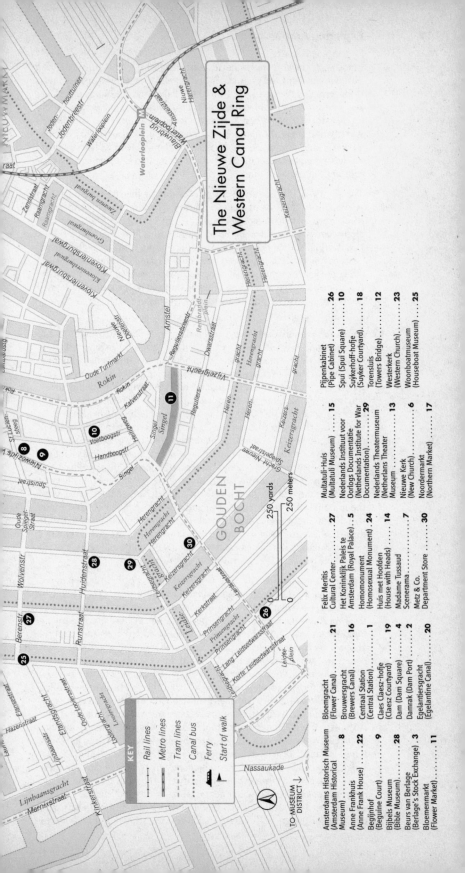

The Nieuwe Zijde & Western Canal Ring

KEY

Rail lines	
Metro lines	
Tram lines	
Canal bus	
Ferry	
Start of walk	

0   250 yards
0   250 meters

GOUDEN BOCHT

TO MUSEUM
DISTRICT →

TIMING   Ignoring all the potential interiors, one can walk this route in a half hour, but plan on doing the grand tour and spend at least three or four hours discovering all the sights. De Koninklijk Paleis and the Nieuwe Kerk are known for their variable hours, so calling ahead might ease any potential heartbreak; Beurs van Berlage is closed on Monday. If you plan to divert to do some shopping, keep in mind that shops are closed Monday mornings, but rejoice in the fact that the whole of Kalverstraat has recently embraced, after much residual Calvinist procrastination, the concept of "Sunday shopping."

HOW TO GET THERE   The Nieuwe Zijde is conveniently accessible by the city transportation systems or by foot from Central Station where most tram and metro routes terminate. Trams Nos. 6, 13, 17 go by Magna Plaza and then along Rozengracht through the Jordaan. Trams Nos. 1, 2 and 5 follow Nieuwzijds Voorburgwal and up Leidsestraat towards Vondelpark. Note that with all the current construction around Centraal Station and along the route of the projected new subway line being built that some routes may change. However, the maps posted at the stops are easy to decipher and will be updated with any changes.

What to See

❽   **Amsterdams Historisch Museum** (Amsterdam Historical Museum). Any city

Fodor'sChoice
★
that began in the 13th century as a sinking bog of a fishing village to slowly evolve as a marketplace for fishermen, eventually becoming the 17th-century's powerful trading city, must have quite a fascinating story to tell, and this museum does it superbly. Housed in a rambling amalgamation of buildings, the complex had become an orphanage in 1580 after being confiscated during the Altercation (when open worship by Catholics was banned) from the St. Lucy Convent, which had existed there the previous two centuries. After the departure of the orphans and an extensive renovation, the building opened as a museum in 1975. Economic downswings, French and Nazi occupations, radical politics, and the growth of multiculturalism round out the city's engaging story to the present day. Although rich with art, models, and plain old treasures, the museum also employs a lot of state-of-the-art technologies: many will delight in the five different **speaking dollhouses** that tell of daily life through the centuries and a "white car" in which you can cruise the city's streets. Budding musicians can even have a go on an old church carillon in one of the building's towers.

On the ground level are the old Boys' and Girls' Courtyards, separated by a loggia. In the boys' section, now the terrace of the **David & Goliath Café**, the rows of wooden lockers once used by the orphans for their meager possessions are adorned with photos and accompanying biographies of some of this city's most prominent 20th-century cultural and artistic heroes. Exiting the opposite end will lead you to the other courtyard, where an immediate left will direct you to the freely accessible atrium, **Schutters Gallery**. This alley—which used to be a narrow canal that separated the boy orphans from the girl orphans—is filled with huge, historic portraits of city militias (some of their red eyes make one suspect that marijuana has always been freely available in this city). Although Rembrandt painted more than a few portraits of the city Civic Guard members, pride of place here is given to works by Dirck Barendsz and Cornelis Anthonisz, notably the latter's *Meal of the 17 Guardsmen of Company H*. Elsewhere, be sure to take in the grand Regents' Chamber, adorned with a magnificent 1656 ceiling painting; the many relics and religious banners dealing with the "Miracle of Amsterdam" and the great religious fervor that rocked the 14th-century city; paintings of the great Golden Age, along with 17th-century city maps and dour Burgomeister portraits; and a stirring photographic panoply that captures the triumphs and tragedies of the modern-day metropolis. ⊠ *Kalverstraat 92 and Nieuwezijds Voorburgwal 357, Nieuwe Zijde* ☎ *020/523–1822* ⊕ *www.ahm.nl* ☜ *€6* ☉ *Weekdays 10–5, weekends 11–5.*

❾ **Begijnhof** (Beguine Court). Here, serenity reigns just a block from the
Fodor's Choice screeching of trams stopping next to the bustling **Spui** square. The richly
★ scenic Begijnhof is the tree-filled courtyard of a residential hideaway, built in the 14th century for the Begijntes, a lay Catholic sisterhood. Created as conventlike living quarters for unmarried or widowed laywomen—of which there were many as a result of the Crusades' efficiency in killing off surplus men—this hof, or almshouse, required them to follow three simple rules: no hens, no dogs, no men. Rent was paid in the form of caring for the sick and educating the destitute. One resident, Cornelia Arens, so loved this spot that she asked to be buried in the gutter here in 1654—so out of respect, don't tap-dance on the slab of red granite on the walkway on the left side of De Engelse Kerk.

This almshouse is typical of many found throughout The Netherlands. At No. 34 is the oldest house in Amsterdam and one of only two remaining wooden houses in the city center. After a series of disastrous fires, laws were passed in the 15th century forbidding the construction of buildings made entirely of timber. On the building's left side there are biblical plaques, which quote scripture and depict scenes from the holy book. The small **Engelse Kerk** (English Church) across from here at No. 48 dates from 1400. To this day, it's unclear why a Scottish Presbyterian church is called the English Church, although it probably has something to do with its having been presented to the Pilgrim Fathers during their brief stay in Amsterdam in 1607 (obviously, the right time: the Altercation of 1578 had seen the church confiscated from the Begijns). Much more recently, its pulpit panels were designed by a young and broke Piet Mondriaan.

Finding themselves churchless, the Beguines built the supposedly clandestine **Mirakel-** or **Begijnhof-Kapel** (Miracle- or Begijn-Chapel), across the lane at No. 29. Built by the Catholic *bouwmeester* (building master, as the architect-carpenters were called in those days) Philips Vingboons in 1671, it once contained the relics of the Miracle of Amsterdam. However, its stained-glass windows are still here to tell the story. ⊠ *Entrances on the north side of Spui and on Gedempte Begijnensloot opposite Begijnensteeg, Nieuwe Zijde* ☉ *Mirakel- or Begijnhof-Kapel Mon. 1–6:30, Tues.–Fri. 9–6:30, weekends 9–6.*

★ ❸ **Beurs van Berlage** (Berlage's Stock Exchange). An architectural turning point, completed in 1903, the Stock Exchange is considered Amsterdam's first modern building. In 1874, when the Amsterdam Stock Exchange building on the Dam showed signs of collapse, the city authorities held a competition for the design of a new one. Fortunately, the architect initially chosen was caught copying the facade of a French town hall, so the commission was awarded to local boy H. P. Berlage. The building that Berlage came up with proved to be a template for its new century. Gone were all the fripperies and ornamentations of the 19th-century "Neo" styles. The new Beurs, with its simple lines and the influence it had on the Amsterdam School architects who followed Berlage, earned him the reputation of being the "Father of Modern Dutch Architecture."

The building—welcoming and quick to absorb by all—is in fact a political manifesto that preaches the oneness of capital and labor. Built upon 4,880 wooden piles, each of the Beurs van Berlage's 9 million bricks is meant to represent an individual, who together form a strong and democratic whole. Berlage showed particular respect for the labor unions by exposing their works and accenting the important structural points with natural stone. What details that do exist, many of them designed by Berlage himself, make comment—as the Dutch are so good at—on the follies of greed. Other details of particular interest come courtesy of Jan Toorop (tile tableaus), Antoon Derkinderen (stained glass), and Mendes da Costa (woodwork).

Perhaps intimidated by all the warnings of blind capitalism, the stockbrokers eventually moved to find more reassuringly Brutalist accommodation (they moved to a stark, modern new building), and today the Beurs serves as a true Palazzo Publico with concert halls (home to the Dutch Philharmonic Orchestra) and space for exhibitions of architecture and applied arts. The small museum has exhibits about the former stock exchange and its architect and offers access to the view from the lofty clock tower. And in 2003, they opened a new and freely accessible café complete with stunning mosaics in which to enjoy some scenic coffee slurping. ⊠ *Damrak 2433–277, Nieuwe Zijde* ☎ *020/624–0141* ⊕ *www.beursvanberlage.nl* ⊠ *€5* ⊙ *Tues.–Sun. 11–4.*

⑪ Bloemenmarkt (Flower Market). No matter that you can stock up on bulbs, fresh cut flowers, or (even) peyote home-grow kits here, drop in on this tourist-friendly site because it is the last of the city's floating markets. In days gone by, merchants would sail up the Amstel loaded down with blooms from the great tulip fields to delight patroons and housewives. Today, the flower sellers stay put, but their wares are still offered on stalls-cum-boats. ⊠ *Singel (between Muntplein and Koningsplein), Nieuwe Zijde* ⊙ *Mon.–Sat. 9:30–5.*

▶ ★ ① Centraal Station (Central Station). The main hub of transportation in The Netherlands, this building was designed as a major architectural statement by P. J. H. Cuypers. Although sporting many Gothic motifs (including a unique wind vane disguised as a clock in its left tower), it is now considered a landmark of Dutch Neo-Renaissance style. Cuypers must have derived great smugness in having designed the city's other main gateway, the Rijksmuseum, which lies like a mirrored rival on the other side of town. The building of the station required the creation of three artificial islands and the ramming of 8,600 wooden piles to support it. Completed in 1885, it represented the psychological break with the city's seafaring past, as its erection slowly blocked the view to the IJ river. Other controversy arose from all its Gothic detailing, which was considered by uptight Protestants as a tad too Catholic—like Cuypers himself—and hence earned the building the nickname the "French Convent" (similarly, the Rijksmuseum became the "Bishop's Castle"). With more than 1,500 trains passing through daily, Centraal Station long ago learned to live with the guilt. And you should certainly not feel guilty about fighting your way through the street performers and backpackers who litter its doorways. If you have time to kill, perhaps take a return trip on the free ferry to Amsterdam North that departs directly opposite the rear entrance; or check out the rather sci-fi-looking multilevel bicycle parking lot to the right when exiting the front entrance. ⊠ *Stationsplein, Nieuwe Zijde* ☎ *0900–9292 (public transport information).*

need a break? A particularly stylish way to wait for a train is at **1e Klas** (⊠ Platform B, Centraal Station, Nieuwe Zijde ☎ 020/625–0131), whose original Art Nouveau brasserie interior, no longer restricted to first-class passengers, is perfect for lingering over coffee, a snack, or a full-blown meal accompanied by fine wine. Whatever the hour, it's a fine place to savor the sumptuousness of fin de siècle living.

❹ Dam (Dam Square). Home to the Koninklijk Paleis and the Nieuwe Kerk, Amsterdam's official center of town is the Dam, which traces its roots to the 12th century, when wanderers from central Europe came floating in their canoes down the Amstel River and thought to stop to build a dam. A city began to evolve when a market was allowed in 1300, and soon this muddy mound became the focal point of the small settlement of Aemstelredamme and the location of the local weigh house. Folks came here to trade, talk, protest, and be executed. Ships once sailed right up to the weigh house, along the Damrak. But in the 19th century the Damrak was filled in to form the street leading to Centraal Station, and King Louis Napoléon had the weigh house demolished in 1808 because it spoiled the view from his bedroom window in the palace across the way. Regardless, the Dam remains the city's true center— which has just been emphasized by the laying of fresh and glistening white cobblestones.

The **National Monument,** a towering white obelisk in the center of the square, was erected in 1956 as memorial to the Dutch victims of World War II. A disconcerting modernist statement, it was designed with De Stijlian echoes by the architect J. J. P. Oud (who felt that De Stijl minimalism was more in keeping with the monument's message). Every year on May 4, it is the national focal point for Remembrance Day, when the queen walks from the adjacent Koninklijk Paleis to the monument to lay flowers. The monument's urns imbedded in its rear contain earth from all the Dutch provinces and its former colonies (Indonesia, Suriname, and the Antilles). Oud designed the steps to be welcoming as seating. He was ultimately successful—to the point that the hippie generation used it for sleeping, and still today, tourists employ it as a favored rest spot from which to watch the world go by. ⊹ *Follow Damrak south from Centraal Station; Raadhuisstraat leads from Dam to intersect main canals.* ✉ *Nieuwe Zijde.*

❷ Damrak (Dam Port). This busy street leading up to Centraal Station is now lined with a mostly barbaric assortment of shops, attractions, hotels, and dispensers of greasy food products. It and its extension, Rokin, was in fact once the Amstel River before evolving into the city's inner harbor, bustling with activity, its piers loaded with fish and other cargo on their way to the weigh house at the Dam or to be stored in the warehouses. During the 19th century it was filled in, and the only open water that remains is a patch in front of the station that provides mooring for canal tour boats. Besides stopping to admire the Beurs van Berlage, it's best to otherwise sail through here quickly. ✉ *Nieuwe Zijde.*

❺ Het Koninklijk Paleis te Amsterdam (Royal Palace, Amsterdam). The

Fodor'sChoice ★ Royal Palace is probably Amsterdam's greatest storyteller. But from the outside, it is somewhat hard to believe that this gray-stained building— with its aura of loneliness highlighted by the fact that it is one of the city's few freestanding buildings—was once called the "Eighth Wonder of the World" when it was built between 1648 and 1665 as the largest nonreligious building on the planet, and that it is still used by the royal family for the highest of state occasions. From the inside, its magnificent interior inspires another brand of disbelief: this palace was actually built as a mere city hall—albeit one for a city drunk with cockiness for having created in a mere 100 years the richest and busiest harbor in the world.

The prosperous burghers of the 17th-century Golden Age, wanting something that could boast of their status to all visitors (in particular, visiting monarchs who belonged to a species that they had always done without), hired the leading architectural ego of his day, Jacob van

Campen, who had traveled to Italy to study the heights of perfection represented by the classical world before the Middle Ages so rudely interrupted. With the commission for building the City Hall, he thought that he finally had the opportunity to create something perfect in its dimensions, spatial relationships, and symbolic meaning—a veritable sermon in stone. The first problem was to create a surface on the blubbery former riverbed that was solid enough to build on. He used the standard local technique of driving wooden piles down to the solid subsurface—a method that inspired Erasmus to comment that Amsterdammers were the only people he knew who lived on treetops. What was less standard was the sheer total, 13,659—a number that is still pounded permanently into the minds of every Dutch schoolchild by the formula of adding 1 to the beginning and 9 to the end of the number of days of the year.

As the building rose, various relatively trivial compromises had to be imposed, but they were sufficient for Campen to give up on the idea of perfection and to leave the rest of the job to his on-site architect, Daniel Stalpaert. Artists and sculptures with such immortal names as Ferdinand Bol, Govert Flinck (both students of Rembrandt, whose own sketches were rejected), and Jan Lievens were called in for the decorating. In the building's public entrance hall, known as the **Burgerzaal,** the world was placed quite literally at one's feet: two maps inlaid in the marble floor show Amsterdam as the center of the world, and the heavens painted above also present the city as the center of the universe. From here, appropriate gods were positioned to point one in the direction of the different rooms whose entranceways had further sculptures to denote their function: hungry rabid rats over the Bankruptcy Chamber, ill-fated Icarus over the Insurance Chamber, a faithful dog looking at its dead master over the Clerks Chamber, and gruesome scenes of torture over the Sentencing Tribunal. In short: this is a place that practically oozes with symbolism.

During the French occupation of The Netherlands, Louis Napoléon, who had been installed as king in 1808 by his brother Bonaparte, wanted to escape The Hague, where his son had recently died, and decided that this was the building most suitable for a royal palace. Soon the city business was moved to the Prinsenhof (now the Grand Hotel) on Oudezijds Voorburgwal, and the prisoners were transferred to the Rasphuis on Heiligeweg to make room for the royal wine cellar. To improve his view of Dam square, he transferred the function of the Waag, the Weigh House, to the one on Nieuwmarkt so that the original one could be destroyed. The ensuing renovation of the interior was actually done quite tastefully, since Campen's 17th-century classicist vision jelled nicely with that of 19th-century France. Objects were covered with tapestries or wooden panels rather than removed. The rectilinear French Empire furniture—much of which remains to this day—blended remarkably well with the interior's tight mathematics.

William V's triumphant entrance into the city in December 1813 marked the beginning of a long-standing debate about who actually owned the palace. Matters were not helped by the fact that Amsterdam and the House of Orange had never really gotten along. The Oranges' endless battles for their dynasty did not sit well with the city's more pragmatic attitude that war was plainly bad for business. However, the city had gotten used to being the country's capital, and when William promised to drop by more often, it was collectively decided that the building would remain a Royal Palace. But, as Geert Mak observed in his definitive book on this building, *De Stadspaleis,* the palace became a symbol of the royal family's absence rather than its presence, with one visitor going so far as to describe the building as a "mummie, wrapped and dried." It was only after World War II that things started to change. Although Queen Wilhelmina, returning from her exile in England with a great admiration for Amsterdam's resistance movement, preferred to live in The Hague, she did begin using the palace for the grandest of state engagements, such as the coronation of her daughter Juliana and the decolonization ceremonies for Indonesia. Renovations began to return the interior to its City Hall glory days. And, most important perhaps, the locals were allowed in to see things for themselves and admire the 17th-century works of art in their original setting. And so things pretty much continued under the current Queen Beatrix, who, however, required a few years to get over her fear of Amsterdam, understandable after her 1966 wedding was disrupted by Provos throwing smoke bombs at her wedding carriage and her 1980 coronation was derailed by riots on the Dam. ⊠ *Dam, Nieuwe Zijde* ☎ *020/620–4060* ⊕ *www.kon-paleisamsterdam.nl* ⊠ *€4.50* ⊗ *Oct.–Dec., Tues.–Thurs. and weekends 12:30–5; July–Sept., daily 11–5; occasionally closed for state events.*

🖐 **❼ Madame Tussaud Scenerama.** This branch of the world-famous wax museum, above the P&C department store, pays its hosting nation ample respect through its depictions of Holland's glitterati, Golden Age names—including a life-size, 3-D rendering of a painting by Vermeer (alas, the lighting is dubious)—and even an understandably displaced-looking Piet Mondriaan. Of course, there is also a broad selection of international superstars, including George W. Bush, who is caught in a suitably presidential mode. Bring your own ironic distance. ⊠ *Dam 20, Nieuwe Zijde* ☎ *020/522–1010* ⊠ *€12* ⊗ *Sept.–June, daily 10–5:30; July and Aug., daily 9:30–7:30.*

★ **❻ Nieuwe Kerk** (New Church). Begun in the 14th century, the Nieuwe Kerk is a soaring Late Gothic structure whose spire was never completed because the authorities—preoccupied with the building of Het Koninklijk Paleis, the city palace next door—ran out of money. Whereas the Oude Kerk had the blessing of the Bishop of Utrecht, the Nieuwe Kerk was supported by the local well-to-do merchant class, which resulted in an endless competition between the two parochial factions. At one point the Oude Kerk led the race with a whopping 38 pulpits against the Nieuwe Kerk's 36, but first prize should go to Nieuwe Kerk for its still-existing pulpit sculpted by Albert Vinckenbrinck, which took him 19 years to complete. Other features include the unmarked grave of the poet Vondel, known as the "Dutch Shakespeare," and the extravagantly marked grave of Admiral Michiel de Ruyter, who daringly sailed his invading fleet up the river Medway in England in the 17th century, to become this country's ultimate naval hero—and who also proved himself to be the ultimate down-to-earth Dutch boy by spending the next day "sweeping his own cabin and feeding his chickens." The Nieuwe Kerk has also been the National Church since 1815, when it began hosting the inauguration ceremony for monarchs. Since this does not occur that often, the church has broadened its appeal by serving as a venue for organ concerts and special—and invariably excellent—exhibitions, which attract a half-million visitors a year. These exhibitions have covered everything from Dutch photography to Buddhist treasures. ⊠ *Dam, Nieuwe Zijde* ☎ *020/628–6909* ⊕ *www. nieuwekerk.nl* ⊠ *Admission varies according to exhibition* ⊗ *During exhibitions Sun.–Wed., Fri., and Sat. 10–6, Thurs. 10–10. In between exhibitions hrs vary.*

⑩ Spui (Spui Square). This beautiful and seemingly relaxed tree-lined square hides a lively and radical recent past. Journalists and the generally well read have long favored its many cafés, and the Atheneum News Center (No. 14–16) and its adjoining bookstore are quite simply the city's best places to peruse an international array of literature, magazines, and newspapers. More cultural browsing can be enjoyed on the Spui's book market on Friday and its art market on Sunday.

But it's the innocent-looking statue of a woolen sock–clad boy, the *Lieverdje* ("Little Darling"—local street slang for wild street boys), that formed the focal point for a particularly wacky and inspired social movement that would prove to have a great influence on the Yippies in America and the Situationists in France. The Provos—taking their name from their ultimate goal, "to provoke"—arose around the "antismoke magician" Robert Jasper Grootveld, who had been hosting absurdist anticonsumerist "happenings" off Leidseplein until the former garage where they were held burned down during a particularly dramatic performance. So in 1964, he moved his show to the Spui around the Lieverdje statue that had auspiciously just been donated to the city by a tobacco multinational. Whereas Grootveld played the clown, anarchist Roel van Duijn set a more purely political agenda through a Provo newsletter. Swelling crowds increased the impatience of police (who were the prime victims of such Provo mind games as repeated drug busts that turned up only bales of hay). In their frustration, the police not only became liberal in their use of billy clubs but even ended up confiscating the white bicycle that the Provos were donating to the city for free use for all in the hope that the city would follow suit.

Another flurry of provocative activity was unleashed for the marriage of present-day queen Beatrix with the German, Claus von Amsberg. It was a touchy subject, and paranoia ran high—fueled by published plans of the Provos to taint the city's water supply with LSD to incite the population, and to taint the streets with lion excrement to craze the horses of the royal carriage. What ended up happening was watched by millions worldwide on television: a simple smoke bomb temporarily obscured the royal carriage from view. When the cloud dispersed, it exposed police showing their billy club expertise; the mayor and the chief of police were fired, and the Provos had won another media war. Some of the more dedicated of the Provos, including Van Duijn, actually ended up getting elected into the city government under the banner of the Kabouters ("forest-dwelling dwarfs"), to annoy the state from within. Currently, Van Duijn continues his political career as a member of a mainstream party, and Grootveld is happily obsessed with bringing floating-garden islands made of Styrofoam to the canals of Amsterdam. In 2003 after decades of experiments and hundreds of thousands of guilders of city investment, a high-tech version of the "White Bicycle Plan" was finally dismissed as unachievable because they could not find a way to make the bikes "hooligan-resistant." ☒ *Bounded by Spuistraat and Kalverstraat, Nieuwe Zijde.*

need a break?

Several of the bar-cafés and eateries on Spui square are good places to take a break, including the ancient **Hoppe** (☒ Spui 18–20, Nieuwe Zijde ☎ 020/420–4420), which has been serving drinks between woody walls and on sandy floors since 1670. Evoking a more rarefied bygone era is the **Café Luxembourg** (☒ Spui 22, Nieuwe Zijde ☎ 020/620–6264). If you just want to eat and run, try **Broodje van Kootje** (☒ Spui 28, Nieuwe Zijde ☎ 020/623–7451) for a classic Amsterdam *broodje* (sandwich).

CITY OF 400 BRIDGES: THE WESTERN CANAL RING & THE JORDAAN

One of Amsterdam's greatest pleasures is also one of its simplest: strolling along the canals. The grand, crescent-shape waterways of the Grachtengordel (canal ring), which surround the old center, are made up of Prinsengracht, Keizersgracht, and Herengracht (Prince, Emperor, and Gentlemen canals), all of which are lined with grand gabled houses built for the movers and shakers of the 17th-century Golden Age. Commentators point to the fact that the Herengracht has always been the top address of the three as proof positive of the Netherlandish admiration for humility. Almost equally scenic are the intersecting canals and streets originally built to house and provide work space for artisans and workers, but which are now magnets to the discerning shopper, diner, and drinker. The construction of the canal girdle that began at the dawn of the 17th century proceeded from west to east. This tour covers the first half-completed section between Brouwersgracht and Leidsegracht; some of its principal highlights are the Anne Frank House, the Westerkerk, and Noordermarkt, but many visitors will give pride of place to the gorgeous panoply of canal-side mansions.

The area behind this stretch was set aside for houses for workers, many of whom were involved in this immense project, and for some of the city's smellier industries such as tanning and brewing. This area—bound by Brouwersgracht, Lijnbaansgracht, Looiersgracht, and Prinsengracht—was to evolve into the city's most singular neighborhood, the Jordaan (pronounced Yoarh-*dahn*). There are various theories on the origins of its name: as the other, more slummy side of the River Jordaan formed by Prinsengracht, or as a mutation of the French word *jardin* (garden), which can be regarded as either a literal reflection of its long-lost richness in gardens (still witnessed by its many streets and canals named after flowers and trees) or simply a sarcastic reference to its once oppressively nonfragrant reality (in days of yore, the area had been home to a group of malodorous industries).

In the 1800s the area became officially pauperized and as such provided a hotbed for the rising socialist and unionist ideas. By the end of the 18th century, things started slowly to improve with the filling in of some of the less aromatic canals and the efforts of the community's growing number of social institutions, but its inhabitants maintained a reputation for rebelliousness and community spirit that gave them a special identity, rather like that of London's Cockneys. Until a generation ago, native Jordaaners would call their elders "uncle" or "aunt"—and many retain a longtime habit of spontaneously breaking out in rousing song. Longtime residents speak "Jordaans," a dialect comparable to London's Cockney slang. These are a people whose dialect harbors as many words for "drunk" as the Eskimos reputedly have for "snow." Locals even have their own kind of music, which began centuries ago as poor people's alternative to opera (don't miss a chance to experience live "Jordaans" music in the local cafes such as the Twee Zwaantjes or Café Nol. In the 1950s, the Jordaan identity reached mythical proportions—aided by nationally popular local singers depicting an idealized vision of a poor but always sharing neighborhood—as its residents successfully fought city plans to fill in the remaining canals.

Since the 1980s, the Jordaan has moved steadily upmarket, and now it is one of the trendiest parts of town. Its 1895 population of 80,000, which made it one of the densest in Europe, has declined to a mere 14,000.

Today, one has a much better chance of hearing the spicy local dialect in Purmerend or Almere, where much of the original population has moved. But in many ways, the Jordaan will always remain the Jordaan, even though its narrow alleys and leafy canals are now lined with quirky specialty shops, excellent restaurants, galleries, and designer boutiques, especially along the streets of Tweede Anjeliersdwarstraat, Tuinstraat, and Egelanteirsstraat. Add to this equation the area's richness in *hofjes* (courtyards), and you have a wanderer's paradise.

When it comes to touring the canals, there are many boats that depart and leave from the piers near the Centraal Station with numerous stops throughout the city. For full information see the section on "Amsterdam Tours" in the Smart Travel Tips chapter.

Numbers in the text correspond to numbers in the margin and on the Nieuwe Zijde & Western Canal Ring map.

a good walk

Exit the **Dam** ④ ▶ on the tiny Eggertstraat—once called Despair Alley when it served as the church graveyard for suicides and the executed—on the right of **Nieuwe Kerk** and turn left onto Gravenstraat (Grave Street), which follows the church's rear walls. Cross the major artery Nieuwezijds Voorburgwal while minding that you do not get grave-bound yourself by a cab or tram at this notoriously dangerous intersection. Enter the narrow Molensteeg and keep going straight to the bridge, **Torensluis** ⑫, over the Singel, dotted with cafés to take advantage of the views up and down the canal. If this early in the tour you needed any liquid blandishment, you might pay tribute to the former home, to the right at **Singel 140,** of one of the richest—although generally regarded as one of the "stupidest"—men in Amsterdam, Frans Banninng Cocq, who is the central character of Rembrandt's *Night Watch.* Now a café, this house is an early example of Dutch Renaissance style and was built by the noted church builder Hendrick de Keyser.

Oude Leliestraat crosses the Herengracht, where you can turn left to reach No. 168, the gloriously beautiful Bartolottihuis, a part of which houses the **Nederlands Theatermuseum** ⑬ (Netherlands Theater Museum). Return to follow Oude Leliestraat's extension, the lovely Leliegracht, which has some excellent specialty bookstores—not to mention a resident comedian who occasionally provides the canal with a radio-powered "corpse." Be sure to stop and admire the unmissable building on the southwest corner of Keizersgracht (No. 174). This former insurance office—note the painting of the guardian angel near its top beneath its nonfunctional clock (if time is of the essence, you can trust the clock belonging to Westerkerk, visible to its left)—was built by Gerrit van Arkel and is one of the city's few examples of *Nieuwkunst,* the Dutch version of Art Nouveau architecture. Its current occupant, Greenpeace, is due to set sail to another location, and there are vague plans afoot to transform this classic building into a classic hotel, so stay tuned. After studying this building, head north and take a right on Keizersgracht's odd-numbered side, where one can admire one of the finest Baroque examples of the Amsterdam renaissance, the **Huis met Hoofden** ⑭, or House with Heads, at No. 123. Continue north and at the end of the block, make a right on Herenstraat—a street lined with interesting shops—crossing Herengracht to head north on the east side of the canal to the **Multatuli-Huis** ⑮, a museum dedicated to the writer whose "genie coming out of the bottle" bust—reflecting his writing on the negative aspects of Indonesian colonialism—you may have noticed crossing the Torensluis bridge. Continue straight to goggle at the gables of various canal-side houses before crossing the bridge over the lovely (and photogenic) **Brouwersgracht** ⑯. Continue along this canal westward

MERCHANTS & MASTERPIECES: THE SPLENDOR OF THE BURGHER BAROQUE

MEN IN BLACK? *As much as Rembrandt's dour, frowning, and Calvinist portraits of town governors may be the image first conjured up by Holland's Golden Age, it should not be the last. As revealed by historian Simon Schama in his landmark 1987 book,* The Embarrassment of Riches: An Interpretation of Dutch Culture in the Golden Age*), a closer look at Dutch 17th-century painting shows that Holland was far from a country where people dressed only in black, wore wooden shoes, and interior decoration flowed in a minor key. Rather, befitting the boom economic years of the second half of the 17th century, Vermeer's sunlighted conversation pieces, Gabriel Metsu's music scenes, and Gerard Terborch's tea parties depict settings fitted out with all the fixings of true bourgeois splendor: alabaster columns, Delftware tiles, Turkish carpets, bouquets of Semper Augustus tulips (often as costly as jewels), farthingale chairs, tables inlaid with ivory, Venetian mirrors, ebony-framed paintings, and parrots from India. Strikingly, all this feather-bed luxury is still on view today in Amsterdam's historic mansions, such as the Museum Willet-Holthuysen, the Museum Amstelkring, the Bartolotti House, and other grachtenhuis (canal houses).*

This Baroque splendor was the result of Amsterdam's transformation into a consumer's paradise in the mid-17th century. Growing fat on the trade of cheese from Friesland, furs from Russia, cattle from Denmark, wine from France, spices from India, and the slave trade from the Java Seas, the rising Dutch burgerij, or burgher class, promptly developed a taste for frills and furbelows. Rose brick gave way to gleaming marble walls; the banketjestukken (breakfast pieces) paintings of the 1620s, often depicting a herring or two and a wineglass, were dropped in favor of the pronkstuk ("showpiece") still life—lobsters and venison set among tall goblets, bowls with strawberries, pewter ware, and silver jugs, all brushed with the sensuality of innuendo.

Civic groups and charitable organizations—not princes and courts—became the standard-bearers of patronage. Not surprisingly, the paintings merchants wanted to hang on their silver-leathered walls depicted the realities of daily life: milkmaids, drunkards, henpecked husbands, genteel music lessons, and elegant parties in tea salets (salons)—not muses and madonnas. All the while, preachers did their best to denounce Queen Money from their pulpits: the Dutch had to remember to be Deugdzaam (virtuous) and Deftzig (to act with propriety and reason). Even landscape paintings should be "cozy." In architecture, Mannerist taste for outlandish and overdone ornament—a holdover from the 16th-century Flemish Renaissance—was tempered by a new style of Italian Classicism, which toned down the clutter of design. Woe betide the burgomaster who did not practice moderation. Look at what happened to poor Rembrandt, who had married above his station, bought one of the grandest houses in the city, and decorated it to the nines, only to default on his mortgage and then liquidate his entire estate.

In the end, the "embarrassment of riches" gave Golden Age art its unique luster. Vermeer may essentially show us private individuals wrapped up in their own thoughts, but what enchants us is his wonderful depiction of an interior space, where his brush lovingly delineates everything from the textures of the deep pile of the Utrecht velvet cushion on a chair to the luxurious sheen of a woman's Lyons silk dress, from Delft tilewares to gleaming pewter chandeliers. The 17th-century Dutch may have come down with a case of advanced consumption—the mercantile, not physical, variety—but their art remains all the richer for it.

for four blocks to then cross back at the bridge over Prinsengracht and proceed down its left bank. No. 7 was formerly the location of the clandestine Augustine chapel "De Posthoorn," which was attached by a secret corridor to the still existing café 't Papeneiland, which you can see across the canal on the corner with Brouwersgracht. Also across the canal is the **Noorderkerk** (Northern Church) and its square **Noordermarkt** 🄧 (Northern Market), which is host to a variety of markets. Before looping back in that direction over the upcoming bridge—crossing it will denote your official entrance into the Jordaan neighborhood—stop and look, if you can sneak a peek, at the two nearby hofjes, located on this block along Prinsengracht, heading south, Van Brienen (Nos. 85–133, closed to the public) and De Zon (Nos. 159–171, open weekdays 10–5), both with plaques telling their stories.

Backtrack north to Brouwersgracht and cross over Prinsengracht, heading south to find Noordermarkt. Here, take the Noorderkerkstraat, which runs along the west side of the church to the once watery Lindengracht, host to a food and clothing market every Friday and Saturday. Hang a left and pause at the next intersection to imagine the bridge that once crossed here and hosted the once popular folk sport of eel pulling. This weekend pursuit involved hanging a slippery eel from a rope tied to the bridge and attempting to yank it off from a tippy boat below. One day in 1885, police tried to untie the rope, and the notorious Eel Riot ensued.

Continuing down Lindengracht a block or so will get you to the entrance to one of the city's most tranquil courtyards, the **Suykerhoff-hofje** 🄲 (at Nos. 149–163). Then turn left down 2e Lindendwarsstraat and you can have a straight "locals' walk"—with the street changing names at every block—all the way to Egelantiersgracht, about a six-block walk. About four blocks in this direction, keep your eyes peeled for the quirky building adornments provided by the Jordaan's artier residents and perhaps poke your head inside another courtyard, the **Claes Claesz-hofje** 🄳 (at 1e Egelantiersdwarsstraat 3). Nearby, along the stately **Egelantiersgracht** 🄴, note the ancient bar at the corner at No. 12, the scenically set Café t'Smalle, one of Amsterdam's tiniest and prettiest. Two blocks south is **Bloemgracht** 🄵, one of the stateliest of canals.

Take the shortest of jags to proceed left and find Prinsengracht, past No. 158, which was home to Kee Strikker, the woman who broke Vincent van Gogh's heart, while noting the crowds across the canal invariably lining up outside the **Anne Frankhuis** 🄶 (Anne Frank House). You may also notice that that side of the canal is about three feet higher than the side you are on in the Jordaan—only the richer Grachtengordel residents could afford the required sand. You certainly won't miss—and the route to get to—the church tower of Anne's neighbor, **Westerkerk** 🄷, behind which is the square of Westermarkt, the home to both the pink granite slabs that form the **Homomonument** 🄸 and was a residence of 17th-century ("I think, therefore I am") philosopher René Descartes (No. 6) until he allegedly took up with his landlord's young daughter (but this story should be taken with a grain of salt: envious philosophers can be such gossips, after all).

After exploring this Jordaan-defining area—even though officially it is on the wrong side of Prinsengracht—cross Rozengracht and proceed down the right bank of Prinsengracht. However, fans of contemporary art might want to break away from the pack and make a small side tour (others should just ignore the rest of this paragraph). Don't cross the street but rather backtrack down Prinsengracht and take the first left up Bloemstraat to **Galerie Fons Welters** (No. 140, ☎ 020/423-3046, open Tuesday–Saturday 1–6) whose bubble entrance built by Atelier van Lieshout denotes the gallery as a great discoverer of both local and international sculptural talents. Taking a side street to the east, crossing Rozengracht (perhaps lingering to track down No. 188, where Rembrandt spent his last days in utter poverty), and hanging a left down Rozenstraat will get you to the **Stedelijk Museum Bureau Amsterdam** (No. 59, ☎ 020/422–0471, open Tuesday–Sunday 11–5) which focuses more on local talent than its celebrated mother ship, the Stedelijk Museum. Now take a right down Prinsengracht and a right again onto the nearest side of Lauriergracht to the often edgy **Torch Gallery** (No. 94, ☎ 020/626–0284, open Thursday–Saturday 2–6), which has long shown remarkable savvy as an early champion of the soon-to-be established: from local folks such as fashion designers Viktor & Rolf and photographer Anton Corbijn to such non-Dutch names as Cindy Sherman and Jake and Dino Chapman. At this point, it's time to return to and proceed right down Prinsengracht.

Take note that the side streets you see across Prinsengracht are part of the **Nine Streets** specialty shopping and dining neighborhood. Docked at the corner of Elandsgracht is the **Woonboatmuseum** ㉕, the Houseboat Museum, where one can glean insight into the lives of the city's floating population. If you proceed right up Elandsgracht, you will first pass Johnny Jordaanplein with its bronze busts of Jordaan's revered singers Johnny Jordaan and Tante Leen and accordionist Johnny Meijer, who all gained a degree of immortality performing songs of lost love and beer in the local bars. Johnny Meijer so loved the neighborhood that he gave up a promising career as side man to the likes of Josephine Baker and Archie Shepp to play locally with his brother-in-law, "the world's worst bassist." A more ancient local legend was called Sjako, the man otherwise known as "Amsterdam's Robin Hood," who together with his gang occupied a confusing maze of a "fort" complete with ample secret escape passages, farther up Elandsgracht at No. 71–77. Although how much he actually gave to the poor is unknown, the stylish way he stole from the rich certainly fed their imagination. In 1717 after several spectacular escapes, he was finally captured, stretched on a rack, then beheaded. **Sjako's Fort** was replaced more than a century ago, but the new building's current owners have installed memorial stone tablets and an informational shrine (the Amsterdams Historisch Museum displays some of Sjako's guns and his self-designed cat burglary ladder).

A still existing maze—but one that facilitates losing oneself in past ages of a kinder, gentler nature—is the rambling downscale antiques market, **Rommelmarkt** (daily 11–5), on Elandsgracht's southern parallel, Looiersgracht, at No. 38. From here, you can reconnect with Prinsengracht. Taking a right here brings you to the relatively banal entrance between No. 338 and 340 that once led to a Golden Age pleasure garden complete with mechanical figures of famous people (a Madame Tussaud's of sorts of its day) and a hedge labyrinth. However, pipe smokers or folks who just want a whiff of Amsterdam's long and obsessive relationship with tobacco will want to take this route farther up Prinsengracht to get to the **Pijpenkabinet** ㉖ (Pipe Cabinet).

Most others will not want to make this ten-block detour, so they should just head straight over the bridge—which denotes the Jordaan and your reentry into the generally more rarified air of the Grachtengordel—and turn left down Prinsengracht's eastern side and then right down Berenstraat into the very browsable heart of the **Nine Streets** specialty shopping area (perhaps checking out those artist-made books at Boekie Woekie at No. 16). Take the first right down Keizersgracht. The 18th-century monolith with the Neoclassic pillars on your right at No. 324 is the **Felix Meritis Cultural Center** ㉗. Farther up at No. 384 are the gates—and only remains of the burned-down Municipal Theater where Vondel's plays premiered—that denote the entrance to the Blakes "designer hotel," a prime example of that term's definer, Anouska Hempel. You may want to take a moment here—while being wary of arriving stretch limos—to imagine this length of canal as it was during the Golden Age when it was host to the Sunday "Slipper Parade," an opportunity for the rich to stroll back and forth to see and be seen.

Taking the next bridge left, proceed down the gustatory Huidenstraat, with its excellent but sweetly priced pastas and sandwiches of Goodies (No. 9) and decadent chocolates and pastries of Pompadour (No. 12), and take the first right down Herengracht. At Nos. 366–8 is the **Bijbels Museum** ㉘ (Bible Museum) in the midst of a row of houses built by that residential architect to the Golden Age stars, Philip Vingboons, who adorned these creations with bull's-eye windows and an ample harvest of stone fruit. An example of a yet more excessive brand of inspired architecture is the building at No. 380 that now houses the **Nederlands Instituut voor Oorlogs Documentatie** ㉙ (Netherlands Institute for War Documentation) and their 3-km-long archive.

To arrive at an optional end point of this tour involves taking the first right down Leidsegracht and then the first left down Keizersgracht, where at the corner of Leidsestraat is the designer-friendly **Metz & Co.** ㉚ department store. The nexus of Keizersgracht and Leidsegracht marks one of the most charming areas of the city, and you can take it all in from on high from the store's *style anglais* sixth-floor café, where you can get an epic view of much of your recent wanderings.

TIMING It is difficult to say how long this walk will take, because it leads you through areas that invite wandering and the exploration of side streets. At a brisk and determined pace, you can manage the route in about two or three hours. But you could also easily while away an afternoon in Jordaan, or take a leisurely stroll along the Prinsengracht. Allow a minimum of an hour for the Anne Frank House, and try to get there early to beat the 10- to 20-minute lines that invariably form by midday.

The best time for canal walks is in late afternoon and early evening—or for you revelers, early in the morning when the darkness gives the water a deep purple color before becoming shrouded by the dawn's mist. If you're planning to go shopping in the Jordaan or the Nine Streets quarter, remember that shops in The Netherlands are closed Monday morning—however, that's the only time that the unmissable Noordermarkt flea market takes place as well as the adjoining textile market along Westerstraat. With its many restaurants and cafés, the Jordaan is also a prime spot for evening frolicking.

HOW TO
GET THERE
The western edge of Amsterdam's "village," the Jordaan, is just a few minutes stroll from the Dam square and Centraal Station. However Trams Nos. 13, 14, and 17 follow Rozengracht and Tram No. 3 follows Marnixstraat to Haarlemmerplein.

Sights to See

㉒ **Anne Frankhuis** (Anne Frank House). With her diary having sold more than 30 million copies, Anne Frank is by far the most successful and famous author of the 20th century, testimony to the inspiring story of a girl who died at age 15 in a tragic denouement of the two-year saga now known to readers around the world. In the precious pages of *The Diary of Anne Frank* (published in 1947 as *The Annex* by her father after her death) the young Anne kept her sad record of two increasingly fraught

Fodor'sChoice
★

years living in secret confinement from the Nazis. Along with the Van Daan family, the Frank family felt the noose tighten, so decided to move into a hidden warren of rooms at the back of this 1635-built canal house.

Anne Frank was born in Germany in 1929; when she was four her family moved to The Netherlands to escape growing anti-Jewish sentiment. Otto Frank operated a pectin business and decided to stay in his adopted country when the war finally reached The Netherlands in 1940. In July 1942, the five adults and three children sought refuge in the attic of the annex "backhouse," or *achterhuis,* of Otto's business in the center of Amsterdam, in a hidden warren of rooms screened behind a hinged bookcase. Here, as one of many *onderduikers* ("people in hiding") throughout all of Amsterdam, Anne dreamed her dreams, wrote her diary, and pinned up movie-star pictures to her wall (still on view). The van Pelsen family, including their son, Peter (van Daan in Anne's journal), along with the dentist Fritz Pfeffer (Dussel) joined them in their cramped quarters. Four trusted employees provided them with food and supplies. In her diary, Anne chronicles the day-to-day life in the house: her longing for a best friend, her crush on Peter, her frustration with her mother, her love for her father, and her annoyance with the petty dentist, Dussel. In August 1944, the Franks were betrayed and the Gestapo invaded their hideaway. All the members of the annex were transported to camps, where Anne and her sister, Margot, died of typhoid fever in Bergen Belsen a few months before the liberation. Otto Frank was the only survivor of the annex. Miep Gies, one of the friends who helped with the hiding, found Anne's diary after the raid and kept it through the war.

A recent expansion by Benthem Crouwel Architects has allowed the recreation of Otto Frank's business in the original house and provided space for more in-depth exhibitions, a bookstore, café, and offices for the employees—which now number 100—of the Anne Frank Foundation. One of the most frequently visited places in the world, this house receives more than 800,000 visitors a year; the wooden stairs behind the swinging bookcase have to be replaced every two years. Anne's diary has now been translated into more than 50 languages, making Anne the international celebrity she always dreamed of being. ⊠ *Prinsengracht 263, Jordaan* ☎ *020/556-7100* ⊕ *www.annefrank.nl* ⊠ *€6.50* ☺ *Sept.–Mar., daily 9–7; Apr.–Aug., daily 9–9.*

㉘ Bijbels Museum (Bible Museum). Although this museum does indeed have a massive collection of Bibles—as well as exhibits with archaeological finds from the Middle East and models of ancient temples that evoke biblical times—what probably draws more people is the building itself. The two enjoined canal houses (dating from 1662) have had their interiors restored, including incredible 18th-century myth-drenched ceiling paintings from the hands of Jacob de Wit, along with the country's best-preserved 17th-century kitchen. The museum is also currently in the midst of efforts geared toward broadening its appeal—such as a "story attic" for children and a modernly landscaped back garden with terraced pools and a "smell cabinet" where one can take a whiff of 16 different biblical essences. ⊠ *Herengracht 366–368, Western Canal Ring* ☎ *020/624-2436* ⊕ *www.bijbelsmuseum.nl* ⊠ *€5* ☺ *Mon.–Sat. 10–5, Sun. 1–5.*

★ ㉑ Bloemgracht (Flower Canal). Lined with suave "burgher" houses of the 17th century, this canal was once so stately it was called the "Herengracht of the Jordaan" (Gentlemen's Canal of the Jordaan). In due course, it became a center for paint manufactories, which made sense, because Egelantiersgracht, an address favored by Golden Age artists, is just one canal to the north. Although modern intrusions have been made, Bloemgracht is still proudly presided over by "De Drie Hendricken," three houses set at Nos. 87 to 91. These 1642 mansions, built by Hendrick de Keyser (hence their nickname) and restored by the De Keyser Foundation, allure with their stepped gables, paned windows, and gable stones, carved with a farmer, a city settler, and a sailor. ⊠ *Between Lijnbaansgracht and Prinsengracht, Jordaan.*

16 **Brouwersgracht** (Brewers Canal). One of the most photographed spots in town, this pretty, tree-lined canal at the northern border of the Jordaan district is bordered by residences and former warehouses of the brewers who traded here in the 17th century when Amsterdam was the "warehouse of the world." Without sacrificing the ancient vibe, most of the buildings have been converted into luxury apartments. Of particular note are the houses at Nos. 188 to 194. The canal is blessed with long views down the main canals and plenty of sunlight, perfect for photo-ops. The Brouwersgracht runs westward from the end of the Singel (a short walk along Prins Hendrikkade from Centraal Station) and forms a cap to the western end of the Grachtengordel. ⊠ *Jordaan.*

19 **Claes Claesz-hofje.** A set of 17th-century hofjes, this was founded in 1616 by the textile dealer Claes Claesz Anslo (note his coat of arms atop one entry). The houses here were renovated and are now rented out to artists, the happiest of whom must occupy the **Huis met de Schrijvende Hand** ("House with the Writing Hand"), the oldest and most picturesque of the lot, topped by a six-stepped gable. ⊠ *1e Egelantiersdwarsstraat 3, Western Canal Ring.*

20 **Egelantiersgracht** (Eglantine Canal). Befitting one of the main canals of the long-ago sylvan Jordaan ("Garden") district, this canal was named after the sweetbrier flower, one of the blooms most favored by Civic Guards and Burgomeisters as a finishing touch to their garments in their 17th-century portraits. The connection grows even more aesthetic since many of the houses along this canal were first occupied by Golden Age painters and artisans. Hidden here is the **St. Andrieshofje** courtyard, found at No. 107 and replete with a Delftware title entryway. Certainly not hidden (it is usually jammed with people) is the world-famed **Café 't Smalle,** found at No. 12. This ivy-covered *proeflokaal* (tasting house), complete with waterside terrace, was where Pieter Hoppe began his *jenever* (Dutch gin) distillery in 1780, an event of such global significance that 't Smalle is re-created in Japan's Holland Village in Nagasaki. The "Very Small" has a delightful tavern interior right out of a Jan Steen canvas, bringing the art referent hereabouts full circle. ⊠ *Between Lijnbaansgracht and Prinsengracht, Jordaan.*

27 **Felix Mauritis Cultural Center.** If we are to believe its name, "Happiness through Achievement," which is chiseled over its entrance, then this is a very happy building indeed—not to mention an enlightened one, since its Neoclassical architecture arose in the year of the French Revolution, 1789. Felix Meritis was a society whose building housed committees dedicated to the study and promotion of economics, science, painting, music, and literature. Its cupola held an observatory, and its concert hall had the likes of Schumann and Brahms dropping by to tickle the ivories. Between 1949 and 1968, the Communist Party took over the building (one result being getting its windows smashed during a protest against the Soviet invasion of Hungary in 1956). Then various experimental theater companies began calling it home before it settled into its current role as European Center for Art and Science, which hosts a plethora of readings, panels, and discussions with the aim of "connecting cultures." Drop by to pick up a program or to check the hours of its Philosophy

Café. ⊠ *Keizersgracht 324, Western Canal Ring* ☎ *020/623–1311* ⊕ *www.felix.meritis.nl* ⊘ *Café has changeable hrs.*

㉔ Homomonument (Homosexual Monument). This, the world's first memorial to persecuted gays and lesbians, was designed by Karin Daan, who employed three huge triangles of pinkish granite—representing past, present, and future—to form a larger triangle. On May 4 (Remembrance Day), there are services here commemorating the homosexual victims of World War II, when thousands were killed of the 50,000 sentenced—all of whom were forced to wear pink triangles. Flowers are laid daily for lost friends, especially on the descending triangle that forms a dock of sorts into Keizersgracht. Particularly large mountains of flowers form on December 1 (World AIDS Day). Signs will lead you to the "Pink Point of Presence," one of the stalls along the east side of Westermarkt, which acts as an information point to visiting gays and lesbians. It is open daily noon–6 during May through September (but there are continued efforts being made to keep it open year-round). ⊠ *Westermarkt, Jordaan.*

★ ⑭ Huis met Hoofden (House with Heads). The Greek deities of Apollo, Ceres, Mars, Minerva, Bacchus, and Diana welcome you—or rather, busts of them do—to this famous example of Dutch Neoclassic architecture, one of the grandest double houses of 17th-century Amsterdam. Delightfully graced with pilasters, pillars, and a step gable, the 1622 mansion is attributed to architect Pieter de Keyser, son of the more famed Hendrick. The heads adorn the entry facade and represent classical deities and are not, as a local tale has it, the concrete-coated skulls of six thieves decapitated by a vigilant but conflicted maid who ended up marrying the seventh. The house is now headquarters to the Monumentenzorg—custodian to many of the city's public monuments—and is not open to the public. ⊠ *Keizersgracht 123, Western Canal Ring* ☎ *020/522–4888* ⊕ *www.bmz.amsterdam.nl.*

㉚ Metz & Co. When the New York Life Insurance Company opened this building in 1891, its soaring six floors brought a touch of Manhattan to Amsterdam's canals—literally, as architect J. van Looy had also designed the company's lofty skyscraper in Manhattan. By 1908, the Metz department store had converted the offices into showcases for Liberty fabrics and De Stijl teapots. Shop if you must, but don't fail to take the circular staircase up from the sixth-floor café to discover the penthouse created by master designer Gerrit Rietveld in 1933 as a showroom to highlight functionalist furniture (his own included). Its glass cupola offers dazzling views of this particularly alluring section of Amsterdam, and the café itself is a favorite time-out spot. ⊠ *Leidsestraat 34, Western Canal Ring* ☎ *020/520–7020* ⊘ *Mon. 11–6, Tues. and Wed. 9:30–6, Thurs. 10–9, Sun. noon–5.*

⑮ Multatuli-Huis. This museum honors the beliefs and work (and continues the legacy) of Eduard Douwes Dekker (1820–1887), a.k.a. Multatuli (from the Latin, meaning "I have suffered greatly"), who famously wrote *Max Havelaar, or the Coffee Auctions of the Dutch Trading Company,* a muckraking book that uncovered the evil of Dutch colonialism. The son of an Amsterdam sea captain, Dekker accompanied his father to the Dutch Indies (Indonesia) and joined the Dutch Civil Service. After years of poverty and wandering, in 1860 he wrote and published his magnum opus, denouncing and exposing the colonial landowners' narrow minds and inhumane practices. Today, Dutch intellectuals and progressive thinkers respect him mightily. ⊠ *Korsjespoortsteeg 20, Western Canal Ring* ☎ *020/638–1938* ⊕ *www.multatuli-museum.nl* ⊘ *Weekends noon–5 and Tues. 10–5.*

29 Nederlands Instituut voor Oorlogs Documentatie (Netherlands Institute for War Documentation). Established in 1945, this institute has collected vast archives of documents, newspapers, 100,000 photos, and 50,000 books relating to the occupation of World War II. It is to this institution that Otto Frank donated his daughter's diary. More recently, the institute has expanded its sights to take in the period between World War I and the present with particular emphasis on the former colony of Indonesia. In 2002, the release of the institute's government-commissioned report on the role of Dutchbat in the 1995 fall of Srebrenica in the former Yugoslavia and the ensuing mass murder of 8,000 Muslim men resulted in Prime Minister Wim Kok stepping down and dissolving his Cabinet. Although the institute is essentially not open to the merely curious, it is very welcoming to people doing academic or family-related research. What can be enjoyed by all is the Loire-style château exterior and its rich and obsessive sculptures of frolicking mythical figures. ⊠ *Herengracht 380, Western Canal Ring* ☎ *020/523–3800* ⊕ *www.oorlogsdoc.knaw.nl* ⊙ *Weekdays 9–5.*

13 Nederlands Theatermuseum (Netherlands Theater Museum). Amsterdam has several Golden Age house museums, but few are as gilded as this one. Currently home to part of the Theater Instituut Nederland (Netherlands Theater Institute), the **Bartolotti Huis** (No. 170–172) is made up of two spectacular examples of 17th-century Dutch Renaissance houses built by Hendrick de Keyser for a brewer by the name of William van der Huvel (who one day thought to spice up his image by calling himself Guillelmo Bartolotti). The rest of the museum takes up the equally delectable White House (No. 168), built in 1638, and which rates as noted designer Philips Vingboons's first work in Amsterdam (and as such sports the city's oldest neck gable). Its original owner, Michiel Pauw—as one of the initiators of the West Indies Company and the founder of a small settlement on the Hudson River—could easily afford its interior of marble-lined corridors, sweeping monumental staircases, densely rendered plasterwork, and ceiling paintings by Jacob de Wit. All of these attributes have been restored to provide a lush backdrop for exhibitions about the history of theater in all its forms: circus, opera, musical, puppetry, and drama. There are costumes, models of stage sets, and other accessories. There is also an extensive library with archives focused on the theatrical scene in The Netherlands. Its stellar back garden—alone worth the price of admission—is the perfect place to sip a coffee from the café while imagining it as the setting for Baroque-era barbecues. ⊠ *Herengracht 168–170, Western Canal Ring* ☎ *020/551–3300* ⊕ *www.tin.nl* ⊠ *€4.50* ⊙ *Tues.–Fri. 11–5, weekends 1–5.*

Fodor's Choice ★

17 Noordermarkt (Northern Market). In 1620, city planners decided to build a church for those too lazy to walk to Westerkerk. **Noorderkerk** (Northern Church), designed by Hendrick de Keyser and completed after his death by his son Pieter, was the first Protestant church that featured a new—more democratic—ground plan, which was formed by the Greek cross (four equal arms) with the pulpit in the middle. The building's religious function was dropped whenever the Jordaan locals deemed it necessary to riot for their rights, then becoming headquarters and barracks for the cavalry and infantry. The soberly Calvinist 18th-century interior can viewed on Monday from 10:30 to 12:30, on Saturday from 11 to 1, and during regular Saturday afternoon concert recitals starting at 2. Until 1688, the surrounding square, Noordermarkt, was a graveyard whose residents were moved to make room for its present—albeit now sporadic—function as a market. The **Maandag Morgen Noordermarkt** (Monday Morning Northern Market), popularly known as the Monday Morning Flea Market, with an enjoining textile market on Westerstraat, is one of the city's most scenic and best-kept secrets. It's also a prime place to see the typically pragmatic sales techniques of the locals in action. All day Saturday (when there's also a more general market along the nearby Lindengracht), there's an organic foods market that often comes supplemented with some more flea-markety stalls of antiques and knickknacks. ⊠ *Bounded by Prinsengracht, Noorderkerkstraat, and Noordermarkt, Jordaan.*

> **need a break?**
>
> The city's most cherished slice of apple pie can be had at **Winkel** (⊠ Noordermarkt 43, Jordaan ☎ 020/623–0223). For a funky setting and perhaps an inspired designer sandwich, head to **Finch** (⊠ Noordermarkt 5, Jordaan ☎ 020/626–2461).

㉖ Pijpenkabinet (Pipe Cabinet). Considering Amsterdam's rich history of tobacco trading and its population's long tradition of rolling its own "shag," there should actually be a much larger museum dedicated to this subject. Perhaps this theoretical museum could relate such local facts as how urine-soaked tobacco was hailed as an able aphrodisiac in the 16th century, how "tobacco-smoke enema applicators" were used until the mid-19th-century as the standard method to attempt the reviving of those seemingly drowned in the canals, and how Golden Age painters employed tobacco and its smoke as an able metaphor for the fleeting nature of life. But as things stand, there is only this focused collection of more than 2,000 pipes, which aims to tell the tale of the Western European "sucking"—as the local parlance used to describe it—tradition. You might also want to check out the library or buy a pipe in the Smokiana shop. At press time, the collection was undergoing a renovation. ⊠ *Prinsengracht 488, Western Canal Ring* ☎ *020/421–1779* ⊕ *www.pijpenkabinet.nl* 🎫 *€5* ☉ *Wed.–Sat. noon–6.*

⑱ Suykerhoff-hofje. For a moment of peace, enter this hof and take in its frighteningly green courtyard, whose houses opened their doors in 1670 to Protestant "daughters and widows" (as long as they behaved and exhibited "a peace-loving humor") and provided each of them with free rent, twenty tons of turf, ten pounds of rice, a vat of butter, and some spending money each year. ⊠ *Lindengracht 149–163, Western Canal Ring.*

⑫ Torensluis (Towers Bridge). Charming views down the Singel are yours from one of the café seats that line this broad bridge, originally built over a 17th-century sluice gate bookended with towers (hence the name), and still one of the widest in Amsterdam. If you do stop at one of the charming terraces here, let the knowledge of the bridge's ancient function as a lockup for drunks—dug deep in its foundations—keep you sufficiently sober. Note the bridge's statue of Multituli, the 19th-century writer who questioned Dutch colonial policies, before heading to the museum devoted to this author nearby at Korsjespoortsteeg 20. ⊠ *Singel between Torensteeg and Oude Leliestraat, Western Canal Ring.*

★ ㉓ Westerkerk (Western Church). Built between 1602 and 1631 by the ubiquitous Hendrick de Keyser and presumed the last resting place of Rembrandt, the Dutch Renaissance Westerkerk was the largest Protestant church in the world until Christopher Wren came along with his St. Paul's Cathedral in London. Its tower—endlessly mentioned in Jordaan songs—is topped by a gaudy copy of the crown of the Habsburg emperor Maximilian I (or, rather, to avoid a potential bar brawl, a later model of the crown used by Rudolph II). Maximilian gave Amsterdam the right to use his royal insignia in 1489 in gratitude for help from the city in his struggle for control of the Low Countries, and the crown's "XXX" marking was quickly exploited by the city's merchants as a visiting card of quality. More recently, Amsterdam's notoriety and the phallic nature of the quickly disappearing *Amsterdammertje* parking poles (which bear a XXX logo, a common civic insignia) has led many to speculate that the poles' markings suggest "Triple-X Rated." Now you know differently. . . .

The tower rates as the city's highest monument. Its gigantic bell (popularly known as the "clock" of this area) rings every half hour but with a different tone to mark the half before the hour—in other words, the 12 rings of 11:30 are different from the rings of 12. The playing of the church's carillon, which still occurs every Tuesday between noon and 1, is often mentioned in the diary of Anne Frank. Another immortal, Rembrandt, lived nearby on Rozengracht 188 during his poverty-stricken last years. He (as well as his son, Titus) was buried in the church in an unmarked grave on October 4, 1669. His posthumous reputation inspired some very surreal television three centuries later, when a body was unearthed that was mistakenly thought to be his. While exposed to the glare of the news cameras, the skull turned to dust. Oopsie. ⊠ *Prinsengracht 281 (corner of Westermarkt), Jordaan* ☎ *020/624–7766* ⊕ *www.westerkerk.nl* ⊙ *Tower June–Sept., Tues., Wed., Fri., and Sat. 2–5; interior Apr.–Sept., weekdays 11–3.*

need a break? Along Westermarkt's southerly side is an excellent fish stall where you can slide a raw herring or some smoked eel down your throat (though there are also less eerily textured options). An equally traditionally Dutch way of keeping eating costs down is to pack one's belly with pancakes. The **Pancake Bakery** (⊠ Prinsengracht 191, Jordaan ☎ 020/625–1333) is one of the best places in Amsterdam to try them, with a menu that offers a near infinite range of topping possibilities—from the sweet to the fruity to the truly belly-gelling powers of cheese and bacon. If you are indeed more thirsty than hungry, head to the brown café **Café Chris** (⊠ Bloemstraat 42, Jordaan ☎ 020/624–5942), up on the next corner; it has been pouring beverages since 1624. Its intrinsic coziness is taken to absurd lengths in its tiny male bathroom, whose cistern's position outside the door means that pranksters can easily shock you out of your reveries with a quick pull of the flusher. Be warned.

✋ ㉕ **Woonboatmuseum** (Houseboat Museum). In Amsterdam nearly 8,000 people (and a whole gaggle of cats at the cat asylum that floats opposite Singel 40—though they may have moved to posher quarters a few boats down from here by now) live on its 2,400 houseboats. This converted 1914-built sailing vessel, the *Hendricka Maria,* provides a glimpse into this unique lifestyle. It almost feels as if you are visiting Grandma—which is also highlighted by the special child-play zone—as you settle into comfy seats to read the information packets. Models and slides help broaden the view. ⊠ *Prinsengracht opposite No. 296, Jordaan* ☎ *020/427–0750* ⊕ *www.houseboatmuseum.nl* ⊠ *€2.50* ⊙ *Mar.–Oct., Wed.–Sun. 11–5; Nov.–Feb., Fri.–Sun. 11–5.*

BEYOND THE "GOLDEN BEND": THE EASTERN CANAL RING & DE PIJP

Amsterdam's 17th-century Golden Age left behind a tidemark of magnificent buildings to line its lovely canals. This is most striking along the famous Gouden Bocht (Golden Bend), where elaborate gables, richly decorated facades, finely detailed cornices, colored marbles, and heavy doors created an imposing architecture that suits the bank headquarters of today as well as it did the grandees of yore. This tour takes in such time-burnished marvels, but—to an even greater degree than with the tour of the Western Canal Ring and the Jordaan—this remains a city area of contrasts. Amsterdam's richest stretches of canals, the Eastern Canal Ring, which still glitter with the sumptuous pretensions of a Golden Age past, will be put against the more "street" (albeit quickly gentrifying) realities of the De Pijp district, which reflect Amsterdam's present as an ultimately global village.

In 1660, city planners decided to continue the western half ring of canals that had been arising since 1613 and had already been proven as a prime and scenic living location for the well-heeled. But the mega-well-heeled observed that the allotments there were too narrow and therefore now had an opportunity to buy two adjoining allotments in the east (this excess is the reason why this area is currently much less residential and much more taken over by banks, businesses, and hotels).

De Pijp ("The Pipe"), named for its narrow streets and towering gables, has been destined to be an "up-and-coming" neighborhood pretty much since it was built in the late 19th century to house working-class families. There's nothing like cheap rent also to attract students, artists, and wacky radicals. This was once a place dense with brothels, where Eduard Jacobs sang his absurd but sharply polemical songs about pimps, prostitutes, and the disenfranchised (thereby laying the groundwork for the typically Dutch form of cabaret that is still popularly practiced by the likes of Freek de Jong and Hans Teeuwen). From his De Pijp grotto, the writer Bordewijk depicted Amsterdam during World War I as a "ramshackle bordello, a wooden shoe made of rock"; Piet Mondriaan began formulating the revolutionary art of De Stijl in an attic studio on Ruysdaelkade (No. 75).

Later, waves of guest workers from Turkey and Morocco and immigrants from the former colonies of Suriname and Indonesia began arriving and were fundamental in revitalizing the area around Albert Cuyp Market—the largest outdoor market in The Netherlands—with shops, restaurants, and family values. By the 1980s, De Pijp was a true global village, with more than 126 nationalities. With a new underground Metro line destined—or doomed, depending on whom you talk to—to run through here within the next decade, yet more upmarket investors are now appearing. But regardless, the Pijp remains a prime spot for cheap international eats and pub-crawling at local bars and cafés.

Numbers in the text correspond to numbers in the margin and on the Eastern Canal Ring & the Museum District map.

a good walk The Muntplein, with the Dutch Renaissance **Munt Toren** ❶ ☛ (Mint Tower) as its focal point, is chaotic—but for a reason. From here you can enter the floating **Flower Market** to the south, witness the walking-and-shopping **Kalverstraat** to the west, or admire the facade to the north of Hotel de L'Europe (which Alfred Hitchcock used as a vertigo inducer in *Foreign Correspondent*).

Some of you may decide first to visit—by taking the road to the right of the tower—the **Torture Museum** (✉ Singel 449, Eastern Canal Ring ☎ 020/320–6642), with its iron maidens and their ilk. It's open daily 10 AM–11 PM. Most, however, will choose to stick temporarily with the chaos and follow the torturous crowds up Reguliersbreestraat's right side, past Easyeverything—a 24-hour cybercafé whose 650 monitors made it the world's largest for a short time in 2000—and the truly grand **Tuschinski Cinema** ❷, a theater that fuses Art Deco with a pure eclectic enthusiasm. For contrast, you might want to glance across the street from here to Nos. 31–33 and admire a classic piece of Functionalist-

The Eastern Canal Ring & the Museum District

OUD WEST

Kinkerstraat

De Costetstraat

Jacob Van Lennepkade

Bosboom Toussaintstraat

Nassaukade

3e Helmersstraat

2e Helmersstraat

1e Helmersstraat

Overtoom

Constantijn Huygensstraat

19

Vondelpark

Marnixstraat

Loiergracht

Loiergracht

Passeerdersstraat

Passeerdersgt

Passeerdersgt

Passeerdersgt

Raamstraat

Leidsegracht

Leidsegracht

Leidsegracht

Vondelstraat

Tesselschadestraat

Visscherstraat

Zandpad

18

Vossiusstraat

Stadhouderskade

Schapenburgerpad

Cornelisz Hooftstraat

Jan Luijkenstraat

Van Baerlestraat

Paulus Potterstraat

17   **16**

Van Eeghenlaan

Van Eeghenstraat

Willemsparkweg

Van Breestraat

Palestrina Straat

J Verhulst Straat

Alexander Boers Str

15

Concertgebouw Plein

Gabriel Metsustraat

de Lairessestraat

Wouwermanstraat

Van Baerlestraat

Nicolaas Maes Straat

Frans Van Mieris Straat

Roysdaelstraat

Cornelis Anthonisz Straat

Wolvenstr

Oude Spiegel Straat

Herengracht

Singel

Singel

Singel

Smitstraat

Nieuwezijds Voorburgwal

Huidenstr

Keizersgracht

Keizersgracht

Keizersgracht

Prinsengracht

Prinsengracht

Leidsegracht

Leidsegracht

Leidse

Keizersgracht

Keizersgracht

Kerkstraat

Prinsengracht

Herengracht

Herengracht

Herengracht

Voetboogstr

Heiligweg

Singel

Handboogstr

Flower Market

GOUDEN BOCHT

Keizers:

Kerkstraat

Prinsen:

Prinsen:

Leidseplein

Leidseplein ▶

12   **11**

13

Korte Leidsedwarsstraat

Lange Leidsedwarsstraat

Prinsengracht

Prinsengracht

Lijnbaansgracht

Weteringschans

Gracht Nieuwe Spiegelstraat

1e Weteringswarsstraat

1e Weteringswarsstraat

1e Weteringswars-straat

Lijnbaansgracht

Nieuwe Weteringstr

Nieuwe Weteringstr

Weteringstr

Wijzelgracht

He

MUSEUM DISTRICT

Museum Plein

14

Hobbemastraat

Hobbemakade

Boerenwetering

Ruysdaelkade

Hendrik M. Van Randwijk-Plantsoen

Stadhouderskade

Straat

Teniers Straat

Vermeer straat

Pieter de Hoochstraat

Johannesms

1e Jacob V. Campen Str

Quellijn Straat

Daniel Stelpert Straat

Seanredamstraat

Helstr

Ferdinand Bolstraat

16

Hobbemakade

Ruysdaelkade

Dusart

1e Jan Steen   Straat

1e Jan V.D. Heijden Straat

DE P

Ferdinand Bolstraat

0		250 yards
0		250 meters

Constructivist architecture from 1934, which was originally a cinema before falling into the hands of Planet Hollywood. But before deciding that the Dutch are folks with impeccable taste, wait until you witness the neon and touristic atrocities in **Rembrandtplein,** where things have changed a lot since it was the city's butter market. Something has gone terribly wrong here, the first clue of which may be the cheap iron (rather than bronze) statue of a cavalier Rembrandt in its center. But in the midst of the infinite middle-of-the-road cafés, clubs, and restaurants, there are some truly classy landmarks: **De Kroon** (No. 17), a shockingly spacious grand café complete with zoological specimens and a balcony, and **Schiller** (No. 26), with its amazing Art Deco interior, which still evokes the bohemian types that used to hang out here.

After loading up on coffee at one of these establishments, exit the square through the enjoining smaller square Thorbeckeplein (although some of you may first want to divert to the right up the very gay-friendly Reguliersdwarsstraat to pick out a restaurant or nightclub for later). The first canal you come to is Herengracht, and to the right lies the opulent Golden Bend, **Gouden Bocht,** with some of the city's most impressive Golden Age residential monuments. However, if you are more interested in looking at the life behind the facades, head left to **Willet-Holthuysen Museum ❸**. Then again, if there's a crack in the clouds, you may want to just hurry straight up Reguliersgracht to the intersection with Keizersgracht, where from the bridge an additional 15 bridges can be viewed.

From here hang a right to reach the majestically opulent interiors on display at **Museum van Loon ❹**. Its neighbor, No. 676, is a former church that now occasionally hosts photographic exhibitions. Before backtracking east to Reguliersgracht to make the right that will get you to **Amstelveld ❺**, a tranquil square, perhaps first pause to observe the Amsterdam School bridge to the west crossing Vijzelstraat. Sit awhile here at the square's famed Moko café—the adjacent blocks and Reguliersgracht combine to form one of the prettiest canal scenes in the city.

Approaching Amstelveld square, you will see on its first corner a wooden church that includes the café Kort, with an exceedingly pleasant terrace, which looks across Prinsengracht to "De Duif" (No. 756); it arose in 1796 as one of the first openly Catholic churches after the Altercation in 1578. The curious may want to check if its renovation is complete before taking Kerkstraat, running along Amstelveld's north side, to the east and crossing the excellently diverse shopping and eating strip of Utrechtsestraat. Continue until you reach the mighty river Amstel. The skinny bridge that crosses it, **Magere Brug ❻**, or Skinny Bridge, is the most photographed bridge in the city, so click your way to the status quo.

Wandering aimlessly along the Amstel is always a worthwhile occupation. If you are feeling particularly ambitious, you can make the 20-minute walk along the river to the south—minding the U-shape jag you have to make to cross Singelgracht—to reach the city archives, **Gemeente Archief ❼**, with its monumental collection of all things Amsterdam. But if you are more motivated by hunger and/or want to check out Amsterdam's most multicultural neighborhood, **De Pijp,** backtrack down Kerkstraat and turn left down Utrechtsestraat, follow its split to the right, cross the bridge, and take the second right to enter Europe's biggest and busiest day market, **Albert Cuypmarkt ❽**. Take the walking side street, 1e Sweelinckstraat, to the left toward the green peace of **Sarphatipark ❾**, on whose opposite end you can connect with another charming walking and terrace street, 1e Van der Helststraat, which will bring you back down to the market. Heading straight will have you passing through

Gerard Douplein with its three funkily mosaic pillars, past Stichting Dodo (No. 21) on the right (where you can pause to invest in some laughably cheap secondhand Euro-bric-a-brac) before turning left on Daniel Stalpertstraat, which will get you to the Marie Heinekenplein. Turning right on Ferdinand Bol and right again on Stadshouderskade will have you at the front door of the **Heineken Brouwerjij** ⑩), a former brewery whose tour remains a must-do for some, a must-avoid for others. But undoubtedly, you've just recently seen a charming spot worthy of partaking in a more relaxed beer. If not, try the many found along the restful, tree-lined, and almost Parisian-flavor Frans Halstraat, which runs as Ferdinand Bolstraat's western parallel. *Proost!*

TIMING   If done briskly, this tour can be completed in an hour and half. Being more of a purely walking, gandering, and following-your-nose tour, there are no major disappointments awaiting you while doing this tour during daylight hours. However, Albert Cuypmarkt is a ghost town on Sunday, and the Museum van Loon does have particularly antisocial hours.

HOW TO   Trams Nos. 16, 24, and 25 follow Vijzelstraat through the canal ring
GET THERE   and into the southern district of De Pijp. Tram No. 4 runs more to the east along Utrechtsestraat towards the RAI convention center.

Sights to See

⑧ **Albert Cuypmarkt** (Albert Cuyp Market). As the biggest and busiest street market in Europe, Albert Cuypmarkt—named after a Golden Age painter like the majority of the streets in De Pijp—welcomes 20,000 shoppers daily during the week and double that number on Saturday. Although you should come here for all your fresh food, textiles, and sundry other needs, the atmosphere alone makes it worthwhile. With a decades-long waiting list for a permanent booth, things can get dramatic—if not occasionally violent—at 9 every morning on the corner of 1e Sweel-inckstraat, where the lottery for that day's available temporary spaces take place. ⊠ *Albert Cuypmarkt between Ferdinand Bolstraat and Van Woustraat, De Pijp* ☯ *Mon.–Sat. 9–5.*

need a break?   De Pijp offers endless options in the world of global snacking and dining. If you want to keep things cheap and speedy, then try such Surinamese (whose history and geography saw the mixing of Indonesian, Chinese, and Caribbean cookeries) purveyors as **Albine** (⊠ Albert Cuypstraat 69, De Pijp ☏ 020/675–5135) or **Warung Spang-Makandra** (⊠ Gerard Doustraat 39, De Pijp ☏ 020/670–5081). Middle Eastern maestros can be found at **Eufraat** (⊠ 1e Van der Helststraat 72, De Pijp ☏ 020/672–0579) and **Falafel Dan's** (⊠ Ferdinand Bolstraat 126, De Pijp ☏ 020/676–3411). For a flavor of the area's reinvented café culture, check out **Kingfisher** (⊠ Ferdinand Bolstraat 23, De Pijp ☏ 020/671–2395), whose stellar kitchen pumps out sandwiches by day and a shockingly inventive and cheap daily special for dinner at night;or the new and remarkably spacious grand café **De Engel** (⊠ Albert Cuypstraat 182, De Pijp ☏ 020/ 675–0544).), where one can linger over a coffee while admiring one's recent market investments.

However, sweet tooths should go directly to the kitschy and kid-friendly **De Taart van m'n Tante** (⊠ Ferdinand Bolstraat 10, De Pijp ☏ 020/776–4600), where a frightening amount of different colorful cakes can be indulged in.

❺ **Amstelveld.** One of the most tranquil corners in the Grachtengordel canal ring, Amstelveld square is landmarked by its **Amstelkerk**, a wooden church that arose in 1668 as one of the first openly Catholic churches after the Altercation in 1578. A Neo-Gothic face-lift was given to the interior in 1840, and the edifice was fitted out with community offices in the 1960s. Services are still held within its nave, however, where its liberal pastor is noted for pulling in the crowds. Others head here to enjoy the exceedingly pleasant terrace of the café Kort, now an adjunct of Amstelkerk, which looks across Prinsengracht to "De Duif" (No. 756) and takes in many of the scenic pleasures—gabled houses, houseboats, canals—of this particularly villagelike area of Amsterdam. ⊠ *Bounded by Kerkstraat, Prinsengracht, Reguliersgracht, and Utrechtsestraat, Eastern Canal Ring.*

❼ Gemeente Archief (Municipal Archives). Established in 1914, this noble institution, which is freely open to the public, is filled with all the archives and collections relevant to Amsterdam. Although you won't be able personally to inspect the piece of paper from 1275 by which Floris V extended toll privileges to the then tiny town and thereby initiated its growth toward global dominance, you can eyeball this parchment, as it is part of their brand-new and permanent "Treasures" exhibition, and do such interactive things as search for your family roots or follow the history of the city's fashion industry. It also holds two temporary city-centric exhibitions per year and harbors an excellent bookstore that sells every available Amster-relevant publication. If all goes to plan, they will move to a new location at the end of 2004, so stay tuned. ⊠ *Amsteldijk 67, De Pijp* ☎ *020/572–0202* ⊕ *www.gemeentearchief.amsterdam.nl* ▧ *Free* ☉ *Mon.–Sat. 11–5.*

★ Gouden Bocht (Golden Bend). This stretch of the Herengracht—which indeed bends—between the Vijzelstraat to the Leidsegracht contains some of Amsterdam's most opulent Golden Age architecture and as such provided homes to the financial and political elite of the 17th and 18th centuries. It speaks of the egalitarian tendencies of the Dutch that such excesses arose here on Herengracht (Gentlemen's Canal) as opposed to the yet snootier-sounding Prinsengracht (Princes' Canal) or Keizersgracht (Emperors' Canal). Actually, some of the exteriors may come across at first glance as more modest than overtly opulent and therefore may reflect the Calvinist owners' "Embarrassment of Riches" so well described in Simon Schama's book of the same name. However, embarrassment did not stop them from importing the exterior's construction materials from afar and stuffing the interiors more overtly. In the late 19th century, most of these buildings were converted into offices for banks and other financial institutions that felt quite comfortable behind the heavy central doors. While there are clusters of wonderful historic facades higher up on the canal, there are several notable addresses on this stretch, including "the most beautiful house in Amsterdam," No. 475 (a Louis XIV-style mansion designed by Hans Jacob Husly in 1703). Also keep your eye posted for 485 (Jean Coulon, 1739); 493 and 527, also in the Louis XVI style (1770); and 284 (Van Brienen House, 1728), another ornate Louis XVI facade. Interestingly, when initially laid out, the great canals, including Herengracht, had no trees, making the city look more than ever like a "Venice of the North." With time, elms were planted, in part to allow for their roots to stablize the canal foundations. ⊠ *Bounded by Vijzelstraat and Leidsestraat, Eastern Canal Ring.*

❿ Heineken Brouwerij (Heineken Brewery). Founded by Gerard Heineken in 1864, the Heineken label quickly become one of Amsterdam's (and therefore the world's) most famous beers. As this factory couldn't keep up with the enormous demand (today, most production rolls on in vast plants in The Hague and Den Bosch), it was transformed into a "Heineken

THE CROWNING TOUCH:
GABLES & GABLE STONES

THE INFINITE ARRAY OF GABLES of Amsterdam's houses, historic and modern, dominates the city's picture-postcard image and is a carefully preserved asset. The lack of firm land meant that Amsterdam houses were built on narrow, deep plots, and one of the only ways to make a property distinctive was at the top, with a decorative gable. The simplest and earliest form is the spout gable in the shape of an inverted funnel. When houses were still made of wood, this protective front could simply be nailed on. Another early form was the step gable, usually a continuation of the masonry of the facade, which rises to a pinnacle. This form was also used in Flemish architecture, as seen in the Belgian city of Bruges. The neck gable was the next development, a brick frontage in the form of a decorated oblong, hiding the angled roof behind. Bell gables are an elaboration of this, with more elaborate carved stone or decorative moldings. Another eye-catching element is the gable stone. These plaster or stone tablets placed above doors or built into walls were houses' identity tags before house numbers were introduced early in the 19th century. The gable stones are simple reliefs, sometimes brightly painted, which usually depicted the craft or profession of the inhabitants. For example, an apple merchant might have a depiction of Adam and Eve. To see a whole selection of rescued gable stones, pop into the Begijnhof courtyard or go to the St. Luciensteeg entranceway of the Amsterdam Historical Museum.

Experience," an interactive center that offers tours of the more-than-century-old facilities. Everything from vast copper vats to beer-wagon dray horses is on view, and if you've ever wanted to know what it feels like to be a beer bottle, the virtual reality ride will clue you in. Others may enjoy the option to drink many beers in a very short time (note this tour is open only to visitors over the age of 18). ⊠ *Stadhouderskade 78, De Pijp* ☎ *020/523–9666* ⊕ *www.heinekenexperience.com* ✉ *€7.50* ☺ *Tues.–Sun, 10–6.*

⑥ **Magere Brug** (Skinny Bridge). Of Amsterdam's 60-plus drawbridges, the Fodor'sChoice Magere is the most famous. Whether or not this is mainly because of its
★ name (which derives from "meager" in Dutch), the legend of its birth—it was purportedly built by two sisters living on opposite sides of the Amstel who wanted an efficient way of sharing that grandest of Dutch traditions, the *gezellig* (socially cozy) midmorning coffee break—or because it is spectacularly lighted with electric lights at night, we can't say. Have your camera ready at all hours, since the bridge is often drawn up to let boats pass by. Many replacements to the original bridge, constructed in 1672, have come and gone, and this, dating to 1969, is but the latest. ⊠ *Between Kerkstraat and Nieuwe Kerkstraat, Eastern Canal Ring.*

① **Munt Toren** (Mint Tower). This tower received its name in 1672 when French troops occupied much of the surrounding Republic and Amsterdam was given the right to mint its own coins here for a brief two-year period. Although the spire was added by Hendrick de Keyser in 1620, the medieval tower and the adjoining guardhouse were part of a gate in the city's fortifying wall from 1490. The guardhouse, which now houses a Dutch porcelain shop, has a gable stone above its entrance, which portrays two men and a dog in a boat. This does not depict that founding legend that has Amsterdam arising on the spot where a dog vomited when finally reaching dry land after being lost and sick in a storm with his two masters but rather a symbolic representation of the already formed city: where warrior and merchant bonded by the loyalty—that would be the dog—are sailing toward the future. The tower's carillon of 38 bells was originally installed in 1666 by the famed Hemony Brothers. Although it is now automated to play every 15 minutes, a live recital often takes place on Friday between 3 and 4. ⊠ *Muntplein, Eastern Canal Ring.*

★ ❹ **Museum van Loon.** Once home to one of Rembrandt's most successful students, Ferdinand Bol, this twin house, built in 1672 by Adriaan Dortsman, fell into the hands of the Van Loon family in 1886, who lived here until 1960. After extensive restoration of the house and facade, designed in a sober classicizing mode, the museum opened to depict opulent canal-side living. Along with wonderful period rooms, the house is filled with 80 portraits of the Van Loon family, which follow their history back to the 17th century when one of them helped found the East Indies Company; subjects include paired marriage portraits, and painters include Dirk Santvoort and Cornelis van der Voort. Up the copper staircase—picked out with the initials of Abraham van Hagen and his wife, Catharine Trip, who presided over the house in the 1750s—you'll find various salons containing trompe l'oeil paintings known as *witjes*, illusionistic depictions of landscapes and other scenes. Don't miss the real landscape out back: an exquisitely elegant garden of trimmed hedgerows, which forms a lovely setting for the Van Loon coach houses (the family was rich enough to elegantly house even its carriages), which magisterially adopt the look of Grecian temples. ⊠ *Keizersgracht 672, Eastern Canal Ring* ☎ *020/624-5255* ⊕ *www.museumvanloon.nl* ⌺ *€4.50* ⊙ *Fri.–Mon. 11–5.*

❾ **Sarphatipark.** This miniature Bois de Boulogne was built by and named after the Jewish jack-of-all-trades and noted city benefactor Samuel Sarphati (1813–66), whose statue deservedly graces the central fountain. This park, with paths undulating along trees, ponds, and expanses of grass, can be considered a kinder, gentler, and definitely much smaller Vondelpark and as such should be exploited for picnicking—on supplies gathered from the Albert Cuypmarkt—when you are in the neighborhood on sunny days. ⊠ *Bounded by Ceintuurbaan and Sarfatipark, De Pijp.*

❷ **Tuschinski Cinema.** Although officially the architect of this "Prune Cake"—as it was described when it first opened in 1921—was H. L. De Jong, the financial and spiritual force was undoubtedly Abram Icek Tuschinski (1886–1942), a Polish Jew who after World War I decided to a build a theater that was "unique." And because interior designers Pieter de Besten, Jaap Gidding, and Chris Bartels came up with a dizzying and dense mixture of Baroque, Art Nouveau, Amsterdam School, Jugendstil, and Asian influences, it is safe to say that he achieved his goal. Obsessed with details, he became known as "Napoléon of Devil's Triangle" (as the surrounding, then seedy neighborhood was called). It began as a variety theater welcoming such stars as Marlene Dietrich, but it soon became a cinema, and to this day viewing a film from one of the extravagant private balconies remains an unforgettable experience—especially if you order champagne. Sobering note: Tuschinski died in Auschwitz. ⊠ *Reguliersbreestraat 26–28, Eastern Canal Ring* ☎ *020/626-2633.*

❸ **Willet-Holthuysen Museum.** Few patrician houses are open to the public

Fodor'sChoice along the Herengracht, so make a beeline to this mansion to see Gracht-
★ engordel (Canal Ring) luxury at its best. In 1895, the widow Sandrina Louisa Willet-Holthuysen donated the house and contents—which included her husband's extensive art collection—to the city of Amsterdam.

Visitors can wander through this 17th-century canal house, now under the management of Amsterdams Historisch Museum, and discover all its original 18th-century interiors, complete with that era's mod-cons: from ballroom to *cabinet des merveilles* (rarities cabinet). Objets d'art of silverware, glass, and goldsmith's work accent the rooms. The biggest salon is the Blue Room, handsomely decked out in blue Utrecht velvet, a ceiling painted by Jacob de Wit, and porcelain bibelots. Note the gilded staircase, whose walls are painted in faux-marble. You can air out the aura of Dutch luxury by lounging in the French-style garden in the back. For a peek at the Downstairs side to this Upstairs coin, be sure to check out the wonderful kitchen. ⊠ *Herengracht 605, Eastern Canal Ring* ☎ *020/523–1822* ⊕ *www.willetholthuysen.nl* ⊠ *€4* ☉ *Weekdays 10–5, weekends 11–5.*

VAN GOGH & COMPANY: FROM LEIDSEPLEIN TO THE MUSEUM DISTRICT

With art, like all good things in life, moderation is the key. The fact remains that you will need to make an exception here, thanks to the efficient fact that Amsterdam's acclaimed density of masterpieces is for the most part concentrated around Museumplein. This sheer quantity of quality can soon render visitors cross-eyed and their other four senses atrophied—thanks to the fact that this square mile offers a remarkably complete lesson in the history of Western art: from the realistic but symbolically obtuse depictions offered by the masters of the Golden Age in the Rijksmuseum, to the artistic revolution of the end of the 19th century when artists—such as Van Gogh (and his colleagues on view in the Van Gogh Museum)—had to reinvent the relevance of painting in a photographic age, through to all the ensuing evolutions and revolutions of the 20th century documented in the Stedelijk Museum.

It is therefore fortuitous that this area of the "Old South," built as a very posh residential area for the rich at the end of the 19th century (when Amsterdam was enjoying a second golden age of sorts), harbors both vast expanses of green to neutralize the eyeballs and the city's best upmarket shopping opportunities to feed one's baser instincts, the former found in the city's beloved Vondelpark, the latter in the antique and couture shops along posh Nieuwe Spiegelstraat. And certainly this tour's starting point of the Leidseplein—just to the northwest of the Museum District proper—with its richness in performance and music venues, offers evening entertainment that may soothe any other senses that may feel neglected.

Numbers in the text correspond to numbers in the margin and on the Eastern Canal Ring & Museum District map.

a good walk

We begin in **Leidseplein** ⑪ ↱, which perhaps at first glance comes across as a lowbrow start to a tour that will take in some of world's greatest art treasures. But if we ignore the sports bars, the faux Irish pubs, and the side streets filled with tourist-preying eateries, we actually find ourselves in the city's central zone for the performing arts—and this does not include the street performers serenading the terraces. Theatergoers flock here for the offerings at the great **Stadsschouwburg** ⑫ theater. Looming over the southwest corner of Leidseplein is the magical castle-like structure of the **American Hotel** ⑬.

Exit Leidseplein via its southeast extension, the Kleine Gartmanplantsoen, which features bronze lizards in the grass parkette on the left, and the political and cultural center–café, De Bali (No. 10) on the right, beside which are large Greek pillars whose mantle is emblazed with the Latin for "Wise men do not piss in the wind." This is the entrance to Max Euweplein, whose surrounding buildings used to be a prison complex that held Nazi resisters during the occupation (but are now dubiously modernized to confine such commercial ventures as a casino). But the square does have a huge chess set—in tribute to Max Euwe, who as a world champion became the nation's chess hero—and also provides a hasty conduit to the gloriously green Vondelpark, this tour's end point.

But to stay on the culture trail continue down Weteringschans, past the Paradiso, until you see the *Night Watch*'s home, the **Rijksmuseum** ⑭, on the right. Here you may choose to go left down the antiques gallery–rich **Spiegelstraat**, or recall it for later as a handy passage back to the historic center of town. Otherwise, one hopes, there will be a violinist or some Mongolian throat-singers on hand to accompany you as you take the acoustically rich arched passage under the museum to reach the freshly revamped **Museumplein** (Museum Square), whose new sense of space is quite at odds with the city's famed crampedness. Visible straight across the wading pool—which can miraculously turn to ice overnight in the heat of summer (thanks to some high-tech wizardry)—is the classical music mecca of the **Concertgebouw** ⑮, cherished by musicians the world over for its superlative acoustics (just imagine if those Mongolian throat-singers could score a gig here). The round titanium-roofed building visible to its right is the new wing of the **Rijksmuseum Vincent Van Gogh** ⑯, whose neighbor is the yet more modern **Stedelijk Museum** ⑰, home to the city's largest collection of contemporary art. From here you can go to the right down Van Baerlestraat to get to the city's green lungs of **Vondelpark** ⑱, perhaps pausing to window-shop along the cross street **PC Hooftstraat**, the nation's poshest high-end designer fashion strip. Film lovers will be sure to check out the park's **Nederlands Filmmuseum** ⑲, set in a lovely 19th-century pavilion.

TIMING   Merely to walk this tour one needs less than an hour. However, to truly absorb all the art treasures along this route requires an additional two weeks—so you might even bring a sleeping bag. For the less ambitious: spend a couple of hours in the Rijksmuseum and Van Gogh Museum, and then take another hour to bring yourselves up to date in the history of art by wandering through the Stedelijk Museum. After seeing infinite representations of light fall, the real thing awaits one in Vondelpark—where just before twilight when it's sunny, one can witness the unique quality of light that has acted as muse for the country's artists for centuries. And attention, shoppers: although PC Hooftstraat offers seven-days-a-week browsing opportunities—with later hours on Thursday—not all its boutiques are open on Sunday and Monday mornings.

HOW TO   From the central square of the Dam it takes about a quarter hour to
GET THERE hike the Leidsegracht or Leidsestraat to reach the southern sector of Amsterdam and the museum district. However, Nieuwe Spiegelstraat is a much more direct and relaxed route towards Museumplein. However you can take Trams Nos. 1, 2, and 5 direct to Leidseplein or Trams Nos. 2 and 5 direct to Museumplein while Tram Nos. 3 and 12 will deposit you at the Concertgebouw. The canals will also get you to the Rijksmuseum, courtesy of the Museumboot and its stop on the Singlegracht.

Sights to See

⑬ **American Hotel.** The architecture of this landmark might drive a professional art historian a little batty. Designer Willem Kromhout grafted Neo-Gothic turrets, Jugenstil gables, Art Deco stained glass, and an Arts & Crafts clock tower onto a proto–Amsterdam School structure, and the result is somewhere between a Venetian palazzo (after all, it does overlook the Singelgracht and has its own boat landing) and a Dutch castle. No matter: this 1902 edifice is a charmer. Inside is the famed Art Deco–style Café Americain, where Mata Hari held her wedding reception. However, this café lost all its street credibility when it banned hippies in the '60s. ⊠ *Leidsekade 97, Museum District* ☎ *020/624–5322* ⊕ *www.amsterdam-american.crowneplaza.com.*

★ ⑮ **Concertgebouw** (Concert Building). The Netherlands' premier and globally acclaimed concert hall has been filled since 1892 with the music of the Royal Concertgebouw Orchestra and an endless stream of international artists. You will recognize the building at once, if not by its Viennese classicist facade then by the golden lyre at its peak. Designed by Al van Gendt to be one of Amsterdam's most sumptuous essays in the Neo-Renaissance style, it continues to charm many of its 800,000 visitors per year. Indeed, this rates as the most visited concert hall in the world. There are two concert halls in the building, the Kleine (Small) and the Grote (Large), the latter being the most acoustically perfect on the planet, according to many pundits. The entrance is through the glass extension along the side. There are no tours of the building, so you will need to buy a ticket to a concert to see beyond the broad lobby, or, if you visit on a Wednesday before 12:30, September to June, you can attend a free lunchtime concert. ⊠ *Concertgebouwplein 2–6, Museum District* ☎ *020/675–4411 24-hr concert schedule and hot line, 020/671–8345 box office* ⊕ *www.concertgebouw.nl.*

> **need a break?**
>
> For Concertgebouwgoers, a posh, popular, and freshly renovated pre- and post-concert dining location is **Bodega Keyzer** (⊠ Van Baerlestraat 96, Museum District ☎ 020/671–1441), whose French-inspired dishes, old-world interior, and uniformed waiters breathe with an appropriately rarified air.

⑪ **Leidseplein** (Leidse Square). In medieval times, Leidseplein was the parking lot for horse-drawn carts since they were banned from the city center—an enlightened policy that today's city planners can perhaps learn from. Today, Leidseplein is where tourists come to park their behinds on the terraces and absorb the infinite crowds and street performers. Hence it is somewhat difficult to imagine that this was long a top hangout for artists and intellectuals; more so, between the wars, this was where Communists and Fascists came to clash. After World War II, much bohemian frolicking took place in such still somewhat evocative cafés as Reindeers (Leidseplein 6), the former resistance hangout Eijlders (Korte Leidsedwarsstraat 47), and the one within the impressively Art Deco American Hotel.

The relatively tamer 1950s crowd around the noted CoBrA painters group, such as Karel Appel, and writers such as Harry Mulisch (now the nation's always dandily dressed grand old man of letters), gave way to a younger and yet more radical and wacky crowd at the dawn of the 1960s. "Anti-smoke magician" Robert Jasper Grootveld started hyping Amsterdam as the "magical center of the universe" and organizing proto-"happenings" from his garage—dubbed the K-Temple ("K" for cancer)—on the Korte Leidsedwarsstraat but eventually moved the show to the Spui to give birth to the more politically motivated Provos. Leidseplein was now left alone to evolve toward its current "international" flavor, but not before going through a "national" stage as the favored spot for football supporters to come celebrate a Dutch victory or exhibit more angry outbursts when they lost. As such, the Leidseplein intellectual aura gave way to mirror the local concept of *pataat cultuur* ("french fry culture"). However, the greasy food dispensers of enjoining Leidsestraat are now slowly disappearing to make way for designer-brand outlets. Certainly the **Stadsschouwburg** provides musical, dance, and theatrical performances for the decidedly highbrow (the generally more hip and youthful go a stone's throw away to the **Melkweg** and **Paradiso** clubs).

Architectural buffs should take time to observe the 1925 **bridge** to the south crossing Singelgracht. Its swoopy Amsterdam School style was the work of Piet Kramer (1881–1961), who designed 220 of the city's existing bridges. Armed with this knowledge (and the fact that his later work became slightly more conservative), you can walk the rest of the city and regularly say "Ah, another Kramer . . . " without worrying too much about being labeled a dilettante. ⊠ *Main entrances: Leidsestraat, Weteringschans, and Marnixstraat, Museum District.*

need a break?

Leidseplein and its surroundings are dense with café-break opportunities. The well-read and politically engaged crowd gathers around the café **De Balie** (⊠ Kleine Gartmanplantsoen 10, Museum District ☎ 020/553–5130). The theatrical crowd can be witnessed at **Café Cox** (⊠ Marnixstraat 429, Museum District ☎ 020/620–7222), part of the Stadsschouwburg building. The lounging American can find a familiar home at **Boom Chicago Lounge** (⊠ Leidseplein 12, Museum District ☎ 020/530–7300), which also provides a terrace option.

★ ⑲ **Nederlands Filmmuseum.** One of the highlights of Vondelpark is the Netherlands Film Museum, which occupies an elegant 19th-century entertainment pavilion, first opened to the public in 1881 as a café. Here's you'll find on display such historic treasures as Amsterdam's first movie theater, the **Cinema Parisien**, replete with its 1910 Art Deco interior, a film poster collection, and public library, as well as shows every day in its two cinemas, drawing on material from all over the world as well as from its substantial archives (which include such gems as hand-tinted silent movies). On Thursday in summer, there are free outdoor screenings beginning at dusk. Even if you're not into film, check out the museum's very popular Café Vertigo, whose terrace tables offer grand views of Vondelpark. It's right near the Roemer Visscherstraat entrance. ⊠ *Vondelpark 3, Museum District* ☎ *020/589–1400* ⊕ *www.nfm.nl* 🖃 *Free* ⊙ *Tues.–Fri. 10–5, Sat. 11–5.*

⑭ **Rijksmuseum** (State Museum). The Netherlands' greatest museum, the **FodorsChoice** Rijksmuseum is home to Rembrandt's *Night Watch*, Vermeer's *The* ★ *Kitchen Maid*, and a near infinite selection of world-famous masterpieces by the likes of Steen, Ruisdael, Brouwers, Hals, Hobbema, Cuyp, Van der Helst, and their Golden Age ilk. This nation's pride (and the information contained herein), however, is soon to be rent by major changes: the Rijksmuseum is set to close between 2004 and 2008 for extensive renovation and rebuilding, following the plans of Seville's architect duo Antonio Cruz and Antonio Ortiz. Only the South Wing—which has now through corporate sponsorship been renamed the Philips Wing—will remain reliably open to house a "Best of" selection. However, with a new exhibition space in Schiphol Airport (Rijksmuseum Amsterdam Schiphol, Holland Boulevard between piers E and F, ☎ 020/653–50 36, Mon.–Fri. 7 AM–8 PM, admission free), and promises of several "roaming" exhibits, visitors can still get an ample dose of Golden Age glory (as long as they call ahead or check the Web site).

Ironically, the Rijksmuseum's fabled collections began life by being housed in the Trippenhuis mansion (⇨ the Oude Zijde section), an act of French sibling rivalry at the dawn of the 19th century during French occupation when King Louis wanted to compete with his brother Napoléon's burgeoning Louvre collection. When architect P. J. H. Cuypers came up with the current location's somewhat over-the-top design in the late 1880s, it shocked Calvinist Holland down to its—one imagines—overly starched shorts. Cuypers was persuaded to tone down some of what was thought of as excessive (read: Catholic) elements of his Neo-Renaissance decoration and soaring Neo-Gothic lines. During the building's construction, however, he did manage to sneak some of his ideas back in, and the result is a magnificent, turreted building that glitters with gold leaf and is textured with sculpture—a fitting palace for the national art collection.

The Rijksmuseum has more than 150 rooms displaying paintings, sculpture, and objects from both the West and Asia, dating from the 9th through the 19th century. The bulk of the collection is of 15th- to 17th-century paintings, mostly Dutch (the Rijksmuseum has the largest concentration of these masters in the world); there are also extensive holdings of drawings and prints from the 15th to the 20th century.

If your time is limited, head directly for the Gallery of Honor on the upper floor, to admire Rembrandt's *Night Watch,* with its central figure, the "stupidest man in Amsterdam," Frans Banningh Cocq. His militia buddies who surround him each paid 100 guilders to be included—quite the sum in those days, so a few of them complained about being lost in all those shadows. It should also be noted that some of these shadows are formed by the daylight coming in through a small window. Daylight? Indeed, the *Night Watch* is actually the *Day Watch,* but it received its name when it was obscured with soot—imagine the restorers' surprise. The rest of this "Best of the Golden Age" hall features other well-known Rembrandt paintings and works by Vermeer, Frans Hals, and other household names—or at least names that you may recognize from wandering the streets of the De Pijp neighborhood.

A clockwise progression through the rooms of the adjoining East Wing takes you past works by some of the greatest Dutch painters of the 15th to the 19th century, which will have you walking by: Mannerist renderings of biblical and mythic scenes where gods and goddesses show an almost yogic ability in twisting their limbs; eerily lifelike portraits with the lighting maximized to flatter the paying subject; landscapes that may either be extravagant and fantastical in both subject and style or conversely dull, flat, and essentially lacking everything but sky; Caravaggio-inspired exercises by the painters of Utrecht School who employed contrast in light and shadow to heighten a sense of drama; straight moralistic paintings of jolly taverns and depraved brothels warning of the dangers of excess; meticulous and shimmering still-lifes of flowers, food, and furnishings; and cold mathematical renderings of interiors that could be used as architectural blueprints. All of these works prove that the nouveau riche of the Golden Age had a hunger for art that knew no bounds.

Unmissable masterpieces include Vermeer's *The Little Street*—a magical sliver of 17th-century Delft life—and his incomparable *The Love Letter,* in which a well-appointed interior reveals a mistress and her maid caught in the emotional eddies of a recently opened and read billet-doux. Note the calm seascape on the back wall—a quiet sea was seen as a good omen by the Dutch; inner anxieties, however, are present in the mistress's face, so much so that the room's clothes hamper, lace-making pillow, and broom all lie forgotten. Ostensibly, a more sedate missive is being read in Vermeer's *Woman in Blue Reading a Letter,* on view nearby. But is this just a matronly dress or is the woman pregnant and thinking about a missing husband (note the seafaring map)?

The walls of this museum here are virtually wallpapered with other masterpieces by Geertgen tot Sint Jans, Cornelis Engebrechtsz, Lucas van Leyden, Jan van Scorel, Joos de Momper, Pieter Aertsen, and Karen van Mander. Especially notable are the group company portraits of Frans Hals, the Caravaggist works by Gerrit van Honthorst, the often funny genre interiors of Jan Steen, and the beloved landscapes of Jan van Goyen, Meindert Hobbema, Aelbert Cuyp, Hendrick Averkamp, and Jacob and Salomon van Ruisdael—these artists created the landscape genre and gave us its greatest achievements. Crowning all are the famous Rembrandt works, topped off by the *Night Watch* and the *Jewish Bride* (which Vincent van Gogh would study for hours) plus many other of the master's paintings; also note the many daubs by his pupils, including Gerrit Dou, Nicolaes Maes, and Ferdinand Bol.

The South Wing contains 18th- and 19th-century paintings, costumes, and textiles and the museum's impressive collection of Asian art, which includes some 500 statues of Buddha from all over the Orient. The Rijksmuseum's collection of drawings and prints is far too vast to be displayed completely, and only a small selection is shown in the Print Room at any one time. Here you might catch a glimpse of Italian Renaissance sketches, Rembrandt engravings, or early-19th-century photographs. Elsewhere in the museum you can wander through room after room of antique furniture, silverware, and exquisite porcelain, including Delftware. The 17th-century doll's houses—made not as toys but as showpieces for wealthy merchant families—are especially worth seeing, as is the collection of expressive Art Nouveau furniture.

A particularly neglected—and freely accessible—part of this museum is its sculpture- and port-filled gardens formed in the triangle by Hobbemastraat and Jan Luijkenstraat. You can also use the alternative entrance found here when the lines seem too long to its main entrance.

For an institution dedicated to antiquity, the Rijksmuseum has shown a remarkable technical savvy in making its vast collection more accessible via its incredible Web site. From the comfort of your home, you can make a virtual tour, chart out a plan of attack, and absorb vast chunks of background information. The museum has also introduced an "ARIA" (Amsterdam Rijksmuseum Inter-Active) system, which allows visitors to ask for information—which may include visuals, text, film, and/or sound—on 1,250 objects and then be given directions to find other related objects. These "create-your-own tours" are available in a room directly behind the *Night Watch*. Whether they will still be available here once the massive renovation of the museum is over remains to be seen. ✉ *Stadhouderskade 42, Museum District* ☎ 020/674-7047 ⊕ *www. rijksmuseum.nl* ✉ €9 (though the price will be markedly lower if areas are closed during renovation) ◷ Daily 10–5.

need a break? After walking through miles of art, there's nothing more invigorating than indulging in the fish-protein infusions on offer at the fish stall on the Rijksmuseum's front east side. **Altena** (✉ Jan Luijkenstraat/ Stadhouderskade, Museum District) also has the bonus of a proprietor who will gladly talk you through the finer points of sliding a raw herring down your throat. On Museumplein, one can sit down on the patio of **Cobra Café** (✉ Hobbemastraat 18, Museum District ☎ 020/470-0111) for a snack from the acclaimed menu, or choose a spot of your own after stocking up at the Albert Heijn supermarket under the grass slope across from the Concertgebouw.

16 Rijksmuseum Vincent Van Gogh (Vincent Van Gogh Museum). Opened in

FodorśChoice
★
1973, this remarkable light-infused building, based on a design by famed
De Stijl architect Gerrit Rietveld, venerates the short, certainly not sweet,
but highly productive career of everyone's favorite tortured 19th-century
artist. First things first: Vincent was a Dutch boy, and therefore his name
is not pronounced like the "Go" in Go-Go Lounge but rather like the
"Go" uttered when one is choking on a whole raw herring.

Although some of the Van Gogh paintings that are scattered throughout the world's high-art temples are of dubious providence, this collection's authenticity is indisputable: its roots trace directly back to brother
Theo van Gogh, Vincent's artistic and financial supporter. The 200
paintings and 500 drawings on display here can be divided into his five
basic periods, the first beginning in 1880 at age 27 after his failure in
finding his voice as schoolmaster and lay preacher. These early depictions of Dutch country landscapes and peasants—particularly around
the Borinage and Nuenen—were notable for their dark colors and a re-
fusal to romanticize (a stand that perhaps also led in this period to his
various failures in romance). The *Potato Eaters* is perhaps his most famous piece from this period.

In 1886, he followed his art-dealing brother Theo to Paris, whose heady
atmosphere—and drinking buddies such as Paul Signac and Henri de
Toulouse-Lautrec—inspired him to new heights of experimentation.
Although heavily inspired by Japanese woodcuts and their hard contrasts and off-kilter compositions, he also took the Neo-Impressionist
obsession with light and color as his own, and his self-portraits (he was
the only model he could afford) began to shimmer with expressive lines
and dots.

With a broadened palate, he returned to the countryside in 1888 to paint
still-lifes—including the famous series of *Sunflowers* (originally meant
to decorate the walls of a single bedroom)—and portraits of locals
around Arles, France. His hopes to begin an artist's colony here with
Paul Gauguin were dampened by the onset of psychotic attacks—one
of which saw the departure of his ear, which, in turn inspired the departure of Gauguin to the South Seas. Recuperating in a mental health
clinic in St-Remy from April 1889, he—feverishly, one is quick to assume—produced his most famous landscapes, such as *Irises* and *Wheatfield with a Reaper,* whose sheer energy in brush stroke makes the
viewer almost feel the area's sweeping winds. In May 1890, Van Gogh
moved to the artist's village of Auvers-sur-Oise, where he traded medical advice from Dr. Paul Gachet in exchange for paintings and etching
lessons. These highly productive last three months of his life were
marred by depression and, on July 27, he shot himself in the chest and
died two days later. His last painting, *Wheatfield with Crows,* remains
the iconic image of this collection.

The permanent holdings also includes other important 19th-century artists,
including those mentioned above, and examples of Japanese woodcuts.
In 1999, a new oval extension was opened. Designed by the Japanese
architect Kisho Kurokawa and built in a bold combination of titanium
and gray-brown stone and connected to the main galleries by an underground walkway, it provides an epic space for a wide range of superbly presented temporary shows of 19th-century art, graphic design,
photography, and sculpture. With all this space, you might be tempted
to take a break at the museum's cafeteria-style restaurant. ⊠ *Paulus Potterstraat 7, Museum District* ☎ *020/570–5200* ⊕ *www.vangoghmuseum.
nl* ⊠ *€9* ☉ *Daily 10–5.*

⑫ **Stadsschouwburg** (Municipal Theater). Somehow managing to retain its central dominance on a square given over to neon and advertising, the Stadsschouwburg has been here since 1784 after the original one on Keizersgracht burned down during mid-performance and killed many in the audience—a tragedy that was to be regarded as poetic justice by the more uptight of Calvinists who thought the proceedings there much too decadent. Their God being a vengeful sort, he may have also been responsible for this Stadsschouwburg also burning down on occasion and having to be rebuilt several times before receiving its current Neo-Renaissance facade and lushly Baroque horseshoe interior in 1890. The decades that followed saw the general state of the nation's theater scene descend into staidness until 1968 when, during a performance of the *Tempest,* the actors were showered with tomatoes. Part of a nationwide protest, the "tomato campaign" expressed the discontent with established theater's lack of social engagement. It resulted in more subsidies for newer theater groups—many of which now form the old guard who regularly play here.

Although the majority of the programming is in Dutch, it should be said that contemporary Dutch theater is marked by a strong visual—and often hilariously absurdist—sense. And naturally, there is also a constant stream of visiting international theater and dance companies. ✉ *Leidseplein 26, Museum District* ☎ *020/624–2311* ⊕ *www.stadsschouwburgamsterdam.nl.*

★ ⑰ **Stedelijk Museum** (Municipal Museum). Hot and happening modern art of this century and the last has one of the world's most respected homes here at the Stedelijk, which occupies, somewhat paradoxically, a wedding-cake Neo-Renaissance structure first opened in 1895. It's a home that is undergoing renovation, however: beginning in 2004, the museum will be undergoing massive refurbishment and perhaps even the addition—pending the finding of funds—of two new wings by Portuguese architect Alvaro Siza, all of which undoubtedly will disrupt accessibility for several years to come. So it's best to call ahead or check the Web site to avoid disappointment (or to be directed to the many planned exhibitions in temporary spaces).

With roots reaching back to when it began as an heiress's collection that included torturous mental health instruments and a bust of her late husband, the Stedelijk began to cover its present course only after World War II. It now has a collection of paintings, sculpture, drawings, prints, photography, graphic design, applied arts, and new media that numbers 100,000 pieces. Although this stunning collection harbors many works by such ancients of modernism as Chagall, Cézanne, Picasso, Monet, and Malevich, there is a definite emphasis on the post–World War II period: with such local CoBrA boys as Appel and Corneille; American Pop artists as Warhol, Johns, Oldenburg, and Liechtenstein; Abstract Expressionists as de Kooning and Pollock, and contemporary German Expressionists as Polke, Richter, and Baselitz. Still, many head here to find the homegrown masterworks of the De Stijl school, including the amazing *Red Blue Chair* Gerrit Rietveld designed in 1918, and the noted Mondriaan canvases on display, including his 1920 *Composition in Red, Black, Yellow, Blue, and Grey.* When not putting together exhibitions culled from this collection, the staff curates large retrospectives or themed programs of the currently acclaimed. Lately, however, these projects have perhaps become a tad too commercial, for instance, by allowing the queen of The Netherlands to play guest curator, and critics have looked askance. ✉ *Paulus Potterstraat 13, Museum District* ☎ *020/573–2911* ⊕ *www.stedelijk.nl* 🎫 *€7* ⊙ *Daily 11–5.*

🖰 ⑱ **Vondelpark.** On sunny days, Amsterdam's "Green Lung" is the most densely populated section of the city. From all walks of life, Vondelpark becomes *the* place where sun is worshiped, joints are smoked, beer is quaffed, picnics are eaten, bands are grooved to, dogs are walked, balls are kicked, lanes are biked and roller-skated on, children frolic, bongos are bonged, lovers kiss, singles seek. By evening, the park has invariably evolved into one large outdoor café. But the chaos is relatively tame and the appeal now much broader compared with that of the summer of 1973, when more than 100,000 camping youths called it home and airlines such as KLM saw bigger profits in advertising tickets to "Hippie Park" instead of its dull surroundings, "Amsterdam."

Such a future was certainly not envisioned in 1865 when Vondelpark was laid out as a 25-acre "walking and riding park" to be enjoyed by the residents of the affluent neighborhood that was arising around it. It soon expanded to cover some 120 acres. In the process, it was renamed after Joost van den Vondel, the "Dutch Shakespeare." Landscaped in the informal English style, the park is an irregular patchwork of copses, ponds, children's playgrounds, and fields linked by winding pathways. Between June and August, one of the park's focal points is the open-air theater where free concerts, plays, comedy, and children's programs are performed Wednesday–Saturday. Children, when they've grown bored with the many playing facilities, will invariably drag their parents to the llama field for some petting action or go in search of the 400 parrots (apparently the progeny of two escaped pets) that miraculously survive every winter. Plant-lovers will follow their noses to the formal and fragrant rose garden. If you do not want to join in on a football game, other forms of specialized exercise are available: at the Amstelveenseweg entrance one can rent in-line skates at the small wooden houses (before perhaps joining the Friday Night Skate crowd who take over the city's streets after meeting in front of the Filmmuseum at 8 PM), and at the van Eeghenstraat entrance one can join the "Oriental laughing sessions" (when people come together to laugh as therapy) every weekday from 8 AM and weekends from 9 AM.

Over the years a range of sculptural and architectural delights have made their appearance in the park. **Picasso** himself donated a sculpture, *The Fish* (which stands in the middle of an overgrown field to deter football players from using it as a goalpost), to commemorate the park's centenary in 1965. There's an elegant 19th-century bandstand, and the famous **Round Blue Teahouse,** a rare beauty of functionalist Nieuw Bouw architecture, built beside the lake in 1937, which attracts every manner of person to its patio during the day and a more clubby crowd by evening. Here, too, is the city's popular **Nederlands Filmmuseum** (*see above*), which is ensconced in a pretty 19th-century pavilion and features the popular Vertigo café. ✉ *Stadhouderskade, Museum District.*

off the
beaten
path

AMSTERDAMSE BOS – The Amsterdam Woods, the largest of Amsterdam's many parks, covers a total area of 2,210 acres and lies a few miles to the south of the city. An extraordinary piece of engineering, all of it was dug, laid out, planted, or constructed from 1934 onward, providing work for 20,000 unemployed people during the Depression. Perhaps even more remarkable is that much of it lies up to 4 m (13 ft) below sea level. This woodland habitat harbors no fewer than 150 tree varieties, but it also has open fields, a boating lake, the Bosbaan rowing course with stadium, and a goat farm. With 137 km (85 mi) of footpaths and 51 km (32 mi) of bicycle paths traversing 50 bridges—many designed in the early-20th-century Amsterdam School style with characteristic redbrick and sculpted stone detailing or more woody versions thereof—it is an easy escape from the city for adults and ideal for children. To get here by bike, cycle through the Vondelpark to its southern tip, then take a left onto the Amstelveenseweg and follow it until you reach the Van Nijenrodeweg. Turn right into the Amsterdamse Bos, and you will find yourself at the stadium end of the Bosbaan rowing course. Buses 170, 171, and 172 take passengers from the Leidseplein to the Van Nijenrodeweg, where you can rent bikes from June to August. Maps and signposting are plentiful throughout the park. At the **Grote Vijver** (Big Pond) you can hire kayaks and rowing boats from April through September. The **Bosmuseum** (✉ Koenenkade 56, Amstelveen ☎ 020/676–2152) has displays about natural history and the management of the woods, and is open daily 10–5. If you didn't pack your own lunch, the neighboring **Boerderij Meerzicht** (✉ Koenenkade 56, Amstelveen ☎ 020/679–2744) is a café-restaurant serving sandwiches and traditional Dutch pancakes with a selection of savory and sweet toppings. ✉ *Amstelveen*.

THE OUDE ZIJDE: THE EASTERN HALF OF THE CENTRUM

As the oldest part of Amsterdam, the Oude Zijde (Old Side) has been very old and very Dutch for a long time. It stands to reason, then, that you'll find, in this mirror quadrant to the Nieuwe Zijde, the entire galaxy of Amsterdam here—everything from the archaeological treasures of the Allard Pierson Museum to the famous "Our Lord in the Attic" chapel to, well, acres of bared female flesh. Yes, here within the shadow of the city's oldest church is the most famous Disneyland of Sex in the world: the Red Light District. Within it, most of the city's 13,000 professionals ply their trade and help generate an estimated 1 billion sex-trade guilders in revenue per year. Although a union, Rode Draad, has been representing sex-for-hire workers since 1984 and the tax man has long finagled a means to take his cut, it's only since 2000 that it has all become perfectly legal—including bordellos, clubs, and sex shops. And pragmatic it is indeed: you may be amazed to find that the area has been grouped according to "predilections" and thereby organized into sections (the turf around the area's ancient heart of the Oude Kerk, for instance, has been staked out by Africans). Although ultimately sleazy, especially in the Walletjes ("little walls")—also called De Wallen and defined by Oudezijds Voorburgwal and Oudezijds Achterburgwal north of Damstraat and their interconnecting streets—this area is also essentially the oldest and once poshest part of town. Edit out the garish advertising and the sweaty breasts hypnotically sandwiched against the red-neon framed windows, and you have some very pretty buildings indeed. But have no fear: this area is also blessed with the city's Chinatown and large sections—as the vast majority of this tour will attest—of pure, unadulterated old worldness.

Even in the reddest of sections, there is a warm—albeit surreal—sense of community where hard-working and -talking tradespeople, pink rinse–haired grandmothers, frolicking schoolchildren, street-savvy nuns (representing the area's historical richness in religious institutions and former convents), prostitutes, and police all interact, oblivious to the fact that they are not actually living in a small town. The cops, especially, come across as cute and cuddly, often distributing fliers that hype them as being "used to weird things" and offering such canny advice as "parking is not free," "when you feel sick after smoking or eating space cake, drink lots of water with sugar," and "if you visit one of the women, we would like to remind you, they are not always women."

A potential annoyance are the junkies and dealers, but even they provide a unifying bond to the rest of the community by being regarded as a shared annoyance. Although a certain alertness is recommended when exploring this area at night by yourself, the area is remarkably safe—there are two basic rules: don't take pictures of prostitutes, and avoid eye contact with dealers. Otherwise just enjoy this dense world of contrasts where sex, religion, history, tourism, dubious coffee shops, food of both the ultimately greasy and posh varieties, and ancient grandeur reign supreme.

Numbers in the text correspond to numbers in the margin and on the Oude Zijde, Plantage & Waterfront map.

a good walk

On exiting Centraal Station you'll see a Catholic church to the left, **Sint Nicolaaskerk** ❶ ▶, at which you may want to stop and check the times of its Gregorian chant vesper services in case you get the urge to purge your soul after this tour. In fact, for this tour you should try to take on the easygoing and forgiving nature of St. Nick, who, as the proto-Santa, was patron saint not only to children but also to thieves, prostitutes, and sailors—not to mention the city of Amsterdam. Sailors have long walked by this church on their way to the stress relief traditionally on offer on the **Zeedijk** ❷. (Perhaps that is why "doing the St. Nicolas" became standard local slang for engaging in the sex act.) Before turning left onto the Zeedijk, you may want to note that walking straight would connect you with the **Warmoesstraat** ❸ or that making a quick right would allow you to pay tribute to that melancholic sailor of jazz notes, Chet Baker, the crooning trumpet player, who made his final decrescendo from a window of the Prins Hendrick Hotel (Prins Hendrikade 53) in 1988 and where now a brass plaque commemorates this adopted native son and junkie. While walking up the infamous Zeedijk, dart up the side canal Oudezijds Kolk for a gander at the famous landmark **Schreierstoren** ❹, from where Henry Hudson began his journey that would lead him to New Amsterdam (the island otherwise known as Manhattan).

Zeedijk is capped by the **Nieuwmarkt** ❺ square, with the evocatively turreted De Waag as its medieval centerpiece. Although the religiously named streets to the right, Monnikenstraat and Bloedstraat (Monk and Blood streets), will ironically lead you to the carnal heart of the **Red Light District,** the more culturally inclined should proceed to the opposite side of the square and head straight up the left side of Kloveniersburgwal to the **Trippenhuis** ❻, the grand Trip House mansion. At the next intersection, on the southwest corner with Oude Hoogstraat, is the Oost Indische Huis, the former offices of the East India Trading Company, which once smelled of exotic spices but now, as part of the University of Amsterdam, exudes more with the fevered sweat of political science students. You might want to pop into its richly ornate courtyard, accessible via Oude Hoogstraat 24, where sailors once came to sign up for voyages. Continuing straight down Kloveniersburgwal's left bank, cross the first bridge to the right, perhaps pausing to browse through the many excellent English-language books on offer at the Book Exchange (Kloveniersburgwal 58), before proceeding straight down Rusland. For a sense of some traditional religion, make the first right down Oudezijds Achterburgwal—perhaps stopping to absorb the modern Dutch design delights in Droog & Co. on the corner—to No. 185, the **Spinhuis,** once the location of the Convent of 11,000 Virgins. After circling this building via the small alleys that surround it, return to Rusland and cross the bridge on the right. Proceed straight down Sint Agnietenstraat, where you can

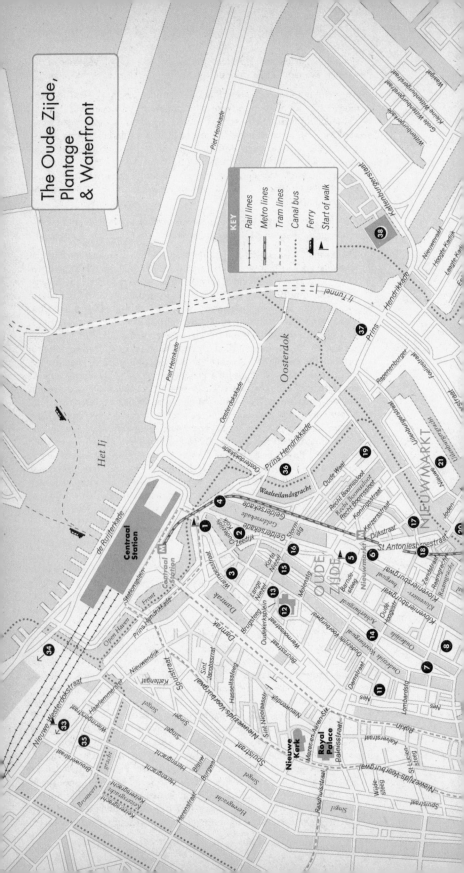

The Oude Zijde, Plantage & Waterfront

KEY

Rail lines
Metro lines
Tram lines
Canal bus
Ferry
Start of walk

Il Tunnel

Oosterdok

Het Ij

Centraal
Station

de Ruijterkade

Prins Heinkade

Piet Heinkade

Oosterdokskade

Prins Hendrikkade

Kattenburgerstraat

Grote Wittenburgerstraat

Kleine Wittenburgerstraat

Waaigat

Nieuwmarkt

NIEUWMARKT

OUDE ZIJDE

Nieuwe
Kerk

Royal
Palace

Damrak

Warmoesstraat

Nieuwendijk

Singel

Herengracht

Keizersgracht

Brouwersgracht

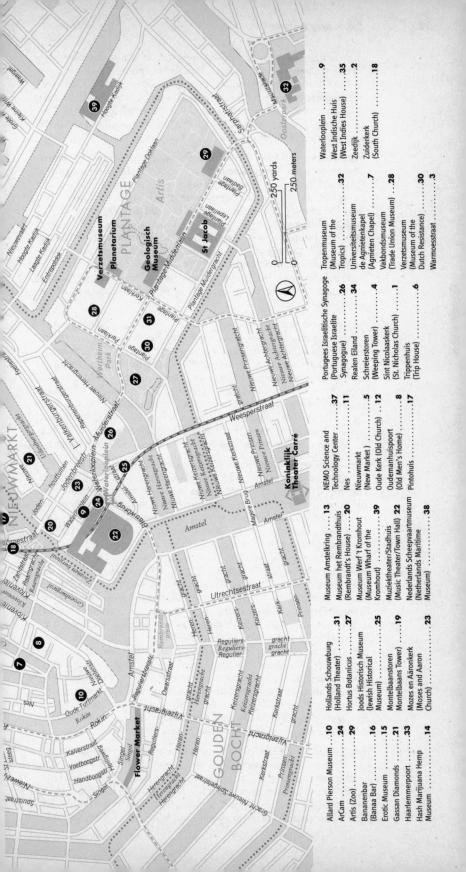

NIEUWMARKT

PLANTAGE

Artis

Verzetsmuseum
Planetarium
Geologisch Museum

St Jacob

Wertheim Park

Koninklijk Theater Carré

GOUDEN BOCHT

Flower Market

250 yards
250 meters

make a right down Oudezijds Voorburgwal, following the curved Amsterdam School wall with its myth-drenched sculptures, past the entrance of Café Roux with its Karel Appel mural in its entranceway, and then right into the entrance of the courtyard belonging to the historically dense **Grand Hotel**. Under the name Prinsenhof, this acted as a City Hall between 1652 and 1655 and 1808 and 1988 and has welcomed such boldface names as William of Orange and Michael Jackson.

Backtracking up Oudezijds Voorburgwal will lead you past the **Universiteitsmuseum de Agnietenkapel** ❼, or University Museum's Agnieten Chapel. A short jaunt to the left lets you cross another bridge; staying to the left, take the archway almost immediately on the right, which will lead you through sliding glass doors into the covered book market **Oudemanhuispoort** ❽, where trading has occurred since 1757. After browsing through this now more youth-oriented corridor—this is the heart of the University of Amsterdam—turn right down Kloveniersburgwal, where almost immediately you must choose to turn left over a drawbridge down Staalstraat, a relentlessly scenic specialty-shopping street and favored filming location, which will lead you to **Waterlooplein** ❾ flea market.

The second drawbridge you will come across was raised during the occupation to cut off the Jews from the rest of the city. After this northerly diversion head back south and westward the way you came to follow Nieuwe Doelenstraat, at whose entrance on the left is a beige-and-redbrick building belonging to Hotel Doelen. Until 1882, there existed a tower dating from 1481 that was part of a fortification wall to defend the city from potential hoards from Utrecht. This tower also acted as the meeting—and imbibing—place for city soldiers who in 1630 asked Rembrandt to paint a portrait of them that they could employ as wall decoration, a bit of interior enhancement that became known as the *Night Watch*.

Continuing straight past the chic Grand Café Jaren on the left, take the right, before crossing the bridge over the canal, down Oude Turfmarkt past the archaeological **Allard Pierson Museum** ❿. Then take the first right down Langebrugsteeg, to the entrance on the left to the theatrical and the old Spinoza stomping ground of the **Nes** ⓫, where on the corner you may want to pause to see what's on offer at the Appenzeller Gallery, a contemporary jewelry and design hot spot. Following the Nes will eventually connect you with the city's main square, the **Dam**. Here, cross the street and take the first alley, Pijlsteeg, to the right running alongside the nearest side of Hotel Krasnapolsky. Between the two sliding glass doors is the entrance, to the left, to the eerily peaceful and green courtyard of Wynand Fonkink, where you can stop for a sandwich or coffee. You may instead choose to pass through the second set of sliding doors to get to its sister establishment, Wynand Fonkink Proeflokaal, an ancient "Tasting Local" and distillery (check out those oak caskets through the windows of No. 41) where one can indulge in a startling array of Dutch Courage in preparation for the full dose of Red Light awaiting you at the end of the alley along the Oudezijds Voorburgwal. Turning left down here will have you reaching the reassuringly religious **Oude Kerk** ⓬ in no time, beyond which lies the **Museum Amstelkring** ⓭ and its celebrated "Our Lord in the Attic" chapel—a must-see for art lovers.

If you want a more leisurely—but no less scholarly—cruise of humanity's darker sides, turn right, then immediately left down Oude Doelenstraat to reach Oudezijds Voorburgwal's parallel canal, Oudezijds Achterburgwal, on which you turn left. Sticking to the left bank of this canal will have you passing such unique institutions as the **Hash Marijuana Hemp Museum** ⓮; the infamous Casa Rosa nightclub at No. 106-

8 (some can't resist posing for a photo in front of the rotating balls of its rather suggestive marble fountain, making sure they include the *krul*, or "curve," a green and aesthetically curved public urinal directly across the canal); and the **Erotic Museum** ⑮. If bicycle-powered dildos and other amazing arcana are not your thing, you may forgo the last institution—and the lore-rich erotic "theater," **Bananenbar** ⑯, across from it—and take the faithful escape route right before it to the left, Oude Kennis-steeg. "Old Friend Alley" will have you praying for your sins at the Oude Kerk in a matter of seconds, although straight beyond it lies the tourist strip of Warmoesstraat.

TIMING This tour will take two to three hours. If you want to enjoy the Red Light District's namesake lighting, mid- to late afternoon might be a good time to start. Such religious institutions as the Oude Kerk and Museum Amstelkring are closed for services on Sunday morning. The Allard Pierson Museum is closed Monday, and you should also note that the more "fringe" museums start and end their days somewhat later than most public museums.

HOW TO You can easily walk to the Oude Zijde from Centraal Station or simply
GET THERE hop on Trams Nos. 4, 9, 16, 24, and 25 to the Dam square, then stroll along Damstraat. Another way to access the neighborhood is Tram Nos. 9 and 14, or use the metro directly to Nieuwmarkt or Waterlooplein.

Sights to See

⑩ **Allard Pierson Museum.** Once the repository of the nation's gold supply, no less, this former National Bank is now home to other treasures. Behind its stern Neoclassical facade, dynamite helped remove the safes and open up the space for the archaeological collection of the University of Amsterdam in 1934. The museum traces the early development of Western civilization, from the Egyptians to the Romans, and of the Near Eastern cultures (Anatolia, Persia, Palestine) in a series of well-documented displays. Although in general it's not exactly a roller-coaster ride, the museum's Egyptian section is particularly well done, with scale models of pyramids, some rather gruesome mummies that look as if they escaped from a B-movie studio lot, and computers that translate your name into hieroglyphics. ✉ *Oude Turfmarkt 127, Oude Zijde* ☎ *020/525–2556* ⊕ *www.uba.uva.nl/apm* ☞ *€4.30* ⊙ *Tues.–Fri. 10–5, weekends 1–5.*

⑯ **Bananenbar** (Banana Bar). Since the 1970s, this ultimately sleazy bar has featured naked barmaids doing tricks "without hands" that use up more than 30 pounds of bananas per evening—impressive, but not exactly something that warrants landmark site status. However, certain events in the 1980s form an "only in Amsterdam" story. The owner at the time realized that because Amsterdam had been defined by religious tolerance for centuries, he could circumvent the problems of impending taxation and a lapsed drinking license by registering as a religion. So he decided to recast the bar as the Church of Satan. By 1988, however, when the church was claiming a membership of 40,000, the tax man was finally motivated enough to seek a loophole. Before legal action could be taken, the owner liquidated the business and flew to warmer climes. Under a new owner, the bar returned to its sleazy—and taxable—roots. ✉ *Oudezijds Achterburgwal 137, Oude Zijde.*

⑮ **Erotic Museum.** "Five floors of highly suggestive trinkets and photos" is probably a better description than "museum." If you're in a when-in-Rome mood, you may want to choose to visit here. Happily, it is all presented rather lightheartedly (although animal-lovers should steer clear of the snapshot gallery). Beatles fans should note that there is an original and satisfyingly suggestive sketch by John Lennon, perhaps rendered when he and Yoko did their weeklong bed-in for peace at the Hilton. Camp fans should note that there is a rich collection dedicated to the patent-leather-clad 1950s muse and proto-dominatrix Betty Page. ⊠ *Oudezijds Achterburgwal 54, Oude Zijde* ☎ *020/624–7303* 🖃 € ☉ *Sun., Mon., and Thurs. 11 AM–1 AM; Fri. and Sat. 11 AM–2 AM.*

⑭ Hash Marijuana Hemp Museum. One would think that some more effort could have gone into the name of this institution—lateral thinking being one of the positive effects of its subject. But regardless, here's your chance to suck back the 8,000-year history of hemp use. The use of pot as medicine was first recorded in The Netherlands in 1554 as a cure for earaches. By this time, its less potent form, hemp, had long been used—as it would until the late 19th century—as the fiber source for rope and hence was fundamental to the economics of this seafaring town. Besides elucidating certain points in history, a variety of displays educates one on such things as smuggling and joint-rolling techniques. A cultivation zone offers handy hints to the green thumb in your family. And, predictably, there's an endless collection of bongs from around the world. ⊠ *Oudezijds Achterburgwal 148, Oude Zijde* ☎ *020/623–5961* 🖃 €6 ☉ *Daily 11–10.*

⑬ Museum Amstelkring ("Our Lord in the Attic" Museum). With its elegant gray-and-white facade and spout gable, this appears to be just another canal house, and on the lower floors it is. The attic of this building, however, contains something unique: the only surviving *schuilkerken* (clandestine church) that dates from the Reformation in Amsterdam, when open worship by Catholics was outlawed. Since the Oude Kerk was then relieved of its original patron, St. Nicholas, when it was de-catholicized, this became the church dedicated to him until the Sint Nicolaaskerk was built. The chapel itself is a triumph of Dutch classicist taste, with magnificent marble columns, gilded capitals, a colored-marble altar, and the *Baptism of Christ* (1716) painting by Jacob de Wit presiding over all. Services and weddings are still offered here, so consider attending a Sunday service in this, one of Amsterdam's most beautiful houses of worship.

Fodor'sChoice
★

The grandeur continues throughout the house, which was renovated by merchant Jan Hartan between 1661 and 1663. Even the kitchen and chaplain bedroom remain furnished in the style of the age, and the drawing room, or *sael,* looks as if it were plucked from a Vermeer painting. With its gold chandelier and Solomonic columns, it's one of the most impressive 17th-century rooms left in Amsterdam. Besides boasting other canvases by Thomas de Keyser, Jan Wynants, and Abraham de Vries, the house also displays impressive collections of church silver and sculptures. ⊠ *Oudezijds Voorburgwal 40, Oude Zijde* ☎ *020/624–6604* ⊕ *www.museumamstelkring.nl* 🖃 €6 ☉ *Mon.–Sat. 10–5, Sun. 1–5.*

⑪ Nes. Originating as a boggy walkway along the Amstel River when Amsterdam was an ever-sinking fishing village, the Nes is now a refreshingly quiet corridor filled with theaters. At the end of the 14th century, the Nes began evolving into a long strip of monasteries and convents before the Altercation of 1578 (or Protestant takeover) saw their eventual decline as Amsterdam became more concerned with commercial pursuits and as it marched toward its Golden Age. The Nes's spiritual life—which had largely made way for tobacco storage and processing—had a slight renaissance when the philosopher Spinoza (1623–77) moved here to escape the derision he was receiving from his own Jewish community for having fused Jewish mysticism with Descartian logic, concluding that body and soul were part of the same essence. Although the still-existing Frascati theater (Nos. 59–65) began life as a coffeehouse in the 18th century, it was not until the 1880s that the Nes began to bloom with cafés filled with dance, song, and operetta performances; stars often represented the less uptight segment of the Jewish community. Adjacent to the southern end of the Nes is **Gebed Zonder End,** the "Prayer Without End" alleyway, which got its name because it was said you could hear prayers from behind the walls of the convents which used to line this alley. ⊠ *Between Langebrugsteeg and Dam, Oude Zijde.*

need a break?

As to be expected from a theatrical neighborhood, the Nes offers some prime drinking holes, which also offer the option of a lingering meal. Fans of Belgian beer should certainly stop at the patio of **De Brakke Grond** (⊠ Nes 43, Oude Zijde ☎ 020/626–0044), part of the Flemish Cultural Center, to partake in one or two of the dozens of options. Coincidentally, on the "Prayer with End" alley, which runs parallel to Nes's south end, is **Captain Zeppos** (⊠ Gebed Zonder End 5, Oude Zijde ☎ 020/624–2057), which is named after a '60s Belgian TV star; this former cigar factory is soaked with jazzy old-world charm.

5 **Nieuwmarkt** (New Market). Home to the striking Waag gatehouse—where Rembrandt came to watch Professor Tulp in action before painting *The Anatomy Lesson*—and also some of the most festive holiday celebrations in town, the Nieuwmarkt has been a marketplace since the 15th century. In those days, de Waag—or Sint Antoniespoort (St. Anthony's Port) as it was then known—formed a gateway in the city defenses. It was not until 17th-century expansion that the current form of Nieuwmarkt was established and farmers from the province of Noord-Holland began setting up stalls to make it a bustling daily market. The **Kruidenwinkel van Jacob Hooy & Co.** (⊠ Kloveniersburgwal 12, Oude Zijde), Amsterdam's oldest medicinal herb and spice shop, and a small row of vegetable stalls are the only vague reminders of those times.

Before the 1796 Civil Liberties Act, when Jews were restricted from most trades, many took up street entertainment and Nieuwmarkt evolved into a favored location for many fairs and circuses complete with acrobat, horse, and freak shows. Nieuwmarkt still maintains these festive roots, especially on Chinese New Year, as the area forms the heart of the city's modestly sized China Town (that is, until New China Town, envisioned as a mini-Singapore, arises in the next years to the east of Centraal Station), which extends down Zeedijk and Binnen Bantammerstraat. The community originates from a 1911 seafarers' strike that motivated the hiring of Chinese sailors from England and Hong Kong. Many more came via Suriname after its 1975 independence from Dutch colonial rule. A slightly more curious celebration is the medieval-rooted Hartjes Dag ("Heart Day") in August, which involves that holy trinity of alcohol, firecrackers, and cross-dressing. Suffering a decline in recent decades, it is now experiencing a renaissance since being embraced by the city's ever-growing transvestite population.

The **Waag** (Weigh House) in the center of the square was built in 1488 (as can be attested by the stone tablet emblazoned with MCCC-CLXXXVIII, placed on the small tower facing Geldersekade), and functioned as a city gate, Sint Antoniespoort, until the early 17th century. During those centuries, the gate would be closed at exactly 9:30 PM to keep out not only the bandits but also the poor and the diseased who built shantytowns outside the wall. When the city expanded, it began a second life as a weighing house for incoming products—in particular such heavier goods as tobacco bales, ship artillery, and an-

chors—after a renovation added a tower and covered the inner courtyard. The top floor of the building came to accommodate the municipal militia and several guilds, including the masons who did the
evocative decorations that grace each of the towers' entrances. One of
its towers housed a teaching hospital for the academy of surgeons of
the Surgeons' Guild. The Theatrum Anatomicum (Anatomy Theater)
with its cupola tower covered in painted coats of arms (many of which
disconcertingly reflect many of the doctors' original trade as barbers),
was the first place in The Netherlands to host public dissections. For
obvious reasons, these took place only in the winter. It was here that
Rembrandt sketched Professor Tulp in preparation to paint his great
Anatomy Lesson. The good professor procured his bodies from those
hanged on the southeast side of the Waag. The surgeons must have
mourned the coming of the guillotine during the reign of King Louis
Napoléon—a time that saw the Waag's importance as weigh house increase when the one on the Dam was cleared to improve the king's view
from his palace. Now the building is occupied by a café-restaurant with
free Internet service and the **Society for Old and New Media** (⊕ www.
waag.org). How things have changed. ⊠ *Bounded by Kloveniersburgwal, Geldersekade, and Zeedijk, Oude Zijde.*

**need a
break?**

You may want to sniff out your own favorite among the many café-
restaurants that line this square. Many will opt for the previously
mentioned **In De Waag** (⊠ Nieuwmarkt, Oude Zijde ☎ 020/422–
7772), which highlights its epic medieval roots with candlelight. An
arty and studenty option is **Lokaal 't Loosje** (⊠ Nieuwmarkt 32–34,
Oude Zijde ☎ 020/627–2635), which is graced with tile tableaus
dating from 1912. The thematically decorated **Café Cuba**
(⊠ Nieuwmarkt 3, Oude Zijde ☎ 020/627–4919) serves relatively
cheap cocktails and offers a jazzy modern-dance sound track that
inspires many of the hipster regulars to light up a joint in the back.
Fans of more traditional jazz should check out the legendary **Cotton
Club** (⊠ Nieuwmarkt 5, Oude Zijde ☎ 020/626–6192), named after
its original owner, the Surinamer trumpet player Teddy Cotton.

★ ⑫ **Oude Kerk** (Old Church). The Oude Kerk is indeed Amsterdam's oldest
church and has been surrounded by all the garnishing and offerings of
humanity's oldest trade (i.e., prostitution) for the vast majority of its
history—a history that has seen it chaotically evolve from single-nave
chapel to hall church to a cross basilica. It began as a wooden chapel
in 1306 but was built for the ages between 1366 and 1566 (and fully
restored between 1955 and 1979), when the whole neighborhood was
rife with monasteries and convents.

As a Catholic church dedicated to St. Nicholas (a forgiving sort who
was relaxed enough also to offer patronage to salacious sailors and fallen
women), it changed denomination during the Reformation when its furnishings were removed by the Iconoclasts—whose arms fortunately
could neither reach the 14th-century paintings still visible on its wooden
roof (which had already miraculously survived the city fires of 1421 and
1452), nor the Virgin Mary stained-glass windows that had been set in
place in 1550. But it did also lose its nickname as the city's "living room"
where beggars and the homeless (and, one suspects, those who had squan-
dered their cash in sins of the flesh) could sleep. When it finally settled
to become Reformed in the 17th century, it became yet more sober, to
be only slightly more balanced with the extravagant placing of its famed
Vater-Muller organ. Among its many haphazard side buildings is the Bridal
Chamber—whose door wisely warns: "Marry in Haste, Mourn in

Leisure"—through which Rembrandt entered to marry Saskia. As it turns out, Saskia was later buried here under the small organ; Rembrandt tried to sell her plot when he was broke. Oude Kerk's haphazard evolution continues unabated: it is now a wholly unique exhibition space for modern-art exhibitions and the annual World Press Photo competition. Its carillon gets played every Saturday between 4 and 5. ⊠ *Oudekerk-splein 23, Oude Zijde* ☎ *020/625-8284* ⊕ *www.oudekerk.nl* ▧ *€4* ⊙ *Mon.–Sat. 11–5, Sun. 1–5.*

❽ Oudemanhuispoort (Old Man's House Alley). Landmarked by its famous chiseled pair of spectacles (set over the Oudezijds Achterburgwal pediment)—a sweet reference to old age—this was once a pensioners' house, an "Oudemannenhuis," first built in 1754. Today, bikes, not canes, are in evidence, as this former almshouse is now part of the University of Amsterdam. One charming trace of its founding days lies in its covered walkway, lined with tiny shops whose rents helped subsidize the 18th-century elderly. Adorned with red shutters, the stalls now house an array of antiquarian booksellers and lead on to Kloverniersburgwal, where a statue of Mother Amsterdam protecting two elders, sculpted by Anthonie Ziessenis in 1786, stands. ⊠ *Between Oudezijds, Achterburgwal, and Klovniersburgwal, Oude Zijde.*

★ ❹ Schreierstoren. Famous as the point from which Henry Hudson set sail to America, this is Amsterdam's most distinctive fortress tower. Although today this tower's innards host a rather frolicsome marine-theme jazz café, it began its life in 1486 as the end point of the city wall. The term *schreiren* suggests the Dutch word for "wailing," and hence the folklore arose that this "Weeping Tower" was where women came to cry when their sailor husbands left for sea and to cry again when they did not return (perhaps followed by the short walk to the Red Light District to begin life as a merry widow?). But the word *schreier* actually comes from an Old Dutch word for a "sharp corner"—and, indeed, the building's rounded harbor face, which looks over the old **Ooster-dok** (Eastern Dock), forms a sharp corner with its straight street face. A plaque on the building tells you that it was from this location that Henry Hudson set sail on behalf of the Dutch East India Company to find a shorter route to the East Indies. In his failure, he came across Canada's Hudson's Bay Company and later—continuing his bad-luck streak—New York harbor and the Hudson River. ⊠ *Prins Hendrikkade 94–95, Oude Zijde.*

▶ ❶ Sint Nicolaaskerk (St. Nicholas Church). The architect A. C. Bleys designed this church, built in 1887, with its dark and eerie interior as a replacement to all the clandestine Catholic churches that arose during the Protestant times. Following in the footsteps of first Oude Kerk and then Museum Amstelkring's "Our Lord in the Attic" chapel, this church became the third and most likely final (unless those darned Calvinists take over again) Sint Nicolaas church. St. Nick (or Sinter Klaas as he is called here), patron saint of children, thieves, prostitutes, sailors, and the city of Amsterdam, arrived with the Catholic church. The eve of his birthday on December 6 is still celebrated as a mellow family feast where everyone exchanges self-made presents and poems. "Sinter Klaas" mutated when he went to the New World and eventually become drawled out as "Santa Claus"; his day shifted to December 25 to synergize with the feast day of Christ. Although the spirit of gross revenue is making its presence felt in Amsterdam, thanks to the efforts of department stores, Christmas remains a more purely religious holiday here. Note that the church is only open when volunteer custodians are available. It hosts a Gregorian chant vesper service September to June on Sunday at 5. ⊠ *Prins Hendrikkade 76, Oude Zijde.* ☎ 020/ 624–8749 🖃 *Free* ⏱ *Mon.–Sat. 11–4.*

★ ❻ **Trippenhuis** (Trip House). As family home to the two Trip brothers, who made their fortune in gun dealing during the 17th-century Golden Age, this noted house's buckshot-gray exterior and various armament motifs—including a mortar-shape chimney—are easily explained. But what is most distinctive about this building is that its Corinthian-columned facade actually hides two symmetrical buildings (note the wall that bisects the middle windows), one for each brother. It went on in the 18th century to house both the Rijksmuseum collection and the Royal Dutch Academy of Sciences before the latter became its sole resident. Be sure to look across the canal to No. 26, the door-wide white building topped with golden sphinxes and the date of 1696, which is known as both the "Little Trip House" and the "House of Mr. Trip's Coachman." The story goes that the smarty-pants coachman once remarked that he would be happy with a house as wide as the Trippenhuis door; not to be outsmarted, Mr. Trip went on to build just that with the leftover bricks. Or so the story goes; the Little Trip House is actually much bigger than it looks, and its completion date was long after either brother died. ⊠ *Kloveniersburgwal 29, Oude Zijde.*

★ ❼ **Universiteitsmuseum de Agnietenkapel** (University Museum Agnieten Chapel). One of Amsterdam's only surviving medieval convents, this Gothic chapel was built in the 1470s. However, it has been emphasizing the secular since 1632, when it became part of the original University of Amsterdam, and thereby rates as the country's oldest lecture hall. Imagine bringing an apple to the likes of Vossius and Barlaeus, two greatly celebrated Renaissance scholars who both taught here. The grand interior solemnly sports stained-glass windows, an impressive Renaissance ceiling painting, and more than 40 paintings of humanists, including everyone's favorite, Erasmus. A renovation around 1919 saw the introduction of some elements of the Amsterdam School to its exterior. ⊠ *Oudezijds Voorburgwal 231, Oude Zijde* ☎ 020/525–3339 🖃 *Free* ⏱ *Mon.–Sat. 9–5.*

❸ **Warmoesstraat.** This densely touristic strip of hostels, bars, and coffee shops began life as one of the original dikes along the Amstel before evolving into the city's richest shopping street (a sharp contrast to its fallen sister, Zeedijk). Imagine, if you will, the famous 17th-century poet Vondel doing business from his hosiery shop at No. 101 or Mozart's dad trying to unload tickets for his son's concert in the posh bars. It entered a decline in the 17th century when the proprietors forsook their above-store lodgings for the posher ones arising on the canal ring; sailors and their caterers started to fill in the gaps. In the 19th century, it evolved, along with its extension **Nes**, into the city's primary drinking and frolicking zone. Karl Marx was known to set himself up regularly in a hotel here not only to write in peace but to have the option to ask for a loan from his cousin-in-law, Gerard Philips, founder of that capitalist machine Philips.

Thanks to a recent revamp, Warmoesstraat is beginning to lose some of its Sodom and Gomorrah edge. Between the cynical tourist traps, there are some rather hip hangouts such as the Hotel Winston; worthwhile specialty stores, such Geels and Co. (No. 67), with its infinite selection of coffees and teas; or the equally complete selection of condoms at the Condomerie Het Gulden Vlies (No. 141)—and even a squatted gallery, the beautifully spacious W139 (No. 139), dedicated to the very outer edges of conceptual art. ⊠ *Between Dam and Nieuwe Brugsteeg, Oude Zijde.*

❾ Waterlooplein. Before its rezoning, this flea market, named after the famous battle, was a swampy neighborhood, bordered by the Leper and Peat canals, that often took the brunt of an overflowing Amstel River and hence housed only the poorest of Jews. In 1886 it became the daily market for the surrounding Jewish neighborhood—a necessity, since Jews were not allowed to own shops. It became a meeting place whose chaos of wooden carts and general vibrancy disappeared along with the Jewish population during World War II. And yet it still provides a colorful glimpse into Amsterdam's particular brand of pragmatic sales techniques. Its stalls filled with clothes, bongs, discarded electronics, and mountains of Euro-knickknacks can sometimes indeed be a battle—albeit a more than worthwhile one—to negotiate. ⊠ *Waterlooplein, Oude Zijde* ☉ *Weekdays 9–5, Sat. 8:30–5:30.*

❷ Zeedijk. Few streets have had a longer or more torrid history; until recently known as the Black Hole of Amsterdam (because of its concentration of drug users), the Zeedijk is now on the up-and-up. As the original dam created to keep the sea at bay, Zeedijk has been around since Amsterdam began life as a fishing hamlet. The building of this dike in 1380 probably represented the first twitchings of democracy in these parts as individual fishing and farming folks were united to make battle with that pesky sea. Less noble democratic forces saw it quickly specialize in the entertaining of sailors—a service it ended up providing for centuries. A more bohemian edge came into the mix in the last century when it provided a mecca for world-class jazz musicians who came to jam in its small clubs and cafés after their more official gigs in the Concertgebouw. One of the more popular was the still-existing Casablanca (No. 26), which regularly saw the likes of local heroes such as Kid Dynamite and Teddy Cotton and more international names such as Erroll Garner, Gerry Mulligan, and Count Basie. However, other, more dingy dens began a lucrative sideline in heroin. By the 1970s, the area had become known throughout the country for its concentration of drug traffickers, where the only tourists were those attached to heavily guided "criminal safaris." But recently Zeedijk has gone through a radical gentrification. Although certainly not sterile of its past, it's now much easier to accept the stray, dubious-looking character as merely part of the street's scenery as opposed to its definition.

As if to tell a tale of rebirth, the first building on the right is the **Sint Olofskapel** (St. Olaf Church), named after the patron saint of dikes, St. Odulphus. This 17th-century structure sports a life-affirming sculpture: grains growing out of a prone skeleton (verily, in times of yore this is what passed for a positive message). After the Altercation, it began a long history of varying functions. Today, it's a convention hall attached by an underground passage to the Golden Tulip Barbizon Palace Hotel on Prins Hendrikkade.

Across the street at No. 1 is one of only two timbered houses left in the city. It does have stone sides—as law dictated after the great fires of 1421 and 1452, the latter of which destroyed a full three-quarters of the town. Dating from around 1550, **in't Aephen** ("In the Monkeys") provided bedding to destitute sailors if they promised to return from their next voyage with a monkey. It worked: it was soon filled with monkeys and their accompanying lice. And to this day if someone is caught scratching his head, the folk response is "You've been staying with the monkeys." The way each floor sticks slightly more outward than the one below it accounts for the way most of Amsterdam's brick buildings lean forward: they were built aesthetically to follow this line (to ape the wooden architectural forms that preceded). An added bonus was that goods being hoisted into upper floors would not hit the windows. When you walk onward, note the first alley on the right, Sint Olofssteeg, which looks down on the "House on Three Alleys," and the way it goes—for Amsterdam's standards anyway—plummeting downward and hence illustrating Zeedijk's roots as dike.

Café Maandje at No. 65 evokes the 1930s, when the first openly gay drinking and dancing dens in the city began popping up here. Its window maintains a shrine to its former proprietor and the spiritual forebear of lesbian biker babes everywhere: Bet van Beeren (1902–67). Although the café opens only on the rarest of occasions, a model of its interior can be viewed at the Amsterdams Historisch Museum. The rest of the street is a quirky mixture of middle-range Asian restaurants, brown cafés with carpeted tables, specialty shops and galleries, and the occasional Chinese medicinal shop. The Chinese community is in full visual effect at the end of the street, where recently the gloriously colorful pagoda-shape **Fo Kuang Shan Buddhist Temple** (No. 118) arose. ⊠ *Oudezijds Kolk (near Centraal Station) to Nieuwmarkt, Oude Zijde.*

need a break?
Zeedijk offers five of the best quick snack/meal stops in town. The most revered is auspiciously placed across from the Buddhist Temple: **Nam Kee** (⊠ Zeedijk 111–113, Oude Zijde ☎ 020/624–3470) is a speedy and cheap Chinese spot whose steamed oysters are so sublime that they provided the title and muse for a local author's novel. **Snackbar Bird** (⊠ Zeedijk 72, Oude Zijde ☎ 020/420–6289) offers wok-fried-in-front-of-your-eyes dishes from Thailand; for a more lingering or less cramped meal, you might want to try its restaurant across the street. The ultimate Dutch snack, raw herring, can be enjoyed at the fresh-fish shop **Huijsmans Cock** (⊠ Zeedijk 129, Oude Zijde ☎ 020/624–2070), which also offers much less controversial options for its deliciously nutty whole wheat buns. A Zeedijk fave, **Cafe Latei** (⊠ Zeedijk 143, Oude Zijde ☎ 020/625–7485) combines a dense interior of quality kitsch (available for the buying!) with the serving of coffee and healthful snacks. **Lime** (⊠ Zeedijk 104, Oude Zijde ☎ 020/639–3020) offers a more slick and minimal lounge but with a nicely unpretentious atmosphere, complete with DJs, cocktails, and all the latest design/arts mags.

EAST OF THE AMSTEL: FROM THE JEWISH QUARTER TO THE PLANTAGE

Although Amsterdam has been Calvinist, Protestant, and Catholic for varying chunks of its history, it has been continuously considered a Jerusalem Junior of sorts by migrating populations of Jews from the medieval to the modern era. In fact, the city came to be known as Mokum (the Hebrew word for "place"), as in *the* place for Jews. And when the Jewish population arrived, so did much of Amsterdam's color and glory. Just witness the legendary diamond trade and feast your eyes upon Rembrandt's *Jewish Bride* in the Rijksmuseum, just one of many canvases the artist painted when, searching for inspiration and Old Testament ambience, he deliberately set up a luxurious household near the heart of the Jewish Quarter.

Since the 15th century, the **Joodse Buurt** (Jewish Quarter) has traditionally been considered the district east of the Zwanenburgwal. The Quarter got its start thanks to the Inquisition, which was extremely efficient in motivating many Sephardic Jews to leave Spain in 1492. Over the next hundred years, their descendants slowly found their way to Amsterdam, where they could reestablish a semblance of their traditional lifestyle. The war with Spain inspired the 1597 Union of Utrecht, which, although formulated to protect Protestants from the religious oppression that came with Spanish invasions, essentially meant that all religions were tolerated. This provided a unique experience for the Jews, for here, unlike elsewhere in Europe, they were not forced to wear badges and live in ghettos. They were still, however, restricted—just like all the other non-Calvinists—from joining guilds and being registered as tradesmen. The only exceptions were in the up-and-coming trades where no guild Mafia had arisen, such as diamond cutting and polishing, sugar refining, silk weaving, and printing. These slim advantages also helped attract many Yiddish-speaking Ashkenazi Jews from Eastern Europe escaping pogroms. The 17th-century Golden Age and the rise of the capitalist saw the weakening of the hard-core Calvinist grip on daily life, and only the Catholics remained barred from open worship. This accounts for the existence of 17th-century synagogues in the city and not of Catholic churches. Rembrandt came to the neighborhood at this time to take advantage of the proximity of all the "biblical faces" that he could employ in his religious paintings.

But it was only in 1796, inspired by the ideals of the French Revolution, that the guilds were finally banned and equal rights instilled. However, although there were always many rich Jewish merchants, poverty was still the essential lot of most Jews until the end of the 19th century, when the rise of the diamond industry meant the spreading of the community away from the old Jewish Quarter. By 1938, 10% of Amsterdam's population was Jewish, and they had long ingrained their influence into the city's psyche (however, the charm factor of one instance in which core supporters of the Ajax football team have long cast themselves as "Jews" was subverted when their archenemies, Rotterdam supporters, started casting themselves as "Palestinians") and into its slang (the Yiddish word *mazzel,* meaning "luck," remains a standard farewell). What remains much more painfully ingrained in the city's psyche, however, is what happened during the Nazi occupation when the Jewish population was reduced to one-seventh of its size. There were many examples of bravery and the opening of homes to hide Jews, but there are many more—and less often told—stories of collaboration. Although the current Jewish population has risen to 20,000, they are now generally dispersed throughout the city, and it is really only the monuments that speak.

Thanks to the devastation of the war and later the demolition to make room for the Stadhuis/Muziektheater (City Hall/Music Theater) and the Metro, the neighborhood is marked by a somewhat schizophrenic hodgepodge of the old and new. The enjoining and more residential **Plantage** neighborhood to the east, which began as a sort of recreation park for the rich before houses for them arose in the 19th century, offers a more cogent and restful atmosphere, with its wide boulevards.

Numbers in the text correspond to numbers in the margin and on the Oude Zijde, Plantage & Waterfront map.

a good walk

While trying to imagine the original 17th-century housing, walk east up Sint Antoniebreestraat from **Nieuwmarkt** ⑤ ▶, which was left as a ghost town for years after the occupation (before experiencing a slight renaissance as a squatters' paradise but then finally getting razed in 1980 to make way for the Metro). One ancient exception remains at Sint Antoniebreestraat 69, the Italian Renaissance–style **Pintohuis** ⑰, a magisterial mansion built in the 17th century, with an opulent interior on view (the house is now a public library).

Across the street lies one of the neighborhood's few wholly successful infusions of modernity, the Theo Bosch–designed Pentagon Apartments, where to its right between No. 130 and 132, one can gain access through a skull and crossbone–adorned gateway to the courtyard of the **Zuiderkerk** 18, the "Southern Church"; here one can climb its 17th-century tower—certainly one of the most beautiful in all Holland—or see models of Amsterdam's many future building projects. Linger on the bridge where Sint Antoniebreestraat turns into Jodenbreestraat, where to the left beside the disconcertingly crooked café, one can take in the view down Oudeschans toward the harbor. The ancient tower on the left is the **Montelbaanstoren** 19, where sailors departed and refugees arrived in small boats that acted as ferries to and from the larger ships anchored in the IJ; this picturesque sight was one of Rembrandt's favorite sketching subjects. Beyond lies a modern green copper building that suggests a sinking *Titanic*: the science and technology museum NEMO (covered in depth in our last neighborhood section). Turning around, you see across the street some stairs leading down to the **Waterlooplein** flea market. The first café-outfitted building on the left corner (Jodenbreestraat 2) is marked with the Hebrew date of 5649 (1889) and adorned with caryatids doing Atlas's dirty work. The house that previously stood here was rented to the art dealer Hendrick Uylenburg, who ran a painting school to which a fresh-faced Rembrandt became aligned when newly arrived from Leiden. Rembrandt ended up becoming much more aligned with Uylenburg's niece Saskia; he married her and eventually bought the red-shuttered house next door, today the famous **Museum het Rembrandthuis** 20, where he spent his salad days.

Ignore the entrance to the Holland Experience—unless, of course, a certain herb inspires you to take in a 3-D tour of Holland's stereotypes—to the left of Rembrandt's former digs and continue down Jodenbreestraat to take the first left after the brutally modern vastness that houses the Amsterdam Academy of Arts' Dance and Theater School, down Nieuwe Uilenburgerstraat. Along this street one can visit the 1879-established **Gassan Diamonds** 21 at No. 173–75, which once hummed with 357 diamond grinders and thereby was a major employer in the neighborhood. Farther down at No. 91, one can admire the facade of a former synagogue that was built in 1766. A straight backtrack will get you to the flea market Waterlooplein. The white building looming ahead is the multitask city hall–music theater, **Muziektheater/Stadhuis** 22. After absorbing the surrounding chaos of carpets and stalls filled with vintage clothing and Euroknickknacks, exit Waterlooplein via its northeast corner, where you can cross the street at the imposing church of **Mozes en Aäronkerk** 23. More contemporary visions can be gleaned once you cross the street at the modern architecture gallery **ArCam** 24, a few doors to the right of the crosswalk. Continue toward the upcoming bridge, **Blauwbrug**, to admire the view down the Amstel River. The "Blue Bridge," built in 1883, was named after its predecessor, a blue wooden bridge, so don't be distressed if it lacks its namesake color. Disconcerting is the fact that during Nazi occupation it was tangled in barbed wire to isolate the Jewish Quarter.

Turning back, take the forking street to the right, Nieuwe Amstelstraat, a walking street where disused tram tracks will tell you that you are at the entrance to a complex of four synagogues that now form the important **Joods Historisch Museum** 25 (Jewish Historical Museum). From here cross the street at Mr. Visserplein—named after a Jewish resistance leader and now sporting a surreal children's playground called TunFun underneath it—toward the rows of tiny houses that form a square around the **Portugees Israelitische Synagoge** 26 to the right of which on the square, Jonas Daniel Meijerplein, is a statue of a husky dock worker, *De Dokwerker*. The statue commemorates the February Strike of February 25, 1941, when dock and transport workers protested the first *razzia* ("roundup") of Jews, with whom they felt united by common union and socialist ideals that had taken hold in the city in the previous decades. Taking Muiderstraat to the left of the synagogue complex, you will soon see the glass structures of the **Hortus Botanicus** ㉗ botanical gardens. Hang left down Parklaan and right down the former diamond mecca of Henri Polaklaan, which is now home to **Vakbondsmuseum** ㉘, the former headquarters of the Diamond Workers Union. The street ends at the **Artis** ㉙ planetarium-zoo, and if you head left, you will come to the World War II resistance subterfuges (used to subvert the occupying Nazis) on display at the excellent **Verzetsmuseum** ㉚ (Resistance Museum).

Reversing down Plantage Kerklaan and then making a right after crossing Plantage Middenlaan will get you to the **Hollands Schouwburg** ㉛, a former theater that is now a memorial to the Jews collected there to await transportation to their fate in the concentration camps. Reversing to continue east down Plantage Middenlaan will get you to the Plantage Westermanplantsoen park on the right, where there is a war monument to the artists' resistance movement and superhero Gerrit van der Veen, who led a party to destroy the records of the city's registry office and later managed to escape wounded after an attempt to free resistance prisoners from the complex around Max Euweplein. Betrayal two weeks later led to his arrest at his hiding place. Because he wanted to die standing, he was shot with his stretcher held vertically by friends. Continuing on the same route, you will eventually reach the imposing **Tropenmuseum** ㉜ (Tropics Museum) and the picnicking opportunities available in **Oosterpark**—perhaps after picking up supplies at the multicultural street market on Dapperstraat.

TIMING To see only the buildings along the main route, block out an hour and a half. Detours to the Tropenmuseum will need an extra 20 minutes' traveling time. Museums along this route need at east a 30-minute visit, though Rembrandthuis, the Jewish Historical Museum, and the Tropenmuseum (whose children's section has very specific visiting times) deserve longer. Also note that the Waterloo flea market does not operate on Sunday.

HOW TO Trams Nos. 9 and 14 will deposit you in the heart of the Plantage, near
GET THERE the Artis zoo and Hortus Botanicus. Metro stop Waterlooplein is also stone's throw from here. Buses Nos. 22 and 32 stop at the Scheepvaart Museum. Tram 6 runs from near Artis and loops around the city via Weteringschans and Marnixstraat.

Sights to See

㉔ **ArCam.** "Architecture Centrum Amsterdam" is dedicated to the promotion of something very much in vogue: modern Dutch architecture. Besides exhibitions, this association organizes lectures, forums, and excellent tours—including to the new landmarks arising along the Eastern Docklands and the artificial residential island of Ijburg. For anybody who considers architect-cum-philosopher Rem Koolhaas to be the leading prophet of the 21st century, this is a must. A new and nearby exhibition space, all swoopy and silver, at the corner of Prins Hendrikkade and Rapenburgerstraat will be opening at the corner of Prins Hendrikkade and Rapenburgerstraat in early 2004. ✉ *Waterlooplein 216, Jewish Quarter and Plantage* ☎ *020/620–4878* ⊕ *www.arcam.nl* ✉ *Free* ✆ *Tues.–Fri. 1–5.*

☽ ㉙ **Artis** (Amsterdam Zoo). Short for Natura Artis Magistra ("Nature Is the Teacher of the Arts"), Artis was mainland Europe's first zoo and rates as the world's third oldest. Built in the mid-19th century, the 37-

acre park is home to a natural-history museum, a zoo with an aviary, a planetarium, and an aquarium. The aquarium does this coastal country proud, with some 500 species on view in both freshwater and saltwater tanks—the highlight may be its evocative cross section of a canal complete with eels and sunken bicycles. As for the zoo proper, a few of its exhibits are cramped, but others are long on inspiration, including the toy ruin, where owls can peer out at you as if on sabbatical from a Hieronymus Bosch painting or, for that matter, a Harry Potter book. A recent expansion, including a new restaurant, has made the zoo bigger and better. In short: it's great for kids of all ages. A special Artis Express canal boat from the Centraal Station is a great alternative for getting here. ⊠ *Plantage Kerklaan 40, Jewish Quarter and Plantage* ☎ *020/ 523–3400* ⊕ *www.artis.nl* ⊡ *€14* ⊙ *Zoo Oct.–May, daily 9–5; June–Sept., daily 9–6; planetarium times vary depending on program.*

㉑ Gassan Diamonds. When diamonds were discovered in South Africa in 1869 (which, along with the then recent opening of the North Sea Channel, led to a second golden age of sorts for Amsterdam), there was a near immediate windfall for Amsterdam's Jewish community, where one-third of the employable worked in the diamond trade (increased wages meant that children could stay in school longer and that families could move to fancier neighborhoods). Built in 1879, Gassan Diamonds was once home to the Boas diamond-polishing factory, the largest in the world, where 357 diamond-polishing machines were on permanent hum. Its essential high-techness was in sharp contrast to the poverty in the Uilenburg neighborhood that surrounded it. World War II led to Amsterdam's loss of top position of the world diamond market to Antwerp, which largely retained its lower-paid polishing population. Today, Gassan offers polishing and grading demonstrations and free one-hour tours (for which it is best to book ahead) of the building and its glittering collection of diamonds and jewelry. If you yourself want to glitter and spend some money, call ahead to see about arranging one of their "diamond and champagne" tours, capped off with a champagne reception (and a diamond gift for one lucky prizewinner). ⊠ *Nieuwe Uilenburgerstraat 173, Jewish Quarter and Plantage* ☎ *020/622–5333* ⊕ *www. GassanDiamonds.nl* ⊡ *Free* ⊙ *Daily 9–5.*

㉛ Hollands Schouwburg (Holland Theater). Between 1892 and 1941, this was *the* theater for Dutch theatrical performances, which came courtesy of such luminaries as writers Herman Heyermans and Esther de Boervan Rijk and such singer-entertainers as Louis Davids (the "Little Big Man"). In 1941, the Nazis shortly deemed it a Jewish-only theater before deciding in 1942 to use it as a central gathering point for the deportation of the city's Jews, first to the national gathering point of Westerbork and then to concentration camps in Germany. In the end, somewhere between 60,000 and 80,000 human souls passed through here for this purpose. In 1993, the Jewish Historical Museum renovated it to include a memorial room displaying the 6,700 family names of the 104,000 Dutch Jews deported and murdered and an upstairs exhibition room that tells the story of the occupation through documents, photographs, and videos. But it is the large and silent courtyard that is perhaps this monument's most effective remembrance. ⊠ *Plantage Middenlaan 24, Jewish Quarter and Plantage* ☎ *020/626–9945* ⊕ *www. jhm.nl* ⊡ *Free* ⊙ *Daily 11–4.*

★ ㉗ Hortus Botanicus. This wonderful botanical garden was originally laid out as an herb garden for doctors and pharmacists in 1682 (after existing at another location since 1632) before it began collecting exotic plants from the East India Company's foreign fields of plunder. Today it is a labyrinth of ornamental gardens and greenhouses set to a variety of climates (desert, swamp, tropical, and subtropical) where a total of 8,000 species are represented—including one of the oldest potted plants in the world, a 300-year-old Cycas palm. Its café-terrace is one of the most peaceful in the city, and buying a coffee here is *alone* worth the price of admission. In fact, you can add some historical resonance to your sipping with the knowledge that Hortus harbors the descendants of the first coffee plants of Europe. A Dutch merchant stole one of the plants from Ethiopia, presented it to this Hortus in 1706, which in turn sent a clipping to a botanist in France, who finally saw to it that further clippings reached their destination of Brazil . . . where an industry was born. ⊠ *Plantage Middenlaan 2a, Jewish Quarter and Plantage* ☎ *020/625–9021* ⊕ *www.hortus-botanicus.nl* 🎫 *€6* ☉ *Apr.–Sept., weekdays 9–5, weekends 11–5; Nov.–Mar., weekdays 9–4, weekends 11–4.*

㉕ **Joods Historisch Museum** (Jewish Historical Museum). Four Ashkenazi synagogues (or *shuls,* as they are called in Yiddish) dating from the 17th and 18th centuries were skillfully combined with glass-and-steel constructions in 1987 into an impressive museum for documents, paintings, and objects related to the four-century history of the Jewish people in Amsterdam and The Netherlands. World War II plunder saw to it that the number of objects of a priceless and beautiful nature is limited, but the museum is still rich with a collection of unusual pieces ranging from the ceremonial to the domestic, from the antique to the modern. Back in the 17th century, Ashkenazi Jews began fleeing the pogroms in Central and Eastern Europe, finding refuge in Amsterdam, if not exactly welcomed with open arms by the already settled Sephardim community, who resented the increased competition imposed by their often poorer brethren. Separate synagogues were consequently built, and four of them make up this complex: the **Neie Sjoel** (New Synagogue, 1752), now given over to exhibits tracing the subject of Jewish identity; the **Grote Sjoel** (Great Synagogue, 1671), where the tenets of Judaism are presented; the **Obbene Sjoel** (Upstairs Synagogue, 1686), where the bookshop and café are found; and the **Dritt Sjoel** (Third Synagogue, 1700). Stars of the collection include an 18th-century Sephardic Torah Mantle, a magnificent carved wood Holy Ark dating from 1791, and the autobiographical art of the Berlin artist Charlotte Solomon (1917–43), who documented her life in 1,000 gouaches accompanied with text and music under the title *Leben? oder Theater?* ("Life? or Theater?"). The museum also features a resource center and one of the city's few purely kosher cafés. Whether or not you tour the collections, check out the excellent tours of the Jewish Quarter conducted by this museum. Just outside the doors is the market at Waterlooplein, where the Jewish community once thrived, and which hosts the famous flea market, as lively as it was in the 17th century. The current Jewish community itself exists largely beneath the surface of Amsterdam, many of its constituents placing Dutch identity before Judaism. ⊠ *Jonas Daniël Meijerplein 2–4, Jewish Quarter and Plantage* ☎ *020/ 626–9945* ⊕ *www.jhm.nl* 🎫 *€6.50* ☉ *Daily 11–5.*

> **need a break?**
>
> While in a refreshingly tourist-free zone, why not check out a friendly local brown café? **Eik & Linde** (⊠ Plantage Middenlaan 22, Jewish Quarter and Plantage ☎ 020/622–5716) is one of the archetypal Amsterdam institutions famed for their brown walls, the result of decades of cigarette and pipe smoking by the patrons. This particular place is noted in recent Jewish history as the radio broadcast location where Ischa Meijer, interviewer extraordinaire, conjoined with his many Jewish guests to confront their own personal stories associated with the Holocaust.

★ ⑲ **Montelbaanstoren** (Montelbaans Tower). Rembrandt loved to sketch this slightly leaning tower, which dates from 1516; in those more perpendicular days, it formed part of the city's defenses against raiding hoards of Gelderlanders. City expansion in 1578 saw it connected by a defensive wall with the Sint Antoniepoort (De Waag in Nieuwenmarkt). It is traditionally thought to be the spot where the first Jewish refugees from the Inquisition in Spain and Portugal arrived. It was certainly the ferrying point to the sailing ships anchored in the IJ that were set to depart to the East Indies. In 1606, the ubiquitous Hendrick de Keyser oversaw the building of a new tower complete with clockworks. But time soon saw the tower leaning toward Pisa, and in 1611 it had to be reset with lots of manpower and ropes on a stronger foundation. Since 1878, it has housed the City Water Office, which maintains the water levels in the canals and engineers the nightly flushing of the entire city waterway system, closing and opening the sluices to change the direction of the flow and cleanse the waters (algae and the use of yacht toilets on houseboats make it a thankless job). ✉ *Oude Schans 2, Jewish Quarter and Plantage.*

㉓ **Mozes und Aäronkerk** (Moses and Aaron Church). Landmarking the eastern corner of the Waterlooplein flea market, this structure once had a warehouse facade to disguise its function as a clandestine Catholic church. If this rarely used church could speak, it would name-drop the great philosopher Spinoza (for it was built on the location of his birth house) and Liszt (for it hosted a recital of his that he considered his all-time best). Originally built in 1649, it was rebuilt in 1841 by architect T. Suys the Elder, then refurbished in 1900 when the twin wood towers were painted in trompe l'oeil fashion to resemble wood. The name of the church refers to the figures adorning two gable stones of the original edifice, now to be seen in the rear wall. Today, the nave hosts very occasional exhibitions and concerts. ✉ *Waterlooplein 205, Jewish Quarter and Plantage* ☎ 020/622–1305 ☉ *Hours vary.*

⑳ **Museum het Rembrandthuis** (Rembrandt's House). One of Amsterdam's more remarkable relics, this house was bought by Rembrandt, flush with success, for his family and is where he lived and worked between 1639 and 1658. Rembrandt chose this house on what was once the main street of the Jewish Quarter because he thought he could then experience daily and firsthand the faces he would use in his Old Testament religious paintings. Later Rembrandt lost the house to bankruptcy when he fell from popularity after the death of Saskia, his wife. When he showed a quick recovery—and an open taste for servant girls—after her death, his uncle-in-law, once his greatest champion, became his biggest detractor. Rembrandt's downfall was sealed: he came under attack by the Amsterdam burghers, who refused to accept his liaison with his amour, Hendrickje.

Fodor'sChoice ★

A recent expansion allowed the house interior to be restored to its original form—complete with one of Rembrandt's printing presses, his rarities collection, and fully stocked studio (which is even now occasionally used by guest artists). The new gallery wing, complete with shop, café, and information center, is the only place in the world where his graphic work is on permanent display—with 250 of the 290 prints that are known to have come from his hand, including the magisterial *Hundred Guilder* and the *Three Crosses* prints. Rembrandt was almost more revolutionary in his prints than in his paintings, so this collection deserves respectful homage, if not downright devotion, by printmakers today. ✉ *Jodenbreestraat 4–6, Jewish Quarter and Plantage* ☎ 020/520–0400 ⊕ *www.rembrandthuis.nl* ✉ €7 ☉ *Mon.–Sat. 10–5, Sun. 1–5.*

REMBRANDT: MAGNIFICENCE AND MISERY

DUTCH ART SPEAKS WITH MANY **VOICES** but in the case of Rembrandt van Rijn (1606–1669)—the greatest painter of Holland's 17th-century Golden Age—it is often sublimely silent. Standing before his reticent and meditative masterpieces, one is aware of a painter who grew great at the art of suggesting rather than laying bare on canvas. Born in Leiden, the fifth child of a miller, Rembrandt quickly became rich from painting and from the tuition paid by his many pupils. In his first works he painted heaps of overornamentation, but then as the years went by, he dug deeper and deeper into the essence of his subjects and portrayed the incessant metaphysical struggle for inner beauty and reason. When his whole material world crashed about him, he unaccountably continued to turn out art that grew bolder and stronger. His greatness as a painter has tended to eclipse the rags-to-riches-to-rags saga of his life.

Heralded as a budding genius of the Leiden School of art by no less a connoisseur than Constantijn Huygens—Secretary to Prince William Henry of Orange—the young Rembrandt arrived in Amsterdam in 1632 to take up residence with Hendrich van Ulyenburgh, an art dealer who helped Rembrandt land his first famous commissions. Here he met Ulyenburgh's cousin, a rich lass named Saskia. Marrying above one's station was considered a clever way to move up Amsterdam's social ladder so Rembrandt prevailed against her family's wishes and made her Mrs. van Rijn in 1634. Heady with the thoughts of her large dowry and swamped by patrons, Rembrandt announced his "arrival" by buying an exceedingly patrician mansion on the Breestraat. Today the Museum het Rembrandthuis, this "double house" came with a vast frontage, its five stories elegantly adorned in brick and a sculpted Palladian pediment. The price was fair— after all, the aristocrats of the area had decided to decamp for the newly chic district of the Grachtengordel, allowing the immigrant set, mostly Portuguese Jews, to colonize the area. If Rembrandt's patrons were clamoring for biblical scenes, what better place to set up shop than in the midst of this "New Jerusalem"?

Shortly after moving in on May 1, 1639, the young couple proceeded to decorate the ground floor to the nines, thanks to Russian leather upholstery, Tournai tablecloths, marble fireplaces, busts of Roman emperors, walls lined with paintings, and a beribboned pet monkey. On the second floor, Rembrandt's own atelier faced the street, with enormous windows and wooden shutters (just the thing to modulate the amount of light and shadow, no?). The year 1642 saw the peak of Rembrandt's fame, with his Night Watch unveiled at the Kloveniersdoelen. But before long, its peat-burning fireplaces had darkened the canvas—a bad omen. Then, on June 14, Saskia died, worn out by tuberculosis and the 1641 birth of their son, Titus. Shortly thereafter, Rembrandt's romance with Geertje Dircx, hired as a baby-sitter, soured with her lawsuit against his broken promise of marriage. As for his new housekeeper Hendrickje Stoffels, by 1654 the Reformed Church fathers had declared that she "confesses that she has engaged in fornication with Rembrandt the painter, is therefore severely reprimanded, and is forbidden to take part in the Lord's Supper." Unmarried though they stayed, a child was born, and Amsterdam was scandalized. Then, because of his many creditors, Rembrandt wound up at insolvency court, was forced to inventory his belongings, see them auctioned off for piddling sums, sell his fabled mansion, then decamp to a simple house on the Rozengracht canal. While patrons still knocked on his door (although he had become "unfashionable" with the rise of the new Frenchified and light Neoclassical style), Hendrickje's death in 1663, Titus's early demise in 1668, and pressing creditors meant that Rembrandt's last years were spent in penury. What he would have made of the fact that one of his smaller portraits, of a dour old lady, was auctioned in 2001 for nearly $24 million we will never know.

Beware: the slant of **Café Sluyswacht** (✉ Jodenbreestraat 1, Jewish
Quarter and Plantage ☎ 020/65–7611) can end up causing nausea
after one too many beers on its patio overlooking Oudeschans. For
more stable fare, just across the street from askew Café Sluyswacht
are the designer sandwiches at **Dantzig** (✉ Zwanenburgwal 15,
Jewish Quarter and Plantage ☎ 020/620–9039), to be enjoyed either
on its patio looking over Waterlooplein or within its modern interior
of mosaics.

㉒ Muziektheater/Stadhuis (Music Theater/Town Hall). Universally known
as the Stopera—not just from the combining of "Stadhuis" (Town Hall)
and "Opera" but from the radical opposition expressed during its construction—this brick-and-marble complex when viewed from the south
resembles, as a local writer once described it, a "set of dentures." Another writer grumbled that its "two for one" nature was a tad too typical of the bargain-loving Dutch. Discontent with this modern complex
began before one stone was in place: what began as a squatter protest
against the razing of the 16th- and 17th-century houses in the old Jewish Quarter and around Nieuwmarkt to make way for the Metro and
this Stopera soon gained neighborhood-wide support. Regardless, the
300 million-guilder building was completed. Perhaps as compensation,
it actually boasts an impressive interior architecture complete with stunning acoustics. The Muziektheater is now home base for the Nederlands
Opera and the National Ballet and the ballet orchestra. It is also a
much-favored stage for other internationally renowned touring companies
of both classical and avant-garde tendencies. Tours of the backstage areas
are run once a week (Saturday at 3) or by prior arrangement. From September to May, the Boekmanzaal is host to a free Tuesday lunch concert.

City Hall provides a rather odd contrast, with its municipal offices and
now gay couple–friendly wedding chamber (Dutch marriages all must
be performed in the Town Hall, with church weddings optional). Also
feel free to wander through the interconnecting lobbies, where there is
interesting sculpture on display that frighteningly illustrates Amsterdam's
position below sea level. ✉ *Waterlooplein 22, Jewish Quarter and Plantage* ☎ *020/551–8911* ⊕ *www.stopera.nl* 🎟 *Tours €4.50* ☉ *Mon.–Sat.
10–6; tours Sat. at 3 or by arrangement.*

★ ⑰ Pintohuis. This Italian Renaissance–style house was grandly renovated
in 1680 by Jewish refugee Isaac de Pinto, a grandee who escaped the
Inquisition in Portugal to come to Amsterdam and become one of the
founders of the East India Company. Six towering Italianate pilasters
break up the impressive facade, remodeled by Elias Bouwman in the 1670s.
The Pintohuis's current function as public library allows easy access to
admire its lush and historic interior—in particular its cherub-encrusted
ceiling painting by Jacob de Wit, the ubiquitous 17th-century master.
The building's history and beauty provided another public service in the
early 1970s when it was successfully squatted by activists protesting its
planned removal to make way for the widening of the street. ✉ *Sint Antoniebreestraat 69, Jewish Quarter and Plantage* ☎ *020/624–3184*
🎟 *Free* ☉ *Mon. and Wed. 2–8, Fri. 2–5, Sat. 11–2.*

㉖ Portugees Israelitische Synagoge (Portuguese Israelite Synagogue). With
Jerusalem's Temple of Solomon as inspiration, Elias Bouwman and
Danield Stalpaert designed this noted synagogue between 1671 and
1675. Its square brick building within a courtyard formed by brick houses
was commissioned by the Sephardic Jewish community that had emi-
grated via Portugal during the preceding two centuries. On its completion it was the largest synagogue in the world, and its spare, elegantly

proportioned wood interior has remained virtually unchanged through the centuries. It is still magically illuminated by candles in two immense candelabra during services. The surrounding buildings that form a square around the synagogue house the world-famous Ets Haim ("Tree of Life") library, one of the oldest in the world, and the winter synagogue for use on those draftier days. ⊠ *Mr. Visserplein 3, Jewish Quarter and Plantage* ☎ *020/624–5351* ✉ *€5* ⊙ *Apr.–Oct., Sun.–Fri. 10–12:30 and 1–4; Nov.–Mar., Mon.–Thurs. 10–12:30 and 1–4, Fri. 10–12:30 and 1–3, Sun. 10–noon.*

🐾 **❸❷** **Tropenmuseum** (Museum of the Tropics). The country's largest anthropological museum, while honoring The Netherlands' link to Indonesia and the West Indies, does a good job of covering many other non-Western cultures. Its skylighted and tiered interior, rich with wood, marble, and gilt, harbors not only endless pieces of antiquity, art, and musical instruments but also many displays and dioramas depicting everyday life. In the space of a couple of hours, one can wander through villages in Java, the Middle East, India, Africa, and Latin America (where you'll also find the city's smallest Internet café, El Cybernetico). There is also a great sunny (that is, if Amsterdam is showing its all too rare tropical side) patio where you can enjoy food from the globe-embracing café.

🐾 Upstairs in the **Kindermuseum** (Children's Museum) children can participate directly in the life of another culture through special programs involving art, dance, song, and sometimes even cooking. Adults may visit the children's section but only under the supervision of a child age 6–12. ⊠ *Linnaeusstraat 2, Plantage* ☎ *020/568–8200* ⊕ *www. tropenmuseum.nl* ✉ *€6.80, Kindermuseum €1.15* ⊙ *Daily 10–5. Kindermuseum activities Wed. at 11, 1:30, and 3:15, weekends at 11:30, 1:30, and 3:15.*

❷❽ **Vakbondsmuseum** (Trade Union Museum). The idea of absorbing the history of Dutch trade unions may perhaps not be enticing to all, but the museum is placed within a monumental building designed by famed architect H. P. Berlage that he himself considered his most successful work. Known as "the castle" and built in 1900 as headquarters for the Diamond Workers Union (the country's first modern union), Berlage's structure mirrored the architect's noted socialist principles, which he had to suppress in the building of that monument to capitalism, the Beurs van Berlage (Stock Exchange). Climbing the tower will lead you to a view and a small display of Berlage's blueprints. The building's stairwell, Committee Room, and Union Hall remain unchanged, and there are fantastic murals by Richard Roland Holst, stained glass depicting the workers' battle, and many other details that savvily fuse Jugendstil with Arts and Crafts stylings. The exhibitions themselves can actually be enjoyed by all. In particular, there is an excellent collection of posters that show the graphic influence of the Soviet avant-garde. And the importance of this union not only for the Jewish community but the worker in general is undeniable. The essentially "third world" conditions of the times were eased by such now fundamental concepts as the banning of child labor and the instilling of the eight-hour day. ⊠ *Henri Polaklaan 9, Jewish Quarter and Plantage* ☎ *020/624–1166* ⊕ *www. deburcht-vakbondsmuseum.nl* ✉ *€3.40* ⊙ *Tues.–Fri. 11–5, Sun. 1–5.*

❸⓿ **Verzetsmuseum** (Museum of the Dutch Resistance). The stirring and suspenseful story of the Dutch resistance to the occupying forces, passive and active, during World War II, is set out here. This museum, which began in another location, was originally set up by resistance members themselves—many of whom were Communist, the only political party at the time to make Nazi resistance part of its platform. Since taking up residence in the Plancius building (whose music-themed facade denotes its history between 1875 and the occupation as the home to Jewish choir and stage companies), the museum has moved toward embracing all the multimedia gizmos and broadening its vision to take on Dutch collaborators and the plain indifferent. But the highlights remain the original selection of the sneaky gadgets, ingenious hiding techniques, and the bicycle-powered printing presses that pumped out fake ID papers and such now-established publications as *De Parool* ("Password") and *Vrij Nederland* ("Free The Netherlands"), which began as illegal underground newsletters. ⊠ *Plantage Kerklaan 61, Jewish Quarter and Plantage* ☏ *020/620–2535* ⊕ *www.verzetsmuseum.org* ⊞ *€3.80* ⊙ *Tues.–Fri. 10–5, weekends noon–5.*

★ ⑱ **Zuiderkerk** (South Church). Gorgeous enough to have inspired both Sir Christopher Wren and Monet, this famous church was built between 1603 and 1611 by Hendrick de Keyser, one of the most prolific architects of Holland's Golden Age. Legend has it this church hypnotized the great British architect Wren, who went on to build London's St. Paul's Cathedral (which spitefully superceded Keyser's own Westerkerk as the world's largest Protestant church); centuries later, Monet committed the Zuiderkerk to canvas. It was one of the earliest churches built in Amsterdam in the Renaissance style and was the first in the city to be built for the Dutch Reformed Church. The church's hallowed floors—under which three of Rembrandt's children are buried and on which the surplus of corpses were stored during the Hunger Winter of 1945—are now under the reign of the City Planning Office and as such are filled with detailed models of Amsterdam's ambitious future building plans. The church tower—a soaring accumulation of columns, brackets, and balustrades—is one of the most glorious exclamation points in Amsterdam; glorious, too, are the panoramic views from its balconies. Its bells are played every Thursday between noon and 1. ⊠ *Zuiderkerkhof, Jewish Quarter and Plantage* ☏ *020/689–2565 for tower* ⊕ *www.zuiderkerk. amsterdam.nl* ⊞ *Free* ⊙ *Church Mon. 11–4; Tues., Wed., and Fri. 9–4; Thurs. 9–8. Tower (tours only) June–Oct., Wed.–Sat. 2, 3, and 4.*

ALONG THE IJ: FROM THE WESTERN ISLANDS TO THE EASTERN DOCKLANDS

Water: Amsterdam was built on it and the town's riches were created by it as the transport medium to foreign seas of trade (and plunder). Psychologists and certainly Taoists could even theorize that water's fluid and flexible nature was also a fundamental influence in creating the famously pragmatic character traits of the Dutch. The fact remains that this city's historical wealth came via its waterfront, whose waters, the Het IJ, give the waterfront its name, the IJ. And before the building of Centraal Station, this waterfront essentially came into the city's center of the Dam and spread out arterially from there.

Today this true fusion of city with water can be witnessed only to the east and west of Centraal Station. To the west, one finds the artificial islands of Westerlijke Eilanden (Western Islands) built during the Golden Age, as the city was tripling in size, for shipbuilding and product storage. Today, it has a charming "village within the city" feel. To the east, the Eastern Docklands, once a squatters' paradise, are arising as a modern boardwalk, complete with a wave-shape cruise-ship passenger terminal, that is hoped to give the waterfront the same sort of international allure that made Sydney, Australia, such a popular travel destination. In short, this tour takes in both the city's aquatic past and its hopefully shimmering future. This is not to say that Amsterdam as a port is dead in the water. Rotterdam has long surpassed it as the world's busiest port, but Amsterdam and its neighboring ports along the North Sea Canal collectively rank as the 15th-busiest port.

Numbers in the text correspond to numbers in the margin and on the Oude Zijde, Plantage & Waterfront map.

a good walk

We find our beginning at **Haarlemmerplein**, a square like Leidseplein in that it began as a parking lot for 17th-century carts. It can be found at the end of the quirky shopping street Haarlemmerdijk (which, together with its westerly extension Haarlemmerweg, began life as the supply road to Haarlem during the Eighty Years' War). If we were to take this route, we would pass the pleasantly green Westerpark, the former gas complex Westergasfabriek (now reinvented as a cultural complex complete with cypress-accented landscaping), and the former water-pumping station reinvented as the Amsterdam restaurant. But since this is a seafaring tour and not one of 19th-century industrial monuments, we just pause briefly at the square's imposing **Haarlemmerpoort** ❸❸, a city gate built for the entrance of King William II on November 27, 1840, before heading north under the elevated train track to take the first right onto Sloterdijkstraat, which has a green-slated, modern, and vaguely ship-shaped building on the right by architect Tymen Ploeg (this man seems to have the monopoly on modernizing this ancient neighborhood).

From the narrow wooden bridge going across to **Prinsen Eiland**, one sees a row of shuttered warehouses (No. 63–73) on the left labeled with their occasionally somewhat odd names (from left to right): Mars, Pants in Waterland, the Golden Head, the Grain Exchange, and the Shellfish. The whole island is worth a circle as you jealously admire all the warehouses reinvented as residences and studio space for artists. The street that intersects the island is called Galgenstraat (Gallow's Street) because of the unobstructed view it once had across the IJ to Volewijk, where the executed were strung up to rot. However, instead of crossing the bridge here to Bickers Eiland and perhaps having this image stamped on your brain, exit the island via the bridge to **Realen Eiland** ❸❹ on the north side opposite No. 49, a warehouse adorned with its building date of 1629, the contorted face of a man, and a quotation that basically extols "laughter as the best medicine."

Now head right down Bickersgracht, with its row of rickety but homey houseboats, beyond which you can see the shipyards of Prinsen Eiland. Take a left down picturesque Zandhoek, admiring its evocative row of house gables before stopping at the "Gouden Reaal" (No. 14)—the large golden coin in its peak is a tribute to the island's original owner, the trade aristocrat Laurens Reael—with its floating terrace and try to imagine this now trendy café-restaurant as a herring-packing plant (then evolving into one of the more infamously rowdy sailor bars in town). This street, Zandhoek (Sand Corner), was designated in 1634 as the spot where sand was unloaded and distributed.

Head back down Zandhoek, cross the bridge to Bickers Eiland, and turn right to walk along Bickersgracht—with its petting zoo and Prinsen Eiland views—to enjoy a scenic walk to Hendrix Jonkerplein, where you can take the passage under the train track. On exiting, glance to the right to see the huge line of artist and designer studios that are now holding up the rest of the train tracks. Time for a bit of window-shopping, perhaps? Window-shopping is certainly still the name of the game if you instead proceed straight down Buiten Oranje and take the left down Haarlemmerdijk. Until less than a decade ago this strip, once a favored home to retired sailors, was a squatters' mecca before evolving into one of the city's more characterful shopping streets and a prime strip of real estate. It is thus ironic that the redbrick **West Indische Huis** ㉟, or West Indies House, on the right was the setting for the commissioning of one of the greatest real estate deals in history: buying Manhattan for 60 guilders.

Before crossing the bridge over the Singel, pause to admire across to the right the dome of the **Ronde Lutherese Kerk** (Round Lutheran Church), once a beautiful bit of 17th-century architecture that Van Gogh immortalized in a painting, now a conference center carefully rebuilt after two disastrous fires. This bridge also crosses the **Haarlemmersluis** (Haarlemmer Sluice), which is essentially the toilet flusher for the canal ring. Cross the bridge, take an immediate left under the road along the bike and walking paths, and keep as straight as is allowed to get to the harbor behind Centraal Station, that edifice that psychologically broke the view to the city's watery past. Directly opposite its main rear entrance, one may opt to take a free ferry ride across the IJ to Amsterdam Noord or eastward to the modern residential architectural mecca of the Eastern Docklands.

Returning to the city side of Centraal Station on its east side, take a left down Oosterdokskade. Between the Botel hotel and the floating pagoda-shape Chinese restaurant, Sea Palace, look across the waters to the rather scarily imposing **Scheepvaarthuis** ㊱, regarded as one of the first—and certainly one of the more excessive—examples of the expressive Amsterdam School of architecture.

The post office—or perhaps, by now, construction site—behind you is where New China Town, envisioned as a mini-Singapore of sorts, is arising between 2004 and 2008. By now, you have long espied the modern green copper building that distressingly suggests a sinking ship but is in fact the science and technology museum, **NEMO** ㊲. Take the shiny silver bridge to get there and find your way up its slanted and easily accessible roof, which offers one of the best views of the city. When your eyes have had their fill, follow the logical way to the **Nederlands Scheepvaartmuseum** ㊳, or Netherlands Maritime Museum, past the new swoopy silver exhibition space of the modern architecture gallery ArCam—though interested parties might want to first hang right to espy the Scheepvaarthuis from close up. If you want to save both for later, turn right into Kadijkplein, which ends with the entrance to **Entrepotdok,** once the biggest warehouse complex in Europe but now an example of tasteful re-invention of the historical past into modern dwellings (the entrance between the "Schiedam" and the "Stavoren" will allow you an inside glimpse). Across the canal you can see—and sometimes smell—the Artis Zoo. When the warehouses end, turn left on the left side of Entrepotdoksluis to find your way to Hoogte Kadijk, where there is the rarely open—but still functioning—shipyard **Museum Werf 't Kromhout** ㊴. If you continue east down Hoogte Kadijk, you will soon find yourself by a windmill that now provides a nice shadow to a brewery that pumps out beer: Brouwerij t'IJ, at Funenkade 7, where one can settle in for a fresh beer in its woody- and sandy-floored interior or on its terrace. After this trek, you deserve it.

TIMING This tour involves covering a lot of space, and hence renting a bicycle is heartily recommended—otherwise you may be walking for three or four hours. Alternatively you can attach the Western Dockland part of the tour to that of Jordaan, and the Eastern with a tour of the Jewish Quarter and the Plantage. You should also note that the Scheepvaartmuseum is closed on Monday in the winter.

HOW TO
GET THERE The Western Islands are accessible via Buses Nos. 18 and 22 (the latter also heads east going by the NEMO museum and the Scheepvaart useum); the Eastern Docklands via Buses Nos. 32, 39, and 43 (32 goes via NEMO and the Scheepvaartmuseum) and, from 2004 on, via the IJTram which will link Centraal Station with the arising residential islands of IJburg.

Sights to See

③③ Haarlemmerpoort. At the northern edges of the Jordaan and veritable gateway to the route that once led to Haarlem, this ornate Neoclassical-style gatehouse was built to honor King William II in 1840 (the landmark is also known as the Willemspoort). Considered a particularly ungraceful work by Cornelis Alewijn, it sits to the east of the Westerpark, one of the city's main retreats of greenery. ⊠ *Haarlemmerplein 50, Waterfront.*

⟳ ③⑨ Museum Werf 't Kromhout (Museum Wharf of the Kromhout). Started by its namesake, a ship's carpenter, in 1757, this is one of Amsterdam's oldest but still functioning shipyards. Almost 300 ships were built here during its most productive period of the last half of the 19th century. During the first part of the 20th century, 't Kromhout produced the diesel engines used by most Dutch canal boats. To this day, old boats are restored here, so expect shuffling your way through wood shavings and succumbing to the smell of tar, diesel, and varnish. Mechanics get particularly excited by the historical collection of 22 old engines. ⊠ *Hoogte Kadijk 147, Waterfront* ☎ *020/627–6777* ⊒ *€3* ⊙ *Tues. 10–3, or by prior arrangements for groups larger than 10.*

★ ⟳ ③⑧ Nederlands Scheepvaartmuseum (Netherlands Maritime Museum). This was originally built in 1656 as a military depot for the Amsterdam Admiralty after Admiral Tromp refused to salute his British counterparts (thereby sparking a war with those touchy trade competitors). Trading vessels of the East Indies Company (VOC) came here to be outfitted for their journeys, with everything from cannons to hardtack. The VOC was the world's first multinational corporation, and, since it was equipped with its own army, which numbered 11,000 at its height of power, it was essentially a state within a state. During its existence between 1602 and 1798, it built 1,450 ships, made 4,700 profit-making voyages, and employed upward of 25,000 people at any given time.

Today, this Dutch Classicist building incorporates room after room of displays related to the development and power of both the Dutch East and West Indies companies, as well as the Dutch fishing industry. At any given time there are 1,000 objects—including epic battle paintings, intricate models, bona fide boats, specialized equipment, and obsessively rendered maps—on display from the 250,000-piece collection. Moored alongside the building at the east end of the old Amsterdam Harbor is a replica of the VOC sailing ship *Amsterdam,* which sank on its maiden voyage off the coast of Hastings in 1749. Fully functional with vast expanses of sail, it generally stays docked for a variety of excellent children's activities. ⊠ *Kattenburgerplein 1, Waterfront* ☎ *020/523–2222* ⊕ *www.scheepvaartmuseum.nl* ⊒ *€7* ⊙ *Oct.–May, Tues.–Sun. 10–5; June–Sept., daily 10–5.*

⟳ ③⑦ NEMO Science & Technology Center. Opened in early 1997, this green copper–clad building, evocative of a ship sinking into the city's boggy surface, was immediately accepted as an architectural landmark. Its architect was no less than Renzo Piano, creator of the Pompidou Centre in Paris. Surrounded by water, the building's colossal volume rises above the entrance to the IJ Tunnel to Amsterdam North. The rooftop café terrace offers a superb panoramic view across the city. But this view can also be enjoyed for free via a staircase on its eastern face and via an elevator just inside the entrance.

The museum recently shortened its name from "NewMetropolis" to NEMO, perhaps to exploit that evocative word's use in *The Odyssey,* as the name of Jules Verne's notorious sea captain, and in Winsor McCay's 100-year-old comic strip, *Little Nemo in Slumberland,* which documented a small boy's surreal adventures of discovery whenever he fell asleep. And indeed, this museum is dedicated to imparting the joys of science—past, present, and futuristic—through high-tech, hands-on experience. Children—and the young at heart—have the options of building hydroelectric power stations, constructing a bamboo house, traveling through brains, indulging in dramatic chemistry experiments, playing with a giant domino set, getting charged on static electricity, and even potentially collapsing economies as a global banker. ⊠ *Oosterdok 2, Waterfront* ☎ *0900/919–1100* ⊕ *www.e-NEMO.nl* ✉ *€10* ♥ *Oct.–May, Tues.–Sun. 10–5; June–Sept., daily 10–5.*

34 Realen Eiland. About a dozen blocks to the west of Centraal Station and due north of the Harlemmerhouttuinen are three off-the-beaten-track islands created from canal landfill back in the 17th century. These Western Islands—known in Dutch as Westelijke eilanden—were then constructed to hold warehouses and now enjoy a quasi-nautical ambience particularly beloved by boaties and other seafaring folk. Most visitors bypass the largest island, Bickers Eiland, jammed as it is with boatyards (and modern apartment buildings) and hew to the west and take the waterside Nieuwe Teruinen for the bridge over to the smallest island, Prinsen Eiland. Forge ahead on its Galgenstraat (Gallows Street—it once framed a vista of the town gallows across the water), then head northward across the wooden drawbridge, to the isle of Realen Eiland. This bridge, Drie Haringbrug, has its name echoed on the gable of the house (Vierwindendwarsstraat 1–3) on its other end on the left: "three herrings" painted silver (perhaps herring storage took place in these parts during days of yore?). Located on the island's eastern shore, the photo-op hereabouts is the waterside **Zandhoek,** a street so named because it used to be the site of the city sand market. Posing for your Nikon is a charming row of 17th-century houses, built by Laurens Reael, a Catholic who became famous for smuggling out treasures from city monasteries before they could be confiscated by authorities. **"De Gouden Reael"** is the name of Reael's own house—quaintly marked with a gold coin on the gable stone—which sits waterside and is now a café, a perfect spot to raise a toast to Reael as you watch boats sail along the Westerdok. ⊠ *Westelijke Eilanden Waterfront, Follow Haarlemmerstraat/ Haarlemmerdijk from Centraal Station and go under the railway tracks at Buiten Oranjestraat or at Haarlemmerplein.*

Schepvaarthuis (Shipping Office). With its extravagantly phantasmagoric zinc-roof detailing spilling over various sculpted sea horses, ship anchors, sea gods (Neptune and his four wives), dolphins, and even shoals of fish, this is one of Amsterdam's most delightful turn-of-the-20th-century structures. Built in 1912 as the headquarters for various shipping firms that had brought back all that booty from Java and the Spice Islands, the structure was one of the opening salvos by the fantastic Amsterdam School of architecture. Piet Kramer, Johan van der May, and Michel de Klerk designed this building to have a suitably prow-shape front. Drink in all the ornamentation on the front facade, but don't forget to amble around the sides to take in the busts of noted explorers, such as Barentz and Mercator, along with such delights as sculpted railings of waves, patterned brickwork, and strutting iron tracery. All of this was highly expensive to create, so it was not surprising that the Amsterdam School's appeal to fantasy suffered an early demise in the 1930s depression. The building now contains offices for Amsterdam's public transport system and is not open to the public. ✉ *Prins Hendrikkade 108, Waterfront.*

㉟ West Indische Huis (West Indies House). These former headquarters of the West Indies Trading Company (WIC) have much historical resonance. The WIC was set up as a means to colonize America and combat Spaniards abroad. Although not as sovereign as the VOC, it was essentially given free trading rein of Africa's west coast, America, and all the islands of the West Pacific and New Guinea. In these rooms, the decision was made to buy Manhattan for 60 guilders, the silver was stored that Piet Hein liberated from the Spanish after winning a sea battle in 1628, and the organization was authorized to oversee the export of 70,000 slaves from West Africa to the Caribbean between 1626 and 1680. Now the building is home to local television production companies and a caterer. You can enter its courtyard, with its statue of Peter Stuyvesant, via its side entrance on Herenmarkt. ✉ *Herenmarkt 93–7, Waterfront.*

WHERE TO EAT

2

FODOR'S CHOICE

Amsterdam, *The Jordaan*

Bakkerswinkel van 90s, *Oude Zijde*

Blue Pepper, *Leidseplein*

Café Bern, *Oude Zijde*

De Kas, *East of Amstel*

D'Vijff Vlieghen, *Nieuwe Zijde and Spui*

Green Planet, *Nieuwe Zijde and Spui*

Inez IPSC, *Eastern Canal Ring*

Supperclub, *Nieuwe Zijde and Spui*

Tempo Doeloe, *Eastern Canal Ring*

Vermeer, *Oude Zijde*

HIGHLY RECOMMENDED

Breitner, *Eastern Canal Ring*

Café de Reiger, *The Jordaan*

De Poort, *Nieuwe Zijde and Spui*

Kantjil en de Tijger, *Nieuwe Zijde and Spui*

Excelsior, *Oude Zijde and De Wallen*

Goodies, *Western Canal Ring*

La Rive, *East of Amstel*

Plancius, *East of Amstel*

Toscanini, *The Jordaan*

VandeMarkt, *East of Amstel*

Wilhelmina-Dok, *Station and Docklands*

Many other fine restaurants enliven Amsterdam. For other favorites, look for the black stars as you read this chapter.

By Steve
Korver

UNTIL A MERE DECADE OR TWO AGO, it seemed that eating in Amsterdam was tinged more with the flavor of Calvinism than with any culinary influence. Certainly colonialism of the past did much to broaden the puritanical Dutch palate, once in the 19th century when the French occupied Holland and imported their delight for delicacies, then during the 17th-century Dutch occupation of Indonesia, whose 1,000 islands offered a roller-coaster ride of exotic spices. But too often the filling yet unenlightened fare of charred fish or meat, overboiled potatoes, and limp vegetables remained the standard. Ironically, this tendency was heightened at the dawn of the 20th century when well-meaning middle-class housewives began producing cookbooks with simple recipes meant to heighten the palate of the working classes. Alas, the only buyers were other middle-class housewives who then began neglecting their own traditional recipes in favor of these fast and easy simplifications. Even so, the Dutch continue to cut loose every now and then, in particular around holiday celebrations. Today, as back when, the drunken gobbling of whole pheasants calls up the boisterous 17th-century depictions of feasts painted by Franz Hals, Jan Steen, and Jacob Jordaens. It's little wonder that a splurge-versus-purge philosophy was a favorite subject of Golden Age painters: the skinny were portrayed as holy people of God and the fat as the precariously mortal spawn of Satan.

Today, happily, the feasting spreads out over the entire year and embraces—thanks to the post–World War II influx of immigrants—every variety of cuisine from all corners of the globe. And international urban eating trends, although perhaps arriving more slowly in Amsterdam than other places, now make it highly probable, on a walk through the city, to encounter a sushi shack, a soup shop, a Thai take-out joint, an organic baker of hearty Mediterranean breads, an olive oil specialist, or a hipster lounge. And, as though to compensate for the long culinary drought, many of the city's former industrial- and harbor-related buildings are being transformed into distinctive or trendy dining establishments. The term "New Dutch Cuisine," although flaunted for years, has come to have meaning only quite recently, thanks to the emergence of young chefs who are finding their inspiration from around the globe—the Dutch are notoriously well traveled after all—while getting their ingredients from local organic farmers (whose businesses are flourishing thanks to the many recent scares associated with mad cow disease and hormone-engorged poultry). Their creations—think foamy-textured pea soup with chanterelles and pancetta, cod smothered in a sauce based on chorizo and fennel, or turbot on a bed of beetroot and nettle leaves—have finally "turned on the style" and succeeded in taking the starch (literally) out of the old mainstays. This no-nonsense obsession in bringing out the best in the ingredients and not drowning them in fusion-for-fashion's sake finery can be seen in the dishes chef Pascal Jalhij creates for the Restaurant Vermeer. He just helped this spot garner a second Michelin star one year after it received its first—a lighting-strikes-twice occurence which has never happened before in The Netherlands.

Although traditional Dutch food with its belly-packing power really shines only in the winter months, there are two imported-but-typically-Dutch culinary trips that cannot be missed: the Indonesian *rijsttafel* ("rice table"), where dozens of vegetables, meats, and fish each get their own spicy twist as a tiny dish and are then served with rice; and cheese fondue, which the Dutch appropriated from the Swiss probably because it appealed to their "one pot, many forks" sense of the democratic. Embracing a sense of the democratic is also the best advice for lunchtime:

just follow the locals into a brown café—one of Amsterdam's iconic cafés labeled such in a reference to their nicotine-stained ambience—or bar (also often called an *eetcafe,* eating café) to have a *broodje* (sandwich), *uitsmijter* (fried eggs with cheese and/or ham served on sliced bread), or salad. If you like what you see and taste, you might also want to ask what their usually very reasonably priced *dagschotel* (daily dish of meat, vegetable, and salad usually based on what was cheapest and freshest at the market that morning) will be at dinnertime. Of course, if you are out only for a cheap, grease-enhanced snack, there are infinite snack bars where you can buy—sometimes via a heated wall *automaat*—deep-fried meat blobs or french fries that you can order with an amazing range of toppings. The many cheap Suri/Indo/Chin (or some such combination) snack bars serve a combination of Suriname, Indonesian, and Chinese dishes, and although they are remarkably consistent, it is perhaps advisable to choose a dish that matches the cook's apparent roots.

But probably the best snacks are those that can be purchased at the many fish stalls found on the city's bridges. The prime taste treat is raw *haring*—herring that has been saltwater cured in vats. This working person's "sushi" variation is at its most succulent—hence, the usual onion and pickle garnish is not required—at the start of the fishing season (late May to early June). If this sounds too radical, there's always a selection of battered and fried fishes, *Noordzee garnalen* (North Sea shrimp, which are tinier, browner, and tastier than most of their brethren) and *gerookte heilbot* (thinly sliced smoked halibut). However, if you decide to indulge, *gerookte paling* (smoked freshwater eel), rich in both price and calories, is the way to go.

If you're the type who likes to make your own discoveries, here are a few tips to keep in mind. In general, except as a lark, avoid the tourist traps around Leidseplein, Rembrandtplein, the Damrak, and the Red Light District. Cheap global eats are concentrated in the De Pijp district. A broad selection of middle-range eateries can be found around Nieuwmarkt, the Jordaan, and Utrechtsestraat. To find posher purveyors for a true blowout, head to Reguliersdwarsstraat or the Nine Streets (the interconnecting streets of the canal girdle between Raadhuisstraat and Leidsestraat) areas.

Note: For a rundown of the best of Amsterdam's famous atmosphere-soaked "brown cafés"—where there is traditionally more imbibing than dining—see Chapter 4, Nightlife & the Arts.

Restaurants by Neighborhood

Nieuwe Zijde & Spui

The historical center's "new side" has the history but none of the neon of the "old side." It's the intellectual heart of Amsterdam and ground central for roaming hipsters, who often load up at a restaurant around Spui square before washing it down with some nightlife in an ancient bar or the latest lounge.

AMERICAN
CASUAL
¢–$

✕ **Caffé Esprit.** The Spui offers several more old-world–evocative eateries, but Esprit (part of the clothing chain of the same name)—with its clean and modern "aluminum design" interior, and windows overlooking the bustling square—does reach out to the homesick by offering contemporary American sandwiches, burgers, pastas, pizzas, salads, and children's menus. Yankee Doodle Sandwich (crisp roll with pastrami, mustard, mayonnaise, and grilled bell peppers), anyone? ⊠ *Spui 10, Nieuwe Zijde and Spui* ☎ *020/622–1967* ⌂ *Reservations not accepted* ☐ *No credit cards* ⊗ *No dinner except Thurs.*

2

Dining Hours
One thing you should be aware of is the Dutch custom of early dining; in fact, the vast majority of the city's kitchens are closed by 10 PM—though happily, many of the newer establishments are moving away from this long-held tradition. It should also be noted that many restaurants choose Monday as their day of rest. Lunches are usually served between noon and 2 PM but note that a goodly proportion of restaurants in Amsterdam are open for dinner only.

Dress
Because Amsterdam is a casual sort of town, "jacket and tie" means more "if you feel like it" than "required." The truly elitist dining spots have long learned to have a supply of jackets on hand for the underdressed.

Reservations
If a restaurant requires reservations, or is so popular they are found to be essential, it is so noted in the individual write-ups. But there's no harm in taking the precaution of calling ahead as far as possible (especially since the process is so easy, with the Dutch seemingly more talented in spoken English than many native English speakers).

Smoking
Although there are strict anti–public smoking laws on the horizon (set to take effect in 2004), the cafés and restaurants of Amsterdam remain puffing paradises. Many restaurants provide no-smoking sections, but the fervently pink-lunged antismoker should really call ahead to get the full scoop.

Tipping
A 15% service charge is automatically included on the menu prices. However, the trend is for most diners to throw in an extra euro or two on smaller bills and €5 or €10 on larger bills.

Prices
Since the introduction of the euro, prices have skyrocketed in Amsterdam. Although we strive to keep abreast of the prices, the rate of inflation, especially taking in the dollar-to-euro exchange, has seemingly overtaken the rate of our updating. But on average, one can expect to pay about €20 for a simple dinner and €6–€12 for a simple lunch. When you hit the blow-out restaurants, the tab can soar into the empyrean.

WHAT IT COSTS In euros				
$$$$	**$$$**	**$$**	**$**	**¢**
AT DINNER Over €30	€22–€30	€15–€22	€10–€15	Under €10

Prices are per person for a main course and include part of the 15% service charge.

DUTCH
$$$–$$$$
Fodor'sChoice
★

✕ **D' Vijff Vlieghen.** The "Five Flies" is a rambling dining institution that takes up five adjoining Golden Age houses. Yet the densely evocative Golden Age vibe—complete with bona fide Rembrandt etchings, wooden *jenever* (Dutch gin) barrels, crystal and armor collections, and an endless array of old-school bric-a-brac—came into being only in 1939. Brass plaques on the chairs, although listing such past visitors as Orson Welles, Walt Disney, and Goldie Hawn, do not tell of its vast popular-

Where to Eat in Amsterdam

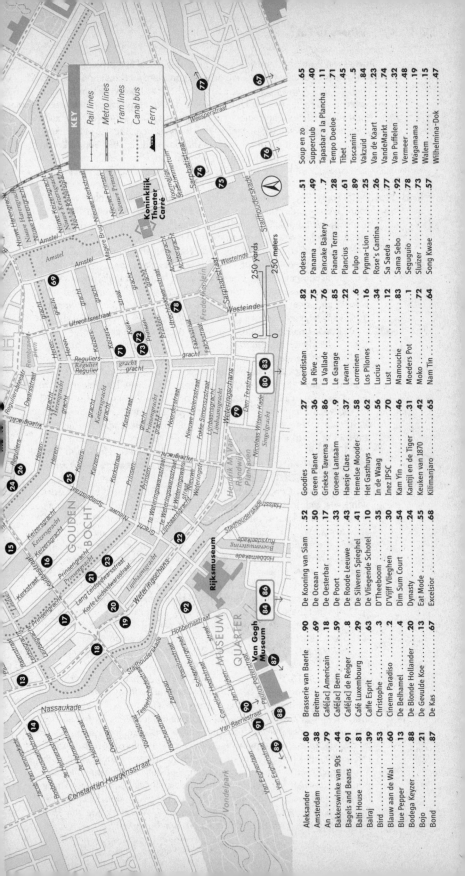

KEY

- Rail lines
- Metro lines
- Tram lines
- Canal bus
- Ferry

Koninklijk Theater Carré

Rijksmuseum

Van Gogh Museum

MUSEUM QUARTER

GOUDEN BOCHT

250 yards
250 meters

Aleksander	80	Brasserie van Baerle	90	De Kooning van Siam ... 52
Amsterdam	38	Breitner	69	De Oceaan ... 50
An	79	Caféjac Americain	18	De Oesterbar ... 17
Bakkerswinkel van 90s	44	Caféjac Bern	59	De Poort ... 33
Bagels and Beans	91	Caféjac de Reiger	8	De Roode Leeuwe ... 43
Balti House	81	Café Luxembourg	29	De Silveren Spieghel ... 41
Balraj	39	Caffe Esprit	63	De Vliegende Schotel ... 10
Bird	53	Christophe	3	D'Theeboom ... 35
Blauw aan de Wal	60	Cinema Paradiso	60	D'Vijff Vlieghen ... 30
Blue Pepper	13	De Belhamel	4	Dim Sum Court ... 54
Bodega Keyzer	88	De Blonde Hollander	20	Dynasty ... 24
Bojo	21	De Gevulde Koe	13	Eat Mode ... 55
Bond	87	De Kas	67	Excelsior ... 68

Goodies ... 27	Koerdistan ... 82	Odessa ... 51	Soup en zo ... 65
Green Planet ... 36	La Rive ... 75	Panama ... 49	Supperclub ... 40
Griekse Taverna ... 86	La Vallade ... 76	Pancake Bakery ... 7	Tapasbar a la Plancha ... 11
Groene Lantaarn ... 9	Le Garage ... 85	Pianeta Terra ... 28	Tempo Doeloe ... 71
Haesje Claes ... 37	Levant ... 22	Plancius ... 61	Tibet ... 45
Hemelse Mooder ... 58	Lorreinen ... 6	Pulpo ... 89	Toscanini ... 5
Het Gasthuys ... 62	Los Pilones ... 16	Pygma-Lion ... 25	Vakzuid ... 84
In de Waag ... 56	Lucius ... 34	Rose's Cantina ... 26	Van de Kaart ... 23
Inez IPSC ... 70	Lust ... 12	Sa Saeda ... 77	VandeMarkt ... 74
Kam Yin ... 46	Mamouche ... 83	Sama Sebo ... 92	Van Puffelen ... 32
Kantjil en de Tiger ... 31	Moeders Pot ... 1	Seguguio ... 78	Vermeer ... 48
Keuken van 1870 ... 42	Moko ... 72	Sluizer ... 73	Wagamama ... 19
Kilimanjaro ... 65	Nam Tin ... 64	Song Kwae ... 57	Walem ... 15
			Wilhelmina-Dok ... 47

ity—you'll find both business folk clinching a deal in a private nook and busloads of tourists who have dibs on complete sections: book accordingly. You do end up paying extra for the Five Flies vibe thanks to an overpriced menu of new Dutch cuisine, which emphasizes local, fresh, and often organic ingredients in everything from wild boar to purely vegetarian dishes. Lack of choice is not an issue here: the size of the menu, the set menus, the wine list, and the flavored jenever are—like the decor—all of epic proportions. ⊠ *Spuistraat 294–302, Nieuwe Zijde and Spui* ☎ 020/530–4060 ⊕ *www.d-vijffvlieghen.com* 🏛 *Jacket and tie* ⊟ *AE, DC, MC, V* ☺ *No lunch.*

★ **$$–$$$$** ✕ **De Poort.** Recently restored in the Old Dutch style (complete with polished woods and ceiling paintings), De Poort—part of the Die Poert van Cleve hotel complex—is, in fact, officially Old Dutch. Its roots as a steak brasserie stretch back to 1870, when it awed the city as the first place with electric light. By the time you read this, De Poort will have served well over 6 million of its acclaimed juicy slabs, served with a choice of eight accompaniments. The menu is supplemented with other options such as smoked salmon, a traditional pea soup thick enough to eat with a fork, and a variety of seafood dishes. ⊠ *Nieuwe Zijde Voorburgwal 176–180, Nieuwe Zijde and Spui* ☎ 020/622–6429 ⊟ *AE, DC, MC, V.*

$$$ ✕ **De Roode Leeuw.** Evoking a sense of timeless classicism along a strip that is decidedly middle-of-the-road, De Roode Leeuw is a brasserie with the city's oldest heated terrace and an impressive champagne list. You'll find poshed-up native fare served up here with even posher silverware, may it be eel (caught fresh from the nearby IJsselmeer before being stewed) in a creamy herb sauce, or Zeeland mussels steamed and served with French fries and served with salad and choice of sauces. Besides attracting passing tourists, they have also built up a sizable local following thanks to having received the coveted "Neerlands Dis" (Netherlands' Dish) award. ⊠ *Damrak 93, Nieuwe Zijde and Spui* ☎ 020/555–0666 ⊕ *www.restaurantderoodeleeuw.com* ⚒ *Reservations essential* ⊟ *AE, DC, MC, V.*

★ **$$** ✕ **Haesje Claes.** Groaning with pewter tankards, stained glass, leaded windows, rich historic paneling, Indonesian paisley *fabriks,* and betasseled Victorian lamps, this is a restaurant after any Meinherr Van Tassel's heart. With a menu to match its "Old Holland" menu, Haesje Claes—the name comes from the lady who founded Amsterdam's orphanage in the 16th-century—specializes in packing in busloads of tourists. But all remains happily cheerful. The food, if occasionally overpriced, is actually quite fine: in particular their pea soup and the selection of *stampotten* (mashed dishes that combine potato with a variety of vegetables and/or meats). On cold winter nights, many opt for the *Hotchpotches* (stews) of steamed beef, sausage, and bacon. Still, we give this a star basically for its Pieter de Hooch–worthy interiors. ⊠ *Spuistraat 273, Oude Zijde* ☎ 020/624–9998 ⊕ *www.haesjeclaes. nl* ⊟ *AE, MC, V.*

¢ ✕ **Keuken van 1870.** This former soup kitchen, where sharing tables is still the norm, offers the best and most economic foray into the satiating world of traditional Dutch cooking. As reassuring as a Dutch grandmother, the kitchen serves such warming singularities as *hutspot* (a hotchpotch of potatoes, carrots, and onions), its more free-ranging variant *stamppot* (a stew of potatoes, greens, and chunks of cured sausage), *erwtensoep* (a sausage-fortified pea soup so thick you could eat it with a toothpick), and, naturally, a full range of meat, fish, vegetable, and potato plates. After a spell of bad luck—namely bankruptcy—its future is somewhat uncertain (though it is impossible to imagine the city without it), so call ahead to check. ⊠ *Spuistraat 4, Nieuwe Zijde and Spui* ☎ 020/624–8965 ⊟ *AE, MC, V* ☺ *No lunch weekends.*

FRENCH
$$$
✕ **De Silveren Spieghel.** Despite appearances, this precariously crooked building near the solid Round Lutheran Church is here to stay. Designed by the ubiquitous Hendrik de Keyser, it has managed to remain standing since 1614, so it should last through your dinner of contemporary Dutch cuisine. In fact, take time to enjoy their use of famous local ingredients, such as succulent lamb from the North Sea island of Texel and honey from Amsterdam's own Vondel Park. There are also expertly prepared fish plates, such as turbot on a bed of beetroot and nettle leaves. Lunch is available by reservation only (phone a day ahead). ✉ *Kattengat 4–6, Nieuwe Zijde and Spui* ☎ *020/624–6589* ⟨ *Reservations essential* ⊟ *AE, MC, V* ☉ *Closed Sun.*

$$$–$$$$
✕ **D' Theeboom.** A favorite of the local French business community, this formal, stylish—done up in Art Deco creams and blacks—and fairly priced purveyor of haute cuisine is behind the Dam in a historic canal-side warehouse. The flavor of, for example, the oven-roasted monkfish with prawns, curry, and grapefruit is particularly enhanced when you take advantage of the sophisticated wine list. Combine this with a sunny day on the terrace and you can definitely settle in for a long and happy linger. ✉ *Singel 210, Nieuwe Zijde and Spui* ☎ *020/623–8420* ⊟ *AE, DC, MC, V* ☉ *No lunch weekends.*

ECLECTIC
$$$$
Fodor's Choice
★
✕ **Supperclub.** The concept is simple but artful. Over the course of an evening, diners casually lounge on white mattresses in a white space while receiving endless courses of food (and drink . . .) marked by irreverent flavor combinations. DJs, VJs, and live performances enhance the clublike, relentlessly hip vibe. Once purely an underground endeavor, the Supperclub is set to go global with a branch already in Rome and more to follow in London, New York City, and Ibiza. Its popularity suggests that one should really go only in large groups; otherwise you may run the risk of being overwhelmed by one of the same. ✉ *Jonge Roelensteeg 21, Nieuwe Zijde and Spui* ☎ *020/638–0513* ⊕ *www.supperclub.nl* ⟨ *Reservations essential* ⊟ *AE, DC, MC, V* ☉ *No lunch.*

★ **¢–$**
✕ **Café Luxembourg.** One of the city's top grand cafés, Luxembourg has a grand interior and a grand view of a bustling square, both of which are maximized for people watching. Famous for its brunches, its classic café menu comes equipped with a mighty fine goat cheese salad, dim sum, and excellent Holtkamp *krokets* (indeed: croquettes, these with a shrimp or meat and potato filling). The "reading table" is sensitively packed with both Dutch and international newspapers and mags. ✉ *Spuistraat 24, Nieuwe Zijde and Spui* ☎ *020/620–6264* ⊟ *AE, V.*

INDONESIAN
★ **$$–$$$**
✕ **Kantjil en de Tijger.** No folkloric shadow puppets adorn the walls at this unusually large and spacious Indonesian restaurant: the interior is serenely Jugendstil (a sort of Austrian Art Nouveau), which provides a refreshing surprise. Although you can order à la carte, the menu is based on three different *rijsttafel* (rice tables), with an abundance of meat, fish, and vegetable dishes varying in flavor from coconut-milk sweetness to distressingly spicy (tip: the sweet and light local *witbier* beer is an excellent antidote). Groups often come here to line their bellies before a night of drinking in the bars around the nearby Spui and Nieuwezijds Voorburgwal. ✉ *Spuistraat 291/293, Nieuwe Zijde and Spui* ☎ *020/620–0994* ⊟ *AE, DC, MC, V* ☉ *No lunch.*

SEAFOOD
$$–$$$
✕ **Lucius.** The plain and informal setting may say "bistro," but don't associate that with speedy service. What we have here is infinitely better: one of the best fish restaurants in town, where you can happily linger over such choices as grilled lobster, a deliciously authentic *plateau de fruits de mer* (fruits-of-the-sea platter), or a positively adventurous sea bass served with buckwheat noodles and mushrooms. Find the perfect

complement in the intelligent list of wines: it spotlights California but—attention oenophiles who think they have heard everything—also sports a Dutch wine from the nation's only vineyard, in Limburg. ✉ *Spuistraat 247, Nieuwe Zijde and Spui* ☎ *020/624–1831* ⊕ *www.lucius.nl* ⌂ *Reservations essential* ⊟ *AE, DC, MC, V* ⊘ *No lunch.*

VEGETARIAN ╳ **Green Planet.** You know this is a serious mecca for vegetarians when
¢–$ 90% of the kitchen's ingredients are organic, the resident cat is a dedicated veg (in both diet and manner), and it is the only restaurant in the country that employs biodegradable packaging for takeout. Their equally noble menu covers everything from wraps to stir-fries but enters true profundity when it comes to the lasagna or Thai carrot cream soup. In short, followers of the fatty diet of the late Dr. Atkins should avoid this place like the plague. ✉ *Spuistraat 122, Nieuwe Zijde and Spui* ☎ *020/625–8280* ⊕ *www.greenplanet.nl* ⊟ *No credit cards* ⊘ *Closed Mon.*

Oude Zijde

The city's "old side" of its historical center, although harboring the decidedly nonedible neon grotesqueries of the Red Light District, is also host to many bargain Asian restaurants and the fine delicacies of some of Amsterdam's most esteemed eateries.

CHINESE ╳ **Kam Yin.** Representative of the many Suriname snack bars found
¢–$ throughout the city, Kam Yin offers this South American country's unique fusion of Caribbean, Chinese, and Indonesian cuisines that arose from its history as a Dutch colony. Perhaps the most popular meal is the *roti,* a flat-bread pancake, which comes with lightly curried potatoes and either vegetable or meat additions. If you are interested only in lunch, try a *broodje pom,* a bun sandwich filled with a remarkably addictive mélange of chicken and root vegetable (mmmmm, root vegetable). Basic, clean, convivial, and noisy, Kam Yin shows extra sensitivity with its speedy service, long hours (daily noon–midnight), and a doggy-bag option. ✉ *Warmoesstraat 6–8, Oude Zijde* ☎ *020/625–3115* ⊟ *No credit cards.*

¢–$ ╳ **Nam Tin.** In the world of culinary imperialism, the Chinese have their formula bolted down. And indeed this massive and massively overlighted restaurant is like thousands of others the world over in ignoring the setting in favor of the flavor within their encyclopedic Cantonese menu. As a hangover-curing bonus, they serve dim sum from noon until 5 PM daily and until 10 PM on Sunday. Clincher of its respected status: the majority of its patrons are Chinese themselves. ✉ *Jodenbreestraat 11, Oude Zijde* ☎ *020/428–8508* ⊟ *AE, DC, MC, V.*

¢–$ ╳ **Tibet Restaurant.** Come here for budget prices or late-night hours (daily 1:30 PM–1:30 AM), but don't expect the Dalai Lama to drop by. Although there are certainly some Tibetan wall adornments and you can get such dishes as *momo* dumplings and various pork offerings that come either in spicy "folk-style" chunks or as milder "family-style" shreds, the majority of the menu is ironically dedicated to fairly standard renderings of Chinese Szechuan fare. ✉ *Lange Niezel 24, Oude Zijde* ☎ *020/624–1137* ⊟ *MC, V.*

¢ ╳ **Dim Sum Court.** The fatigue induced by travel—or an excess of partying—sometimes calls for but one thing: the obsessive stuffing of your face. Here for a mere €7.50, one can do just that for one hour. Granted, the fare is not representative of the heights of Chinese cookery, but the belly-packing and energizing properties of dim sum are still renowned the world over, and the ones found here are turned out by the city's leading producer of these steamed and sticky hors d'oeuvres of sorts. The buffet is supplemented by more dubious approximations of fried rice, noodles, vegetable dishes, and crispy fried pork and chicken. Another bonus is that this place stays open late: until 11 Monday to Wednesday and until midnight Thursday to Sunday. ⊠ *Zeedijk 109, Oude Zijde* ☎ *020/638–1466* ⊠ *Rokin 152* ☎ *020/638-1249* ⚒ *Reservations not accepted* ⊟ *No credit cards.*

CONTEMPORARY
$$–$$$
✕ **Blauw aan de Wal.** In the heart of the Red Light District is a small alley that leads to this charming oasis, "Blue on the Quay," complete with the innocent chirping of birds. Auspiciously set in a courtyard that once belonged to the Bethanienklooster monastery, this place offers a restful ambience with multiple dining areas (one is no-smoking), each with a unique and serene view. Original wood floors and exposed-brick walls hint at the building's 1625 origins, but white tablecloths, an extensive and inspired wine list, and an open kitchen that employs fresh local ingredients in its Mediterranean-influenced masterworks speak more of an unpretentious and contemporary take on chic. After starting on a foamy pea soup with chanterelle mushrooms and pancetta, you may want to indulge in a melt-in-the-mouth cod seductively smothered in a sauce of chorizo and fennel. ⊠ *Oude Zijde Achterburgwal 99, Oude Zijde* ☎ *020/330–2257* ⊟ *AE, MC, V* ☺ *Closed Sun. No lunch.*

DUTCH
$
Fodor'sChoice
★
✕ **Café Bern.** This dark and woody café, as evocative as a Jan Steen 17th-century interior, has been serving the same cheese fondue for decades and for good reason: it's just about perfect, especially if you enhance digestion—and the frolic factor—with plenty of orders from the fully stocked bar. Like the Dutch, you, too, may be inspired to establish cheese fondue as your own celebratory meal of choice. ⊠ *Nieuwmarkt 9, Oude Zijde* ☎ *020/622–0034* ⚒ *Reservations essential* ⊟ *No credit cards* ☺ *No lunch.*

$
✕ **Het Gasthuys.** In this bustling and student-filled eetcafé near the university you'll be served handsome portions of traditional Dutch home cooking, choice cuts of meat with simple sauces, fine fries, and piles of mixed salad. Sit at the wood bar or take a table high up in the rafters at the back, surrounded by ancient wallpapers. In summer you can watch the passing boats from the enchanting canal-side terrace or watch the junkies selling bikes off the nearby bridge. ⊠ *Grimburgwal 7, Oude Zijde* ☎ *020/624-8230* ⊟ *No credit cards.*

¢
Fodor'sChoice
★
✕ **Bakkerswinkel van 90s.** This genteel yet unpretentious bakery/tearoom evokes an English country kitchen, one that lovingly prepares and serves breakfasts, high tea, hearty-breaded sandwiches, soups, and the most divine—and dare it be said, most manly—slabs of quiche you will probably ever taste. There's little sense of privacy within their closely clustered wooden tables, but this remains a true oasis for those out to indulge in a healthful breakfast or lunch. Not only do they open at 7 AM daily, but they also have another handy location, complete with garden patio, in the Museum District. ⊠ *Warmoestraat 69, Oude Zijde* ☎ *020/489-8000* ⊟ *No credit cards* ☺ *No dinner. Closed Mon.* ⊠ *Roelef Hartstraat 68* ☎ *020/662-3594* ⊟ *No credit cards* ☺ *No dinner. Closed Mon.*

FRENCH
★ $$$$
✕ **Excelsior.** For when only the poshest and most classically elegant will do, take your primped-up selves here. To the tinkling of a grand piano, solicitous waiters, knowledgeable sommeliers, towering dessert trolleys, and preparation carts all waltz together in a setting of towering palms, tall candelabras, and shimmering chandeliers. Even more delicious is the Excelsior's mouthwatering view over the Amstel River toward either the Muntplein and its medieval tower on one side or the Music Theater on the other. If you have not already guessed, the kitchen here is traditional French. But the inspired chef, Jean-Jacques Menanteau, also knows some twists, such as a sublime lobster bisque and a

grilled turbot with shrimp and Parmesan risotto. The truly adventurous should opt for his fixed-price *menu gastronomique*, which will feature not only seasonal specialties (think truffles) but occasionally also the acclaimed reveries he creates from such unprepossessing meats as liver and kidney. Rest assured, there are four more fixed-priced menus to choose from. ⊠ *Hotel de l'Europe, Nieuwe Doelenstraat 2–8, Oude Zijde* ☎ *020/531–1705* ⊕ *www.leurope.nl* ⋔ *Jacket and tie* ⊟ *AE, DC, MC, V* ⊙ *No lunch Sat. and Sun.*

$$$$
Fodor'sChoice
★

✕ **Vermeer.** With its milk-white walls, dramatic black-and-white patterned floors, Delft plates, fireplace hearths, and Stern Old Dutch chandeliers, this stately place does conjure up the amber canvases of the great Johannes (if he ever did the decor for a fancy hotel chain, that is). Its very posh vibe, however, suggests that no milkmaid on Earth that will be able to afford the prices of this restaurant set within the 17th-century wing of the NH Barbizon Palace Hotel. Young chef Pascal Jalaij received a Michelin star a year in the past two years and indeed his creations are cosmic in the way they balance texture and contrast (what this man does with fois gras!). He sums up the current ambitions of local chefs: buying the produce from organic farmers (and going so far as to get his fish from bona fide rod fishermen), building up dishes steeped in classical French, then infusing them with a nouvelle "anything goes as long as it's honest and it works" sensibility. A poached Anjou dove with juniper berry sauce and a crunchy potato pie, anyone? And of course, an army of waiters are on hand to insure that the service is always impeccable. If you are in feasting mode, opt for Grand Bouffe excess by spending €100 to have a taste of everything on the menu. ⊠ *Prins Hendrikkade 59–72, Oude Zijde* ☎ *020/556–4885* ⊕ *www.restaurantvermeer.nl* ⊟ *AE, DC, MC, V* ⊙ *No Sat. lunch. Closed Sun.*

$$

✕ **In de Waag.** The lofty, beamed interior of the historic Waag (weigh house) has been converted into a grand café and restaurant. Although the reading table houses computer terminals with free Internet access, a strict dinner lighting policy of "candles only"—from a huge wooden candelabra, no less—helps maintain the building's medieval majesty. The approach is heartily Burgundian with such entrées as baked fillet of salmon with braised endives and Noilly Prat sauce or tournedos of entrecôte with roasted beets, potato, puffed garlic, and veal gravy. The long wooden tables make this an ideal location for larger groups, and if you happen to belong to a party of eight, you should definitely book the spookily evocative tower room. Daytime hunger pangs are also catered to from 10 AM, when you can enjoy a sandwich, a salad, or a snack on the spacious terrace. ⊠ *Nieuwmarkt 4, Oude Zijde* ☎ *020/422–7772* ⊕ *www.indewaag.nl* ⊟ *AE, DC, MC, V.*

PAN-ASIAN
¢

✕ **Eat Mode.** One can easily imagine this sleek steel- and Formica-rich snack bar, which is dedicated to the more popular dishes of Asia, set on a Tokyo subway platform. So it just adds to the charm that it is, in fact, on Amsterdam's oldest street. Order some cheap but tasty yakitori, sushi, noodles, or whatever they happen to have as specials that day and then wait for your number to be called out. Is this the beginning of a new eating trend? We hope so. ⊠ *Zeedijk 105-7, Oude Zijde* ☎ *020/330–0806* ⊟ *No credit cards.*

THAI
$$

✕ **De Kooning van Siam.** This Thai restaurant, sitting smack in the middle of the Red Light District, takes delight in the fact that Brad Pitt (who incidentally just went local by buying a home in the Jordaan) once came to dine. It should take more from the fact that it is favored by local Thai residents. Although the old beams and wall panels are still visible in this old canal house, the furniture and wall decorations refreshingly dilute the sense of Olde Dutchness. Sensitive to wimpier palates, the menu balances such scorchers as stir-fried beef with onion and chili peppers with milder options such as the chicken with Chinese vegetables seasoned with coconut, curry, and basil. ☒ *Oude Zijde Voorburgwal 42, Oude Zijde* ☎ *020/623–7293* ☲ *AE, DC, MC, V* ☽ *Closed Feb. No lunch.*

$–$$ ✕ **Bird.** After many years of success operating the chaotic and tiny Thai snack bar across the street, Bird's proprietors opened this expansive 100-seat restaurant. Now they have the extra kitchen space to flash-fry their options from an expanded menu, and enough room to place the chunky teak furnishings they had imported from Thailand. The best tables— where you can enjoy coconut-chicken soup with lemongrass followed by fruity curry with mixed seafood—are at the rear overlooking the canal. ☒ *Zeedijk 72–74, Oude Zijde* ☎ *020/620–1442* ☲ *AE, DC, MC, V.*

¢–$ ✕ **Song Kwae.** Here's yet another Thai spot that seems to be usurping the kind of offerings more traditionally associated with Amsterdam's Chinatown. Perhaps influenced by their Chinese competitors, this buzzing joint offers speedy service and high-quality food for a budget price. Alongside the traditional red and green Thai curries and the stir-fry options, there are specialties such as green papaya salad with crab and *potek*, a searingly spicy mix of meats and fish. In the summer, the seating spills over onto the street with its views of Nieuwmarkt. They have also just opened a nearby sister restaurant Song Kwae Sukiyaki that specializes in the always socially convivial fondue. ☒ *Kloveniersburgwal 14, Oude Zijde* ☎ *020/624–2568* ☲ *AE, DC, MC, V* ☒ *Binnenbantammerstraat Oude Zijde and De Wallen* ☎ *020/422–2444* ☲ *AE, DC, MC, V.*

VEGETARIAN ✕ **Soup en Zo.** Only in the last couple of years, perhaps because *Sein-*
¢ *feld* runs a few seasons behind here, has the concept of speedy soup purveyors hit Amsterdam. "Soup etc." leads the pack by being particularly speedy (at least between 10 and 7:30 daily), as well as health conscious. They attempt to make their four daily available soups, served with chunky slices of whole-grain breads, from as many organic ingredients as possible, and their menu also offers salads and exotic fruit juices imported from Brazil as frozen fruit pulp. Fortified, you can now rush back to searching for bargains at the Waterlooplein flea market or window shopping for arts and antiques around its new, second location. ☒ *Jodenbreestraat 94a, Oude Zijde* ☎ *020/422–2243* ⊕ *www.soupenzo.nl* ☲ *No credit cards* ☒ *Nieuwe Spiegelstraat 94a, Museum District* ☎ *020/330–7781* ☲ *No credit cards.*

Western Canal Ring

The intrinsically posh sector of the Grachtengordel ring and its intersecting streets is a foodie paradise. Meals here come equipped with the potential for an after-dinner romantic walk to aid the digestion.

CONTEMPORARY ✕ **Lust.** Before you get the wrong idea: "lust" is a much softer word in
¢ Dutch and suggests a calmer desire best translated as "appetite." And if you have worked up a lunchy one while wandering the Nine Streets specialty shopping area, this is a truly satiating place for healthful club sandwiches, bagels (their tuna spread being particularly sublime), fruit shakes, stir-fries, pastas, and salads. Few leave disappointed from this trendy lunchroom, especially if they included a visit to the wacky washroom. ☒ *Runstraat 13, Western Canal Ring* ☎ *020/626–5791* ☲ *No credit cards* ☽ *No dinner.*

CONTINENTAL ✕ **De Belhamel.** This restaurant, set on the edge of the Jordaan, is blessed
$$ with Art Nouveau detailing and wallpaper that is so darkly evocative of fin-de-siècle living it may inspire a thirst for absinthe and Symbolist poetry. But the views of the Herengracht canal and the attentive and

friendly service help create a more purely romantic setting in which to settle down and enjoy the French-inspired menu, which in the winter emphasizes hearty game dishes (venison with a red-wine and shallot sauce) and in the summer—when the seating spills out into the street—offers lighter fare with unusual but inspired flavor combinations. ⊠ *Brouwersgracht 60, Western Canal Ring* ☎ *020/622–1095* ⊕ *www.belhamel. nl* ⊟ *AE, MC, V* ☉ *No lunch.*

$$ ⨉ **Van Puffelen.** Dual-natured, the woody and classically ancient Van Puffelen, on a particularly mellow stretch of canal, offers both a startling array of herbed and spiced jenevers in its role as a *proeverij* ("tasting house") and, in addition, it has a huge restaurant section in which to settle the belly. The menu is of modern café variety, but it's the daily special—duck breast with passion-fruit sauce, to name one—that draws the many regulars. Red meat tends to be done rare, so let them know if you prefer medium to well done. Things can indeed get somewhat boisterous here, but one can always escape to the more secluded and intimate mezzanine or, in the summer, the terrace. Reservations are essential for the restaurant (also essential is a visit to their "liquor vat" washrooms). ⊠ *Prinsengracht 375–377, Western Canal Ring* ☎ *020/624–6270* ⊟ *AE, DC, MC, V.*

DUTCH ⨉ **Pancake Bakery.** As a well honed art form that delicately balances thin-
¢–$ ness with belly packing power, one can't really go wrong when going out for Dutch pancakes. But the quaint Pancake Bakery rises above the pack with its medieval vibe, canal-side patio, and a mammoth menu with over 70 choices of sweet and savory toppings. They also do a convincing take on the folk dish of *erwtensoep* (a smoked sausage imbued pea soup that is so thick that you can eat it with a toothpick). ⊠ *Prinsengracht 191, Western Canal Ring* ☎ *020/625–1333* ⊟ *No credit cards.*

FRENCH ⨉ **Christophe.** When Algerian-born Frenchman Jean-Christophe Royer
$$$$ opened his canal-side *eettempel* (eating temple) in the 1980s, it was almost immediately lauded for both its William Katz–designed interior, which evokes this artist's acclaimed ballet scenery, and Royer's own culinary vision, which embellishes French haute cuisine with Arabic and African influences. In short: Christophe's cooking awards are well deserved. The ever-changing menu—always loaded with vegetarian options—may include entrées such as ragout of lobster with cocoa beans, pimientos, and coriander, or sweetbreads of veal in a sauce of *vin jaune* (a deep golden wine from the Jura region in France) with white cabbage and chanterelles. ⊠ *Leliegracht 46, Western Canal Ring* ☎ *020/625–0807* ⊕ *www.christophe.nl* ⌕ *Reservations essential* ♔ *Jacket required* ⊟ *AE, DC, MC, V* ☉ *Closed Sun. and Mon., 1st wk in Jan., and 2 wks in July and Aug. No lunch.*

ITALIAN ⨉ **Pianeta Terra.** This multilevel, marble-clad, and softly lighted intimate
$$ setting is perfect for enjoying a menu that embraces the whole Mediterranean region and pays respect to vegetarians and organic farmers. Trust the daily set menus, especially if they include a carpaccio of swordfish with Pecorino cheese, octopus and mussels prepared in a traditionally Moroccan *tagine* (clay pot) and served on a bed of arugula, or a dish employing pasta, which, like the bread, is made on the premises from only organic ingredients. ⊠ *Beulingstraat 7, Western Canal Ring* ☎ *020/626–1912* ⊕ *www.pianetaterra.nl* ⌕ *Reservations essential* ⊟ *AE, DC, MC, V* ☉ *No lunch.*

★ **$–$$** ⨉ **Goodies.** Free of all pretension, this spaghetteria is merely out to serve fresh homemade pastas, healthful salads, and tasty meat and fish dishes of the highest quality for the friendliest of prices. You will, however, be packed like a sardine at the wooden tables and benches (moved

ON THE MENU

A TYPICAL DUTCH MEAL is often derided for its boldly honest approach to the food groups: meat, vegetable, potato. But all you need is one restaurant meal that seems home cooked by a particularly savvy mother to see that Dutch cuisine is filled with unexpected nuances and can be positively skeee-rumptious.

There are usually many different meals on offer, including very traditional winter fare such as zuurkool met spek en worst (sauerkraut with bacon and sausage); hutspot (a hotchpotch of potato and carrots served with sausage); stampot (a hotchpotch of potato and sauerkraut served with sausage); and erwetensoup, also called snert, which is a thick pea soup that comes fortified with a variety of meats.

Let the good local burghers save this magnificent brew for ice-skating time; we like this about 364 days of the year. It can be loaded with spicy sausages and pork fat; it's as thick as diesel oil, as rich as supercondensed cream, as inert as infantry pancakes, and sometimes as indigestible as green sawdust—but is it good!

More-summery options are the famed asperges, the white and tender local asparagus that comes into season in May, and mossellen, or mussels, that are matured by mid-August in the pristine waters of Oosterschelde in Zeeland.

Fancier summer starters may be a seasonal salad with smoked salmon or eel, or a carpaccio made with sole. Desserts invariably include homemade custards and some version of profiterole, which is a liquor-soaked thin pancake usually filled with ice cream and drowned in dark chocolate.

And although it may be handy to learn that kip means "chicken" and biefstuk means "beefsteak," a much easier and common shortcut to understanding a Dutch menu is to ask for an English menu (or a quick translation of "recommendations"). Keep in mind one local menu quirk: an entrée is, in fact, a starter and not a main course. Those are called hoofdgerechten.

For snack and sandwich best bests, see the Close-Up box "Refuel Around Town."

Of course, any visitors to Amsterdam will want to familiarize themselves with the much more exotic fare of Indonesian restaurants (and their more down-market and non-rice-table-serving cousins, the speedy Surinamese/Chinese/Indonesian snack bars).

Starters include many different skewered satés of meat, which are served with either a spicy peanut sauce or a sweetened thick soy sauce; a fortifying soto ayam, a spicy chicken stew; or a loempia, a much larger take on the Chinese eggroll. Fuller meals are usually formed around bami goreng (spiced-up noodle) or nasi goreng (spiced-up rice), which are then supplemented with several ladlefuls of different spiced meats and vegetables, and hence can be regarded as one-plate "rice tables."

Vegetarians are always well served by gado-gado, a crunchy mix of vegetables (and an optional sliced egg) that is drowned in a spicy peanut sauce. Desserts are either fruity like a plate of fresh lychees, or cold like ice cream made with young coconut.

The one meal that stresses the Suriname part of Suri/Chin/Indo snack bars is the roti, the flat Caribbean-style pancake that comes with a choice of curried vegetables and meats, making perhaps the most economical of tasty meals on offer in the city.

Many of the above Indo dishes come together in the world-famous rijsttafel (pronounced rye-staffel, and translated as "rice table"). See the Close-Up Box "Indonesian Delights" on these multiplatter feasts.

onto the street on warmer days). By day, Goodies switches modes and becomes a popular café serving filling sandwiches on wedges of hearty bread, plus salads and deliciously thick fruit shakes. ⊠ *Huidenstraat 9, Western Canal Ring* ☎ *020/625–6122* ⌘ *Reservations essential for dinner* ▭ *AE, MC, V.*

Leidseplein: Center Canal Ring

Leidse "square" is the heart of Amsterdam's nightlife. Although the connecting streets are packed with middle-of-the-road restaurants, there are a number of culinary treasures to be found in and around the central canal belt.

CONTEMPORARY ✕ **De Gevulde Koe.** "The Stuffed Cow" is as friendly and socially cozy
¢–$ as its upstairs bar, "The Cow," but it's never so crowded as the skinny kitchen where sardined cooks manage to pump out wonderfully prepared dishes from an ever-changing menu that tends to favor less— strange, considering it's name—beef and more fish and ostrich (in truffle sauce!). In short: this is the ultimate in earthy Dutch eating cafés where a Yuppie is yet to be sighted. Their menu changes every day but one constant is a daily special priced at a mere €7.95. ⊠ *Marnixstraat 381, Leidseplein* ☎ *020/625–4482* ⊕ *www.cafedekoe.nl* ▭ *AE, DC, MC, V* ⊗ *No lunch.*

DUTCH ✕ **De Blonde Hollander.** In a setting of wood, candlelight, and Delft blue
$–$$ accents, "The Blond Dutchie" serves up large-portioned and well-practiced interpretations of traditional dishes. In other words: lots of chunky soups, slabs of meat, and hotchepotches of mashed potatoes with vegetables. As a bonus at this local culinary oddity, the kitchen stays open until 11:30 PM on weekends. ⊠ *Leidsekruisstraat 28, Leidseplein* ☎ *020/627–0522* ⌘ *Reservations not accepted* ▭ *AE, DC, MC, V* ⊗ *No lunch.*

CONTINENTAL ✕ **Café Americain.** Though thousands of buildings in Amsterdam are
$$–$$$ designated historic monuments, few like the Americain have their *interiors* landmarked as well. And for good reason: it's an Art Deco display of arched ceilings, stained glass, leaded-glass lamps, wall paintings, and a huge antique reading table (Mata Hari had her wedding reception here). As a hybrid restaurant-café serving everything from light snacks to full dinners, the food usually rates less "heavenly" than the interior. But the coffee and cakes are always excellent accompaniments to inhaling the singularly delicious decor. ⊠ *American Hotel, Leidsekade 97, Leidseplein* ☎ *020/624–5322* ⌘ *Reservations not accepted* ▭ *AE, DC, MC, V.*

ECLETIC ✕ **Walem.** As if ripped from the pages of *Wallpaper* magazine, this
$–$$ sleekly hip and trendy all-day *grand café* serves elegant breakfast and brunch options on crunchy *ciabatta* bread with both cappuccino and champagne on hand to wash it down. Dinnertime is fusion time, as the chefs create salads of marinated duck and chicken, crispy greens, and buckwheat noodles; or slather a roast duck with bilberry sauce and serve it with a hotchpotch of arugula. In the summer, you can relax in the formal garden or on the canal-side terrace, and late at night, guest DJs spin hip lounge tunes for an appreciative crowd. ⊠ *Keizersgracht 449, Leidseplein* ☎ *020/625–3544* ▭ *AE, MC, V.*

INDONESIAN ✕ **Blue Pepper.** One of the more widely acclaimed of recent newcomers
$$–$$$ in town, this blue-toned Indo features the inspired cooking of a chef whose
Fodor'sChoice previous restaurant won her a Michelin star. Blue Pepper will un-
★ doubtedly follow the same course towards the culinary stars since here you can just sit back and put your utter faith in any of the specials of the day (which, unlike at most other Indos, do not pile a thousand dif-

ferent dishes on your plate but rather focus on just a few obsessively prepared ones) or one of their full menus (€45–55) with bliss as your dessert. Of course, one should heighten the tongue-ballet by heeding more smart advice when ordering a bottle from their savvy selection of wines. So be warned: the price of the mains is deceiving because you will always be inspired to spend more than you planned. ✉ *Nassaukade 366, Leidseplein* ☎ *020/489–7039* ▤ *DC, MC, V* ⊙ *No lunch. Closed Sun.*

¢–$ ✕ **Bojo.** There are plenty of mediocre late-night eateries in this touristic zone, but the bambooed Bojo—although not representative of the heights of the Indonesian kitchen—does serve huge portions of enjoyable food. They have it all, from *saté* (skewered and barbecued meats) snacks to vegetarian *gado-gado* (where raw vegetables are drowned in a spicy peanut sauce) to the monumental rice table where dozens of different small side dishes are served. With your belly nicely filled, you could return to your night-frolicking, as this place is open until 1:30 AM during the week and 3:30 AM on the weekend. ✉ *Lange Leidsedwarsstraat 51, Leidseplein* ☎ *020/620 4989* ▤ *AE, DC, MC* ⊙ *No lunch.*

JAPANESE   ✕ **Wagamama.** Name seemingly to the contrary, Wagamama is no Italian restaurant run by a large-bottomed matriarch, but rather a slick and minimalist London-based chain re-creating the centuries-old traditions of Japanese ramen shops. It's noodly, fresh, fast, and fairly cheap. Just fill out a choice-rich menu and hand it to one of the waitstaff, and moments later they'll be sliding a heartening bowl of noodly goodness supplemented with your choice of meats, fish, and vegetables under your nose. Further empowerment comes in the form of fruit and/or vegetable shakes. ✉ *Max Euweplein 10, Leidseplein* ☎ *020/528–7778* ⊕ *www.wagamama.com* ▤ *AE, EC, MC, V.*

MEDITERRANEAN   ✕ **Van de Kaart.** This sub-canal-level newcomer with a restful interior $$$ blows most starred restaurants out of the water with its savvy and stylish balancing of Mediterranean tastes. Since the menu is in continual flux, cross your fingers that it may include their highly feted shrimp sausages, their octopus with a salad of couscous, basil, and black olives, or their warm polenta cake of goose liver. One can also opt for one of their three surprise menus with matching wines (€34 (+15 for wines) for three courses, €40 (+20) for four courses, and €45 (+25) for five courses). ✉ *Prinsengracht 512sous, Leidseplein* ☎ *020/625–9232* ▤ *AE, DC, MC, V* ⊙ *No lunch. Closed Sun.*

MEXICAN   ✕ **Los Pilones.** There's no sign of Tex in this very friendly Mex. In fact, ¢–$ one could wager that few Texans have the courage to try their cactus salad (even though the main ingredient is happily de-spiked) or their version of the popular Day of the Dead dish, the enchilada with mole (which also happily is more about a cocoa-based sauce than blind rodents). But all visitors are invariably charmed by the young service and the relaxing-in-the-barrio environment. And they ably pass the ultimate tests: their selection of tequilas is deliciously ample, and their margaritas have all the requisite bite and zest you could ever wish for. ✉ *Kerkstraat 63, Leidseplein* ☎ *020/320–4651* ▤ *AE, DC, MC, V* ⊙ *No lunch. Closed Mon.*

SEAFOOD   ✕ **De Oesterbar.** The Oyster Bar has long been a local institution with $$–$$$ many regulars, including the country's grand old dandy of letters, Harry Mulisch. Its Parisian-style ambience and service make a bow to legendary Atlantis, thanks to the eerily lighted fish tanks that line the walls and are refilled twice a day with dining options (a scenario that is sure to give angst to animal-lovers). Although a tad overpriced, top selections here are their oysters Rockefeller fresh from the Oosterschelde in the south of The Netherlands and/or the straight and honestly prepared catch of the day. Depending on your tastes, avoid or embrace getting booked

REFUEL AROUND TOWN

THERE ARE NO REAL FAST-FOOD CHAINS in Amsterdam, other than the ubiquitous multinationals of middle-of-the-road dining such as McDonald's and Burger King that keep popping up around town (though you can check under the listings for Soup en Zo and Bagels and Beans, both nicely spaced throughout town).

Snack bars such as FEBO are the exception by serving fries (with a stunning variety of topping options) along with a stunning variety of deep-fried meat and cheese products. Although not for the grease-adverse, their kaas soufflé (cheese soufflé) is actually quite savory and tasty, and their kroketten (croquettes with a potato and meat or shrimp melange) on a bun with mustard is always a surefire hit with kids of all ages.

Most slagers (butchers) and bakkers (bakers) supplement their incomes by

preparing broodjes (sandwiches) of every imaginable topping. Besides broodjes, tostis (grilled cheese and/or ham sandwiches), and appeltaart (apple pie), most local brown bars and cafés also serve a standard range of snacks that really come into their own when washed down with beer. Bitterballen ("bitter balls"—really just more dainty versions of croquettes), kaas blokjes ("cheese blocks," which are always served with mustard), and vlammetjes ("flame-ies," which are pastry puffs filled with spicy beef and served with Thai sweet chili sauce) all work to keep your belly happy through to dinnertime.

Coffee Company is expanding quickly—to, it is hoped, beat out the imminent arrival of Starbucks to mainland Europe and the sad development that coffee will taste the same everywhere—and provide folks on the move with their caffeine and sugar fixes.

---

into the upstairs dining room, which was seemingly designed by a 1950s bordello owner. ⊠ *Leidseplein 10, Leidseplein* ☎ *020/623–2988* ⚏ *Reservations essential* ▤ *AE, DC, MC, V.*

TURKISH ✕ **Levant.** Welcome to Istanbul Junior, where in a simple and modern
$$ setting, you can indulge in grilled meats and meze—and the appropriate firewaters to wash them down with—while your children are invariably entertained by the extraordinarily warm staff. This hidden treasure comes with an even more hidden treasure of a canal-side terrace (from which, on your way out, you can pay your respects to the bustling kitchen staff). Reservations are especially recommended. ⊠ *Weteringschans 93, Leidseplein* ☎ *020/662–5184* ⊕ *www.restaurant-levant.nl* ▤ *AE, DC, MC, V* ☯ *Closed Sun. No lunch.*

Eastern Canal Ring, Rembrandtplein & De Pijp

The eastern sector of the Grachtengordel canal ring and the nightclub-rich Rembrandtplein come equipped with some of the city's poshest restaurants. But for a less rarified air, head to the excellent and economic ethnic eateries that dot the more casual De Pijp neighborhood.

AFRICAN ✕ **Pygma-Lion.** As a major port country, South Africa has been fine-tuning
$–$$$ a fusion kitchen for the last 350 years by happily absorbing influences from not only its home continent but also Asia, Portugal, England, and The Netherlands. Hence, the menu here balances such exotic meats as crocodile, zebra (served as a minced sausage to disguise the stripes, no doubt), and antelope with a vast array of vegetarian options. They also have a long list of tasty and unique sandwiches for the lunch-hungry. ⊠ *Nieuwe Spiegelstraat 5a, Eastern Canal Ring* ☎ *020/420–7022* ⊕ *www.pygma-lion.com* ▤ *AE, MC, V* ☯ *Closed Mon.*

CONTEMPORARY ✕ **Inez IPSC.** As the final project of the late and great artist-designer-poet
$$ Peter Giele (who had made his name with the famed Amsterdam RoXY
Fodor's Choice nightclub), Club Inez stands as a hip and happening testament to a man
★ who could fuse explosive colors and heavy ornamentation into a curi-
ously soothing whole. Add to this a panoramic urban view and food as
inspired as the decor and you'll quickly understand its popularity among
clubbers, business suits, and food-lovers alike. The "international mod-
ern free-style" cooking of chef Michiel van Berge employs the freshest
of ingredients and tricks of the flavor trade from around the world. ⊠ *Am-
stel 2, Eastern Canal Ring* ☎ *020/639–2899* ⚑ *Reservations essential*
🖃 *MC, V* 𝕆 *Closed Sun. No lunch.*

$$ ✕ **Moko.** Although its patio on a scenic square is perhaps its greatest
feature, there is also something to be said for Moko's funky '70s eclec-
tic yet romantic interior, complete with fish tanks and, after 10 PM, hipster DJs. Located in a wooden church that once served as stable for
Napoléon's horses, this spot serves fresh and generally non-French classics of the world filtered through a typically Australian oh-my-God-we-
live-in-the-middle-of-Asia fusion sense. Cinnamon quail with ginger
carrot salad and pomegranate, anyone? Another option is to just drop
in for a cocktail or a lunchtime snack or sandwich after a scenic walk
in the 'hood. ⊠ *Amstelveld 12, Eastern Canal Ring* ☎ *020/626–1199*
🖃 *AE, DC, MC, V.*

CONTINENTAL ✕ **Sluizer.** Sluizer is actually a twin restaurant with a bistrolike atmo-
$–$$ sphere that serves meat on one side and fish on the other. Both areas
are simply decorated and unpretentious and are known for good food
prepared without an excess of either fanfare or creativity. Because the
prices are right and the service swift, it is crowded every night with a
predominantly business crowd. ⊠ *Utrechtsestraat 43–45, Eastern Canal
Ring* ☎ *020/622–6376 (meat), 020/626–3557 (fish)* 🖃 *AE, DC, MC,
V* 𝕆 *No lunch weekends.*

EASTERN ✕ **Aleksander.** With walls dense with knickknacks and paintings evok-
EUROPEAN ing the Balkans, this Dalmatian grill sums up the often forgotten spirit
$–$$ of this region, where hospitality and food—particularly grilled meats
and fish—reign supreme. Walking in, one is often offered a complimentary
shot of their slivovitz, a plum-based hard liquor. Unless you want to rent
the whole restaurant for a celebration, things remain fairly quiet here:
the clientele is mostly mature locals out for a quiet evening and to take
advantage of the three-course daily special for €13. ⊠ *Ceintuurbaan
196, De Pijp* ☎ *020/676–6384* 🖃 *MC, V* 𝕆 *No lunch.*

FRENCH ✕ **Breitner.** Whether for romance or the pure enjoyment of fine contem-
★ **$$$–$$$$** porary dining, Breitner gets high marks. With a formal interior of rich
red carpeting and muted pastel colors, and a view across the Amstel River
that takes in both the Muziektheater-Stadhuis (Music Theater–City Hall
complex) and the grand Carre Theater, this spot serves French-inspired
dishes, many of which pack a flavorful punch. Their seasonal menu may
include a starter of baked quail with goose liver and bacon and entrées
such as skate with Indonesian-style vegetables or smoked rib of beef with
a sauce of whole-grain mustard and marinated vegetables. Foie gras, fab-
ulous desserts, and an innovative wine list allow you to step into the realm
of pure decadence. As to be expected, the service is flawless and the pa-
trons do their part to reflect Breitner's high standards by dressing smartly.
⊠ *Amstel 212, Eastern Canal Ring* ☎ *020/627–7879* ⚑ *Reservations
essential* 🖃 *AE, DC, MC, V* 𝕆 *Closed Sun. No lunch.*

INDIAN ✕ **Balti House.** If you find yourself craving curry even though you are
$–$$ closer to Centraal Station than to the Rijksmuseum, head to Balraj; otherwise come to this excellent purveyor of Indian cuisine where dishes have

CloseUp

INDONESIAN DELIGHTS

HOLLAND'S FAMED *RIJSTTAFEL*, OR RICE TABLE, *was the ceremonial feast of the Dutch colonists in Indonesia centuries ago. Partake of a serious one and you may be confronting 36 separate platters—platters, not full dishes—so you may wish to starve yourself all day. When you sit down to face the dizzying array, put two spoonfuls of rice in the center of your plate and limit yourself to one small taste of everything. Otherwise, you're licked from the start. Restaurants provide minifeasts for a party as small as two, even one. The number of dishes usually runs a dozen to a score or more, and most restaurants offer three main choices with varying emphasis on meat, fish, or vegetables. Go with jasmine tea or beer; few wines can hold their own in this sea of flavors. If you are ravenous, go for an appetizer of soto ajam, a clear chicken broth with rice noodles, or* loempia, deep-fried rolls of bean sprouts, vegetables, and meat. After this, the staff will bring a number of hot plates, warmed by candles, to the table. The ritual of describing the dishes is a ceremony in itself. The dishes are often arranged according to their level of spiciness. Standard delights include saté, a skewer of bite-size morsels of babi (pork) or ajam (chicken), drenched in a rich peanut sauce. Gado-gado is a mix of cold, cooked vegetables, also in peanut sauce. Seroendeng, a mix of fried coconut and peanuts, or sayur lodeh, vegetables cooked in coconut milk, can help take the bite out of peppery spiciness. Daging is meat, often beef, stewed lovingly in no less than 11 spices. Bali is the name for dishes made with sambal, a red chili–based sauce with a bite, which may be used for meats and fish such as mackerel.*

---

an actual subtle variance in flavors as opposed to unsubtle variance in tongue-blistering potential. Some of their more addictive choices are any one of their soups or tandooris, the butter chicken, the garlic *nam* bread and the homemade *kulfi* ice cream. The patio's quite nice in the sunshine as well. ⊠ *Albert Cuypstraat 41, De Pijp* ☎ *020/470–8917* ▤ *AE, MC, V* ⊘ *No lunch.*

INDONESIAN ✕ **Tempo Doeloe.** For decades, this has been a safe and elegant—albeit
$$–$$$$ somewhat cramped—place to indulge in that spicy smorgasbord of the gods, the Indonesian rice table. Stay alert when the waitstaff point out the hotness of the dishes; otherwise you might stretch your wallet with the downing of gallons of antidotal *witbier* (a sweet local wheat beer). Tempo's more informal neighbor, **Tujuh Maret** (Utrechtsestraat 73, 020/427–9865), offers a cheaper but no less taste bud–tantalizing alternative (with takeout as an option). ⊠ *Utrechtsestraat 75, Eastern Canal Ring* ☎ *020/625–6718* ⌂ *Reservations essential* ▤ *AE, DC, MC, V* ⊘ *No lunch.*

ITALIAN ✕ **Segugio.** Two local and long-respected Italian chefs came together to
$$–$$$ open this temple to the taste buds. And perhaps as tribute to the ancient family recipes they brought as their heritage, they even got one of their papas to stucco the walls Venetian style to give a nice, simple, and spacious feel to the proceedings. In the summer you can have aperitifs on the patio, and in the winter you can request a table by the open fire. No matter what the season, however, foodies will love the chef's five-course menu for €48.50. But going with one main course, such as the always sublime risotto of the day, or a roasted rabbit hopped up with capers and olives, usually proves fail-safe, too. ⊠ *Utrechtsestraat 96, Eastern Canal Ring* ☎ *020/330–1503* ⊕ *www.segugio.nl* ▤ *AE, MC, V.*

JAPANESE ✕ **An.** This long-worshiped Japanese takeout has just moved across
$–$$ the street so it could score not only some space for tables but also a
license zoned to serve alcohol. After all, many of the diners here enjoy
washing down their Japanese working-class street treats with excellent plum wine (*umeshuu*). Although it focuses on sushi, An also prepares fantastic baked tofu (*atsuage*) and some super-delicious *gyoza*
dumplings. You may still choose to forgo dining in their oddly Mediterranean interior for a takeout to a nearby bench on the Amstel or within
the green expanses of Saraphatipark. ✉ *Weteringschans 76, Eastern
Canal Ring* ☎ 020/624–4672 ▭ *No credit cards* ⊗ *Closed weekends.
No lunch.*

MIDDLE EASTERN ✕ **Koerdistan.** Holland is in that part of Europe that is sadly north of
¢–$ the garlic border. Hence the Dutch are still babes in the woods when it
comes not only to spicing but also to charcoal grilling. However, Middle Easterners have been mastering grilling technology since the dawn
of time, and it really shows in this shockingly inexpensive Kurdistan grill
restaurant, where you can score a three-course meal for a mere €12 (with
a friendly lesson in Middle Eastern politics thrown in for free). Everything here is simply delicious: from the fish to the meat to the mezes.
✉ *Ferdinand Bolstraat 23, De Pijp* ☎ 020/676–1995 ▭ *DC, V* ⊗ *No
lunch. Closed Mon.*

MOROCCAN ✕ **Mamouche.** All signs of this location's past as a Hell's Angels bar has
$$ been erased with a North African teahouse vibe and an almost Parisian
delight in detail. This romantic and posh purveyor of Moroccan cuisine
was a big culinary hit—with its couscous with saffron-baked pumpkin
cited as their triumphant icing on the cake—when it opened in 2002 in
the appropriately gentrifying and ultimately "multiculti" Pijp neigh-
borhood. Chocoholics will say a heartfelt amen if they round off their
meal with the Ahram, a dark, mysterious pyramid embellished with a
nut caramel sauce. ✉ *Quelijnstraat 104, De Pijp* ☎ 020/673–6361
▭ *AE, DC, MC, V* ⊗ *Closed Mon. No lunch.*

PAN-ASIAN ✕ **Dynasty.** Although its name certainly does not refer to the soap opera,
$$$ its regular clientele of showbiz types and football heroes dangling arm
candy does sometimes resemble a casting call for a reality TV version
of that show. Hence, although it's not required, you might want to dress
up a bit. The interior is certainly fanciful: the Art Deco starting point
blurs into an Asian frenzy of rice-paper umbrellas and Buddhas. In the
summer, you should try for a table on the "dream terrace" set in a majestic Golden Age courtyard. Chef K. Y. Lee's menu, which is full of Can-
tonese, Thai, Malaysian, and Vietnamese culinary classics, is as ambitious
as the decor and bears such enticing names as Phoenix and Dragon and
Secret of the Spicy Ox. A particular success is his Drunken Prawns, and
they smartly live up to their billing: jumbo shrimps marinated in an in-
toxicating broth of Chinese herbs and Xiaoxing wine. ✉ *Reguliersdwarsstraat 30, Rembrandtplein* ☎ 020/626–8400 ▭ *AE, DC, MC, V*
⊗ *Closed Tues. No lunch.*

TEX-MEX ✕ **Rose's Cantina.** Rose's fills a sad void in the Amsterdam dining mar-
$$ ket as one of the few places serving heaps of Tex-Mex food and dare-
devil margaritas. However, connoisseurs should prepare themselves to
deem the food merely "sufficient," and those with sensitive ears should
certainly bring their own earplugs, as the noise levels careen up the deci-
bel scale. In summer you can sit in the gardens facing the backs of the
stately mansions on the Herengracht. ✉ *Reguliersdwarsstraat 38, Rem-
brandtplein* ☎ 020/625–9797 ▭ *AE, DC, MC, V* ⊗ *No lunch.*

Jordaan

De Jordaan is Amsterdam's most colorful and authentic neighborhood, so it is no surprise that it has some of the most colorful and authentic— whether Italian or Indian—restaurants. Afterward, you can order your digestive at a friendly local bar.

DUTCH
$$–$$$

✕ **Groene Lantaarn.** Traditionally Swiss, cheese fondue has long been the party dish of choice for the Dutch, and this place offers a beautiful Old World setting to enjoy this or another of many cheese delights. The menu documents fondue's evolution and infinite global variants, offering such options as the communal deep-frying of meats and the shared steaming of dim sum. Of fundamental importance: the bar is fully stocked with a variety of grease-cutting choices. ⊠ *Bloemgracht 47, Jordaan* ☎ *020/620–2088* ♠ *Reservations essential* ☰ *AE, MC, V* ☺ *Closed Mon.–Wed. No lunch.*

¢

✕ **Moeders Pot.** "Mother's Pot" does not refer to a beer-swilling matriarch (nor to your mother's lesbian lover as the local parlance would interpret it) but rather to those local old-school home-cooking recipes that deem that each meat, potato, and vegetable should rightly have the life completely fried out of it. But don't be frightened: rarely will you find such mass amounts of staple foods costing less or an interior more charmingly kitsch-addled. And since one man does all the work here, please be sensitive to the fact that he might have to rush off to flip a steak in mid-order. If you want your local cuisine served up quickly and Cultural, head here. ⊠ *Vinkenstraat 119, Jordaan* ☎ *020/623–7643* ☰ *No credit cards* ☺ *No lunch. Closed Sun.*

CONTINENTAL
$–$$
Fodor'sChoice
★

✕ **Amsterdam.** Getting here requires going west of the Jordaan, and beyond the Westergasfabriek cultural complex. Like that neighbor (which began its days as a gas factory), this spot is an industrial monument— for a century, this plant pumped water from coastal dunes. Now, under a sky-high ceiling, one can dine on honestly rendered French and Dutch dishes in a bustling atmosphere favored by families and larger groups. If it's too noisy for you, seek refuge on the peaceful terrace. ⊠ *Watertoren 6, Jordaan* ☎ *020/682–2666* ☰ *AE, DC, MC, V.*

★ $$

✕ **Café de Reiger.** This excellent neighborhood brown café ("brown" because of its ancient woody, nicotine-stained nature) has a long history— reflected in its tile tableaux and century-old fittings—of being packed with boisterous drinkers and diners. The Dutch fare is of the bold meat-potato-vegetable variety always wonderfully prepared and sometimes even with an occasional adventurous diversion, such as the sea bass tastily swimming in a sauce of fennel and spinach. At lunchtime there is a menu of sandwiches and warm snacks. ⊠ *Nieuwe Leliestraat 34, Jordaan* ☎ *020/624–7426* ♠ *Reservations essential* ☰ *AE, MC, V.*

$$

✕ **Lorreinen.** There are many nooks and crannies for the romantic-minded to hide in and a general historical ambience that fuses nicely with the evocative square on which Lorreinen is situated (and where the terrace is set up during the summer). The reasonably priced and conscientiously prepared French-based Continental menu usually plays it safe but can also surprise with a white fish smothered with fennel and served with an all-herb salsa, or a more seasonal dish that stews a venison steak to succulence with the aid of pears, endive, and red wine. ⊠ *Noordermarkt 42, Jordaan* ☎ *020/624–3689* ☰ *AE, DC, MC, V* ☺ *Closed Tues. No lunch.*

INDIAN
$

✕ **Balraj.** For a quarter of a century, Balraj has been a favorite of curry connoisseurs. People do not come for the ambience—though it's clean and certainly does not lack charm (the plastic flowers are always impeccably fresh)—but for the friendly fellows who serve unimpeachable snacks, soups, and meals from their homeland. You will break out in the happiest of sweats when indulging in the chicken Madras, which you can wash down with sweet cardamom tea. ⊠ *Haarlemmerdijk 28, Jordaan* ☎ *020/625–1428* ⊟ *No credit cards* ☉ *No lunch.*

ITALIAN ★ $$ ✕ **Toscanini.** In the heart of Amsterdam's most authentic neighborhood is a true-blue Florentine trattoria, one that is a perennial favorite with professionals and media types alike. The open kitchen, skylighted ceiling, wooden floors and tables, and the ultimately personable service all work to create a sense that you have just stepped into Grandmama's country kitchen. The cooks pride themselves on the ability to create any regional dish, but you will undoubtedly find your favorite already listed in the extensive menu. The risottos are profound, the fish dishes sublime, the desserts decadent, and the wine list inspired. What more can one ask? ⊠ *Lindengracht 75, Jordaan* ☎ *020/623–2813* ⚓ *Reservations essential* ⊟ *AE, DC, MC, V* ☉ *Closed Sun. No lunch.*

$ ✕ **Cinema Paradiso.** This former art-house cinema has been reinvented as a designer spot serving excellent starters—both their *bresaola* (an antipasto of air-dried salted beef that has been aged for two months, sliced thin, and then moistened with olive oil and lemon) and *gambas* (prawns) are manna to the tongue—which can easily form a full meal when supplemented with their pizza-oven baked bread. But for the Full Montini, you can also choose from a wide array of simple pastas and pizzas. They do not take reservations, but they do have a bar to linger at and lean on while you wait (sometimes for quite a stretch) for a table. ⊠ *Westerstraat 186, Jordaan* ☎ *020/623–7344* ⊟ *AE, MC, V* ☉ *Closed Mon. No lunch.*

SPANISH $ ✕ **Tapasbar a La Plancha.** With their tortilla and garlicky gamba prawns both being perfect, Plancha passes the standard tapas test. Indeed all their tapas rate among the best in town. You'll quickly realize, as communications invariably break down with the friendly service, that they are also the most authentic. This place is very popular with neighborhood locals and so tiny that the bull's head over the bar barely fits, but booking ahead or dropping by during a quieter time during their long hours (till 1 AM on weekdays and 3 AM on weekends) should have you squashed in no time. ⊠ *1e Looiersdwarsstraat 15, at Looiersgracht, Jordaan* ☎ *020/420–3633* ⊟ *MC, V* ☉ *Closed Mon.*

VEGETARIAN ¢–$ ✕ **De Vliegende Schotel.** The Flying Saucer has been ably probing the more tasty and inexpensive recipes of vegetarian cooking for a couple of decades now. With buffet-style ordering and an innately left-wing squatter's aesthetic, this is alternative Amsterdam at its best, one that you will grow to appreciate all the more if you wash your dinner down with some organic beer or wine. If they are full or your need for fiber occurs more around lunchtime, the more kitschy but no less vegan-friendly De Bolhoed (Prinsengracht 60, 020/626–1803), complete with patio, is but a short stroll away. ⊠ *Nieuwe Leliestraat 162, Jordaan* ☎ *020/625–2041* ⊟ *AE, DC, MC, V* ☉ *No lunch.*

Museum District & South Amsterdam

Monuments to culture, acres of lush greenery, and residences for the rich combine to make this area rich with high-end culinary favorites.

CONTINENTAL $$$ ✕ **Bodega Keyzer.** In the shadow of the golden lyre that tops the Concertgebouw (Concert Building), this institution has been serving musicians and concertgoers alike for almost a century and a recent renovation has sought to maintain this tradition. You can come at almost any hour, for either a drink or a full meal. The appropriately classical, dimly lighted Old Dutch interior—comfortable as an old shoe—is paneled with dark wood and the tables are covered with Oriental rugs. Aside from such relative oddities as *ris de veau* (veal sweetbreads) with orange and green-pepper sauce, the tournedos- and schnitzel-rich menu leans toward tradition, with a sole meunière being the house specialty. We can only hope that it maintains this tradition when it reopens in early 2004 after a long renovation. ✉ *Van Baerlestraat 96, Museum District and South Amsterdam* ☎ *020/671–1441* ▭ *AE, DC, MC, V.*

$$–$$$ ✕ **Brasserie van Baerle.** If it's Sunday and you want to brunch on the holiest of trinities—blini, caviar, and champagne—look no further than this brasserie. The elegant modern decor and the professional yet personal service attracts a business crowd at lunch, as well as late-night diners still on an aesthetic roll after attending an event at the nearby Concert Building. The imaginative chef knows how to put on an inspired show with a fusion menu that includes both light and spicy Asian salads and heavier fare such as veal tartlet with sweetbreads, tongue, and winter truffles. There is outdoor dining in good weather. ✉ *Van Baerlestraat 158, Museum District and South Amsterdam* ☎ *020/679–1532* ▭ *AE, DC, MC, V* ⊘ *Closed Sat.*

CONTEMPORARY   ✕ **Le Garage.** This former garage is now a brasserie of red-plush seating and kaleidoscopically mirrored walls—handy for local glitterati
$$$–$$$$ who like to see and be seen. This is the home of the celebrity "Crazy Chef" Joop Braakhekke, whose busy schedule of TV appearances necessitates his leaving his "kitchen of the world" in other—ironically more capable—hands. The food is invariably excellent and uses French haute cuisine as the basis on which to embrace the world. Particularly sublime is the Flemish *hennepotje,* a starter pâté of chicken, snails, and rabbit, and the Moroccan *pastilla d'anguille,* which seals a mélange of duck liver and eel in a thin pastry dough. Although champagnes, fine wines, and caviar accent the essential poshness of it all, the daily set lunch menu is quite reasonably priced. They now also have a sister establishment, En Pluche (471–4695) next door serving "global street foods" and fancy cocktails. ✉ *Ruysdaelstraat 54, Museum District and South Amsterdam* ☎ *020/679–7176* ⚠ *Reservations essential* 🔒 *Jacket and tie* ▭ *AE, DC, MC, V* ⊘ *No lunch weekends.*

ECLECTIC   ✕ **Vakzuid.** This sprawling bar-café-lounge-restaurant is in Section
$$–$$$ South of the looking-like-new 1928 Olympic Stadium, an architectural monument designed by one of the founders of De Stijl, Jan Wils. Vakzuid fits right in with its contemporary take on the functionally modern. This is indeed a space for all desires: a huge, sunny patio (accessible by water taxi) with plush comfortable seating and umbrellas; a solo-friendly bar specializing in coffee and designer sandwiches by day and cocktails and sushi by night; a comfortable lounge area with a view over the track field; and a raised restaurant section with an open kitchen and "wok bar," serving a fusion of Mediterranean and Asian cooking. Weekend evenings see this spot transform into something resembling a nightclub, complete with noise, smoke, bouncers, and DJs. Reservations are essential for the restaurant. ✉ *Olympisch Stadion 35, Museum District and South Amsterdam* ☎ *0900/825–9843* ▭ *AE, DC, MC, V.*

¢   ✕ **Bagels and Beans.** It was a truly momentous moment in culinary history when the world discovered that you don't have to be Jewish to love bagels. And this low-key, choice-rich, and always bustling hot spot is just what the Jewish doctor ordered. He would also recommend their fresh juices and fresher coffee. They also have locations at Ferdinand Bolstraat 70 in the Pijp and Keizersgracht 504 near Leidseplein, but the Museum District location wins out with its remarkably pleasant and peaceful back patio. ✉ *Van Baerlestraat 40, Museum District and*

WITH CHILDREN?

BEFITTING A CASUAL AND CHAOTIC TOWN, *children are pretty much universally welcomed in Amsterdam.*

Most eating cafés include a children's menu (and Wilhelmina Dok even goes so far as to provide scissors with their spaghetti). The industrial monument Café-Restaurant Amsterdam, the Turkish Levant, and the Chinese Nam Tin also all have a great reputation for their kid sensitivity (for all four check the listings).

Pannenkoeken (pancakes), with both sweet and savory topping options, are also a regular mainstay on the menu of both cafés and such specialty places as the Pancake Bakery (Prinsengracht 191, Jordaan, 020/625-1333), the Upstairs Pannenkoekenhuis (Grimburgwal 2, Old Side, 020/626-5603) and the Boerderij Meerzicht (Koenenkade 56, Buitenveldert,

0290/679-2744), which is an out-of-the way petting zoo and playground in the heart of Amsterdamse Bos (Amsterdam Forest).

De Taart van m'n Tante (Ferdinand Bolstraat 10, De Pijp, 020/776-4600), "My Aunt's Cake," looks like the edible set of some cult children's show, with every funky table surrounded by funky chairs and decorated with a wacky and colorful pie and cake. Quiche forms the only nonsweet option on the menu.

But certainly the most child-friendly place in town is the KinderKookKafe (Oudezijds Achterburgwal 193, Oude Zijde, 020/625-3257), a "children's cooking café," which gives Dutch-language cooking lessons during the week and then has the kids running the whole place on weekends and serving a simple, cheap and healthful fixed menu.

South Amsterdam ☎ 020/672-1610 ⊕ *www.bagelsbeans.nl* ▤ AE, MC, V ⊘ *No dinner.*

GREEK | ✕ **Griekse Taverna.** They serve no souvlaki or gyros, nor do they offer
$ | the option of plate throwing as a *digestif* like their esteemed fellow-Greek neighbors, I Kriti (Balthasar Floriszstraat 3, 020/664–445). But this woody and comfortable taverna does allure with its late hours (until midnight) and its excellent, affordable, and fresh herbed starters (€3.50/plate), which they bring to your table en masse for you to choose from. Since these easily make a full meal, you won't have to worry about choosing one of their grilled main dishes until your inevitable next visit. ⊠ *Hobbemakade 64/65, Museum District/De Pijp* ☎ 020/671-7923 ▤ No credit cards ⊘ No lunch.

INDONESIAN | ✕ **Sama Sebo.** Taking care that the incendiary level is palatable, this small,
$$ | busy, and relaxed neighborhood restaurant acts as a good, albeit not too adventurous, Intro to Indo course. Near Museumplein, for the last 30 years Sama Sebo has been dishing out *rijsttafel*, a feast with myriad exotically spiced small dishes, in an atmosphere characteristically enhanced by rush mats and shadow puppets. There are also simpler dishes such as *bami goreng* (spicy fried noodles with vegetables and meat options) and *nasi goreng* (same, but with the noodles replaced by rice). There's also a bar where you can wait, have a beer, and get to know the regulars. ⊠ *P. C. Hooftstraat 27, Museum District and South Amsterdam* ☎ 020/662-8146 ▤ AE, DC, MC, V ⊘ *Closed Sun.*

MEDITERRANEAN | ✕ **Bond.** Bond. Jan Bond. With its golden ceiling above and lush lamps,
$$ | sofas, and sounds below, Bond is equally as double-oh-so-'70s as it is comfortably experimental. Ditto for the menu, which darts from rabbit braised to perfection to steak grilled with heirloom mushrooms to

fish roasted with corn, wild parsnips, and oranges. Being close to the similarly gilded Concert Building, Bond can also be a great location for, say, a post-Rossini martini. Lunchtime sees things a tad more restrained, with choices running more along the lines of club sandwiches and decidedly non-McDonalds-like caesar salads. ⊠ *Valeriusstraat 128b, Museum District and South Amsterdam* ☎ *020/676–4647* ⊟ *No credit cards.*

$$ ⨉ **Pulpo.** This trendy hot spot suggests a simple Italian trattoria at first glance before the eyes settle on the '70s shag carpeting on the walls. The surprises continue, thanks to Pulpo's remarkable friendliness and great price/quality ratio. So, settle back, groove to jazzy tunes, and splash some Mediterranean sunshine down with a glass of fine Italian wine. The main courses are simple but always decidedly delish—few will be able to resist the signature marinated squid with *rucola* (arugula) and lime, nor will many fans of candied duck find one more quackalicious. And if you arrive before 6:45 PM a three-course, preconcert menu will set you back only €25. ⊠ *Willemsparkweg 87, Museum District and South Amsterdam* ☎ *020/676–0700* ⊟ *AE, DC, MC, V* ☺ *Closed Mon. No lunch Sun.*

East of Amstel

Head away from the historical center, east of the Amstel River, and toward the tranquil neighborhood known as the Plantage for a truly leisurely meal.

ECLECTIC   ⨉ **Plancius.** With an arty but calming interior of leather walls and pri-
★ **$$**   mary color accents, Plancius offers a refreshing sense of space after the chaos of the Artis zoo or the cramped exhibits at the Resistance Museum. After breakfast and lunch service, evenings see it emerge as a fashionable restaurant with the tables set more closely together, compounding the conviviality factor. The superb menu is adventurous, mixing and matching everything from Italian *panzarotti* (a folded-over pizza of sorts) to Indian dal-lentil soup to fish steaks with teriyaki and tahini sauce. Everything is homemade from scratch, right down to the tapenade. ⊠ *Plantage Kerklaan 61a, East of Amstel* ☎ *020/330–9469* ⊟ *AE, DC, MC, V.*

FRENCH   ⨉ **La Rive.** La Rive was once home to the Netherlands' most famous chef,
★ **$$$$**   Robert Kranenborg, who left in 2001 to open his own place in the hopes of finally getting that elusive third Michelin star (sadly, his dreams were dashed when his restaurant Vermeer went bankrupt in the summer of 2003). But all continues normally at La Rive with the former Vermeer chef, Edwin Kats, who has had no problems maintaining their two-star status. Located within the Amstel Hotel—the accommodation of choice for royalty, dignitaries, and rock stars—La Rive is the city's unparalleled purveyor of refined French and Mediterranean cuisines. The setting is chic, with views over the Amstel and formal service that is solicitous but not stuffy. If one is there purely for the food, request a spot on their chef's table. Otherwise, chubby-walleted epicureans should settle in for one of the three five-course choices on offer, priced €80, €95, and €135. Complex flavors arise out of the combining of contrasting and flown-in fresh ingredients of an often exotic nature. Terrine of Jabugo ham with goose liver and simmered beef served with oxtail jelly and Sichuan peppers is a typical starter, while main choices reflect a marked truffle fetish; in particular if they happen to be serving their much lauded turbot and truffle wrapped in potato spaghetti and served with veal sauce–stewed chard stalks. A meatier choice is their roasted rack of lamb enriched with pulverized rillettes of lamb shoulder, curry, ginger juice, and chorizo chips. To tap into this cornucopia, you'll need

to book two weeks ahead to guarantee a table. Or just opt for the hotel's more relaxed Amstel Bar & Brasserie which comes with a river-level bar, very suitable for admiring the dance of reflected colors at night. ⊠ *Amstel Inter-Continental Hotel, Professor Tulpplein 1, East of Amstel* ☎ *020/520–3264* ⓜ *Jacket and tie* ⊟ *AE, DC, MC, V* ☿ *Closed Sun. No lunch Sat.*

$$$–$$$$
Fodor'sChoice
★

✕ **De Kas.** This 1926-built municipal "greenhouse" (not to be confused with a coffee shop of the same name) must be the ultimate workplace for chefs: they can begin the day picking the best and freshest of homegrown produce before building an inspired French-based menu around them. For diners it's equally sumptuous, especially since the setting harbors two such very un-Dutch commodities as maximum light and a giddy sense of vertical space. One can also opt for the whole hog on the chef's table, which will set you back €102.50, including wine. Reservations are essential since this place was quick to chart high in the culinary orbit when it opened in 2002. ⊠ *Kamerlingh Onnelaan 3, East of Amstel* ☎ *020/462–4562* ⊟ *AE, DC, MC, V* ☿ *Closed Sun. No lunch Sat.*

$$$

✕ **La Vallade.** A candlelighted, cozy café atmosphere and revered French country cooking inspire many to take Tram 9 to this outlying restaurant on the Ringdijk, the city's perimeter dike. Every night a new four-course menu is posted, for just €30, the only constant being a diverse cheese board. A lovely terrace in the summer slightly increases the chances of being able to book a table. ⊠ *Ringdijk 23, East of Amstel* ☎ *020/665–2025* ⊟ *No credit cards* ☿ *No lunch.*

ITALIAN
$$–$$$

✕ **Sa Seada.** Named after a Sardinian dish, this slightly out-of-the-way newcomer near Ooster Park has some of the best pizza and calzone in town (including one particularly *delizioso* number with ricotta cheese) and also sports a great patio if the indoor coziness gets a little cramped. It's just a shame that European Union regulations no longer allow the importing of the famed Sardinian worm cheese. It's not only a crime against cheese plates everywhere but also prevents this place from being the ultimate in authenticity. But here we can blame the EU, and not this wonderful little treasure. ⊠ *1e Oosterparkstraat 3–5, East of Amstel* ☎ *020/663–3276* ⊟ *AE* ☿ *Closed Tues. No lunch.*

MEDITERRANEAN
★ **$$**

✕ **VandeMarkt.** "From the Market" states its intent: each course of the three- (€32) or four- (€42) course feast is made from the freshest ingredients found at the market that morning. Certainly unique for this neighborhood, the setting is sleek and up-to-the-minute trendy, with simple pine floors and tables contrasting with the eye-arresting walls of bright color blocks. Also accented is the pan-Mediterranean approach, which belies a particular respect for Morocco with the sauces often given substance with nuts and chickpeas. The menu will include anything from a lobster bisque with prawn wonton parcels to wild duck with sage sauce. ⊠ *Schollenbrugstraat 8–9, East of Amstel* ☎ *020/468–6958* ⚐ *Reservations essential* ⊟ *AE, DC, MC, V* ☿ *Closed Sun. No lunch.*

Station & Docklands

Amsterdam's historical harbor is getting the finishing touches on what is hoped to be an image-polishing boardwalk that will perhaps evolve into the city's premier entertainment zone. And naturally, many once purely industrial buildings have been transformed into dining hot spots.

AFRICAN
$–$$

✕ **Kilimanjaro.** This relaxed and friendly pan-African place serves dishes from all over the continent—including one that may well inspire the outburst from the hammier among us: "this is darn crocodilicious!"—but focuses in on the often vegetarian *enjera* pancake-based meals of Ethiopia (which you famously eat with your hands). Perfection is achieved by seating yourself on their summer patio, ordering either a *mongooza* beer (served in a calabash) or a fruity cocktail (species: exotic), and then later rounding off the meal with a freshly hand-ground Ethiopian coffee served with popcorn before taking a digestive stroll around the harbor. ⊠ *Rapenburgerplein 6, Station and Docklands* ☎ 020/622–3485 ☰ *AE, DC, MC, V* ☺ *Closed Mon. No lunch.*

CONTEMPORARY ✗**Odessa.** With its Docklands port, this floating restaurant attracts
$$–$$$ hipsters and boaties alike. Although this expat Ukrainian trawler makes you pay a pretty price for its international fusion meals, you do get a trendy and loungey '70s Bond film interior plus views of acclaimed modern residential architecture. The vibe enters overdrive in the summer when the deck is open to diners and on sporadic Sundays when they do an all-you-can-eat barbecue. Dancing begins after dark. They plan to moor a sister steamship beside the good ship Odessa by 2004 to broaden both its appeal and its seating capacity. ⊠ *Veemkade 259, Station and Docklands* ☎ 020/419–3011 ⊕ *www.de-odessa.nl* ☰ *AE, DC, MC, V.*

$$ ✗**De Oceaan.** "The Ocean" is suitably located on the city's Borneo island with an outlook over old ships. No matter if those plucky Dutch transformed this bay of seawater into a freshwater lake, sea fish still form the bulk of the ever-changing menu, which hops erratically across the globe for inspiration. You may choose to aid digestion by taking a walk along the very odd Schipstimmermanstraat (that wacky street filled with wacky modern residential architecture), as this restaurant is in the heart of a modern architecture mecca. It is also open for a less-fishy-oriented breakfast. ⊠ *RJH Fortuynplein 29, Borneo Island, Station and Docklands* ☎ 020/419–0020 ☰ *MC, V* ☺ *Closed Mon.*

CONTINENTAL ✗**Panama.** A posh pioneer in the Eastern Docklands in the harbor's
$$–$$$ former power station, Panama serves authentic dishes from around the world, with a special emphasis on fish. Although the original 19th-century industrial architecture is retained, design bureau VASD has brought the space up to date in furnishings. Plan to continue your evening in the attached nightspot, where the warm use of red, blue, and gold evokes a vision of an old-fashioned jazz club but one where the far-out programming includes genre-expanding circus acts, big bands, and tango combos. ⊠ *Oostelijke Handelskade 4, Station and Docklands* ☎ 020/311–8686 ⊕ *www.panama.nl* ⌂ *Reservations essential* ☰ *AE, DC, MC, V.*

$$ ✗**Hemelse Modder.** This bright, stylish, informal, and vegetarian-friendly restaurant is on one of the city's broadest canals and has a long-standing reputation for high quality at a great price. Patrons select from fixed-price formulas with three to five courses, costing from €23 to €28. The inspired choices show a global sweep but invariably come to rest within the borders of Italy and France. For a supplement of €6 you can tuck into one of the mountainous grand desserts, including the "heavenly mud" mousse of dark and white chocolate that gives the restaurant its name. ⊠ *Oude Waal 9, Station and Docklands* ☎ 020/624–3203 ☰ *AE, DC, MC, V* ☺ *Closed Mon. No lunch.*

★ $–$$ ✗**Wilhelmina-Dok.** Getting to this former haven dock involves seafaring—you take a fun ferry ride along the Noordzeekanaal (North Sea Canal) departing from a dock directly behind Centraal Station. Set on two levels, this cube-form, large-windowed restaurant is abuzz over the unique view back across the IJ river to Amsterdam's redeveloped docklands—a view totally unblocked when sitting at the picnic tables put out in the summer. And the changing daily menu fits the setting: rich in fish (from soup offerings to grilled choices) yet still kid-friendly enough to serve spaghetti with scissors (blunt-nosed ones, we assume). A heavily laden dessert trolley offers to energize you for the voyage back to town. The establishment also serves sandwiches and soups during the day. Note that there is ferry service every 10 minutes to IJplein in Amsterdam-Noord from Steiger 8 (Pier 8). Turn right off the ferry, follow the banks of the canal, and you will find the restaurant in five minutes. You can also take the restaurant's own boat from Steiger 9 (Pier 9), but call in advance. ⊠ *Noordwal 1, Amsterdam-Noord, Station and Docklands* ☎ *020/632–3701* 🖃 *AE, DC, MC, V* ⊙ *Closed Jan.*

WHERE TO STAY

3

FODOR'S CHOICE

Ambassade, *Western Canal Ring*

Amstel Inter-Continental, *The Plantage*

Blakes's, *Western Canal Ring*

Dikker and Thijs Fenice, *Leidseplein*

Grand Sofitel Demeure Amsterdam, *Oude Zijde*

Het Canal House, *Western Canal Ring*

Hotel de l'Europe, *Oude Zijde*

Park, *Leidseplein*

Piet Hein, *Vondelpark*

Quentin England, *Vondelpark*

Seven Bridges, *Rembrandtplein*

Seven One Seven, *Western Canal Ring*

HIGHLY RECOMMENDED

Acadia, *Jordaan*

Crowne Plaza Amsterdam-American, *Leidseplein*

Flying Pig Palace Hostel, *Vondelpark*

Hotel de Filosoof, *Vondelpark*

Nadia, *Jordaan*

Prinsen, *Vondelpark*

Prinsengracht, *Western Canal Ring*

Pulitzer Sheraton, *Western Canal Ring*

Rembrandt, *The Plantage*

Toren, *Jordaan*

Washington, *Museum District*

Many other fine hotels enliven Amsterdam. For other favorites, look for the black stars as you read this chapter.

By Jonette
Stabbert

A 17TH-CENTURY CANAL HOUSE GUEST ROOM: Late-morning sunshine streams through a drift of tulle curtains on windows set into the gray stone structure (if the ivy creepers will let you see them). Outside floats a Vermeer-worthy view of the Keizersgracht, the most elegant of Amsterdam's canals. Set a mere yardarm away from the moored boats, the hotel seems not only on—but almost literally *in*—the H_2O. After lolling under crisp sheets, the down-stuffed duvet, and a bed canopy Louis XV *à la Hollandaise,* you get ready to face the day by heading for breakfast, stepping nimbly down the steep and narrow canal-house stairway, whose bottom is too perpendicular to see. As if this is not daunting enough, the steps themselves are too shallow to rest your entire foot on—and you begin to wonder how any Dutchman can dare to ever drink too much. You enter a breakfast nook that is the epitome of *gezellig*, a term that embodies the notions of coziness, comfort, and pleasure. The table is set with ham, rolls, jams, and cheeses, and the lady serving you is as courteous as the *ontbijtkoek* (gingerbread cake) is velvety and rich.

For those who view hotels as an integral part of their travel experience—and not simply as somewhere to spend the night—it is thrilling to stay in a listed monument such as a 17th-century house, especially one furnished with antiques. These lovely gabled buildings often overlook a canal, and many have a garden out back (if not an elevator, which is considered too much of a modernization for many such historic abodes). Amsterdam has more than a fair share of such hostelries, which provide the chance to experience in the most direct way the ambience and lifestyle of the luckiest Amsterdammers. To walk down medieval passages on the way to sleep in a four-poster bed, sit down to dinner before a baronial fireplace, have breakfast on a terrace overlooking a river that has flowed through history—all these flesh out the shadows that an addicted traveler feels surrounded by on his or her journey. And, more practically, staying in a historic hotel creates a ready base for exploring the historic qualities of the Dutch capital, thus getting a head start on sizing up all that Amsterdam has to offer. But it is also true that not everyone wants to revel in the 18th century over morning coffee.

Here, too, Amsterdam comes through, as the city is equally famous for its vast array of spruce and sleek "office-for-a-day" hotels, custom-tailored for the modern business traveler. The overriding principle apparent at these havens is that everything function *exactly* as it should, in a very proper Dutch manner. Of course, because so many of them seem to have been squeezed from the same designer tube, the resulting interpretation of 21st-century functionality has a greater appeal for the Dutch vacationer than for those hailing from less historic realms elsewhere. Fortunately, there are top places such as Blake's and the Pulitzer that combine the best of the old and the new. They offer a kind of *trompe l'oeil* experience: the exteriors are historic, but their sleek interiors proffer modern sparkle and design. No matter where you stay, chances are your room was scrubbed only hours, or mere minutes, before you arrived, because nearly every Dutch hostelry can serve as Mother Hubbard's cupboard. If cleanliness is next to godliness, then Amsterdam's moteless hotels attain heavenly heights. As they should, for they have had centuries of practice. Sooner or later, most travelers to Europe pass through Amsterdam. From the Holy Roman Emperor Maximilian I to John and Yoko (who staged their famous "bed-in" for peace at the city's towering Hilton), the rich and famous have always visited this city. Today, many heads of state book into one of Amsterdam's mythically grand hotels, such as the spectacular Amstel, the newly opened Grand Amsterdam, the old-world Krasnapolsky, or the grande dame American, where all can enjoy doorknob-to-bedpost luxe. Pop stars favor the Wiechmann; literati, the Ambassade.

The larger hotels, including the expensive international chains, are clustered around Centraal Station, at Dam Square, and near Leidseplein. If you want all the mod cons and to be in the thick of things, you'll be happy staying at one of these, where stepping out the door places you in the midst of the madding crowd. But maybe all you want is a bed for the night and you don't give a hoot about the art on the walls. If you love to boogie, Rembrandtplein is where it's all happening, and you'll find a good lodging selection in the area. Want to wake to birdsong and enjoy breakfast in the garden? You'll be spoiled for choice if you are considering one of the many refined hotels around the leafy, quiet streets in South Amsterdam and its Museum District. These neighborhoods are rich in brasseries and outdoor café terraces. Enjoy a morning stroll in Vondelpark and continue on to the major art museums and the exclusive P. C. Hooftstraat shopping street, all literally minutes away on foot. Despite their prime location, the charming, small family-run hotels next to the Vondelpark are often relatively inexpensive. The Jordaan has a character unlike any other part of the city. Explore the maze of small streets and narrow canals and discover its hidden *hofjes* (almshouses/ courtyards). Hotels in this area tend to have small, cozy rooms, with staff even friendlier than elsewhere, if possible. But all parts of the city are interesting, with points of interest on nearly every corner, so even the Plantage or Oost neighborhoods (in East Amsterdam) will not be a disappointment if you stay there. Public transportation connects you efficiently and inexpensively.

All in all, Amsterdam's span of hotels befits a dowager who is 10 centuries old but growing younger every day. Like an old-timer that has grown weary but swallowed a whacking dose of pep pills, it offers home-away-from-homes that often combine the best of the old and the new. For a burst of that nostalgia of bygone grace that is somehow yet within reach, why not opt for lodgings in an archetypal canal house? Just remember to keep a steady eye, and hand, out when navigating those traditional Dutch staircases. For the nimble-footed who wants the full Dutch treatment, this need not be a deterrent; otherwise check in advance to find out if you need to walk stairs at your hotel—how many, what type, and the degree of incline. And watch out for that last step out the door; if not careful, you might end up doing a slow breaststroke.

The Canal Rings

When in Rome, you know what to do. So, when in Amsterdam, consider opting for a stay in an evocative Grachtengordel (canal ring) lodging with all the Golden Age trimmings. As for neighborhoods, these canal-side hotels are listed as either in the Western Canal Ring, which is northwest of the Golden Bend area, or the Eastern Canal Ring, which is southeast of the Golden Bend area.

$$$$ ✕▥ **Blake's.** Known for her chic London hotels, Anouska Hempel
FodorsChoice   opened this Amsterdam outpost as the city's first "designer" hotel. For
★   discerning travelers, this place has everything—even history: its stone-arch entranceway marks this as the site of the 17th-century Municipal Theater before a fire, occurring tragically in midperformance, literally brought down the house. An 18th-century canal house that replaced it long served as a poorhouse and an orphanage. The structure that then replaced the poorhouse now ranks, with its East-meets-West decor, as one of the city's most elegant buildings. The furnishings are accented with lacquered trunks, mahogany screens, modernist hardwood tables,

3

Prices

Although Amsterdam used to be fabled as one of the "bargain" cities of Europe, there are few dime-store palaces to be found. Budget travelers, backpackers, and students will all find comfortable, affordable options; most are near Centraal Station and the Dam. But for the discerning pilgrim, Amsterdam's finer hotels can have prices as altitudinal as Paris if not as legally larcenous as London's. The prices begin to verge on the shocking when you deal with the middle-tier hotels because, invariably, although the exterior can be cute and picturesque, the room furnishings are standard issue in allure. You'll get the most for your money staying at small family-run hotels in the Jordaan or around Vondelpark. In general, hotels located in the the posh southern part of town—the Museum District and Oud Zuid—and town houses alongside canals in the Grachtengordel will be expensive, but you'll be able to satisfy your daydreams of historic Amsterdam.

We always list the facilities that are available—but we don't specify whether they cost extra. For instance, although Amsterdam is a biker/pedestrian's paradise, it is a driver's nightmare, and few hotels have parking lots (and if they do, charge accordingly). In fact, cars are perhaps best abandoned in one of the city's multistory lots for the duration of your stay. Most of the pricing includes a V.A.T. (Value Added Tax) of 6%, and in some cases the city tax of 5% may be included. Many hotels operate on the European Plan (with no meals) and some on the Continental Plan (with a Continental breakfast). Breakfast (*ontbijt*) can vary from packaged juice, coffee, rolls, and butter to a generous buffet. Price categories are assigned based on the range between their least and most expensive standard double rooms in nonholiday high season, based on the European Plan (with no meals) unless otherwise noted.

WHAT IT COSTS In euros				
$$$$	$$$	$$	$	¢
HOTELS Over €230	€165–€230	€120–€165	€75–€120	Under €75

Prices are for two people in a standard double room in high season, including the 6% VAT (value-added tax).

Reservations

Pricey or not, Amsterdam's hotels get jammed to the rafters in the summer. Because of the squeeze every year brought on by the amphibious invasion of millions of tourists, you'll want to reserve way in advance from early April to late October. Bulb time (April to June) can be the thorniest period. But because Amsterdam is such a tourist mecca, reservations are advised at any time of the year. Annual conventions also fill the city for weeks in the beginning of September. Some of the hotels are very small and benefit from excellent word of mouth, so they book quickly. The Amsterdam tourist office, known as the VVV (Vereniging voor Vreemdelingenverkeer), can book hotel rooms for you in all categories if you arrive without reservations. The VVV books for everything—including tickets for tours, theater, and concerts—and the offices are ridiculously crowded in summer with all manner of visitors needing same-day booking, but it's worth waiting to get reliable referrals from the VVV.

Where to Stay in Amsterdam

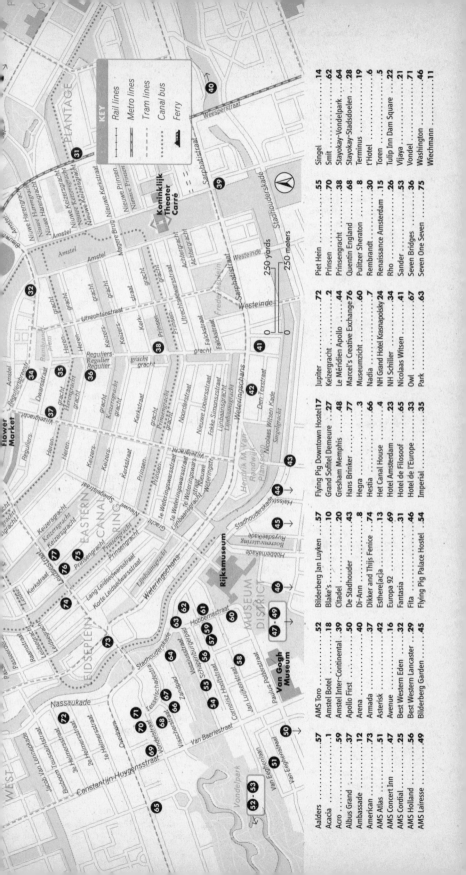

and cushy cushions in fine fabrics. One suite commands a view of the canal; other rooms overlook a central courtyard and are serenely quiet. The palette of each room exudes a Zen-like calm: gray to blue, terracotta to chocolate brown, ruby red to cream. The flow of water in the bathroom sinks acts more like a fountain than a tap. The hotel's exclusive restaurant now offers an acclaimed Asian-Western menu. All the delicious luxury on offer in this hotel is happily accented by the youthful but able service. ⊠ *Keizersgracht 384, 1016 GB, Western Canal Ring* ☎ *020/530–2010* 🖷 *020/530–2030* ⊕ *www.slh.com/blakes* ⬿ *22 rooms, 19 suites* ⚿ *Restaurant, cable TV, in-room data ports, boating, bar, meeting rooms* ⊟ *AE, DC, MC, V* ❠⊙❠ *EP.*

$$$$ ▦ **Estheréa.** On a convenient and quiet part of the Singel canal, this hotel has been run by the same family for three generations—hence, tradition and hospitality have become its chief hallmarks. Six 17th-century houses form the hotel, which was modernized without erasing the burnished sheen of the lobby, still filled with antiques, brass chandeliers, and 1930s furniture. The somewhat smallish rooms are bright white with pastel highlights in the Adamesque ceilings and doors, and each has individual features, some with clever headboards made of finely upholstered pillows hung from brass rods. The owners and staff are young, enthusiastic, and highly professional. If you can't manage to book a room with a view of the canal, you can always enjoy that view while breakfasting. There is no charge for using the Internet terminal in the lounge, where free coffee and tea are available 24 hours a day. ⊠ *Singel 303–309, 1012 WJ, Western Canal Ring* ☎ *020/624–5146* 🖷 *020/623–9001* ⊕ *www.estherea.nl* ⬿ *70 rooms* ⚿ *Room service, in-room data ports, in-room safes, cable TV, bar, dry cleaning, laundry service; no a/c* ⊟ *AE, DC, MC, V* ❠⊙❠ *EP.*

★ **$$$$** ▦ **Pulitzer Sheraton.** A clutch of 17th- and 18th-century houses—25 in all—were combined to create this rambling hotel sprinkled with landscaped garden courtyards. It faces the Prinsengracht and the Keizersgracht canals and is just a short walk from both the Dam Square and the Jordaan. The place retains a historic ambience: most guest rooms—which are surprisingly spacious compared with its labyrinth of narrow halls and steep stairs—have beam ceilings and antique stylings. An appropriately historical sound track is provided every half hour when the nearby Westerkerk chimes the time. However, a certain irreverent postmodern quirkiness is occasionally evident by the paintings, belonging to the hotel's own extensive collection, decorating the hallways, rooms, and restaurant (where a "Frans Hal" harbors such time warps as Heineken cans and cell phones). The hotel was completely refurbished in 2000 to increase comfort and convenience—for instance, heated bathroom floors mean that your toes will remain toasty. Other perks, such as a prizewinning wine cellar and a wooden boat for touring, guarantee the Pulitzer its own award: a steady stream of returning guests. Note, there are several lower-priced rooms usually available here. ⊠ *Prinsengracht 315–331, 1016 GZ, Western Canal Ring* ☎ *020/523–5235* 🖷 *020/627–6753* ⊕ *www.luxurycollection.com/pulitzer* ⬿ *224 rooms, 6 suites* ⚿ *Restaurant, café, room service, in-room data ports, in-room safes, cable TV, bar, baby-sitting, dry cleaning, laundry service, business services, some pets allowed* ⊟ *AE, DC, MC, V* ❠⊙❠ *EP.*

$$$$ ▦ **Seven One Seven.** Signed with only its house number, "717" is more like an exclusive "home away from home" than a hotel—or would be, if you happened to reside in a classical 19th-century canal-side guest house. Fusing grandeur with tasteful glamour, its designer and former proprietor, Kees van der Valk (who has since retired to warmer climes), was a fashion designer who savvily applied men's suiting fabrics as upholstery for the overstuffed armchairs and sofas. The guest rooms also reflect his discerning eye; set up as minimuseums, they are filled with classical antiquities, framed art, flowers, and objets and candles on tables and fireplace mantels. Each of the splendid suites pays homage to a different composer, artist, or writer. Breakfast can be served in the suites or downstairs in the Stravinsky Room, where coffee, tea, cakes, wine, and beer are available for the asking throughout the day and evening from the discreet but always willing help. There is an extensive DVD selection in the plush library, a setting designed after Sherlock Holmes's own heart. However, literary pursuits are perhaps best enjoyed on the lush back patio. ⊠ *Prinsengracht 717, 1017 JW, Western Canal Ring* ☎ *020/427–0717* 🖷 *020/423–0717* ⊕ *www.717hotel.nl* 🛏 *8 suites* ⚭ *Minibars, in-room data ports, in-room safes, cable TV* ⊟ *AE, DC, MC, V* ⌸ *CP.*

$$$ 🛏 **Ambassade.** Ten 17th- and 18th-century houses have been folded into
Fodor'sChoice this hotel on the Herengracht near the Spui square, whose Friday book
★ market might explain the Ambassade's popularity with book-world people: not only did Howard Norman set part of his *Museum Guard* here, but also such renowned surnames as Lessing, Le Carré, Eco, and Rushdie are known regulars. Two lounges—one of which functions as breakfast room—and the library are elegantly decorated with Oriental rugs, chandeliers, clocks, paintings, and antiques. The canal-side rooms are spacious, with large floor-to-ceiling windows and solid, functional furniture. The rooms at the rear are quieter but smaller and darker. Attic rooms have beam ceilings, providing a period atmosphere. In short: there's a room for practically every desire. Service is attentive and friendly, and if by the smallest of chances you do end up getting out of sorts, you can always seek refuge in the flotation tanks. ⊠ *Herengracht 341, 1016 AZ, Western Canal Ring* ☎ *020/555–0222* 🖷 *020/555–0277* ⊕ *www. ambassade-hotel.nl* 🛏 *59 rooms, 8 suites, 1 apartment* ⚭ *Room service, breakfast room, in-room safes, cable TV, spa, bar, baby-sitting, dry cleaning, laundry service, business services* ⊟ *AE, DC, MC, V* ⌸ *EP.*

$$–$$$ 🛏 **Het Canal House.** The owners have put a lot of love and style into this
Fodor'sChoice 17th-century (1640) canal-house hotel. It's a beautiful old home with
★ high plaster ceilings, antique furniture, old paintings, and a backyard garden bursting with plants and flowers. Every room is unique—but you can probably count on a grandmotherly quilt on the bed—in both size and decor, and there isn't a television set in sight (although, oddly for this sort of setup, there is an elevator). The elegant chandeliered breakfast room with burled-wood grand piano overlooks the garden, and there is a small bar in the front parlor. Wandering the halls is a treat. ⊠ *Keizersgracht 148, 1015 CX, Western Canal Ring* ☎ *020/622–5182* 🖷 *020/624–1317* ⊕ *www.canalhouse.nl* 🛏 *26 rooms* ⚭ *In-room data ports; no a/c, no room TVs* ⊟ *AE, DC, MC, V* ⌸ *CP.*

$$ 🛏 **'t Hotel.** On a romantic canal in the Jordaan, the small and intimate 't Hotel is in an 18th-century house. Because this is a listed monument, they aren't permitted to add an elevator. Those unable to navigate traditional steep and narrow Dutch staircases need not completely despair, as one of the apartments is only three steps down. Rooms are larger than the norm in a hotel this size. Those in the rear are especially quiet, and the top back room has a garden view. Little wonder guests return year after year. Antiques are for sale in a small shop within the hotel. ⊠ *Leliegracht 18, 1015 DE, Western Canal Ring* ☎ *020/422–2741* 🖷 *020/626–7873* ⊕ *www. thotel.nl* 🛏 *8 rooms, 1 apartment* ⚭ *In-room data ports, cable TV, some pets allowed; no a/c* ⊟ *AE, DC, MC, V* ⌸ *CP.*

★ **$–$$** 🛏 **Prinsengracht Hotel.** With vast town-house windows overlooking the houseboat-graced Prinsengracht Canal, these three 18th-century canal houses are a popular choice. When the weather is fine, it is delightful to breakfast in the hotel's garden. Guests can also choose to stay in the small "house" in the garden, a simple affair that sleeps up to four. Front rooms have a view of the Prinsengracht, and back rooms overlook the garden.

A short walk takes you to the Rembrandtplein, the Flower Market, and the main shopping area by the Kalverstraat. ✉ *Prinsengracht 1015, 1017 KN, Western Canal Ring* ☎ *020/623–7779* 🖷 *020/623–8926* ⊕ *www.prinsengrachthotel.nl* ⮡ *33 rooms, 1 garden house* ⚒ *In-room data ports, in-room safes, cable TV, bar; no a/c* ▤ *AE, DC, MC, V* ⍥ *CP.*

$ ⊡ **Armada.** The Hotel Armada offers a superb canal-side location at the corner of the Utrechtsestraat, an area of excellent shopping and dining. The rooms are simple, and some doubles can be adjusted to accommodate additional guests. Twelve of the rooms have neither bath nor shower but share facilities down the hall. The breakfast room has an aquarium, and—in 17th-century style—small Oriental carpets cover the tables. ✉ *Keizersgracht 713–715, 1017 DX, Eastern Canal Ring* ☎ *020/623–2980* 🖷 *020/623–5829* ⮡ *26 rooms, 14 with bath* ⚒ *Cable TV, bar, some pets allowed* ▤ *AE, MC, V* ⍥ *CP.*

$ ⊡ **Keizersgracht.** Appealing to youthful and budget-minded travelers, the Hotel Keizersgracht is on its namesake canal within a five-minute walk of Centraal Station. The hotel is very plain, but the staff is friendly and helpful with advice regarding your Holland itinerary. All rooms have private toilets and shower facilities, and there is an elevator. Guests gather in the downstairs bar to socialize, watch TV, and play pool, pinball, or video games. Light meals and snacks can be ordered throughout the day. ✉ *Keizersgracht 15–17, 1015 CC, Western Canal Ring* ☎ *020/625–1364* 🖷 *020/620-7347* ⮡ *26 rooms* ⚒ *Restaurant, bar; no a/c, no room phones, no TV* ▤ *AE, DC, MC, V* ⍥ *EP.*

¢–$ ⊡ **Hegra.** In a 17th-century building on the Herengracht canal, the Hotel Hegra is what the Dutch call *klein maar fijn* (small but good). Rooms are unpretentious but comfortable and the ones in front have a canal view. Not all rooms have private baths. The absence of facilities is offset by the cordiality of the family that runs the hotel, the great location (with a proximity to the Anne Frank House, shopping streets and the major art museums), not to mention the relatively gentle price tag. ✉ *Herengracht 269, 1016 BJ, Western Canal Ring* ☎ *020/623–7877* 🖷 *020/623–8159* ⮡ *11 rooms, 8 with bath* ⚒ *No a/c, no room phones, no room TVs* ▤ *AE, DC, MC, V* ⍥ *CP.*

De Pijp & Amsterdam South

Both budget and posh, the homey and the businesslike, accommodations come together in the more quiet residential neighborhoods of De Pijp and the high-toned Oud Zuid (Old South). They are set a mere 15-minute canal ride away from Centraal Station, but far enough removed from center-city crowds.

$$$$ ✕⊡ **Bilderberg Garden.** With its modern bulk looming over a tree-lined street in Oud Zuid (Old South), Amsterdam's poshest neighborhood, south of Museumplein, the Bilderberg Garden Hotel is most noted for its top restaurant, the Mangerie De Kersentuin (or Cherry Orchard). With tables therefore as important as mattresses at the Bilderberg, it is perhaps not surprising to see that guest rooms are hued culinarily: salad green, salmon pink, grape blue, or cherry red. And let's not forget the truffle-hue headboards, oyster-tone walls, and red wine chairs. Bedrooms and suites are a cossetting cocoon of Swedish woods, palm trees, thick velvet comforters, and plate glass windows, the better to enjoy this leafy and verdant district. Luxe is on offer, too: all accommodations include a Jacuzzi, bathrobes, and slippers for guests, turn-down service, fruit before bedtime, and a trouser press in every room. What is not on offer at this hotel that particularly welcomes business travelers is any sort of historic allure, but, happily, you can find plenty of that within walking distance: the Vondelpark, Concertgebouw,

the Museum District, and the elegant shops in the Apollolaan are just short strolls away. ⊠ *Dijsselhofplantsoen 7, 1077 BJ, Amsterdam South* ☎ *020/570–5600* 🖷 *020/570–5654* ⊕ *www.gardenhotel.nl* ↴ *122 rooms, 2 suites* ♢ *Restaurant, in-room data ports, minibars, cable TV, some pets allowed* ⊟ *AE, DC, MC, V* ⍥ *CP.*

$$$$ ✕⊡ **Le Méridien Apollo.** Amsterdam is often called the "Venice of the North" and situated, as it is, at the confluence of five canals, the Apollo nearly lives up to this title itself. A modernist palace framed by lovely trees and repoussoired by an enormous and gorgeous body of water, this spot offers a location that we are tempted to list as "out-of-town." Geographically, however, it is in the swank and suave Apollolaan, known for its elegant shops and within easy distance of the RAI congress center as well as the Museum Quarter. Guest rooms are luxurious and Le Méridein modern, a bit generic with lots of polished wood, bright textiles, and light accent pieces. Downstairs, the tangerine and terra-cotta-hued La Sirene offers a French-Mediterranean menu crafted by the famous Parisian chef Michel Rostang. Few can resist feasting on fish on the restaurant's beautiful canal-side terraces (higher-priced rooms also offer great views of the canals). As *un touche finale,* the hotel even has its own private marina. ⊠ *Apollolaan 2, 1077 BA, Amsterdam South* ☎ *020/673–5922* 🖷 *020/570–5744* ⊕ *www.lemeridien.com* ↴ *215 rooms, 15 suites* ♢ *Restaurant, in-room data ports, minibars, cable TV, fitness center, some pets allowed* ⊟ *AE, DC, MC, V* ⍥ *EP.*

$$$ ⊡ **Apollo First.** The big neon marquee here seems more suitable for a cinema, but inside, graciously, the interior matches the fashionable elegance of its famed throughfare, the Apollolaan. Black walls, gold trim, overstuffed chairs, and glittering chandeliers and sconces make the lobby a modern jewel box. Upstairs, you'll want to opt for a room at the back—quieter, these chambers allow you to fully savor the tranquility of the hotel's sylvan garden terrace. This is a family-run spot, presided over by the Venman family for two generations, with all the pluses that implies. A few steps out the door the chic shops start and you are also within walking distance of Museum Square. ⊠ *Apollolaan 123, 1077 AP, Amsterdam South* ☎ *020/577–3800* 🖷 *020/675–0348* ⊕ *www.apollofirst.nl* ↴ *39 rooms, 1 suite* ♢ *In-room data ports, in-room safes, cable TV, some pets allowed; no a/c* ⊟ *AE, DC, MC, V* ⍥ *CP.*

¢–$ ⊡ **De Stadhouder.** The Canalboat service stops right in front of this simple, well-kept hotel, in a century-old canal house just a few minutes' walk from the Museum District. Though facilities are limited, there is an elevator, unusual for hotels in this price category—and necessary, given the steep and narrow *trappenhuis* (walk-up) stairway. The lovely couple who own the hotel have, with their friendly dog, created a cozy atmosphere, and the delightful breakfast room is filled with blue-and-white Delft-style pottery and red flowers. There is an additional 5% charge if you pay with a credit card. ⊠ *Stadhouderskade 76, 1072 AE, De Pijp* ☎ *020/671–8428* 🖷 *020/664–7410* ↴ *20 rooms, 10 with bath* ♢ *Cable TV; no a/c, no room phones* ⊟ *AE, MC, V* ⍥ *CP.*

Jordaan

While wandering this most singular of neighborhoods, you may decide it is your most favorite of all—so why not stay in it? The bells from the Westertoren take you back in time. Sleepy little canals and narrow cobblestone streets with lopsided 17th-century houses give the Jordaan a special charm. On the surface, the neighborhood still looks very much as it did when Anne Frank lived here, although behind the weather-worn exteriors it now sports numerous fascinating boutiques and antique shops.

★ $$–$$$ ⊡ **Toren.** The historic setting for the founding of the Free University in the 17th century, this is a perfect example of a canal-side hotel. Occupying two buildings from 1638, the Toren has an evocative garden and offers every modern convenience (such as whirlpool baths in the higher-priced rooms) for both business travelers and honeymooners. A 1999 renovation gained it four-star status, but its service often exceeds even that. Family-run for several generations, the Hotel Toren is in the shadow of the Westerkerk *toren* (Western Church tower) in the Jordaan, but the "toren" is also the family name. There is a beautiful carved wooden and mirrored bar. The unique and charming garden cottage is on call to serve as a delightful bridal suite. ⊠ *Keizersgracht 164, 1015 CZ, Jordaan* ☎ *020/622–6033* 🖷 *020/626–9705* ⊕ *www.toren.nl* ↩ *37 rooms, 2 suites, 1 garden cottage* ⌂ *Room service, in-room data ports, in-room safes, cable TV, bar, elevator, some pets allowed* ⊟ *AE, DC, MC, V* ⊺⊙⊺ *EP.*

★ $$ ⊡ **Wiechmann.** A favorite with rock musicians—of both the punk (Sex Pistols) and country (Emmy Lou Harris) persuasions—the Wiechmann's main claim to fame is announced by a collection of gold records displayed in the lobby, the pride and joy of the owner, Mr. Boddy, who has run this hotel for 50 years. There are delightful personal touches throughout the lobby and adjoining breakfast room, where Mrs. Boddy's fantastic collection of teapots, toys, and antiques adds a cheerful note. The hotel seems like a maze of hallways leading through three buildings to the guest rooms (which are of wildly varying sizes). It's worth the extra money for the ones with views over the canal. Although the hotel's facilities could use some upgrading, it, along with its owners, is enchanting. ⊠ *Prinsengracht 328–330, 1016 HX, Jordaan* ☎ *020/626–3321* 🖷 *020/626–8962* ⊕ *www.hotelwiechmann.nl* ↩ *38 rooms* ⌂ *In-room data ports, cable TV; no a/c* ⊟ *MC, V* ⊺⊙⊺ *CP.*

★ $ ⊡ **Acacia.** As the Jordaan is Amsterdam's friendliest neighborhood, the small family-run Acacia is a good ambassador for the nabe, thanks to its quiet, clean, and welcoming vibe. The public rooms here are oh-so-cozy and grandmothery, but you might opt to "go native" and book one of the two self-catering houseboats moored out front. The Acacia is within walking distance of the Anne Frankhuis and the Westertoren, and is right next door to a typical Jordaan café, noted for its charming *gezelligheid*, as is, of course, the whole district, full of interesting, quirky shops offering collectibles, handmade jewelry, and antiques. ⊠ *Lindengracht 251, 1015 KH Jordaan* ☎ *020/622–1460* 🖷 *020/638–0748* ⊕ *www. hotelacacia.nl* ↩ *20 rooms (4 on houseboats), 2 apartments* ⌂ *Cable TV; no a/c* ⊟ *MC, V* ⊺⊙⊺ *CP.*

¢–$ ⊡ **Di-Ann.** Just a few minutes' walk from the Westertoren, Anne Frankhuis and the Royal Palace, this friendly family hotel is in a gorgeously historic building, replete with gable roofs, romanesque balconies, and half-moon windows. Perched above a ground floor filled with shops, overlooking the regal Herengracht, and several blocks from the hectic Dam square, the Di-Ann is right in the middle of all the action (perhaps too so: delicate sleepers should opt for a room in the rear). When you enter, you need to climb a traditional narrow, steep staircase, so the hotel is not recommended for less athletic types. Some of the attractively modern guest rooms have balconies, and those in the rear overlook a garden. Other rooms have views of the Westertoren, Royal Palace, or the canal. The breakfast room allures with crown moldings, chandelier, and flowered wallpapers. ⊠ *Raadhuisstraat 27, 1016 DC Jordaan* ☎ *020/623–1137* 🖷 *020/624–3598* ⊕ *www.diann.nl* ↩ *33 rooms* ⌂ *In-room data ports, in-room safes, cable TV; no a/c* ⊟ *AE, MC, V* ⊺⊙⊺ *CP.*

★ ¢–$ ⊡ **Nadia.** The Nadia is the sister hotel to the Hotel Di-Ann (located just down the street on the same block) and may have it one-up on its mate because this building is even more of an 19th-century architectural extravaganza, complete with kiosk corner turret, Art Nouveau-y portals, and red-brick trim. Inside, rooms are white, modern, and casual, and some have adorable views overlooking the canals (sleepers bothered by noise should opt for rooms in the rear) and framed by the building's architectural trim. The breakfast room is idyllic, bathed in a rosy orange glow, topped by a chandelier, with leafy views out the windows. Like the Di-Ann, this enjoys a great location for seeing the sights. ⊠ *Raadhuisstraat 51, 1016 DD Jordaan* ☎ *020/620–1550* 🖷 *020/428–1507* ⊕ *www.nadia.nl* ↩ *38* ⚷ *In-room data ports, in-room safes, cable TV; no a/c* ☰ *AE, MC, V* |○| *CP.*

Leidseplein

It can be noisy in the city's busiest square, but then again sometimes it pays to be centrally located.

★ $$$$ 🏨 **Crowne Plaza Amsterdam-American.** Housed in one of the city's most fancifully designed buildings—one that is said to form the missing link between Art Nouveau and the Amsterdam School—the American (the name everyone knows it by) is a beloved Amsterdam landmark. Directly on Leidseplein, this 1902 castlelike structure is an agglomeration of Neo-Gothic turrets, Jugenstil gables, Art Deco stained glass, and an Arts & Crafts clock tower. Gloriously overlooking the Singelgracht canal (one reason why the hotel has its own boat landing), this place is a charmer. As for location, it is in the middle of everything—nightlife, dining, sightseeing, and shopping are all at hand. Guest rooms are sizable, bright, and furnished in a modern Art Deco style, and you have a choice between canal and bustling-square views—the latter option having the bonus of small balconies. The hotel entered the new millennium under new ownership and has been upgraded—sort of: readers report some rooms with leaky air-conditioning and dysfunctional heating. The decor at the overpriced and sometimes snooty (readers report) Café Americain is one of the finest in Amsterdam, with original Art Deco lighting fixtures, and murals from 1930 depicting *A Midsummer Night's Dream*. Newlyweds might want to indulge in the Mata Hari Honeymoon Suite, named after the spy fatale who celebrated her own wedding here. ⊠ *Leidsekade 97, 1017 PN, Leidseplein* ☎ *020/556–3000* 🖷 *020/556–3001* ⊕ *www.amsterdam-american.crowneplaza.com* ↩ *174 rooms, 11 suites* ⚷ *Restaurant, room service, in-room data ports, cable TV, gym, sauna, 2 bars, dry cleaning, laundry service, meeting rooms* ☰ *AE, DC, MC, V* |○| *EP.*

$$$$ 🏨 **Park.** At first glance, the Park looks like everyone's dream of a grand
FodorsChoice Netherlandish hotel, topped out by a picturesque pepper-pot tower, its
★ 18th-century building set with regal windows, topped off by a roof aflap with colorful flags, and mirrored charmingly in the Singel river. Then you note that although this stately Amsterdam fixture has one foot in history, the other is firmly entrenched in today, thanks to a 1950s wing, guest rooms done up with Le Meridien's traditional-but-modern luxe (cozy colors, swagged curtains, bright patterned bedspreads), and amenities that business travelers love. If the neon lights of Leideplein's shops, casino, and clubs are around the corner, the sylvan glades of Amsterdam's gorgeous Vondelpark are just across the road, beckoning you to take an early morning jog. Convenience is another plus for the Park: major art museums are within walking distance and you can also take a canal boat tour from the mooring a few feet away. Of course, the best views are reserved for the hotel's higher-priced rooms. Some, but not all rooms, have air-conditioning and minibars. ⊠ *Stadhouderskade 25, 1071 ZD Leidseplein* ☎ *020/671–1222* 🖷 *020/664–9455* ⊕ *www.lemeridien.com* ↩ *181 rooms, 6 suites* ⚷ *Restaurant, cable TV, hair salon, bar, baby-sitting, dry cleaning, laundry service, some pets allowed* ☰ *AE, DC, MC, V* |○| *EP.*

$$$–$$$$ ▣**Dikker and Thijs Fenice.** "Lavish," "classical," and "cozy" are some
Fodor's Choice of the adjectives typically used to describe this hotel, which has a regal
★   address on the Prinsengracht canal. The hotel, first opened as a shop
in 1895, has been renowned for fine dining since its founder, A. W.
Dikker, entered into a partnership in 1915 with H. Thijs, who had ap-
prenticed with the famous French chef Escoffier. The busy location—
happily, all the majestic sash windows are double-glazed—is convenient
to the major shopping areas and one block from the Leidseplein,
nightlife center of the city. The Art Deco–style rooms are fully mod-
ernized, and the hotel underwent a complete renovation in 2001. Of
the upper-price hotels, this is one of the few that includes breakfast
in the basic room rate. ⊠ *Prinsengracht 444, 1017 KE, Leidseplein*
☎ *020/620–1212* 🖷 *020/625–8986* 🌐 *www.dtfh.nl* ⟋ *42 rooms*
⚴ *Restaurant, room service, in-room data ports, cable TV, bar, baby-
sitting, laundry service, business services, some pets allowed; no a/c*
🖃 *AE, DC, MC, V* ⦿|⦿ *CP.*

$ ▣**Marcel's Creative Exchange Bed & Breakfast.** How would you like to
stay in a renovated 17th-century home decorated with fine antiques and
original works of art, located in the heart of the city and all for a sweetly
gentle price? The owner is fascinating, with mucho worldwide artistic
connections and will share his information about the city and the art
scene like a personal mentor. Yes, this is all possible, but the catch is
that you have to be interesting enough to pass muster—exclamation
point—with the host. Internationally renowned artist/designer Marcel
van Woerkom has been renting rooms in his house since 1970 and has
since hosted royalty, travelers, and artists from a variety of disciplines.
All guests surely drool over the moderne interiors with their furniture
from Charles and Ray Eames, Alvar Alto, Philippe Starck, and Marcel
Breuer. Because of the location on the Leidsestraat next to De Uitkijk,
Amsterdam's oldest existing art cinema (Marcel is one of the owners),
you're right in the thick of things and can watch the city from a bal-
cony. ⊠ *87 Leidsestraat, 1017 NX, Leidseplein* ☎ *020/622–983* 🌐 *www.
marcelamsterdam.com* ⟋ *4 rooms* ⚴ *Cable TV; no a/c* 🖃 *V* ⦿|⦿ *EP.*

$ ▣**Nicolaas Witsen.** If you're just looking for a place to hang your hat
and get a quiet night's sleep, the Nicolaas Witsen is a good choice. Run
by the same affable family for two generations, the redbrick-and-white-
trim hotel is on a peaceful street within walking distance of the Ri-
jksmuseum and the Heineken Brewery. Windows let in lots of light
onto the standard-issue guest rooms, your usual array of white walls,
Swedish-wood furniture, and modern bathrooms. The breakfast room
is cheery, and there is a family room that sleeps up to four people. ⊠ *Nico-
laas Witsenstraat 4, 1017 ZH Leidseplein* ☎ *020/623–6143* 🖷 *020/620–
5113* 🌐 *www.hotelnicolaaswitsen.nl* ⟋ *29* ⚴ *In-room data ports,
cable TV; no a/c* 🖃 *AE, MC, V* ⦿|⦿ *CP.*

¢   ▣**Hans Brinker.** It may be housed in a brick building that was a monastery
about half a century ago, but no one comes here any longer to get reli-
gion. The rooms are no-frills but sparkling clean, with white walls and
blue floors. The dorms have bunk beds, the private rooms have bath-
room facilities. As basic as it all is, it's never boring. You can boogie in
the disco, drink at the bar, enjoy incredibly cheap meals (guests only)
in the restaurant and surf the 'net on one of the hostel's three comput-
ers. From five to six, you'll find your fellow backpackers guzzling beer
in the bar during Happy Hour. And it's all "happening" at Leidseplein,
just around the corner. What more could you want? ⊠ *Kerkstraat 136,
1017 CR, Leidseplein* ☎ *020/622–0687* 🖷 *020/638–2060* 🌐 *www.
hansbrinkerhotel.com* ⟋ *6 rooms, 5 dormitories* ⚴ *Restaurant, bar; no
phones, no a/c, no room TV* 🖃 *MC, V* ⦿|⦿ *CP.*

Museum District & Vondelpark

If you came to Amsterdam for its reputation as the city of the arts, then convenience and tastes dictate that you book a room in this quarter. With the city's top museums located here—and the priciest shopping area just around the corner—plus the city's sylvan Vondelpark situated just to the west, it is little wonder that this entire area has been colonized by fine hotels.

$$$$ ☐**Gresham Memphis.** Classically proportioned, mansard-roofed, and ivy-covered—what more do you want from an Amsterdam hotel facade? This elegant, exceptionally spacious hotel was once the private residence of Freddy Heineken, of brewery fame. Formerly decorated in a classical style, the entire hotel was renovated in 2003 to give it a fresh, modern, and airy look, so if you want Vermeer, look elsewhere. But the new design is energizing, not to say empowering (lots of businesspeople stay here): the breakfast room is bright and welcoming, the bar-lounge is sleek contempo, the guest rooms modern and tranquil. As formal but not as expensive as the deluxe hotels, and embraced by a serene residential neighborhood, the Memphis is near the Concertgebouw. Extra beds are available, and children under 12 are welcome at no additional charge. The large bar has comfortable armchairs and tables and serves light meals as well. ⊠ *De Lairessestraat 87, 1071 NX, Museum District* ☎ *020/673-3141* 📠 *020/673-7312* ⊕ *www.gresham-hotels.com* 🛏 *74 rooms* ⟁ *Cable TV, gym, bar, dry cleaning, laundry service, no-smoking rooms* ☰ *AE, DC, MC, V* � *EP.*

$$$$ ☐**Vondel.** On a quiet street next to Vondelpark and very close to the Leidseplein, this hotel is refined and contemporary. The lobby and bar, all beige and light wood, are filled with comfortable suede sofas, sunlight, and flowers. The similarly colored rooms, generous in size, are enhanced with flashes of crimson, while a small garden terrace makes for a verdant oasis. Suites are on the top floor and have large windows that follow the shape of the roof and give you a scenic swoop of the neighborhood. Throughout the hotel are paintings by Amsterdam artist Peter Keizer. The hotel, like the park, gets its name from the 17th century poet, Joost van den Vondel, and the rooms are named after his poems. A lavish breakfast buffet is available, but is not included in the rate. ⊠ *Vondelstraat 28–30, 1054 GE, Vondelpark* ☎ *020/612–0120* 📠 *020/685–4321* ⊕ *www.hotelvondel.nl* 🛏 *67 rooms, 3 suites* ⟁ *Room service, in-room data ports, in-room safes, minibars, cable TV, bar, baby-sitting, dry cleaning, laundry service, business services* ☰ *AE, DC, MC, V* aÌ *EP.*

$$$-$$$$ ☐**AMS Lairesse.** Small and refined, in cherry brick and white trim, the AMS Hotel Lairesse is within walking distance of the Concertgebouw and the major art museums, as well as a large selection of good restaurants and trendy brasseries. Because of its proximity to the Concertgebouw, the paintings on the walls are music-related. The Vondelpark is very nearby, but you can enjoy your own little piece of private heaven in the hotel's tranquil Japanese garden. Rooms are attractively furnished and are light and airy. ⊠ *De Lairessestraat 7, 1071 NR Museum District* ☎ *020/671–9596* 📠 *020/671–1756* ⊕ *www.ams.nl* 🛏 *34 rooms* ⟁ *Room service, in-room safes, cable TV, laundry service* ☰ *AE, DC, MC, V* aÌ *CP.*

$$$-$$$$ ☐**AMS Toro.** In a prim and proper 19th-century-style villa on the southern border of Vondelpark, this hotel offers a relaxing atmosphere. The views of the park and a small lake, and an interior tastefully dotted with antiques, oil paintings, and chandeliers provide a special homelike environment that is rare in Amsterdam. Rooms are bright and spacious, and some have balconies. Set near the area of the park far from the museum quarter and its shops, slightly outside the city center in a chic residential area, the hotel is, nevertheless, convenient to tram lines and lends itself to a lovely stroll through the park from the heart of Amsterdam— that is, if you ever become motivated to leave. ⊠ *Koningslaan 64, 1075 AG, Vondelpark* ☎ *020/673–7223* 🖷 *020/675–0031* ⊕ *www.ams.nl* 🛏 *22 rooms* ♧ *In-room safes, cable TV, bar, laundry service; no a/c* ⊟ *AE, DC, MC, V* ⑩ *CP.*

★ **$$$–$$$$** 🖭 **Bilderberg Jan Luyken.** This small, formal, and stylish town house hotel is nicely located for those who want a subdued environment complete with peaceful garden and restrained Art Nouveau stylings. Located in a trio of quaint 19th-century five-story town houses, its exterior is fitted out with wrought-iron balconies, cute gables, and the usual ugly roof extension. The keynote of the interior decor is *Wallpaper*-modern—tripod lamps, "paper" steel ashtrays, Knoll-ish chairs—but every so often a blast from the past is sounded, as in the main salon's faux-baronial fireplace. Guest rooms can be on the snug side, and service and housekeeping leave a bit to be desired, according to some readers. The hotel is nestled among homes and offices in a 19th-century residential neighborhood yet is just one block away from the Museumplein and fashionable shopping streets—perhaps this explains its popularity with musicians in town to play the nearby Concertgebouw. The personal approach is a relaxing alternative to the large business hotels, but the Jan Luyken is itself well equipped to handle the needs of the business traveler. There is a lovely little "relaxation" room with a tanning lounge, Turkish bath, and hot tub. The hotel's trendy bar, Wines and Bites, serves high-quality wine along with snacks and lunches. ⊠ *Jan Luykenstraat 58, 1071 CS, Museum District* ☎ *020/573–0730* 🖷 *020/676–3841* ⊕ *www.janluyken.nl* 🛏 *62 rooms* ♧ *Room service, in-room data ports, in-room safes, cable TV, bar, dry cleaning, laundry service, business services, some pets allowed* ⊟ *AE, DC, MC, V* ⑩ *EP.*

$$–$$$ 🖭 **AMS Atlas.** Set just a block from Amsterdam's green-lung Vondelpark, the Atlas, housed in a quaint Art Nouveau mansion, is renowned for its personal, friendly, and generally relaxing atmosphere and discreetly blends into its well-to-do residential area. Despite the hotel being within easy walking distance of the museums, the convivial nature of its lounge-bar-restaurant seems to exert a holding suction effect on many of the guests. ⊠ *Van Eeghenstraat 64, 1071 GK, Vondelpark* ☎ *020/676–6336* 🖷 *020/671–7633* ⊕ *www.ams.nl* 🛏 *23 rooms* ♧ *Restaurant, cable TV, bar, laundry service; no a/c* ⊟ *AE, DC, MC, V* ⑩ *CP.*

$$–$$$ 🖭 **AMS Concert Inn.** The AMS Hotel Concert Inn is across from the glorious Concertgebouw and offers simple, basic accommodations. The rooms are immaculate; most are at the back of the hotel and thus easy on the ears, with blackout blinds offering rest for your eyes as well. For longer stays there are rental apartments equipped with kitchenettes and fax machines. There is a large, lush Japanese-style garden where guests can lounge or enjoy a traditional Dutch breakfast. Bicycles are also handily available for rental. ⊠ *De Lairessestraat 11, 1071 NR, Museum District* ☎ *020/305–7272* 🖷 *020/305–7271* ⊕ *www.ams.nl* 🛏 *28 rooms, 6 apartments* ♧ *Cable TV, laundry service; no a/c* ⊟ *AE, DC, MC, V* ⑩ *CP.*

★ **$$** 🖭 **Prinsen.** Architect of the Rijksmuseum and Centraal Station, P. H. H. Cuijpers created several of the city's stateliest landmarks, but he rarely came up with such an adorable edifice as this one, built around 1870. Chalet roof, dormers, bay window, jigsaw trim, neoclassical columns, and sculpted reliefs of cats (one showing a kitty chasing mice) all enchant the eye. The storybook feeling, sadly, ends with one foot in the door. Although it has been gutted and renovated, however, the Prinsen has lots of cheery and gracious bedrooms. On the ground floor, the yellow breakfast room is made even brighter by opening up on a lovely garden. Set on a quiet street next to the Vondelpark, the hotel makes all its guests very welcome and is particularly gay-friendly. ⊠ *Vondelstraat 36–38, 1054 GE, Vondelpark* ☎ *020/616–2323* 🖷 *020/616–6112* ⊕ *www.prinsenhotel.demon.nl* ↩ *45 rooms* ⌂ *In-room data ports, in-room safes, cable TV, bar, dry cleaning, laundry service, babysitting, some pets allowed; no a/c* ☐ *AE, DC, MC, V* |◯| *CP.*

$$ ▦ **Smit.** Despite its location, at the foot of the exclusive PC Hooftstraat and south entrance to the Rijksmuseum, this hotel is anything but pretentious. It's a lively and friendly place and a good choice for those who want to enjoy the Leidseplein nightlife. The neighboring restaurant is open for lunch and snacks but closes at 6 PM. The rooms are very plain and the recently remodeled bathrooms are relatively spacious. Some of the rooms facing the tram lines are less quiet. ⊠ *P. C. Hooftstraat 24–28, 1071 BX, Museum District* ☎ *020/671–4785* 🖷 *020/662–9161* ⊕ *www.hotelsmit.com* ↩ *63 rooms* ⌂ *Restaurant, cable TV, some pets allowed; no a/c* ☐ *AE, DC, MC, V* |◯| *CP.*

$–$$ ▦ **Aalders.** Occupying a cozy, grandmotherly town house, this busy little hotel has reasonably sized rooms with large windows on a quiet street. All rooms have shower or bath, and computers can be connected to the telephone lines with an adapter that the hotel does not provide. All the double rooms have twin beds. Breakfast is served in a large and beautiful second-floor room. ⊠ *Jan Luykenstraat 13–15, 1071 CJ, Museum District* ☎ *020/662–0116* 🖷 *020/673–4698* ⊕ *www.hotelaalders.nl* ↩ *28 rooms* ⌂ *Cable TV, bar; no a/c* ☐ *AE, DC, MC, V* |◯| *CP.*

$–$$ ▦ **AMS Holland.** You would expect to find expensive luxury hotels here, to match the elegance of the P. C. Hooftstraat, the most exclusive shopping street in Amsterdam, yet the Holland is unpretentious and appeals to budget travelers. Set in a cookie-cutter bland building, this place is not far from the Stedelijk museum, Rijksmuseum, and Van Gogh Museum, as well as the Vondelpark (which can be viewed from the breakfast room). The many club pennants displayed on the walls of the bar show that football fans like to stay here. ⊠ *P. C. Hooftstraat 162, 1071 CH, Museum District* ☎ *020/676–4253* 🖷 *020/676–5956* ⊕ *www.ams.nl* ↩ *62 rooms* ⌂ *Cable TV, laundry service; no a/c* ☐ *AE, DC, MC, V* |◯| *CP.*

$–$$ ▦ **Fita.** The couple who run the Hotel Fita, Mr. and Mrs. de Rapper, place an emphasis on the spic-and-span. Therefore, this peaceful hotel, which is set in a gracious, turn-of-the-20th-century, five-story townhouse, is not only dustless but is off-limits to smokers. As though they were members of the family, guests are served Mrs. Rapper's fresh-baked bread and homemade jam, along with freshly squeezed orange juice, at the buffet breakfast. Another plus: you won't be charged for telephone calls within Europe and to the United States. The Rijksmuseum, Van Gogh Museum, Stedelijk Museum, and Concertgebouw are literally around the corner. ⊠ *Jan Luykenstraat 37, 1071 CL, Museum District* ☎ *020/679–0976* 🖷 *020/664–3969* ⊕ *www.fita.nl* ↩ *16 rooms* ⌂ *Elevator, in-room safes, cable TV, dry cleaning, laundry facilities, some pets allowed; no a/c* ☐ *AE, DC, MC, V* |◯| *CP.*

$–$$ ▦ **Hestia.** Located on a street of extraordinary 19th-century houses, the Hestia is parallel to Vondelpark and close to the Leidseplein. Fitted out with red brick, white trim, and a mansard-cute roof, the Hestia is family-operated, with a helpful and courteous staff, and is the kind of place that reinforces the image of the Dutch as a clean and orderly people. The hotel's breakfast room has a view of the garden, and a large family room has a charming sitting area in a bay window with stained glass, which also overlooks the garden. The rooms are basic, light, and simply modern. Four of the rooms are very small, but so is their cost. Larger rooms can be adjusted to accommodate parties of four or five.

✉ *Roemer Visscherstraat 7, 1054 EV, Vondelpark* ☎ *020/618–0801* 🖷 *020/685–1382* 🌐 *www.hotel-hestia.nl* ➦ *18 rooms* ♿ *In-room safes, cable TV, some pets allowed; no a/c* 🚫 *AE, DC, MC, V* ⊙ *CP.*

★ **$–$$** ⊡ **Hotel de Filosoof.** Looking for something a little bit different? How about bona fide Amsterdam philosophers, regularly to be found ensconced in this hotel's comfy armchairs. It turns out the Filosoof hosts monthly lectures and discussion evenings for the locals and guests, many of whom are, needless to say, artists, writers, and even thinkers. Even the decorator gets into the act: each of the guest rooms is decorated with a different cultural or ideological motif, from Zen to feminism. There is an Aristotle room furnished in Greek style, with passages from the works of Greek philosophers hung on the walls, and a Goethe room adorned with Faustian texts. Some of the rooms are a little silly—the Walden, for instance, sports some landscape daubs on the wall—but the Spinoza is a total knock-out: an homage to Golden Age style, complete with black-and-white floors, 19th-century library lamp, and framed paintings, it is a jewel that fancier hotels in town could well take as a model. Enjoy breakfast, or merely relax, in the large garden. ✉ *Anna van den Vondelstraat 6, 1054 GZ, Vondelpark* ☎ *020/683–3013* 🖷 *020/685–3750* 🌐 *www.hotelfilosoof.nl* ➦ *38 rooms* ♿ *In-room data ports, cable TV, library; no a/c* 🚫 *AE, MC, V* ⊙ *CP.*

$–$$ ⊡ **Piet Hein.** Not all chocolates have a gooey center. When in 2003 it
FodorśChoice came time to refurbish this ornate brick Vondelpark mansion, the own-
★ ers decided to go for the modern, the light, the airy, the less-is-not-a-bore, and they have gorgeously succeeded. Salons don't come any sleeker than these, thanks to cube-shape chairs, straight-as-an arrow sofas, gleaming Swedish woods, sisal-like carpeting, white-on-white hues, and bright bursts of navy blue, perhaps in homage to Piet Hein, the legendary 17th-century Dutch privateer and vice admiral. Other maritime touches include paintings of sailing ships, navy blue carpets with patterns of seaman's knots, and cozy rooms that make you feel like you're in a ship's cabin. Some bedrooms here are so sprightly done up you will feel ten years younger. Real color lies outside the windows, as front rooms here have fine views of the park (always in demand—even booking far in advance doesn't guarantee you one of these rooms). Those in the back aren't out of luck, as a garden allures at the rear. Here, too, is a *dépendance* annex with additional rooms. Step out the front door and you are within walking distance of the fashionable P. C. Hooftstraat, the Concertgebouw, and the city's major art museums. And making this place even more popular with the *Wallpaper* crowd are the relatively gentle room rates. ✉ *Vossiusstraat 52–53, 1071 AK Museum District* ☎ *020/662–7205* 🖷 *020/662–1526* 🌐 *www.hotelpiethein.com* ➦ *61 rooms* ♿ *In-room data ports, in-room safes, cable TV, bar, dry cleaning, laundry service* 🚫 *AE, DC, MC, V* ⊙ *CP.*

★ **$–$$** ⊡ **Washington.** This small hotel is set a discreet stone's throw from the Museumplein and often attracts international musicians in town to perform at the nearby Concertgebouw—except perhaps those carrying a cello (there's a steep staircase here). The owners are helpful and will lend from their collection of guidebooks. The breakfast room and lounge are filled with antiques and marvelous brass chandeliers, and the hotel is meticulously polished and sparkling clean. The rooms are simply and charmingly decorated in white and pastel shades. Large windows let in a flood of light. The apartments consist of four rooms and even contain a piano. ✉ *F. van Mierisstraat 10, 1071 RS, Museum District* ☎ *020/679–6754* 🖷 *020/673–4435* 🌐 *www.hotelwashington.nl* ➦ *17 rooms, 4 apartments* ♿ *Cable TV; no a/c* 🚫 *AE, DC, MC, V* ⊙ *CP.*

$ ⊡ **Acro.** This is a simple, clean, and pleasant tourist hotel, with a friendly staff. The hotel, with a light slate-blue interior, is geared to the leisure traveler and can accommodate up to four in a room. There is a breakfast room and the 24-hour bar serves snacks. The bar has been redecorated to resemble a traditional Dutch "brown café." You can buy postcards and newspapers at the desk. ✉ *Jan Luykenstraat 44, 1071 CR, Museum District* ☎ *020/662–5538* 📠 *020/675–0811* 🌐 *www.acro-hotel.nl* ⇆ *65 rooms* ◊ *Cable TV, bar, some pets allowed* ▭ *AE, DC, MC, V* 🍴 *CP.*

$ **Europa 92.** You can't miss the Europa: it has a neon sign nearly larger than its four-story house. Within easy walking distance of the Vondelpark and the elegant shopping street P. C. Hooftstraat, this family-run hotel has a lovely garden, which you may wish to escape to after realizing that the No. 1 tram passes the front—be sure to opt for the quieter rooms at the back, two of which contain small kitchenettes and provide a garden view. ✉ *1e Constantijn Huygenstraat 103–105, 1054 BV Vondelpark* ☎ *020/618–8808* 📠 *020/683–6405* 🌐 *www.europa92.nl* ⇆ *47 rooms* ◊ *In-room data ports, in-room safes, cable TV, bar, some pets allowed* ▭ *AE, DC, MC, V* 🍴 *CP.*

★ $ **Museumzicht.** When they call themselves "Museum View," they mean it: the hotel is directly across the street from the Rijksmuseum. The owner formerly had an antiques shop, so the house is filled with wonderful objects. The breakfast room–lounge is special, with a Murano glass chandelier and Art Deco pottery on the chimney walls. The rooms are simple but delightful, with pastel-striped wallpaper and little etchings. The hotel is on the top floors of the building, and guests must climb a narrow and steep stairway with their luggage to the reception desk and to the rooms—the owners highly recommend traveling light. ✉ *Jan Luykenstraat 22, 1071 CN, Museum District* ☎ *020/671–2954* 📠 *020/671–3597* ⇆ *14 rooms, 3 with shower* ◊ *In-room data ports; no a/c* ▭ *MC, V* 🍴 *CP.*

$ **Owl.** Architecturally aflutter with white-trimmed turret, mansard roof, and bay windows, this friendly, family-run hotel is on charming Roemer Visscherstraat. In the entrance, in fact, is an architect's elevation drawing from the turn of the 20th century showing the original facade of what is now the hotel with its two adjoining houses. Inside, all is rather dispiritingly standard issue, so all eyes are quickly drawn to the lounge's glass showcase, filled with a collection of owls, all sent as gifts to the family from satisfied guests. From the back garden, you can keep your eye out for the parrots that fly free in the adjoining Vondelpark (and maybe even an owl or two). ✉ *Roemer Visscherstraat 1, 1054 EV, Vondelpark* ☎ *020/618–9484* 📠 *020/618–9441* 🌐 *www.owl-hotel.nl* ⇆ *34 rooms* ◊ *Room service, in-room data ports, cable TV, bar, babysitting, dry cleaning, laundry service; no a/c* ▭ *AE, DC, MC, V* 🍴 *CP.*

$ **Quentin England.** The intimate Quentin England is one of a series of adjoining buildings dating from 1884, each of which is built in an architectural style of the country whose name it bears. A connoisseur's delight—adorned with a Tudor gable and five-step gable—the Quentin occupies the England and Netherlands buildings. Rooms are simple and vary greatly in size but are cozy and clean. The tiny breakfast room is particularly enchanting, with flower boxes on the windowsills, dark-wood tables, and fin-de-siècle decorations. Behind the reception desk is a small bar and espresso machine (perhaps on loan from the neighboring Italian building?). The hotel offers tremendous character and attention in place of space and facilities. There is an additional 5% fee for using a credit card. ✉ *Roemer Visscherstraat 30, 1054 EZ, Vondelpark* ☎ *020/689–2323* 📠 *020/685–3148* 🌐 *www.quentinhotels.com* ⇆ *50 rooms* ◊ *Cable TV; no a/c* ▭ *AE, DC, MC, V* 🍴 *EP.*

Fodor'sChoice ★

$ **Sander.** Inexpensive, and fortunate in having a good location for museum-going, the Hotel Sander offers rooms best described as traditionally Dutch: comfortable and simple. Seating areas in window bays give some rooms additional charm. The bar and breakfast room open out onto a garden. The hotel is also particularly gay-friendly. ✉ *Jacob Obrechtstraat 69, 1071 KJ, Museum District* ☎ *020/662–7574* 🖷 *020/ 679–6067* ⊕ *www.hotel-sander.nl* 🗗 *20 rooms* ♿ *In-room safes, cable TV, bar; no a/c* ⊟ *AE, MC, V* 〶 *CP.*

★ ¢–$ 🏨 **Flying Pig Palace Hostel.** For those backpackers who like to chill out, have their Simpsons done up in psychedelic pink hair (as a wall mural here attests), and save a load of money, the Pig Palaces—there is one in the city center and another in the posher neighborhood of Vondel-park—are the favored choice of "piggies" everywhere. The Flying Pig Downtown is a bit frantic, so why not opt for the Pig near the park and steps away from the Museum District? The policy is strict: if you're not a backpacker aged 18 to 35, look elsewhere. Not only breakfast and sheets are included in the price, but also free Internet and e-mail service and the use of in-line skates (so lace up and explore the park, or join the once-weekly night skate throughout the city). It gets even better: the downstairs bar claims to serve the cheapest beer in town, and you can cook with other guests in the kitchen. The staff is also comprised of back-packers, and a happy guest provided the paintings on view throughout the hostel. If you're traveling with an amour or don't mind sharing with a friend, the best deal is to book a queen-size bunk bed in one of the dorms. The city center hostel is slightly more expensive, but then it hosts a disco twice a week. ✉ *Vossiusstraat 46, 1012 GJ, Vondelpark* ☎ *020/ 400–4187* 🖷 *020/421–0802* ⊕ *www.flyingpig.nl* 🗗 *2 rooms, 20 dor-mitories* ♿ *Lockers, bar; no TV, no phones, no a/c* ⊟ *AE, MC, V* 〶 *CP* ✉ *Flying Pig Downtown: Nieuwendijk 100, 1012 MR, Nieuwe Zijde* ☎ *020/420–6822* 🖷 *020/421–0802* 🗗 *2 rooms, 20 dormitories* ♿ *Lockers, bar; no TV, no phones, no a/c, no private bath* ♿ *Reser-vations not accepted* ⊟ *No credit cards* 〶 *CP.*

¢–$ 🏨 **Jupiter.** On a quiet residential street not far from the Vondelpark, the Jupiter hotel has a plain, homey interior. The hotel has an elevator. You're a short walk away from the Rijksmuseum and the Concertgebouw, as well as the shops in the chic P. C. Hooftstraat. ✉ *2e Helmersstraat 14, 1054 CJ Vondelpark* ☎ *020/618–7132* 🖷 *020/616–8838* ⊕ *www. jupiterhotel.nl* 🗗 *10 rooms, 6 suites* ♿ *In-room data ports, cable TV, some pets allowed; no a/c* ⊟ *No credit cards* 〶 *CP.*

¢–$ 🏨 **Stayokay Amsterdam-Vondelpark Hostel.** Word of mouth has made this hostel so popular that over 75,000 backpackers stay here every year. Hidden on a small side path within the Vondelpark, the location is al-most like being in a secret forest, despite being only minutes away from the hustle and bustle of the city. Put your bike in the hostel's covered shed, breakfast on the terrace and ogle the parrots in the trees, then do a few rounds of the park (a great place to connect with new people). Accommodations range from rooms that sleep two to dormitories for twenty, and sheets are included in the price. In the spacious lounge, you can use the Internet, watch TV, play pool, or get acquainted with back-packers from around the world. Some rooms are available for those with disabilities. This is probably the cleanest hostel anywhere—your mom would definitely approve. ✉ *Zandpad 5, 1054 GA, Vondelpark* ☎ *020/ 589–8996* 🖷 *020/589–8955* ⊕ *www.stayokay.com* 🗗 *105 rooms, 536 beds* ♿ *Restaurant, brasserie, lockers, laundry facilities; no phones, no a/c, no private bath* ⊟ *MC, V* 〶 *CP.*

Nieuwe Zijde

If you want to stay in the pulsing aorta of Amsterdam, the "New Side" is ground zero. Crowds centered around the Dam square mean you'll have plenty of company.

$$$$ ✕⛶ **NH Grand Hotel Krasnapolsky.** Competing for prominence with the Royal Palace on Dam Square and Amsterdam's "Hilton" of the 19th century, this was Holland's biggest hotel until the real Hilton came along. For a while this was Holland's best, and you can revisit that gilded age by taking a table in the Kras's soaringly beautiful Wintertuin (Winter Garden), still Amsterdam's loveliest place for luncheon. Sitting in this masterpiece of 19th-century allure, replete with potted palms, greenhouse roof, Victorian chandeliers, and buffet tables stocked with cakes and roses, will make you feel like a countess or duke. If only the rest of this 1866 landmark was as sugared. Unfortunately, a mishmash of revamping over the years was done with a progressively penurious attitude toward living space. When it first opened its doors, guest rooms flaunted the latest in luxury—centralized heating, French-parquet floors, and electric lights. Last renovated in 2003, the guest rooms—now numbering more than 450—vary greatly in size and tend toward serviceable functionality, somewhat of a disappointment after such a grand beginning. Its extravagance shows itself again with its business facilities (including 22 conference rooms), which are some of the best in the city, and its evocative dining opportunities. Who wants to linger in their room when one can be drinking a *jenever* gin cocktail at the Proeflokaal Wynand Fockink (Tasting House Wynand Fockink), dining in a Bedouin tent, feasting on Japanese delights, or taking a tipple in the Art Deco–style bar? But for those with more domestic desires, there are also furnished apartments available. In the end, you can be delighted with your room here (keep in mind, prices are wildly variable and bargains can be had) or chagrined. Abristle with hustle and bustle, this "village on the Dam" can delight those in search of the big city lights. Those in search of peace and tranquility will want to head elsewhere, or just camp out in the glorious Winter Garden. ✉ *Dam 9, 101 JS, Nieuwe Zijde* ☎ *020/554–9111* 🖷 *020/626–570* ⊕ *www.nh-hotels.com* ⟿ *431 rooms, 7 suites, 36 apartments* ⟁ *5 restaurants, in-room data ports, in-room safes, cable TV, hair salon, bar, convention center, some pets allowed* ▭ *AE, DC, MC, V* ⦿ *EP.*

$$$$ ✕⛶ **Hotel Amsterdam.** Located since 1911—but with roots back to the 16th century—at the hub of the city's business and shopping areas and close to the Centraal Station, on the corner of Dam Square and across from the leading department store, De Bijenkorf, the Hotel Amsterdam is a cut above other hotels on the Damrak. The guest rooms on the elegant 18th-century facade have soundproof windows to buffer the outside world, and rooms at the back or on the "executive floor" are also safe bets. Rooms that accommodate three people and extra beds are available, and the hotel's restaurant, De Roode Leeuw, has built up a sizable following thanks to its heated terrace, Dutch haute cuisine, and encyclopedic champagne list. The restaurant is the recipient of the coveted *Neerlands Dis* (Netherlands' Dish) award. ✉ *Damrak 93–94, 1012 LP, Nieuwe Zijde* ☎ *020/555–0666* 🖷 *020/620–4716* ⊕ *www. hotelamsterdam.nl* ⟿ *79 rooms* ⟁ *Restaurant, room service, in-room data ports, in-room safes, cable TV, laundry service, business services* ▭ *AE, DC, MC, V* ⦿ *EP.*

$$ ⛶ **Rho.** Few hotels have as marvelous a lobby as this one, thanks to the building's origins as a 1910s theater. Jugendstil ornament, tile trim, and etched glass all conjure up the soigné style of the turn of the 20th century. A rich maroon color is carried out in furnishings throughout the hotel, conveying a bit of the music-hall tinkle; guest room furnishings for the most part, however, are modern and standard issue. Happily located on a quiet side street off the Dam square, the Rho is within walking distance to theaters, nightlife, and shopping. ✉ *Nes 5–23, 1012 KC Nieuwe Zijde* ☎ *020/620–7371* 🖷 *020/620–7826* ⊕ *www.rhohotel.com* ⟿ *167 rooms* ⟁ *Cable TV, bar, dry cleaning, laundry service, some pets allowed; no a/c* ▭ *AE, MC, V* ⦿ *CP.*

$$$ ▣ **Tulip Inn Dam Square.** Just around the corner from the Royal Palace, and right in the very heart of the city, this hotel is a surprising oasis of quiet because of its site on a narrow, pedestrians-only street. Within a half-minute's walking distance, you're immersed in the hustle and bustle of the main shopping center. The Amsterdam School–style building is adorned with storybook-ornate brick and stone trim and a gabled roof, so to view it is to step back in time. Inside, rooms are modern and comfortable with terracotta and dark green furnishings. The building once housed a liquor distillery, and you can still enjoy a visit to the tasting house next door. A nice plus here is the hotel's level of service—at times, the staff coddles you. It's no surprise that visitors return again and again. ⊠ *Gravenstraat 12–16, 1012 NM Nieuwe Zijde* ☎ *020/623–3716* 🖷 *020/638–1156* ⊕ *www.tulipinndamsquare. com* ↪ *34 rooms, 4 suites* ⚒ *In-room data ports, cable TV, bar* ☰ *AE, DC, MC, V* ⫟Ⓞ⫠ *CP.*

$$ ▣ **Avenue.** The Avenue Hotel is in several historic buildings, one a listed monument that used to be a warehouse for the United East India Company. The hotel interior underwent renovation in 2000, and the new modernization brings bright and cheerful contemporary style to rooms that are small but comfortable. The large and varied breakfast buffet gets raves from guests. ⊠ *Nieuwezijds Voorburgwal 27, 1012 RD, Nieuwe Zijde* ☎ *020/530–9530* 🖷 *020/530–9599* ⊕ *www.avenue-hotel.nl* ↪ *77 rooms* ⚒ *Room service, cable TV, laundry service, elevator, some pets allowed; no a/c* ☰ *AE, DC, MC, V* ⫟Ⓞ⫠ *CP.*

$$ ▣ **Citadel.** Set in a spiffy eight-story building, brown brick with white trim, and topped out with a jaunty two-story mansard roof, the Citadel is a particularly cheery option. Set on a busy main street just a hop, skip, and a jump from the Royal Palace, Dam Square, and the Magna Plaza shopping mall, it's hard to find a more central location. Higher rooms and rooms at the back are a bit quieter. Top-floor rooms at the front provide a sweeping view. The guest rooms themselves are modern, alluring, and comfortable. ⊠ *N.Z. Voorburgwal 100, 1012 SG Nieuwe Zijde* ☎ *020/627–3882* 🖷 *020/627–4684* ⊕ *www.lempereur-hotels.nl* ↪ *38 rooms* ⚒ *Cable TV, bar, dry cleaning; no a/c* ☰ *AE, DC, MC, V* ⫟Ⓞ⫠ *CP.*

$$ ▣ **Singel.** Old meets new at this spot, comprised of three renovated 17th-century canal houses, as charmingly lopsided as their peers elsewhere in Amsterdam. Fairly unprepossessing (at least compared to the surrounding buildings in the historic Koepelkwartier), the facade is cheerily adorned with striped window canopies. The exterior belies the modern furnishings and comforts you'll discover within, including an elevator. If you want a view of the Singel canal, book a front or side room. From the hotel, it's just a short stroll to the Kalvertoren and Magna Plaza shopping malls, as well as the Dam Square. ⊠ *Singel 13, 1012 VC Nieuwe Zijde* ☎ *020/626–3108* 🖷 *020/620–3777* ⊕ *www.lempereur-hotels.nl* ↪ *32 rooms* ⚒ *In-room data ports, cable TV, bar, some pets allowed; no a/c* ☰ *AE, DC, MC, V* ⫟Ⓞ⫠ *CP.*

$$ ▣ **Terminus.** Ten 18th-century town houses make up the Terminus, which is between the Berlage Exchange and has its back to the Oudekerk (Old Church), two famed historic monuments. Bless the Old Church, as it is the oldest in Amsterdam, but, unfortunately, its bell chimes every half hour around the clock, which means it can be heard in some rooms even through double-glazed windows. The modern glass-panelled entrance manages not to detract from the traditional beauty of the buildings. The room decor is nothing to write home about as it is elegantly modern, comfortable, and boring (actually it may be good to have that kind of difference, or you could get caught in a time warp in historic Amsterdam). You're in the heart of the city, surrounded by landmarks and in the major shopping district. ⊠ *Beursstraat 11–19, 1012 JT*

Nieuwe Zijde ☎ 020/622–0535 🖷 020/627–2216 ⊕ *www.terminus. nl* ➦ *96 rooms* ♺ *Cable TV, bar, dry cleaning, laundry service; no a/c* ⊟ *AE, DC, MC, V* ¶⊖¶ *CP.*

$ 🖼 **AMS Cordial.** Young international travelers are drawn to this hotel because it is easy on the budget, informal, and centrally located. Front rooms face the busy Rokin shopping street or you can people-watch while enjoying a drink on the terrace in front of the hotel. The cold breakfast buffet (included in the price) is accompanied by warm homemade bread rolls. ⊠ *Rokin 62–64, 1012 KW Nieuwe Zijde* ☎ 020/626–4411 🖷 020/623–5744 ⊕ *www.ams.nl* ➦ *50 rooms, 40 with bath* ♺ *Cable TV, bar; no a/c* ⊟ *AE, DC, MC, V* ¶⊖¶ *CP.*

¢–$ 🖼 **Asterisk.** A touch of the 19th century still hovers about this very friendly (they love children) hotel. Some guest rooms feature ceiling moldings and chandeliers, and more-modern touches make this a comfy option for all. Major art museums, the Leidseplein, the Flower Market, and the Rembrandtsplein are all within walking distance of the hotel, which is on a quiet street. For children, cots and high chairs can be used if requested in advance. Breakfast is included in the price only if you pay cash in advance. ⊠ *Den Texstraat 16, 1017 ZA Nieuwe Zijde* ☎ 020/ 626–2396 🖷 020/638–2790 ⊕ *www.asteriskhotel.nl* ➦ *40 rooms* ♺ *In-room safes, cable TV* ⊟ *MC, V* ¶⊖¶ *EP.*

Oude Zijde

The adjacent Red Light District may cast a less-than-rosy glow, but the Old Side, for the most part, remains one of the city's most historic neighborhoods.

$$$$ ✕🖼 **Grand Sofitel Demeure Amsterdam.** For captivating elegance, nothing
Fodor'sChoice   tops the facade of the Grand, a Neoclassical courtyard replete with white
★ sash windows, carved marble pediments, and roof abristle with chimneys and gilded weather vanes. If it all seems unchanged since the days of Rembrandt, that's because this hotel's celebrated city-center site has a long and varied history as far as lodgings go. It started simple in the 14th century as a convent dedicated to St. Celia and St. Catherine, before going poshly secular by becoming a *Prinsenhof* (Prince's Courtyard) in 1578 and welcoming such illustrious guests as William of Orange and Maria de Medici. For a time it became the offices of the Amsterdam Admiralty before the buildings were yet again rezoned—by Napoléon, no less—to become Amsterdam's city hall from 1808 to 1988 and thereby providing the setting for Queen Beatrix's civil wedding in 1966. Today's incarnation, opened in 1992, is one of the city's most deluxe hotels, a suitable home-away-from-home for such guests as Mick Jagger and President Jacques Chirac of France. Once inside, the time machine zooms forward to the 20th century. The lobby and public salons are all fairly sedate, done in champagnes and browns, and accented with marble floors, Jugendstil stained-glass windows, and scattered tapestries. More tranquil, low-key style comes with your key—guest rooms offer eye-soothing scenery, with traditional-luxe furniture, fine fabrics, and quiet hues, plus every manner of business mod con. If you want fireworks, repair to the Café Roux, an oak-and-black-trim Art Deco-ish brasserie supervised by the famed Albert Roux. It sports a mural that Karel Appel created early in his career to repay a debt to the city and some of the most stylish French dishes in town, such as a superb flan of scallops with tiger prawns and Roquefort and innovative Pavé of turbot served with a green pea–mint risotto. Nearby is the Admiralty, a more casual nook that opens out onto a glorious courtyard for the enjoyment of afternoon tea. And try to take a peek at the hotel's Marriage Chamber meeting room and its amazing Jugenstil interior. ⊠ *Oudezijds Voorburgwal 197, 1012 EX,*

Oude Zijde ☎ 020/555–3111 📠 020/555–3222 ⊕ *www.thegrand.nl*
🛏 *160 rooms, 6 suites, 16 apartments* ♿ *Restaurant, room service, in-room data ports, in-room safes, cable TV, indoor pool, massage, sauna, Turkish bath, bar, baby-sitting, dry cleaning, laundry service, some pets allowed* ⊟ *AE, DC, MC, V* ⎸◯⎸ *EP.*

$$$$ 🏨**Hotel de l'Europe.** Owned by Freddy Heineken's daughter, this hotel
Fodor'sChoice is one of the comeliest tulips on the Amsterdam hotel scene. Quiet, gra-
★ cious, and plush in both decor and service, this queen has a history extending back to 1638, although its delightful, storybook facade dates
only to the 19th century. Overlooking the Amstel River, the Muntplein,
and the Flower Market, it may be familiar to those who remember the
setting of Hitchcock's *Foreign Correspondent*. The chandeliered lobby
leads off to the lounge, aglow with ruby and tangerine hues and glittering with gold-trimmed ceiling coves and blackamoor lamps—the
perfect setting in which to perfect the art of high tea (served in full glory
here). Guest rooms are furnished with reserved, classical elegance: the
city-side rooms are full of warm, rich colors; riverside rooms are in brilliant whites and have French windows to let in floods of light. All
rooms have luscious swags of Victorian-style draperies as canopies over
the beds. And all this 19th-century sense of splendor is backed up with
every 21st-century convenience. The Excelsior restaurant pairs splendid river views with a palacelike interior, complete with enchanting ceiling mural. The fine French food is ooh-la-la. ⊠ *Nieuwe Doelenstraat
2–8, 1012 CP, Oude Zijde* ☎ 020/531–1777 📠 020/531–1778 ⊕ *www.
leurope.nl* 🛏 *77 rooms, 23 suites* ♿ *2 restaurants, room service, in-room
data ports, minibars, cable TV, indoor pool, gym, hair salon, hot tub,
sauna, bar, business services, some pets allowed* ⊟ *AE, DC, MC, V* ⎸◯⎸ *EP.*

$$$$ 🏨**Renaissance Amsterdam.** It's not every day that a 17th-century church
is part of a hotel, but an underground passage connects the Renaissance
with the domed Koepelkerk, an erstwhile Lutheran church that is now
the hotel's conference center. Smack dab in the middle of the Centrum
(city center), between Dam Square and Centraal Station, this ultramodern hotel's top floors provide panoramic views of the city. Another
high point is the hotel's highly popular fitness center, Splash, where you
can have a complete workout or relax with a massage, steam bath, whirlpool, or sauna. The soaring lobby is basically modern, trimmed out with
wood and topped off with a chandelier, so do make a point and ask the
concierge to let you see the Koepelkerk. ⊠ *Kattengat 1, 1012 SZ Oude
Zijde* ☎ 020/621–2223 📠 020/627–5245 ⊕ *www.renaissancehotels.com/
amsrd* 🛏 *376 rooms, 6 suites, 23 apartments* ♿ *Restaurant, in-room
data ports, minibars, cable TV, health club, hair salon, sauna, bar, some
pets allowed* ⊟ *AE, DC, MC, V* ⎸◯⎸ *EP.*

$ 🏨**Amstel Botel.** This floating hotel, moored near Centraal Station, is an
appropriate lodging in watery Amsterdam. However, it is more *Love
Ferry* than *Love Boat*. The clean and modern rooms are cabinlike, but
the portholes have been replaced by windows that provide fine views
of the city across the water. If you want a room with a view, try to avoid
rooms on the land side of the vessel, which look out on a strictly utilitarian postal sorting office. ⊠ *Oosterdokskade 2–4, 1011 AE, Oude
Zijde* ☎ 020/626–4247 📠 020/639–1952 ⊕ *www.amstelbotel.com*
🛏 *175 rooms* ♿ *Cable TV, bar; no a/c* ⊟ *AE, DC, MC, V* ⎸◯⎸ *EP.*

$ 🏨**Vijaya.** As with many 18th-century canal-house hotels, the exterior
here is eye-catching—this one has a particularly ornate gable—and the
inside is modernized. Comfortably furnished rooms in front have a
canal view, but the rooms at the back are quieter. The family room sleeps
five. Near Dam Square, the main shopping streets and Centraal Station,
you are also just a short tram ride away from the major museums. ⊠ *O.
Z. Voorburgwal 44, 1012 GE Oude Zijde* ☎ 020/638–0102 📠 020/

626–9406 ⊕ *www.hotelvijaya.com* 🛏 *30 rooms* ⚇ *Cable TV, baby-sitting; no a/c* 🖃 *AE, DC, MC, V* ⦿ *CP.*

¢ 🖥 **Stayokay Amsterdam-Stadsdoelen Hostel.** Located in a canal house at the edge of the Red Light district, this hostel is a backpacker's Ritz. Usually filled with young, friendly international travelers, it has a reputation as the most *gezellig* place to stay in Amsterdam. Some say if you're looking for simple accommodation at a bargain-basement price, you can't do better. The dormitories are immaculate with breakfast and bedsheets included in the price. You can get meals and drinks at the café or do your own cooking in the guest kitchen. Everyone congregates in the lobby to make new friends, watch TV, or use the Internet. ✉ *Kloverniersburgwal 97, 1011 KB, Oude Zijde* ☎ *020/624–6832* 📠 *020/639–1035* ⊕ *www.stayokay.com* 🛏 *10 dormitories, 170 beds* ⚇ *Café, lockers, laundry facilities; no phones, no room TV, no a/c* 🖃 *MC, V* ⦿ *CP.*

The Plantage

Head away from the historical center to the small tranquil neighborhood known as the Plantage for a more relaxed stay. The Hortus Botanicus, Artis Zoo, and the Tropenmuseum dominate this *Oost* (East) Amsterdam area. The Tropenmuseum backs on to the Oosterpark neighborhood, which is bordered by the Linneausstraat, Populierenweg, Amstel River and Mauritskade. It's a mainly residential area with the exception of the busy Wibautstraat.

$$$$ ✕🖥 **Amstel Inter-Continental.** Welcome to a decidedly old-world vision
FodorśChoice of heaven and one that rates extra points for its scenic location along
★ the Amstel River. Elegant enough to please a queen, extroverted enough to welcome Madonna, the Rolling Stones, and Michael Jackson, this grand dowager has wowed all onlookers since it opened its doors in 1867. With its palatial five stories, sash windows, and historic roof dormers, this lily was gilded in 1992 with a renovation by Pierre Yves Rochon of Paris, whose emphasis on its long-established grace and elegance made it possible not only to imagine the svelte Audrey Hepburn here but to understand why she became a fixture in this environment. You'll feel like a visiting dignitary when entering the magnificent lobby, a soaring salon covered with wedding-cake stucco trim and replete with a grand double staircase that demands you glide, not walk, down it. The guest rooms are the most spacious in the city (though they shrink considerably on the top floor), and the decor creates the ambience of a home personalized by Oriental rugs, brocade upholstery, Delft lamps, and a color palette of warm tones inspired by Makkum pottery. Fresh tulips are placed in all of the rooms, and the bathrooms spoil guests with showerheads the size of dinner plates. The generous staff-to-guest ratio, the top-notch food—in particular, at the award-winning La Rive restaurant—the riverside terrace, the Amstel Lounge (perfect for drinks), and the endless stream of extra "little touches" (such as yacht service), will make for a truly baronial experience. ✉ *Professor Tulpplein 1, 1018 GX, Plantage* ☎ *020/622–6060* 📠 *020/622–5808* ⊕ *www.amsterdam.intercontinental.com* 🛏 *55 rooms, 24 suites* ⚇ *2 restaurants, room service, in-room data ports, cable TV, indoor pool, health club, bar, dry cleaning, laundry service, business services* 🖃 *AE, DC, MC, V* ⦿ *EP.*

$$$ 🖥 **Arena.** This grand complex set in a former 19th-century Roman Catholic orphanage consists of the hotel, a café-restaurant, a patio, a back garden, and a dance club (complete with frescoed walls that reflect its former function as a clandestine church). For those who like spare minimal style the hotel is strikingly austere—as if it were torn from the pages of *Wallpaper* magazine. The lobby is minimalist white, which draws attention to the impressive cast-iron staircase leading to the rooms. The hotel used the hottest young Dutch architects and designers to supervise the recent renovation, which has helped erase the shadow of its past as a youth hostel. Rooms—some of which are split-level to form a lounge area—are painted in white, gray, and mauve tones and are furnished with modernist furniture by Gispen, Eames, and Martin Visser. With all these features, guests often forget to explore Amsterdam itself. ⊠ *'s-Gravesandestraat 51, 1092 AA, Plantage* ☎ *020/850–2417* 🖷 *020/850–2425* ⊕ *www.hotelarena.nl* ↘ *121 rooms* ♿ *Restaurant, cable TV, bar, dance club; no a/c* ⊟ *AE, DC, MC, V* |○| *CP.*

$$–$$$ ⊡ **Best Western Lancaster.** This neighborhood is greener than many in the city, and the higher-priced rooms in the hotel have a welcoming view of the park. Family rooms sleep up to four people. The Artis zoo is opposite the hotel, and the Tropenmuseum (Tropical Museum) is within walking distance. ⊠ *Plantage Middenlaan 48, 1018 DH Plantage* ☎ *020/535–6888* 🖷 *020/535–6889* ⊕ *www.edenhotelgroup.com* ↘ *92* ♿ *In-room safes, cable TV; no a/c* ⊟ *AE, DC, MC, V* |○| *EP.*

$ ⊡ **Fantasia.** Peace and quiet await you in this small, friendly family hotel in a circa 1733 canal house not far from the Plantage. The hotel owner's father was a farmer, which explains the owner's collection of ornamental cows, found everywhere in the hotel. There's a room to suit everyone, from a small attic room (complete with bath) to a family room that sleeps four. ⊠ *Nieuwe Keizersgracht 16, 1018 DR Plantage* ☎ *020/623–8259* 🖷 *020/622–3913* ⊕ *www.fantasia-hotel.com* ↘ *19 rooms, 18 with bath* ♿ *Some pets allowed; no a/c, no room TVs* ⊟ *AE, MC, V* ☉ *Closed Dec. 16–26, Jan. 6–Feb. 28* |○| *CP.*

★ $ ⊡ **Rembrandt.** Because it is close to the University of Amsterdam, the Artis zoo, Hortus Botanicus, and Tropenmuseum, the Hotel Rembrandt is often populated with academics and museum people—so perhaps bring a seriously titled book if you want to gain entry. The rarified air is particularly thick in the remarkable breakfast room: the 18th-century paintings and exquisitely painted woodwork on the ceiling, and the wood paneling and beams carved in and dated 1558, were transported to their current location in the 19th century. Most of the rooms at the back of the hotel facing the garden are quiet. Duplex Room 21, in the front, can accommodate a family of six, and six rooms can house three or four. All rooms are immaculately clean. ⊠ *Plantage Middenlaan 17, 1018 DA, Plantage* ☎ *020/627–2714* 🖷 *020/638–0293* ⊕ *www.hotelrembrandt.nl* ↘ *16 rooms, 1 suite* ♿ *Cable TV, library; no a/c* ⊟ *AE, MC, V* |○| *CP.*

Rembrandtplein

Rembrandtplein may be a glaring tribute to neon and nightclubs, but its location is close to everything.

$$$ ⊡ **Albus Grand.** One of the newest hotels in Amsterdam, the Albus Grand's exterior has been graciously designed to conjure up the look of yesteryear. Inside, seven floors offer rooms of a comfortable size. Even the street-side rooms are remarkably quiet because of their double-paned windows, which are needed since the hotel is in the bustling center overlooking the Munt tower and Flower Market, with the Rembrandtplein nearby. The hotel lobby and guest rooms are tastefully decorated with wicker chairs and contemporary paintings from the owners' collection. The buffet in the light and cheerful breakfast room has the usual fare plus Dutch specialties. ⊠ *Vijzelstraat 49, 1017 HE, Rembrandtplein* ☎ *020/530–6200* 🖷 *020/530–6299* ⊕ *www.albusgrandhotel.com* ↘ *74 rooms, 2 apartments* ♿ *In-room data ports, cable TV, some pets allowed; no a/c* ⊟ *AE, DC, MC, V* |○| *EP.*

$$$ ■ **Best Western Eden.** This area gets very noisy when the discos empty in the wee hours, but this gigantic hotel is perfectly situated for those who like the club scene and surrounding nightlife. Rooms in front have views of the Amstel River, whereas rooms elsewhere have few views but are quieter. The street appears to be down at the heels, but the inside of the hotel is clean, comfortable, and modern. ✉ *Amstel 144, 1017 AE Rembrandtplein* ☎ *020/530–7878* 🖶 *020/624–2946* ⊕ *www.edenhotelgroup. com* 🛏 *320 rooms* ⚐ *Restaurant, in-room safes, hair salon, bar, babysitting, dry cleaning, laundry service* ☰ *AE, DC, MC, V* ⧉ *EP.*

$$$ ✕■ **NH Schiller.** Frits Schiller built the hotel in 1912 in the Art Nouveau variant known as Jugendstil. He may have been an artist of modest ability, but a huge number of his paintings, whose colors inspired the inventive decor of the modernized rooms, are proudly displayed throughout the hotel. His friends, bohemian painters and sculptors, came to the Schiller Café, which became a famous meeting place and is still an informal and popular bar with Amsterdammers. From the lobby lounge you can check your e-mail to the hum of the espresso machine from the Brasserie Schiller. A winter film series is held on Sunday afternoons in the restaurant, with cocktails and dinner included. Rooms are conveniently stocked with coffeemakers, trouser presses, and hair dryers, and six are large enough, with two double beds, to suit families. ✉ *Rembrandtplein 26–36, 1017 CV, Rembrandtplein* ☎ *020/554–0700* 🖶 *020/ 624–0098* ⊕ *www.goldentulip.com* 🛏 *91 rooms, 1 suite* ⚐ *Restaurant, in-room data ports, cable TV, bar, baby-sitting, laundry service* ☰ *AE, DC, MC, V* ⧉ *EP.*

$$–$$$ ■ **Seven Bridges.** One of the more famous canal sights in Amsterdam
Fodor's Choice is the lineup of seven consecutive bridges that can be seen gracing Reg-
★ uliersgracht. This atmosphere-y little retreat takes its name from them as its hotelscape provides some idyllic views of this canal. Set in an 18th-century house in the heart of "Golden Bend" country (yet just a few blocks from Rembrandtplein), this hotel offers uniquely stylish guest rooms, all meticulously decorated with dark woods, Oriental rugs, Art Deco lamps, and marble sinks. The proud owner scouts the antiques stores and auction houses for furnishings, and all have thorough documentation. Handcrafted and inlaid bed frames and tables supplement the antique decorations for a whimsical atmosphere. Top-floor rooms are the smallest and priced accordingly; the first-floor room is practically palatial. No. 5 is a cargo of charm, complete with private terrace. The one catch is that there is no common area or salon, but even here another plus results: breakfast is delivered to your room. Nail down your reservation well in advance. ✉ *Reguliersgracht 31, 1017 LK, Rembrandtplein* ☎ *020/623–1329* 🛏 *8 rooms* ⚐ *In-room data ports, cable TV; no a/c* ☰ *AE, MC, V* ⧉ *CP.*

$$ ■ **Imperial.** The outside of this hotel has a Parisian appearance. It's on a pedestrian-only, tree-lined street with cobblestones and a terraced square. Each room is individually decorated, some masculine, some feminine, and in styles ranging from sedate to cheerful to bold, to appeal to every kind of taste so that each guest feels at home. This is a nonsmoking hotel. Most rooms provide the luxury of a Jacuzzi shower. There is no elevator, and although the stairs are modern (as opposed to steep traditional Dutch staircases), you must walk up at least two flights of them. ✉ *Thorbeckeplein 9, 1017 CS, Rembrandtplein* ⊕ *www. imperial-hotel.com* 🛏 *14* ⚐ *In-room data ports, in-room safes, cable TV; no a/c* ☰ *MC, V* ⧉ *CP.*

NIGHTLIFE
& THE ARTS

FODOR'S CHOICE

Bimhuis, *le jazz hot near the Red Light District*

Café Schiller, *historic ambience on Rembrandtplein*

Concertgebouw, *Amsterdam's "Carnegie Hall"*

Muziektheater, *the place for opera and ballet*

Stadsschouwburg, *red-and-gold plush on the Leidseplein*

Seymour Likely, *half lounge, half scene-arena*

t'Smalle, *the quintessential historic "brown café"*

HIGHLY RECOMMENDED

Café Vertigo, *with a great Vondelpark terrace*

Café Wildschut, *for people-watching near the Amstel*

Engelse Kerk, *Baroque chamber music in the Pilgrims' church*

Paradiso, *the "Pop Temple" in the Leidseplein area*

Supper Club, *a hipster's fave in the Nieuwe Zijds*

Tuschinski, *the Art Deco cinema near Rembrandtplein*

Vondelpark Openluchttheater, *for summer arts in the park*

Wynand Fockink, *the place to raise a glass of Dutch jenever*

By Steve
Korver

NIGHTLIFE AND THE ARTS HAVE ALWAYS WALKED HAND IN HAND—like the most yin and yang of intimate lovers—in this land. One just has to look at the selection of Golden Age paintings by Jan Steen and his colleagues depicting frolicsome bar scenes that grace the walls of the Rijksmuseum to get the idea that there's nothing like a beer after a long day of more noble and artistic pursuits. The organizers of Amsterdam's annual Museum Night suavely tapped into this long legacy and came up with the city's most popular new event to come along in decades. For one night in early November, all the major museums stay open until the wee hours to host a variety of themed parties—tangos under the *Night Watch,* house beats in the Jewish Historical Museum, easy tunes in the Stedelijk, ghost stories for kids in the Bible Museum (to name but a few and, in fact, the relatively sedate of the many often surreal combinations that have occurred).

Coincidentally, a group of nightclub DJs and party organizers, under their auspicious moniker of "The Night Watch," were elected the "Night Mayors" of Amsterdam in 2003. They see their role as fighting against the frumpiness that cast a shadow over this city as Amsterdam cleared away the squats—the deserted buildings that had become the usual settings for some of the city's more famed and wild events—to make room for corporate headquarters that Amsterdam hoped to lure as "Gateway to Europe." Hopefully they will oversee a renaissance in Amsterdam's long and cherished reputation as a true night-life capital. But the short-term visitor will notice little of these dips and valleys of the scene. The city is still rich with inspired folk who are willing to organize a video art festival in a cruise ship terminal, a gentle Bach recital in an ancient church, an arts festival in an abandoned factory, a house party in a football stadium, or some heart-stopping theatrical spectacle in a park. And the beautiful thing about this country is that if by the smallest—and we do mean smallest—of chances Amsterdam is slow one night, a short train trip to Rotterdam or the Hague will undoubtedly have you at the center of some cultural storm.

Of course, some visitors throughout the centuries have found it difficult to find the right balance between taking advantage of both Amsterdam's acclaimed arts scene (without burning out the eyes) and the equally famed nightlife scene (without incurring toxic shock). Alas, we can help only by narrowing down some of the infinite options this town has to offer and by emphasizing the fact that most visitors survive unscathed, not only richer for the experience but also equipped with a desire to return to do it all over again.

NIGHTLIFE

Fasten your seat belts. Amsterdam's nightlife can have you careening between smoky coffee shops, chic wine bars, mellow jazz joints, laid-back lounges, and clubs either intimate or raucous. The bona fide local flavor can perhaps best be tasted in one of the city's ubiquitous brown café-bars—called "brown" because of their woody walls and nicotine-stained ceilings (although lately many have let in some light and international styles). Here, both young and old, the mohawked and the merely balding, come to relax, rave, and revel in every variety of coffee and alcohol.

The city's nightlife is centered on two of its main squares. Leidseplein, rich with cafés and discos that attract younger visitors to the city, also has the city's two major live venues, Melkweg and, around the corner, Paradiso. The area around Rembrandtplein, whose cafés cater to a more local crowd, harbors the trendier nightspots and many of Amsterdam's gay venues (the latter being particularly concentrated along Reguliersdwarsstraat).

Warmoestraat and other streets in the Red Light District provide the spicy setting for leather-oriented gay bars and the more throbbing rock clubs. The lounge phenomenon, although a bit late in arriving, is now in full bloom, offering a kinder, gentler club vibe. Hipsters and those employed in the commercial arts are attracted to the venues concentrated around Nieuwezijds Voorburgwal, but others are springing up throughout the city that invariably have DJs spinning the mellower dance tunes.

Amsterdam, being one of the most liberal cities in the world, is known for having a tolerant attitude toward prostitution and soft drugs. It is somewhat shocking for first-time visitors to see the world-famous Red Light District and the hundreds of "coffee shops" scattered throughout the city. It is essentially legal to deal small amounts of marijuana and hashish via the "front door" of a coffee shop where the customer enters. However, the "back door," through which the product arrives, is linked to the illegal world of the supplier. Although it is fine to smoke marijuana in these coffee shops—takeout to a more discreet spot is another option—many people frown upon smoking in restaurants, bars, and cafés (though a simple query to the bar staff will usually get you a friendly answer).

The Dutch are a very sociable people and enjoy going out either after work or after dinner. Sunday and Monday nights tend to be quiet, whereas things tend to get very lively on weekends. Most bars and cafés close around 1 or 2 AM during the week and stay open an extra hour or two on weekends. However, *Nachtbars* (night bars) open after 10 PM and are licensed to stay open until about dawn—just ask somebody who looks like a potential bon vivant to point you to the nearest one.

Bars

Although brown cafés are probably the most authentically "local" places to stop in for a coffee or something stronger, there are also plenty—and we do mean plenty—of places that have scrubbed their windows and let in some light in the form of sun and international styles and music. Others have soundproofed their windows in the name of privacy, and later and louder hours.

The youthful, late-houred, and grottolike **Absinthe** (⊠ Nieuwezijds Voorburgwal 171, Nieuwe Zijds and Spui ☎ 020/320–6780) offers the option of true hallucinations if you happen to overindulge in their liquid namesake, rumored to be the trigger for Van Gogh's act of self-mutilation. And no worries: this is a legal recipe. The trendy, sleekly minimal, and cheekily no-signed **Bar With No Name** (⊠ Wolvenstraat 23, Grachtengordel West ☎ 020/320–0843) ironically attracts a lot of commercial arts and advertising types. It also happens to be open all day for great breakfasts, lunches, and dinners. The theatrical crowd can be witnessed eating, drinking and being generally merry at **Café Cox** (⊠ Marnixstraat 429, Museum District ☎ 020/620–7222), part of the Stadsschouwburg building. **Café de Koe** (⊠ Marnixstraat 381, Leidseplein ☎ 020/625–4482) takes seriously both its name (Cow) with the decor's bovine accents and its goal to provide a hip and relaxed refuge for local musicians and students. On the "Prayer with End" alley, which runs parallel to Nes's south end, is **Captain Zeppos** (⊠ Gebed Zonder End 5, Oude Zijde ☎ 020/624–2057), a former cigar factory which is soaked with jazzy old-world charm that gets enhanced with music on Sundays. The well-read and politically engaged crowd gathers around the café/bar belonging to the political and cultural arts center **De Balie** (⊠ Kleine Gartmanplantsoen 10, Museum District ☎ 020/553–5130).

As to be expected from a theatrical neighborhood, the Nes offers some prime drinking holes and fans of Belgian beer should certainly stop at the patio or the clean interior of **De Brakke Grond** (⊠ Nes 43, Oude Zijde ☎ 020/626–0044), part of the Flemish Cultural Center, to partake in one or two of the dozens of options. **De Buurvrouw** (⊠ St. Pieterspoortsteeg 29, Oude Zijds ☎ 020/625–9654) is a small sawdust- and kitsch-strewn haven for the more studenty and alternative of heart who don't mind yelling over the latest in loud guitars and funky beats. The always welcoming and cozy **De Still** (⊠ Spuistraat 326, Nieuwe Zijds and Spui ☎ 020/620–1349) is for the whiskey obsessive with ambitions to try as many as possible of the 600 varieties on offer here. The mazelike **Dulac** (⊠ Haarlemmerstraat 118, Jordaan ☎ 020/624–4265) attracts all types by offering sensory overload in the form of a hallucinatory decor that suggests it was built by a Gaudi who was reborn as an inspired junkyard artist. With a funky interior and epic views of a canal and a church square, **Finch** (⊠ Noordermarkt 5, Jordaan ☎ 020/626–2461) does a good job of attracting the local and thirsty arts scene. Forming the center focal point of Vondelpark, the blue space-ship–shaped **Het Blauwe Theehuis** (⊠ Vondelpark, Museum District ☎ 020/662–0254) has a massive terrace that attracts all manner of folks by day and a more clubby hip crowd by night. DJs are often on hand to provide a gentle but beat-driven soundtrack.

For a flavor of the Pijp's reinvented café culture, check out **Kingfisher** (⊠ Ferdinand Bolstraat 23, De Pijp ☎ 020/671–2395), which fills up most nights with thirsty locals. The arty and the studenty come together at the **Lokaal 't Loosje** (⊠ Nieuwmarkt 32–34, Oude Zijde ☎ 020/627–2635), which is graced with tile pictures dating from 1912. **The Tara** (⊠ Rokin 89, Oude Zijds ☎ 020/421–2654) is a labyrinth of an Irish bar that is large enough to harbor live music and large-screen football (soccer) matches while still having enough cozy nooks left over for those who want to eat, drink, or cuddle in private—in short: the best pub in town. **Twstd** (⊠ Weteringschans 157, Grachtengordel East ☎ no phone ⊕ www.twstd.nl) is the small cozy bar-lounge belonging to the organizers of the annual mega Dance Valley festival (www.dancevalley.nl), so don't be surprised if a top DJ drops by to spin some latest dance groove.

Brown Cafés

Coffee and conversation are the two main ingredients of *gezelligheid* (a socially cozy time) for an Amsterdammer, and upon occasion a beer or two (with perhaps a *jenever* [Dutch gin] added to the mix) as the evening wears on. The best place for these pleasures is a traditional brown café, or *bruine kroeg*. Wood paneling, wooden floors, comfortably worn furniture, and walls and ceilings stained with eons' worth of tobacco smoke give the cafés their name—though today a little artfully stippled paint achieves the same effect. Traditionally, there is no background music, just the hum of chitchat. You can meet up with friends or sit alone, undisturbed for hours, enjoying a cup of coffee and a thorough read of the newspapers and magazines from the pile at hand. The Jordaan district is a particularly happy hunting ground for this phenomenon.

Intensely evocative if out of the way, **Bierbrouwerij 't IJ** (⊠ Funenkade 7, East of Amstel ☎ 020/622–8325) is a microbrewery perched under a windmill and is open Wednesday–Sunday 3–8. **Café Chris** (⊠ Bloemstraat 42, Jordaan ☎ 020/624–5942) has been pouring beverages since 1624 when it was used as the local bar for the builders of the Western Church. Its coziness is enhanced by having the smallest washrooms in town. Beware: the slant of **Café Sluyswacht** (⊠ Jodenbreestraat 1, Jewish Quarter and

CloseUp

PROOST!: DUTCH BEERS & BREWS

WITH BRANDS SUCH AS HEINEKEN and Grolsch available around the world, you can be sure that the Dutch know their beers. Although most breweries have moved outside Amsterdam, an aromatic cloud of malt and hop vapors occasionally envelops the city. The Dutch are especially fond of their pils, a light golden lager usually served with a large head of foam. Locals claim—in fact, science backs them up—that their pils tastes better if sipped through the foam, so asking for a top-off pour may offend. There are stronger beers, generally referred to as bokbier—usually seasonal, they are made with warming spices in the winter. In summer, witte bier (white beer) is a refreshing drink, a zesty brew served cool with a twist of lemon. The indigenous liquor of The Netherlands is jenever, a potent gin, in fact, the original gin, which the English went on to make more bitter. It is usually served neat in tall, narrow glasses. It comes in varieties from jonge (young gin), with a rough edge (though Ketel's mellower recipe has managed to become a huge trend in cocktail bars across the globe), to the more sophisticated oude (mature gin), aged in vats for years. Locals knock back their gin borrel (in one gulp), but beware. When served accompanying a beer it is known as a kopstoot ("headbang"). The name should be taken as a warning to the uninitiated. There are also fruit-flavor gin variants, with currant or lemon juice, for those with a sweeter tooth. Try out Dutch liquors at a proeflokaal or proeverij, an old-fashioned "tasting house." An after-work phenomenon, most of the tasting houses close in the early evening.

Plantage ☎ 020/65–7611) can end up causing nausea after one too many beers on its patio overlooking Oudeschans. Once the tasting house of an old family distillery, **De Admiraal** (⊠ Herengracht 319, Grachtengordel East ☎ 020/625–4334) still serves potent liqueurs—many with obscene names. **De Doktertje** (⊠ Rozenboomsteeg 4, Nieuwe Zijds and Spui ☎ 020/626–4427), or "the Doctor," has been prescribing beers and liquors for against what ails you (most likely: too much sightseeing) for centuries in a tiny brown bar not much wider than the alley it's found on. Decidedly, a classic.

Decidedly ancient and brown, **De Engelse Reet** (⊠ Begijnensteeg 4, Nieuwe Zijds and Spui ☎ 020/623–1777) is like stepping back into some lost age when beer was the safest alternative to drinking water. Like many cafés in the Jordaan, **De Prins** (⊠ Prinsengracht 124, Jordaan ☎ 020/624–9382) is blessed with a canal-side patio. **De Reiger** (⊠ Nieuwe Leliestraat 34, Jordaan ☎ 020/624–7426) has a distinctive Jugendstil bar and serves food. If you want to hear the locals sing folk music on Sunday afternoon, stop by **De Twee Zwaantjes** (⊠ Prinsengracht 114, Jordaan ☎ 020/625–2729). A busy, jolly brown café, **In de Wildeman** (⊠ Kolksteeg 3, Nieuwe Zijds and Spui ☎ 020/638–2348) attracts a wide range of types and ages.

Nol (⊠ Westerstraat 109, Jordaan ☎ 020/624–5380) resonates most nights with lusty-lunged, native Jordaaners having the time of their lives. **Rooie Nelis** (⊠ Laurierstraat 101, Jordaan ☎ 020/624–4167) has kept its traditional Jordaan atmosphere despite the area's tendency toward trendiness. Set with Golden Age chandeliers, leaded-glass windows, and the patina of centuries, the gloriously charming **'t Smalle** (⊠ Egelantiersgracht 12, Jordaan ☎ 020/623–9617) is one of Amsterdam's most delightful spots. The after-work crowd always jams the waterside terrace here, but opt instead for the historic interior, once home to one of the city's first jenever distilleries. It is not surprising to learn that a literal copy of this place was created for Nagasaki's Holland Village in Japan. One of Amsterdam's most famous *proeflokaal* ("tasting houses"), **Wynand Fockink** (⊠ Pijlsteeg 31, Oude Zijds ☎ 020/639–2695) offers top tasting options for Dutch jenever between 3 and 9 PM daily in a more cramped yet equally evocative locale (and also offers lunch earlier in the day in its atmospheric hidden garden courtyard).

Cabarets

Boom Chicago (⊠ Leidseplein 12, Leidseplein ☎ 020/423–0101 ⊕ www. boomchicago.nl), at the Leidseplein Theater, belongs to a bunch of zany ex-pat Americans who opened their own restaurant-theater to present improvised comedy inspired by life in both Amsterdam and the world. Dinner and seating begin at 7, with show time at 8:15. **Kleine Komedie** (⊠ Amstel 56–58, East of Amstel ☎ 020/624–0534) has for many years been the most vibrant venue for cabaret and comedy (mainly in Dutch). For some straight—and often English—stand-up comedy, check the schedule of **Comedy Café Amsterdam** (⊠ Max Euweplein 43, Leidseplein ☎ 020/638–3971 ⊕ www.comedycafe.nl). **Toomler** (⊠ Breitnerstraat 2, Amsterdam South ☎ 020/670–7400 ⊕ www.toomler.nl) is a popular comedy-club option with often English-friendly programming.

Casino

The **Holland Casino Amsterdam** (⊠ Max Euweplein 62, Leidseplein ☎ 020/521–1111) is part of the Lido complex near Leidseplein. It is one of the largest casinos in Europe (more than 90,000 square feet) and offers everything from your choice of French or American roulette to computerized bingo, as well as the obligatory slot machines to eat up your supply of loose euros. On your way out of town via Schiphol airport, Holland Casino has lounges tucked away in many of the wings of the airport leading to your gate.

Cocktail Bars & Grand Cafés

The lounging American can find a familiar home at **Boom Chicago Lounge** (⊠ Leidseplein 12, Museum District ☎ 020/530–7300), part of the comedy club of the same name, which also provides both a terrace option and an array of fruity cocktails. The thematically decorated **Café Cuba** (⊠ Nieuwmarkt 3, Oude Zijde ☎ 020/627–4919) serves relatively cheap cocktails and offers a jazzy modern-dance sound track that inspires many of the hipster and student regulars to light up a joint in the back. Exceedingly popular, the riverside **Café de Jaren** (⊠ Nieuwe Doelenstraat 20, Oude Zijds ☎ 020/625–5771) is a large, airy multilevel bar/café/restaurant with a lovely terrace overlooking the Amstel. **Ciel Bleu Bar** (⊠ Hotel Okura, Ferdinand Bolstraat 333, De Pijp ☎ 020/ 678–7111) has a glass-wall lounge set 23 stories high, where you can enjoy sunsets over Amsterdam and watch the night lights twinkle to life. Part of the Nederlands Filmmuseum, **Café Vertigo** (⊠ Vondelpark 3, Museum District ☎ 020/612–3021) has a stunningly scenic terrace for watching the chaos that is Vondelpark.

In the Stopera complex next to the Waterlooplein Market is the lovely **Dantzig** (⊠ Zwanenburgwal 15, Oude Zijds, ☎ 020/620–9039). With a view of the Amstel River, it is the perfect location before or after the ballet or opera. The relatively new grand café **De Engel** (⊠ Albert Cuypstraat 182, De Pijp ☎ 020/ 675–0544) offers a sense of epic space in a decidedly non-spacious neighborhood. **De Kroon** (✉ Rembrandtplein 17, Rembrandtsplein ☎ 020/625–2011) is a grand café with intimate seating arrangements and a U-shape bar surrounding old-style wooden museum cases filled with zoological specimens. The bar attracts a fashionable yuppie clientele in the evenings. **Freddy's** (✉ Hotel de l'Europe, Nieuwe Doelenstraat 2–8, Rembrandtsplein ☎ 020/623–4836), cozy and stylish, is a favorite meeting place for businesspeople. Comfy leather chairs and soft lighting give the **Golden Palm Bar** (✉ Grand Hotel Krasnapolsky, Dam 9, Oude Zijds ☎ 020/554–9111) something of the atmosphere of a British gentlemen's club. **Luxembourg** (✉ Spui 22–24, Nieuwe Zijds and Spui ☎ 020/620–6264) has an Art Deco–style interior and a glassed-in terrace for people-watching on Spui square. One of Rembrandt-

Fodor'sChoice plein's few redeeming features, **Schiller** (✉ Rembrandtplein 26,
★ Rembrandtplein ☎ 020/624–9846), part of the hotel of the same name, has a faded glory and a real sense of history thanks to a wooden fin-de-siècle interior that other grand cafés would sell their souls for. This re-

★ mains a favorite with the media crowd. In the afternoon, **Wildschut** (✉ Roelof Hartplein 1-3, Museum District ☎ 020/676–8220), in a 1920s Amsterdam School edifice, is a delightful place for coffee; it's also the place to meet suited yuppies in the evenings. The terrace is large and has great views for architecture enthusiasts.

Coffee Shops

Generally, the "coffee shops" where marijuana and hashish are smoked are not the most delightful of local places, but the following are among the more acceptable of these establishments. Observers commonly note that one should use caution if indulging, because the available product is very good and those unaccustomed to its high quality may overreact, chemically speaking.

Hidden in a small alley, **Abraxas** (✉ Jonge Roelensteeg 12-14, Nieuwe Zijds and Spui ☎ 020/625–5763) supplements its smokeables with a menu of ganga cakes and shakes in an atmosphere that suggests a hip and multilevel home of a family of hobbits. **Barney's** (✉ Haarlemmer-straat 102, Jordaan ☎ 020/625–9761) brings together two stand-alone concepts: a wide variety of smokeables and all-day breakfasts of the world. Artful mosaics provide background at the **Greenhouse** (✉ Oude Zijds Voorburgwal, Oude Zijds ☎ 020/627–1739), renowned for the "quality" of both its weeds and its seeds. **Kandinsky** (✉ Rosmarijnsteeg 9, Nieuwe Zijds ☎ 020/624–7023) offers mellow jazz and scrumptious chocolate-chip cookies. The clientele at the **Other Side** (✉ Reguliersd-warsstraat 6, Rembrandtplein ☎ 020/625–5141) is primarily gay. **Paradox** (✉ 1e Bloemdwarstraat 2, Jordaan ☎ 020/623–5639), a storefront in the charming Jordaan, is more like a health-food café than a
★ coffee shop. The very popular **De Rokerij** (✉ Lange Leidsedwarsstraat 41, Leidseplein ☎ 020/622–9442) has a magical-grotto feel that requires no extra indulgences to induce a state of giddiness. The mellow **Yo-Yo** (✉ 2e Jan van der Heijdenstraat 79, De Pijp ☎ 020/664–7173) is the quintessential "friendly neighborhood coffee shop" in the heart of the multicultural Pijp.

Dance & Rock Clubs

Since the heady '50s, Amsterdam is the place where perhaps 90% of the world's musicians dream of playing some day. And happily for them, the city's venues are geared towards making such dreams come true (so much so that the town locals are often relegated to playing clubs on the national circuit). Two legendary locations took up the slack after the fading of jazz. The Melkweg and the Paradiso have savvily kept their fingers on the pulse—or even a few beats ahead—of every major musical trend since those culturally defining times of the late '60s. After the hippies, punk rock took over.

Many mourn the passing of the city's once much more vibrant dance club scene, thanks to the loss of the squat clubs and the world-famous Roxy, with its savvy vibe of unpretentious glamour, which burned down in 1999. But short-term visitors will notice little in this downswing when they scan the event flyers at the AUB Ticketshop on Leidseplein. The famed sense of flamboyance is still alive and well. Many party organizers currently seem taken by themed nights that enforce a dress code—may it be "all in white" or the less virginal theme of "Pimp and 'Ho." One warning: visiting bands and DJs sometimes cannot but help overindulge in Amsterdam's mythic reputation. The long clichéd unholy trinity of "sex, drugs, and rock' n' roll" may not define Amsterdam as well as it used to but the city remains one of the defining places for musicians world-wide to indulge in dreams of excess.

Arena (⊠ 's-Gravensandestraat 51, East of Amstel ☎ 020/694–7444 ⊕ www.hotelarena.nl), part of the Arena hotel complex, is popular for its hip roster of DJs and club nights, which take place in a reinvented, formerly clandestine church. **Back Door** (⊠ Amstelstraat 32, Rembrandtsplein, ☎ 020/620–2333) is as laid-back as a back porch in terms of door policy, crowd, and tunes: mostly classic soul, funk, and disco from the '60s and '70s. The huge and popular **Escape** (⊠Rembrandtplein 11–15, Rembrandtsplein ☎ 020/622–1111 ⊕ www.escape.nl) can handle 2,500 people dancing under laser lights to DJs spinning techno and its derivatives, with things getting particularly pumped up on the international, star-studded "Chemistry" evenings. The brand-spanking-new and rather-out-of-the-way **Heineken Music Hall** (⊠ Arena Boule vard 590, Amsterdam Southeast ☎ 0900–2173 ⊕ www.heineken-music-hall.nl), with a capacity for 5,000, offers a sterile but acoustic-rich environment for touring bands that have outgrown the Melkweg and Paradiso. **iT** (⊠ Amstelstraat 24, Rembrandtsplein ☎ 020/625–0111 ⊕ www.it.nl), with four bars, special acts, bands, and celebrities, has forsaken its famously gay and extravagant crowds (although they have retained one "Real" night, the third Saturday of every month) for a more polysexual and studenty mix. **Korsakoff** (⊠ Lijnbaansgrach 161, Jordaan ☎ 020/625–7854 ⊕ www.korsakoff.nl) is a dark but friendly magnet for the pierced and tattooed among us who like their music industrially rough and ready. **Mazzo** (⊠ Rozengracht 114, Jordaan ☎ 020/626–7500 ⊕ www.mazzo.nl), especially acclaimed for its VJs, is a hip, relaxed place that is especially savvy at keeping abreast, or even ahead, of the latest dance sounds. As of press time (winter 2004), it was unclear whether the new owners and makeover will manage to keep this on course.

★ The legendary **Melkweg** (⊠ Lijnbaansgracht 231, Leidseplein ☎ 020/531–8181 ⊕www.melkweg.nl) has a broad programming policy that takes in everything from club nights to world music. This Milky Way, named after the building's previous function as a milk factory, began as a hippie squat in the '60s before savvily evolving with the times and providing a venue for the major trends that followed—from punk to house to world music. Today it's a slickly operated multimedia center equipped with two concert halls, a theater, cinema, gallery, and café-restaurant. On any day of the week you may walk into an evening of rock, reggae, drum'n'bass, hip-hop, soul, punk, or any other imaginable genre. **More** (⊠ Rozengracht 133, Jordaan ⊕ www.expectmore.nl) has been attempting to fill the void, with varied success, left by the sadly burned down RoXY club, which had been internationally acclaimed for its theatrical and glamorous crowd who happily grooved to house and techno DJs. If you feel like dancing in a gracious old canal house, head for **Odeon** (⌂ Singel 460, Nieuwe Zijds and Spui ☎ 020/624–9711 ⊕ www.odeontheater.nl), where hip-hop, R&B, house, and disco get played in different rooms, many of which retain their spectacular painted and stucco ceilings.

★ The country's most famous concert venue, and former church, **Paradiso** (⌂ Weteringschans 6-8, Leidseplein ☎ 020/626–4521 ⊕ www.paradiso.nl), known as the "pop temple" for its vaulted ceilings and stained glass, began its days as a hippie squat allowed by the local government who hoped it might help empty the Vondelpark (then serving as a crash pad for a generation). To this day, the Paradiso remains an epic venue to witness both music's legends and up-and-comers, regardless of their genre. Most concerts are followed by a club night to the early hours that showcases the latest dance sounds. Flexible staging arrangements also make this a favorite venue for performance artists and multimedia events. Amsterdam's relatively new megaclub **The Power Zone** (⌂ Daniel Goedkoopstraat 1-3, Museum District ☎ 020/681–8866 ⊕ www.thepowerzone.nl) can pack in thousands of revelers and often does, thanks to having no door policy and plenty of room for both lounging and dancing to the latest happy house tunes.

If it is a much smaller scale you're out for, **Winston** (⌂ Warmoesstraat 129, Oude Zijds ☎ 020/623–1380 ⊕ www.winston.nl) is ambitious when it comes to programming—from spoken word to punk to DJs—but its ultimate night remains Sunday, when Club Vegas re-creates a happy, kitschy, and always danceable vibe with hosts Erin Tazmania and DJ Pollack. A favorite with tourists, **The Last Waterhole** (⌂ Oude Zijds Armsteeg 12, Oude Zijds ☎ 020/624–4814, ⊕ www.lastwaterhole.nl) usually features a blues and rock cover band of usually dubious distinction—but it remains a fun place to trade tales of the road. **Maloe Melo** (⌂ Lijnbaansgracht 163, Jordaan ☎ 020/420–4592 ⊕ www.maloemelo.com) is a charming and friendly hangout dive and a venue for rock, blues, and roots musicians who are often joined on stage by more international names coming from their gigs at more reputable venues. A former squat, **OCCII** (⌂ Amstelveenseweg 134, Museum District ☎ 020/671–7778 ⊕ www.occii.org) has retained its punky vibe over the years with programming that often also embraces world music.

World-music buffs should check the listings for the Melkweg and Paradiso before checking out the offerings at **Akhnaton** (⌂ Nieuwezijds Kolk 25, Nieuwe Zijds and Spui ☎ 020/624–3396 ⊕ www.akhnaton.nl), renowned for their tight and sweaty African and salsa club nights. **Badcuyp** (⌂ 1e Sweelinckstraat 10, De Pijp ☎ 020/675–9669 ⊕ www.badcuyp.demon.nl) packs in locals for jams of both the jazz and world persuasion. Some of the bigger legends of both world music and dance wind up performing in the rarefied venue (*see* Exploring Amsterdam chapter) of the famous **Tropenmuseum** (⌂ Linnaeusstraat 2, Amsterdam East ☎ 020/568–8200 ⊕ www.tropenmuseum.nl).

Potential pleasure-palace extraordinaire (and not open at press time), the **Westergasfabriek** (⌂ Haarlemmerweg 8-10, Amsterdam West ☎ 020/586–0710 ⊕ www.westergasfabriek.nl) reopened in the autumn of 2003 as an arts and cultural center. Covering the historic 19th-century Western Gas Factory grounds, its site consists of 13 monumental buildings of various sizes and shapes, which play host to film and theater companies, fashion shows, corporate functions, movie shoots, art shows, operas, techno parties, and assorted festivals, plus bars, nightclubs, and restaurants. Visitors interested in all matters of culture should certainly check out how things are shaping up there. Out for a truly unique club location? Check out the multifunctional **Vakzuid** (✉ Olympisch Stadium 35, Amsterdam South ☎ 020/570–8400 ⊕ www.vakzuid.nl), in the 1928 Olympic Stadium; this attracts more of a working commercial arts crowd to its changing roster of weekend DJs.

Gay & Lesbian Bars

Tankards and brass pots hanging from the ceiling in the woody **Amstel Taveerne** (✉ Amstel 54, Rembrandtsplein ☎ 020/623–4254) reflect the friendly crowd of Amsterdammers around the bar whose members burst into song whenever the sound system plays an old favorite. **April** (✉ Reguliersdwarsstraat 37, Rembrandtsplein, ☎ 020/625–9572), which gets going only after 11, has a lounge in the front and a fabulous rotating bar in the back, which management opens when the place becomes particularly crowded on the weekends. April's late-night multi-level bar and disco, **April's Exit** (✉ Reguliersdwarsstraat 42, Rembrandtsplein ☎ 020/625–8788) attracts a smart young crowd of gay men and is women-friendly. The always-packed **Soho** (✉ Reguliersdwarsstraat 36, Rembrandtsplein ☎ 020/330–4400) is an English-style pub that provides the backdrop to some outrageous flirting.

Club Havana (✉ Reguliersdwarsstraat 17, Rembrandtsplein ☎ 020/620–6788) has a comfortable atmosphere with large wicker chairs and banquet seating with an upstairs dance area that throbs on weekends. For a heavy cruise scene, the men-only and leather-rich **Cockring** (✉ Warmoestraat 96, Oude Zijds ☎ 020/623–9604) runs well into the morning hours. **Downtown** (✉ Reguliersdwarsstraat 31, Rembrandtsplein, ☎ 020/622–9958) is a pleasant daytime coffee bar with a sunny terrace. **Getto** (✉ Warmoesstraat, Oude Zijds ☎ 020/421–5151) is an ultimately friendly and pansexual lounge-bar that also serves excellent meals. **Le Montmartre** (✉ Halvemaansteeg 17, Rembrandtsplein ☎ 020/620–7622) attracts a hip crowd of younger gay men, who stop for a drink and perhaps a sing-along before heading out clubbing. Leather, piercing, and tattoos predominate at the **Web** (✉ Sint Jacobstraat 6, Nieuwe Zijds and Spui ☎ 020/623–6758).

Amsterdam offers lesbians very few places to meet and party. Women should check at the bars, the women/lesbian bookstore Xantippe Unlimited (Prinsengracht 290, Grachtengordel West, 020/623–5854), or the COC (Rozenstraat 8, Jordaan, 020/623 4596, www.coc.nl), a national organization that deals with all matters gay and lesbian, for women's parties and events. But there is an official dance club—**You II** (✉ Amstel 178, Rembrandtsplein ☎ 020/421–0900)—that has tried to fill the void. Amsterdam's best lesbian bar, **Saarein** (✉ Elandsstraat 119, Jordaan ☎ 020/623–4901), has a cozy brown-café atmosphere in the Jordaan and a relatively new "mixed" policy. The lesbian perennial **Vive-la-Vie** (✉ Amstelstraat 7, Rembrandtsplein ☎ 020/624–0114) has a lively bar scene and is both men- and straight-friendly.

Jazz Clubs

Amsterdam has provided a happy home-away-from-home for jazz musicians since the early '50s, when such legends as Chet Baker and Gerry Mulligan would wind down after their official show at the Concertgebouw by jamming at one or another of the many bohemian bars around the Zeedijk. For the last quarter century, the world-statured but intimate Bimhuis has taken over duties as the city's major jazz venue with an excellent programming policy that welcomes both the legendary jazz performer and the latest avant-garde up-and-comer.

In the smoky, jam-packed atmosphere of **Alto** (⊠ Korte Leidsedwarsstraat 115, Leidseplein ☎ 020/626–3249), you can hear the top picks of local bands. **Bamboo Bar** (⊠ Lange Leidsedwarsstraat 64, Leidseplein ☎ 020/624–3993) has a long bar and cool Latin sounds. At **Bimhuis** (⊠ Oude Schans 73–77, Oude Zijds ☎ 020/623–3373), the best-known jazz place in town, you'll find top musicians, including avant-gardists, performing on Friday and Saturday nights, and weeknight jam sessions—call ahead, since they are due to move to the Eastern Docklands at the dawn of 2004. **Bourbon Street Jazz & Blues Club** (⊠ Leidsekruisstraat 6–8, Leidseplein ☎ 020/623–3440) presents mainstream blues and jazz to a largely tourist clientele. Fans of more traditional jazz should check out the legendary **Cotton Club** (⊠ Nieuwmarkt 5, Oude Zijde ☎ 020/626–6192), named after its original owner, the Surinamer trumpet player Teddy Cotton. While the music is not usually live, its gregarious crowd is certainly lively. **Casablanca** (⊠ Zeedijk 26, Oude Zijds ☎ 020/625–5685), on the edge of the Red Light District, is an institution in the neighborhood, with jazz during the week and karaoke on weekends. **Café Meander** (⊠ Voetboogstraat 3b, Nieuwe Zijds and Spui ☎ 020/625–8430) offers a mixed selection of live music, from soul to swing. **Joseph Lam Jazz Club** (⊠ Van Diemenstraat 242, Amsterdam West ☎ 020/622–8086) specializes in Dixieland and is open only on Saturday. A pioneer on the up-and-coming nightlife and culture zone of the Eastern Docklands, **Panama** (⊠ Oostelijke Handelskade 4, Waterfront ☎ 020/311–8686 ⊕ www.panama.nl) is a nightclub with a difference: plush and golden interior combined with inspired programming—including everything from tango orchestras to circus acts to big bands unafraid of appropriating contemporary dance beats—that effectively updates a 1920s jazz-club ambience for the 21st century.

Lounges

NL-Lounge (⊠ Nieuwezijds Voorburgwal 169, Nieuwe Zijds and Spui ☎ no phone), taking its name from the national car code NL, is probably one of the hipper and most "classic" of local lounges, with decor that makes you feel as if you have been transported to New York City. Since it opened, **Bep** (⊠ Nieuwezijds Voorburgwal 260, Nieuwe Zijds and Spui ☎ 020/626–5649) has attracted a smart artist crowd for mellow afternoons and lively evenings. **Lime** (⊠ Zeedijk 104, Oude Zijde ☎ 020/639–3020) offers a more slick and minimal lounge but with a nicely unpretentious atmosphere, complete with DJs, cocktails, and all the latest design/arts mags. A group of artists runs **Seymour Likely** (⊠ Nieuwezijds Voorburgwal 250, Nieuwe Zijds and Spui ☎ 020/627–1427); it was one of the first hip lounges to become the rage and often spotlights funky DJs. Don't get confused if they have changed their name: the song will undoubtedly stay the same. **Lux** (⊠ Marnixstraat 397, Nieuwe Zijds and Spui ☎ 020/422–1412) has a fantastic 1960s decor and an attractive young crowd. Part of the ultimately lounging-oriented Supper Club (*see* Chapter 2), the **Supper Club Lounge** (⊠ Jongeroelensteeg 21, Nieuwe Zijds and Spui ☎ 020/638–0513) is quintessentially hip with a snooty door policy to match, where you can groove to equally hip tunes or squeeze in around tables in a heavenly white room.

THE ARTS

Although a relatively small city, Amsterdam packs a giant cultural wallop through its numerous venues—from former churches and industrial monuments to the acoustical supremacy of the Concertgebouw—and festivals that invariably feature both homegrown and international talent.

Although healthy subsidies play a role, it is more the interest of a culturally inclined people that supports a milieu whose spectrum ranges from the austerely classical to the outrageously avant-garde. So book that ticket fast. Amsterdam's theater and music season begins in September and runs through June, when the Holland Festival of Performing Arts is held. *What's On in Amsterdam* is a comprehensive, albeit a tad dull, English-language publication distributed by the tourist office that lists art and performing-arts events around the city. Culture hounds are better directed to browse through the many fliers, pamphlets, booklets, and magazines—including the Dutch-language but still somewhat decipherable and certainly complete *Uitkrant,* or the more alternative-inclined English-language listings magazine *Shark,* also on-line at (⊕ www.underwateramsterdam.com). Autumn 2003 should also see the debut of an English-language cultural listings and reviews weekly called—appropriately enough—*Amsterdam Weekly.* All of these are available at the **AUB Ticketshop** (⊠ Leidseplein, at Marnixstraat, Leidseplein ☎ 0900/0191, 9–6 daily ⊕ www.aub.nl), open Monday–Saturday 10–6, Thursday until 9. Tickets can also be purchased in person at the tourist information offices through the **VVV Theater Booking Office** (⊠ Stationsplein 10, Centraal Station), open daily 10–5, or at theater box offices. Reserve tickets to performances at the major theaters before your arrival through the AUB Web site or the **National Reservation Center** (⌂ Postbus 404, 2260 AK, Leidschendam ☎ 3170/ 320–2500 ⊞ 070/320–2611).

Film

Have you ever wondered how the Dutch came to speak impeccable English? One of the reasons may be the fact that English films shown in Holland are merely subtitled, not dubbed—good news for both late-night hotel-TV viewers and city-cinema visitors. This Dutch command of English has allowed many Dutch directors—alienated by the long lackluster local scene—to make the shift to Hollywood (the notorious Paul Verhoeven being the most famous example, as witnessed in his *Basic Instinct* and *RoboCop*). But visitors returning home should really harass their local video store for the latest generation of directors who have decided to stay put and produce their own personal and happily genre-free films that are inspired by the efforts of local heroes and international festival darlings Alex Van Warmerdam (*Abel, De Noorderlingen*), Eddie Terstall (*Hufters and Hofdames, Rent-a-Friend*), and Robert Jan Westdijk (*Zusje*). Some names to look out for (or look up) are Paula van der Oest, Lodewijk Crijns, Martin Koolhoven, Erik de Bruijn, and Karim Traidia.

And true film buffs should certainly consider timing their vacation around such internationally renowned events as the International Film Festival Rotterdam (⊕ www.filmfestivalrotterdam.com) in late January/early February (it's only an hour away by train, after all); the International Documentary Film Festival Amsterdam (⊕ www.idfa.nl) in November; or the Festival of Fantastic Film (⊕ www.filmevents.nl) in April.

Although there are cinema programs available or on display at most every bar and café in town, and such Dutch-language mags as the free *De Filmkrant* or the "Saturday PS" supplement of *De Parool* newspaper are easy enough to decipher, it may help to have some general information about the scene. Mainstream cinemas are concentrated near the Leidseplein; the largest and most Hollywood blockbuster–oriented is the seven-screen (and monument of functionalist architecture) **City 1–7** (⊠ Kleine Gartmanplantsoen 13–25, Leidseplein ☎ 0900–1458). **Cinecenter** (⊠ Lijnbaansgracht 236, Leidseplein ☎ 020/623–6615), with a sleek modern lounge decor, uses its four screens for the artier and more internationally acclaimed films. If you cannot decide between two films, then choose the one with the best setting—for instance the widely eclectic Art Deco reverie on display at the **Tuschinski** (✉ Reguliersbreestraat 26, Rembrandtplein ☎ 0900/1458). A full-swing 1920s ambience is on view at the **Movies** (✉ Haarlemmerdijk 161, Jordaan ☎ 020/624–5790). The canal-side and popcorn-free **De Uitkijk** (✉ Prinsengracht 452, Leidseplein ☎ 020/623–7460) ranks as the city's oldest cinema, having opened in 1913.

Fodor'sChoice
★

But there are also several repertory cinemas that show a savvy blend of classics and latest offerings of world cinema. **Filmhuis Cavia** (✉ Van Hallstraat 521, Amsterdam West ☎ 020/681–1419) offers programming that is decidedly edgy and politically alternative. **Kriterion** (✉ Roetersstraat 170, East of Amstel ☎ 020/623–1708) is run by students and reflects their world-embracing tastes (especially during its late shows that embrace the more cultish of movies). **Rialto** (✉ Ceintuurbaan 338, De Pijp ☎ 020/662–3488) is noted for world cinema and the more highbrow of film classics.

Film buffs should definitely pay a visit to the **Nederlands Filmmuseum** (Netherlands Film Museum; ✉ Vondelpark 3, Museum District ☎ 020/589–1400 ⊕ www.filmmuseum.nl) for its public library and schedule of revivals culled from a collection of more than 35,000 films. It also has occasional special programs that comprise outdoor screenings and silent films accompanied by live piano music.

Music

There are two auditoriums, large and small, under one roof at The Netherlands' premier concert hall, the **Concertgebouw** (✉ Concertgebouwplein 2–6, Museum District ☎ 020/671–8345 ⊕ www.concertgebouw.nl). Its Viennese Classicist facade surmounted by a golden lyre, this hall draws 800,000 visitors per year, many of whom flock here to enjoy Bach and Beethoven performed under nearly perfect acoustic conditions. In the larger of the two theaters, the **Grote Zaal**, Amsterdam's critically acclaimed **Koninklijk Concertgebouworkest** (Royal Concert Orchestra), whose recordings are in the collections of most self-respecting lovers of classical music, is often joined by international soloists. Their reputation has only grown in the last decade under the baton twirling of conductor Riccardo Chailly who has just passed the honor to the highly regarded Latvian Mariss Jansons. Guest conductors read like a list from the musical heavens: Mstislav Rostropovich, Nikolaus Harnoncourt, and Bernard Haitink. Visting maestros like these naturally push the prices up but the range remains wide: expect to pay anything between €5 and €100. But throughout July and August, tickets for the Robeco Summer Concerts, which involve high-profile artists and orchestras, are an excellent bargain. The smaller hall, the **Kleine Zaal**, is a venue for chamber music and up-and-coming musicians and which is the usual setting for the free lunchtime concerts on Wednesdays at 12:30. The architectural landmark and progenitor of the Amsterdam School, the **Beurs van Berlage** (✉ Damrak 213, Oude Zijds ☎ 020/627–0466 ⊕ www.beursvanberlage.nl) also has two concert halls—including the definitely unique glass-box "diamond-in-space" AGA Zaal—with The Netherlands Philharmonic and The Netherlands Chamber Orchestra as the in-house talent. The **IJsbreker** (✉ Weesperzijde 23, East of Amstel ☎ 020/693–9093 ⊕ www.ysbreker.nl), due to move to a new location on the arising new nightlife and culture zone of the Eastern Docklands in late 2004 (call ahead for details around that time), is at the cutting edge of contemporary music and often hosts festivals of international repute.

Fodor'sChoice
★

Many of the city's churches are being exploited by music-lovers and players (*see also* Nieuwe Kerk, Noorder Kerk, Nicolaas Kerk, and Oude Kerk *in* Exploring Amsterdam). A former monastery, **Bethanienklooster** (⊠ Barndesteeg 6B, Oude Zijds ☎ 020/625–0078) still provides a calm and holy setting for regular chamber music concerts. The former Pilgrims' hang-

★ out, the **Engelse Kerk** (⊠ Begijnhof 48, Nieuwe Zijds and Spui ☎ 020/624–9665) has weekly concerts of Baroque and classical music that al-

★ ways seek to employ period instruments. The 17th-century **Waalse Kerk** (⊠ Oudezijds Achterburgwal 157, Oude Zijds, ☎ 070/236–2236) is a small, elegant, and intimate church that once was the Huguenots' home base in Amsterdam. Concerts here are organized by the Organisatie Oude Muziek, a group devoted to early music played on period instruments that arranges upward of 100 concerts in the country each year. Musicians from both The Netherlands and abroad play here on a relatively regular basis.

Skaters, joggers, cyclists, and sun worshippers gather in Vondelpark each summer to enjoy the great outdoors. However, between late May and

★ September, they're joined by culture vultures, who head to the **Vondelpark Openluchttheater** (⊠ Vondelpark, Museum District ☎ 020/673–1499 ⊕ www.openluchttheater.nl) for its program of music, theater, and children's events (theatrical events have, in fact, been held in the park since 1865). During the festival, Wednesdays offer a lunchtime concert and a midafternoon children's show; Thursday nights find a concert on the bandstand; there's a theater show every Friday night; various events (including another theater show) take place on Saturday; and theater events and pop concerts are held on Sunday afternoons.

Opera & Ballet

Fodor'sChoice The grand and elegant **Muziektheater** (⊠ Waterlooplein 22, Oude Zijds
★ ☎ 020/551–8911 ⊕ www.muziektheater.nl) seats 1,600 people and hosts international opera, ballet, and orchestra performances throughout the year and is home to **De Nederlandse Opera** (Netherlands National Opera) and **Het Nationale Ballet** (Netherlands National Ballet), whose repertoires embrace both the classical and the 20th century. Muziektheater's huge and flexible stage acts as a magnet to directors with a penchant for grand-scale decors, such as Robert Wilson, Willy Decker,
Fodor'sChoice and Peter Sellars. The red-and-gold plushness of **Stadsschouwburg** (⊠ Lei-
★ dseplein 26, Leidseplein ☎ 020/624–2311 ⊕ www.stadsschouwburg.nl), home to the underrated **Nationale Reisopera** (National Travelling Opera), regularly hosts visiting companies. Although more focused on commercial and large-scale musicals, former circus theater **Koninklijk Theater Carre** (⊠ Amstel 115–25, East of Amstel ☎ 020/622–5225) also schedules many acclaimed Eastern European companies performing ballet and opera classics.

Dance

While many associate the Dutch dance scene with two names—Nationale Ballet and Nederlands Dans Theater—there are lot more local companies that are busy jumping around and being innovative. Certainly the Hungarian expat Krisztina de Châtel (www.dechatel.nl) has turned Amsterdam into a jumping-off point for international acclaim thanks to her physical approach that also often employs the latest technologies in the visual arts. A certain multimedia savvy is also seen in the works of other acclaimed Amsterdam-based troupes such as Dance Company Leine & Roebana, the Shusaku & Dormu Dance Theater & Bodytorium, and the absurdity- and mime-loving Hans Hof Ensemble. One annual event that should not be missed by dance-lovers—that mixes both local and international names of a cutting-edge nature—is the month-long Julidans (www.julidans.nl) that is centered around the Stadsschouwburg.

The relatively small stage of the multimedia center **Melkweg** (✉ Lijnbaansgracht 234a, Leidseplein ☎ 020/531 8181) brings together both local and international dance names to a more intimate setting. The grand and spacious **Muziektheater** (✉ Waterlooplein 22, Oude Zijds ☎ 020/551–8911 ⊕ www.muziektheater.nl) is not only home to the **De Nederlandse Opera** (Netherlands National Opera) and **Het Nationale Ballet** (Netherlands National Ballet), but also often hosts the **Nederlands Dans Theater** (National Dance Theater) which has evolved into one of the most celebrated of modern dance companies in the world under choreographers Jiri Kylian and Hans van Manen. Hosts of the Julidans festival, **Stadsschouwburg** (✉ Leidseplein 26, Leidseplein ☎ 020/624–2311 ⊕ www.stadsschouwburg.nl) often has a variety of modern dance offerings in an epic setting of gilding and red velvet. Part of the Tropics Institute, **Tropeninstituut Theater** (✉ Linnaeusstraat 2, East of Amstel ☎ 020/568—8500) hosts international companies dedicated to non-Western dance—from classical Indian to re-invented tango.

Theater

The red-velvet **Stadsschouwburg** (✉ Leidseplein 26, Leidseplein ☎ 020/624–2311) focuses primarily on Dutch theater but has occasional English and multicultural performances where understanding the language becomes less of an issue. For lavish, large-scale productions, the place to go is **Koninklijk Theater Carre** (✉ Amstel 115–125, East of Amstel ☎ 020/622–5225), originally built in the 19th century as permanent home to a circus.

Amsterdam's Off Broadway–type theaters are centered along the Nes, an alley leading off the Dam. Part of the Flemish cultural center, **Brakke Grond** (✉ Nes 45, Oude Zijds ☎ 020/626–6866 ⊕ www.brakkegrond.nl) often hosts the more experimental of theater and dance performances from Holland's neighbor to the south. **Cosmic Theater** (✉ Nes 75, Oude Zijds ☎ 020/622–8858 ⊕ www.cosmictheater.nl) was formed 15 years ago in the Caribbean and, after a spell in New York, ended up in Amsterdam. The company has toured widely and has developed an international reputation for its productions that address the modern world's multicultural reality. **De Engelenbak** (✉ Nes 71, Oude Zijds ☎ 020/626–3644, ⊕ www.engelenbak.nl) is best known for "Open Bak," an open-stage event each Tuesday where virtually anything goes. It's the longest-running theater program in The Netherlands, where everybody gets their 15 minutes of potential fame; arrive at least half an hour before the show starts to get a ticket. Otherwise, the best amateur groups in the country perform between Thursday and Saturday. **Frascati** (✉ Nes 63, Oude Zijds ☎ 020/626–6866 ⊕ www.nestheaters.nl) has three stages that all lend intimacy to both performers and audience (only reinforced on their regular open-stage nights where they welcome audience members to take the stage). Although the **Muiderpoorttheater** (✉ 2e Van Swindenstraat 26, East of Amstel ☎ 020/668–1313 ⊕ www.muiderpoorttheater.nl) is not within the Nes zone, it also follows an Off Broadway path by presenting new faces of the international theater and dance scene in an intimate setting.

Handily located near the Waterlooplein, **International Theaterschool** (✉ Jodenbreestraat 3, Oude Zijds ☎ 020/527–7700 ⊕ www.the.ahk.nl) brings together students and teachers from all over the world to share their experiences, and both to learn and create in the fields of dance and theater. Dance performances—some of which are announced in *Uitkrant*—vary from studio shots to evening-long events in the Philip Morris Dans Zaal theater. Also worth checking out is the international theater school festival they host every June.

Alternative "forms" of theater are *very* Amsterdam. The former gas-factory complex **Westergasfabriek** (✉ Haarlemmerweg 8-10, Amsterdam West, ☎ 020/586–0710 ⊕ www.westergasfabriek.nl) (*see* Dance and Rock Clubs) will undoubtedly continue employing its singular performance spaces for a variety of shows and festivals that often embrace the more visual, and more avant-garde, of the entertainment spectrum. **Warner en Consorten** (Warner and Company; ☎ 020/663–2656 ⊕ www.warnerenconsorten.nl), formed in 1993, is an interdisciplinary concept of street theater, where sculpture, dance, physical acting (such as mime), and music collide and challenge the concepts of theater, urban life, and reality. The results are often delightfully, Dada-istically hilarious. Public space is the starting point—streets are analyzed, crowd behavior is studied, passersby are observed. During the winter months, the company finds abandoned warehouses and factories for venues; in the summer, city streets are the "theaters." Such internationally statured companies as **Dogtroep** (⊕ www.dogtroep.nl) and **Vis-a-Vis** (⊕ www.vis-a-vis.nl) are specialists in the typically Dutch school of "spectacle theater," which is not bounded by language and goes in search of unique locations to strut its stuff. All or one of these three groups usually take part (with many others of like mind from around the world) in the amazing annual **Over het IJ Festival** (⊕ www.ijfestival.nl), which takes place every summer in an abandoned shipyard in Amsterdam North, and gathers together dozens of dance and theater troupes dedicated to the more wild and physical aspects of the theatrical arts. Finally, if you happen to be in town for the first two weeks of August, don't miss **Parade** (✉ Martin Luther Kingpark, Amsterdam South ☎ 033/465–4577), a traveling tent city that specializes in quirky performances and a social and carnivalesque ambience.

SPORTS & THE OUTDOORS

5

FODOR'S CHOICE

Ajax, *the most entertaining soccer team on the planet*

Ice-skating, *on the rink behind the Rijksmuseum*

HIGHLY RECOMMENDED

Bloemendaal, *a beach that comes complete with DJs*

Sauna Deco, *a health club with historic ambience to spare*

Revised and
updated by
Steve Korver

REMBRANDTS, DIAMONDS, CANALS, AND RED LIGHT DISTRICTS: it may
not be totally surprising that with this sort of competition, sports does-
n't register in a big way for travelers to Amsterdam. But as the tallest
nation on earth, Holland remains, in fact, a nation as infatuated with
outdoor activities as any. So much so that they've even invented a few
sports of their own, notably a mutation of basketball called korfball,
thought up by an Amsterdam schoolteacher in 1902. Although it has
only about 100,000 practitioners countrywide, it remains notable for
two reasons: as a pioneer in allowing men and women to play together,
and because of its failure to extend beyond Belgium. It thereby—oh, those
crafty Dutch!—ensures The Netherlands' lock on their world champion
status for millennia to come.

Happily, the Dutch have proven themselves more than able to export
their skills in such other, more globally recognized sports as tennis, cycling, skating, rowing, and field hockey. Swimming in particular got a
shot in the arm recently when Peter van den Hoogenband walked away
with a stack of medals from the Sydney Olympics. And a few years ago,
cafés across the country started upgrading their dartboards when the
Dutch found themselves a new—and most unlikely—national sports icon
in the decidedly nonathletic-looking world darts champion Raymond
van Barneveld.

But essentially the local world of Dutch athletics revolves around one
sport: football (called soccer by the more North American–inclined).
Forget the Royal Family or coffee shops: football is the one and only
unifying national obsession. And the man who personifies the sport—
not to mention all that is good, just, and pragmatic in this world—is
the former star footballer/manager and local Amsterdam boy Johann
Cruijff, who long ago surpassed Erasmus as the country's most respected
philosopher. Developer of the concept of "total football," Cruijff's ob-
servations on both life and football—terms that are in fact synonymous
to his disciples (who refer to him as the Redeemer and rather irrever-
ently point toward his initials J. C. as proof thereof)—have regularly
entered the vernacular, whether or not they are straightforwardly pragmatic ("if you don't score, you don't win") or, more enigmatically, Zen
riddlelike ("every disadvantage has an advantage"). And the team that
most reflects Cruijff's ideals remains the Amsterdam Ajax, where he
first shot—not to mention dribbled, headed, defended, and offended—
his way to prominence. It should be no surprise then that Ajax (pronounced *eye*-axe) has always rated superior technique and artistry as
the fundaments for high-quality football. This attitude is in sharp contrast with their eternal competitor—and an equal in attracting certain
hooligan elements—Rotterdam Feyenoord, whose more working class
roots have always reflected a more straightforward and bulk-oriented
"boat worker's football."

Ajax's heady combination of confidence, bluff, and big-mouth arrogance
makes them perhaps the most entertaining team on the planet, even if
viewed only from the bleachers (but good luck in getting a ticket). Their
playing style gives a balletlike illusion of effortlessness. But because Ajax
can rarely afford the high prices paid to today's star players (namely
David Beckham-types), the team often ends up losing their best to higher
bidders—just think of all those Dutch names on the jerseys of teams from
Manchester to Milan—that has resulted recently in a few slow seasons.
In the last couple of years, however, Ajax has attempted to quell this
talent drain by quickly training young players in the mysteries of Ajax's
highly effective team play, and 2003 saw a team reflecting anew the same
champion potential of past glory years.

The famously smart-ass nature of the Amsterdam football player is reflected in other athletes (the cyclist Gerrie Kneteman, when asked what was going through him when he won a world championship responded, "Some white blood cells, some red blood cells"), as well as in their spectators (before World War II, visiting Nazis who were *sieg heil*-ing their national team would be shouted down by locals supporting the Dutch national team with "Hey, don't worry, it's not raining yet"). Certainly, whether you decide to watch a game at the Arena or to join in one in Vondelpark, you will find yourself being tested both physically and mentally.

Perhaps the best way to stay in shape in Amsterdam, naturally, is to pursue the more solo—but no less stressful, especially on the city's busy streets—pursuit of renting a bike and pointing it around town or even beyond, down the Amstel River or toward the fishing villages of North Holland. And if you happen to get a flat tire, you can pretty much count on someone stopping to question both your biking and patching skills (before lending a hand, of course.)

Beaches

After their typically long, dreary winter, Amsterdammers count the days until they can hit the beaches at **Zandvoort,** a beach community directly west of the city, beyond Haarlem, where clean beachfront stretches for miles and many of the dunes are open for walking. The train station is close by, and there are lifeguards on duty. Separate areas of the beach are reserved for nudists, though topless bathing is common practice everywhere in The Netherlands. The city's more hip and youthful, however, invariably head to the long line of beach shacks and lounges (complete
★ with DJs) along **Bloemendaal** beach, which can be reached via train taxi (a ticket for which you must buy with your train ticket) from Haarlem Centraal Station. And Amsterdam now has its own beach in the form of the artificial islands of **Ijburg,** east of the Eastern Docklands. In coming years, these will house tens of thousands of residents, but meanwhile its sandy nature is being exploited for its beachlike properties. And while the surrounding water is, in fact, fresh since the plucky Dutch built a massive dike to keep the sea at bay, it is more than clean enough to swim in (and happily warms up more quickly than the quite aptly named North Sea.). By the end of 2003, the IJ Tram should be running from Centraal Station and could have you diving into the water within 10–15 minutes of your arrival.

Biking

Take a cue from the Amsterdammers and bike your way around the city—it's fun, it's healthful, and it's easy. But keep in mind there are nearly half a million *fiets* (bikes—pronounced feets), so be sure to keep your eyes moving and your bike locked up when you park (there are lots of thefts). Probably one of the more convenient places to rent a bicycle is **Centraal Station** (⊠ Stationsplein 12, 1012 AB, Centraal Station, ☎ 020/624–8391), A long time favorite is **MacBike, Marnixstraat** (⊠ Marnixstraat 220, 1016 TL, Jordaan, ☎ 020/626–6964). **MacBike, Mr Visserplein** (⊠ Mr Visserplein 2, 10111 RD, Jewish Quarter, ☎ 020/620–0985) can have you exploring the Plantage and Jewish neighborhood in no time. **MacBike, Weteringschans** (⊠ Weteringschans 2, 1017 SG, Leidseplein, ☎ 020/528–7688) besides renting bikes also organizes bike tours of the city and its surrounds. **Bike City** (⊠ Bloemgracht 70, 1015 TL, Jordaan, ☎ 020/626–3721) is conveniently located within the scenic Jordaan neighborhood. **Frederic** (⊠ Brouwersgracht 78, 1013 GZ, Jordaan, ☎ 020/ 624–5509) is not only friendly but sensitive (because they do not emblazon their bicycles with their name like other bike rental places and hence you are not recognized immediately as a tourist).

Expect to pay from €8 per day, plus a deposit of €30–€100 per bicycle. You'll need a passport or other identification. You may just want to ask your hotel for a bike shop most convenient to your neighborhood. For ground rules on biking, *see* Amsterdam on Wheels *in* the Destination chapter.

Cycling

As a national obsession, there are cycle races—from track to road to Tour de Nederland circuits—to be witnessed on most weekends of the nonwinter months. The best way to stay abreast is to contact the Royal Dutch Cycle Racing Association, **KNWU** (⊠ Postbus 136, 3440 AC, Woerden, ☎ 0348/484–084, ⊕ www.knwu.nl).

Football (American)

Amsterdam has only recently embraced its one pro football (as in pigskin) team, the **Amsterdam Admirals,** who, although not showing great results, still manage to pack in more than 15,000 spectators per game, which they, like Ajax, play at the **Amsterdam Arena** (⊠ Arena A Boulevard 29, 1101 AX, Amsterdam South-East ☎ 020/311–1444, ⊕ www.admirals.nl).

Golf

The modern and luxurious **BurgGolf** is outside Amsterdam in Noord Holland province. It is a 27-hole course, comprising a 9-hole course and a more difficult 18-hole course. ⊠ *Golden Tulip Hotel Purmerend, Westerweg 60, 1445 AD, Purmerend,* ☎ *0299/481–666* ⊠ *Greens fee €40 weekdays, €45 weekends.*

Closer to home than the BurgGolf course, but still out in the sticks of Amsterdam South-East, is the public, 18-hole, polder course, **De Hoge Dijk-Olympus** ⊠ *Abcouderstraatweg 46, 1105 AA, Amsterdam South-East,* ☎ *0294/281–241* ⊠ *Greens fee €37, club rental €15.*

Health Clubs

Several hotels in Amsterdam have fitness facilities for guests, usually including exercise machines, weights, sauna, and whirlpool. **Barry's Fitness Centre** (⊠ Lijnbaansgracht 350, 1017 XB, Jordaan, ☎ 020/626–1036) has excellent standards when it comes to its equipment, training (by appointment), massages, and sauna. **The Garden** (⊠ Jodenbreestraat 158, 1001 NS, Oudezijds and De Wallen, ☎ 020/626–8772) offers all your physical abuse needs—weights, aerobics, stretching, and calisthenics—while retaining probably the cheapest prices in town. The **Holiday Inn Crowne Plaza** (⊠ Nieuwezijds Voorburgwal 5, 1012 RC, Nieuwezijds and Spui, ☎ 020/620–0500) has a large indoor swimming pool. One of the more comprehensive hotel-based fitness facilities is **AAA Barbizon Palace** (⊠ Prins Hendrikkade 59–72, 1012 AD, Centraal Station ☎ 020/556–4899). Probably the hippest of all the options, **Shape All-In** (⊠ 2e Hugo de Grootstraat 2–6, 1052 LC, Jordaan ☎ 020/684–5857) is truly "all-in" by supplementing a full array of fitness options with a delightful patio, great food, exotic cocktails, and even DJs after dark—only for those who can resist or want to embrace temptation. **Splash Renaissance** (⊠ Kattengat 1, 1012 SZ, Nieuwezijds and Spui ☎ 020/621–

2223) usually offers personal training, aerobics, weight training, massage, solarium, Turkish bath, sauna, and whirlpool. **Sporting Club Leidseplein** (⊠ Korte Leidsedwarsstraat 18, 1017 RC, Leidseplein ☏ 020/620–6631) offers fitness facilities, sauna, and superfast tanners. Day rates at all of the above are around €12, with extra charges for special services. You may also want to check the Amsterdam Yellow Pages under "Fitnesscentra."

★ If you're interested in relaxing, sensual (not sexual) activities, plan to spend a delightful fall or winter evening at Amsterdam's most amazing "health club," the **Sauna Deco** (⊠ Herengracht 115, 1015 BE, Grachtengordel (West) ☏ 020/623–8215), an institution for Amsterdam literati and cognoscenti. On entering the canal house designed by Hendrik P. Berlage (in his early "Neoclassical" period), you descend several steps and are dazzled: the interior is truly spectacular with an Art Deco environment salvaged from some historic landmarks, including Paris's Au Bon Marché department store, the Dutch Twentsche Bank, and chairs from the Hotel Suisse. People come here to read, relax, chat—little wonder many guests take up residence for hours. In short: this is the most beautiful sauna in town. Surrender to their Turkish bath and Finnish sauna, bake in their solarium or revitalise yourself in their cold plunge bath. You can also arrange an a variety of beauty treatments (which use the all-natural products of Algologie and Revita-Apiserum), manicures, pedicures, shiatsu, and massage. Complete day packages can also be arranged that include drinks and a light lunch.

Horseback Riding

There are two places that organize horseback riding in the Amsterdamse Bos (Amsterdam Woods). One of them, the **Hollandsche Manege,** an 1882 landmark beside Vondelpark, is worth a visit in itself since it is a remarkable re-creation of Vienna's famed wooden Spanish Riding School, complete with café and an orchestra balcony to admire the horse-work below. ⊠ *Vondelstraat 140, 1054 GT, Museum District,* ☏ *020/618-0942,* ⊕ *www.dehollandschemanege.nl* ✍ *€17.50/hour.* **Nieuw Amstelland Manege** is the other horse specialist that will see to it that you will be trotting throught the forest in no time. ⊠ *J. Tooropplnts 17, 1182 AC, Amstelveen,* ☏ *020/643–2468,* ⊕ *www.nieuwamstelland. nl,* ✍ *€16/hour.*

Ice-Skating

Although utterly and completely obsessed with ice-skating the Dutch rarely get the chance to show off either their famed speed or their distance-skating capabilities—global warming is considered the culprit. But if conditions allow, the 124-mile Elfstedentocht (Eleven City Route) takes place in Friesland (way up in northern Holland) and as many as 10,000 people take part. Those who do not take an active part either go to watch, or stay home and do their own ice-skating on Amsterdam's canals. Unfortunately, because Amsterdam is not far from the sea, the canals rarely freeze over in the inner city, so if you have your heart set on being a Hans Brinker, head to the Museumplein area to see if they have finally found FodorśChoice a steady contractor to run the high-tech **pond behind the Rijksmuseum** for ★ more than sporadic times. This rink is often artificially induced to freeze and skates are available for rental. On rare occasions, the city canals are solid enough to do a double lutz and the city celebrates appropriately— at various places, stalls are set up to serve hot concoctions and loudspeakers blare Bach. The die-hard skater, whatever the season, can head to the outdoor and year-round indoor skating rinks of **Jaap Edenbaan**. If you don't get to do your Hans Brinker routine on the canals (word to the wise: the ice thaws first along the canal edges and under the bridges), you can also enjoy the Oosterpark pond and the Grote Vijver and Bosbaan in the Amsterdamse Bos park area. ✉ *Radioweg 64, 1098 NJ,* ☎ *020/694–9652* 🖃 *Admission €3.70, skate rental from 5€ a day.*

Jogging

Sunday morning is about the only time when Amsterdam's city center gets enough of a break from foot, bike, and car traffic to allow for a comfortable jog. Beyond the city near the suburb of Amstelveen, **Amsterdamse Bos** (Amsterdam Woods) is a large, spacious place to run. **Oosterpark** (Eastern Park), behind the Tropenmuseum, **Beatrixpark**, near the RAI convention center, and, of course, **Vondelpark**, near the art museums, are the only parks within the city proper that do not require having to endlessly repeat the same circuit.

Roller Skating & In-line Skating

Vondelpark is ground zero for folks attracted to having wheels under their feet—especially on Fridays, when **Friday Night Skate** (⊕ www.fridaynightskate.nl) gathers together a crowd to take over and swoop through the streets of Amsterdam en masse. They'll know all about it at the nearby **Balance** ✉ *Overtoom 464-6, 1054 JX, Museum District* ☎ *020/489–4723* 🖃 *From €7.* Find out about all roller-skating/in-line events at **Rent a Skate** ✉ *Vondelpark 7 (near park entrance at Amstelveenseweg), 1075 VR, Museum District* ☎ *020/664–5091* 🖃 *From €7.*

Rowing

In the Amsterdamse Bos (Amsterdam Woods), the recently widened Bosbaan canal is the setting for an infinite variety of rowing races. The best way to stay abreast is to contact the Royal Dutch Rowing Association. **KNRB** (✉ Bosbaan 6 , 1182 AG, Amstelveen, ☎ 020/646–2740, ⊕ www.knrb.nl).

Snooker

Of course, the natural environment in which to play pool, or, as the Dutch call it, snooker, is in an equipped bar or café, of which there are many in this town. But there are also places where you can truly focus on the game at hand. **De Keizer** (✉ Keizersgracht 256, 1016 EV, Grachtengordel (West), ☎ 020/623–1586, 🖃 €5–8/hour) has a bevy of private rooms with not only a pool or snooker table but also a phone to order a drink or snack. The charm of this place has attracted such luminaries as English snooker champion Alex Higgins (although it is said that those same drink options may also have caused his downfall). **Amsterdam Zuid Pool- and Snookercentrum** (✉ Van Ostadestraat 97hk, 1072 ST, De Pijp, ☎ 020/676–7903, 🖃 €7–8/hour) is a huge mazelike multifloor pool and snooker oasis (but call first, because some nights are members-only).

Soccer

Soccer is a near obsession with the Dutch, and if you want to impress an Amsterdam host, you would best be advised not only to refer to it FodorsChoice as football but also to know the current standing of the local team, **Ajax** ★ relative to that of its archrivals, Rotterdam's Feyenoord (pronounced *feya*-nort) and Eindhoven's PSV (Philips Sports Vereniging). Making a Dutch friend in this way may be the only way to get a very scarce ticket. The Dutch soccer season runs from August to June, with a short break in midwinter; matches are played at the **Amsterdam Arena** (✉ Arena A

Boulevard 29, 1101 AX, Amsterdam South-East, ☎ 020/311–1444 ⊕ www.ajax.nl).

Swimming

When heading to a swimming pool in Amsterdam, always call ahead to save yourself from the potential shock/embarrassment of coming in on hours dedicated to lessons, sexual orientation, and/or nudity.

Mirandabad (✉ De Mirandalaan 9, 1079 PA, Amsterdam South, ☎ 020/ 546–4444, ✉ €3) attracts the masses on sunny days to its outdoor pool and on normal days to the subtropical temperatures of its indoor pool. They also have whirlpools, slides, and squash. Chaotic fun for the whole family! **Zuiderbad** (✉ Hobbemastraat 26, 1071 ZC, Museum District, ☎ 020/671–2217, ✉ €3) is one of the country's oldest pools, and a recent renovation has seen the mosaic tiling shining with epic life again. Very Euro.

SHOPPING

FODOR'S CHOICE

Coster Diamonds, *carat, color, clarity, and cut*

Couzijn Simon, *a children-of-all-ages extravaganza*

De Klompenboer, *the best handpainted Dutch clogs*

Exclusive Oilily Store, *for their kaleidoscopically colored togs*

The Frozen Fountain, *trendmeisters love this home decor shop*

Hogedoorn & Kaufman, *for ceramics and crystal fit for a king*

Marlijn, *move over, Jean-Paul Gautier*

"Negen Straattjes," *a charmer of a shopping district*

P. C. Hooftstraat, *the Faubourg St-Honoré of Amsterdam*

Shoebaloo, *for those Day-glo tiger-stripped stillettos*

The Spigelkwartier, *tiptoe through the tulipwood armoires here*

HIGHLY RECOMMENDED

Albert Cuypmarkt, *the most exotic street market in town*

Antiquariaat Kok, *a bookstore with vintage works on Amsterdam*

Bloemenmarkt, *the floating flower market on the Singel*

Puccini Bomboni, *Death by Dutch chocolate*

Metz & Company, *in a gorgeous 1908 building*

Pinokkio, *for that step-gabled wooden doll house*

Puccini Bomboni, *Death by Dutch chocolate*

Skatezone, *when you want to do your Hans Brinker routine*

Many other fine stores enliven Amsterdam. For other favorites, look for the black stars as you read this chapter.

By Jonette
Stabbert

AS OLD AS AMSTERDAM IS, some things never seem to change. The bustle and noise of crowds of shoppers in the area surrounding Dam Square is reminiscent of the cattle drives that only a few centuries ago thundered to market through the Kalverstraat (Calf's Street), now one of the major shopping streets. The city's mercantile roots go as far back as Rembrandt's day, when the maritime Dutch West India and East India companies were busy colonizing a trading empire so far-flung the sun never set on it entirely. The resulting plunder—spices from Java, porcelains from China, furs from Russia, rugs from Turkey—produced the first wave of shop-till-you-drop Amsterdammers. Today, thanks to the six-centuries-old Dutch history of savvy trading, you can save the money that a world cruise would cost and instead stay here to shop from a bounty of delights. A folkloric *koekeplank* (cookie mold)? A Makkum ceramic herring platter? A pair of handpainted wooded *klompen* clogs (which the Dutch often nail to the wall and fill with plants)? A cutting-edge vest styled by Viktor & Rolf? A 17th-century miniature *spiegel* mirror? A psychedelically hued ski cap from Oilily? Or one of those household objets d'art that have made contemporary Dutch design the darling of high-style fans the world over? Whether you go for Baroque or for Postmillennium, the variety of goods available in Amsterdam energizes a continuous parade of boutiques, street markets, and department stores. Hunting in Amsterdam for that special purchase is akin to grand entertainment.

DIAMONDS TO
DELFT: TOP
TEMPTATIONS

What gifts "say" Amsterdam? Diamonds have always been an Amsterdammer's best friend. Starting with the Spanish conquest of 1576, many diamond experts fled north, from Antwerp to the Netherlandish capital. Shiploads of raw diamonds from India or Brazil led to a spate of feverish activity, lasting until the cargo was cut and the finished stone sent off, usually to Paris. This stream became a flood when the children of a Dutch farmer living near Hopetown, South Africa, discovered that pebbles in a nearby stream made marvelous toys. Soon, the diamond rush was on and Amsterdam became famed as the home of diamond cutters. A visit to one of the city's modern diamond centers (there are several around the Rokin) offers the visitor a brief education in this fascinating business. We are told it can take an entire day to process a single carat. Note how often the size of a gem is proportionate to the number of gray hairs on the head of its worker, as it takes about 15 years to become expert at polishing the big stuff. But buyers should take heart. For if Amsterdam's stone sculptors fashioned for King Edward II of England the 3,000-carat Cullinan—the largest diamond in the world—they also cut, as an even more challenging demonstration of master technique, the world's smallest. It weighs ¼ of a milligram, or 1/2,500,000th of the Cullinan. Be it a tiny bauble or a boulder-size rock, you could do worse than choose a sparkling diamond as a lifelong souvenir of your visit to Holland—for one thing, it will cost considerably less here than elsewhere.

Droolingly, we recommend one of the city's noted "chocolateries." Holland is a chocoholic's mecca and everyone knows the mmmm-boy flavors crafted by Droste and Van Houten. Those good Dutch chocolates are available in prepackaged bars, but head to a shop such as Puccini Bomboni, centrally located on the Singel canal, to stock up on large slabs or handmade bonbons with exotic fillings. Stored at room temperature, they'll keep all the way back home and make yumptious gifts.

Many visitors like to delve into Delft and purchase a piece of authentic Delftware. The key word is "authentic." A variety of blue and white "delft" is available in a range of brands and prices, and you can pick up attractive souvenir-quality "delft" pieces at any giftware shop. But the real McCoy is known as Royal Delft and it can be found in the better giftware shops, such as those on the Rokin and the P. C. Hooftstraat. These wares bear the worthy name of De Porceleyne Fles. On the bottom of each object is a triple signature: a plump vase topped by a straight line, the stylized letter "F" below it, and the word "Delft." Blue is no longer the only official color. In 1948, a rich red cracked glaze was premiered, depicting profuse flowers, graceful birds, and leaping gazelles. There is "New-Delft," a range of green, gold, and black hues, whose exquisite minuscule figures are drawn to resemble an old Persian tapestry; the Pynacker Delft, borrowing Japanese motifs in rich oranges and golds, and the brighter Polychrome Delft, which can strike a brilliant sunflower-yellow effect. When shopping, keep in mind that there are many companies creating "delft," but only one crafting the porcelain that has colored the world since the 17th century with its unique blue. Holland's other famous ceramic is Makkum pottery, whose only genuine objects come from the firm of Koninklijke Tichelaar Makkum (Royal Tichelaar). Collectors, museum curators, and antiques dealers routinely shop Amsterdam for old Delft and Makkum treasures. The Spiegel Quarter is home to elegant antiques shops whose beautiful displays include a variety of antique art, maps, furnishings, jewelry, and clocks.

The chic-to-the-cuticles crowd knows that avant-garde Dutch fashion is one of the hottest things going. However, if magazine editors in the Big Apple and Milan like to drop the names of such supernovas as Viktor & Rolf, this designing pair is less appreciated in Holland (Van Gogh had the same problem). Still, trendmeisters will find Amsterdam a great place for threads; be on the look-out in stores along P. C. Hooftstraat for clothing by Frans Molenaar, new talent like Marlijn Franken (who dresses opera divas and rock stars), and up and coming couture stars Ronald Kolk and Marissa. For knock-your-socks-off color, head over to Oilily, the famed children's and women's fashion store—it's no surprise to encounter so many smiles when you walk in the door here. But if you want to see the Dutch pull out all the stops, check out their home designs. Perhaps its due to their Calvinist background, which causes them to favor functionality over fashion, but interior decorating rules in Amsterdam. Amsterdammers love their home design shops, from the megastore Pakhuis to such trend-setting boutiques as The Frozen Fountain.

BARGAINS TO BLOW-OUTS   Fashionistas melt their credit cards on Amsterdam's priciest street, the P. C. Hooftstraat in the Museum Quarter, affectionately called the P. C. (pronounced Pay Say). Elegant stores compete to sell designer-label goods, jewelry, and other luxe items; staff members are exceptionally courteous and treat customers like visiting royalty. Ferraris and BMWs are parked along the street, and the smell of money is in the air. Many shop interiors mimic stately Dutch mansions, with marble floors, crystal chandeliers, and antique furnishings arrayed for your comfort. Even if shopping the P. C. is beyond your budget, you might indulge voyeuristic tendencies and drink an overpriced glass of wine at one of the chic outdoor terraces while watching the Beautiful People, including well-turned-out tots, parade by. Don't neglect the Van Baerlestraat and the Willemsparkweg, (just steps away from the P. C. Hooftstraat), where you're likely to discover a stunning lamp, or home accessory. Quirky little boutiques abound in the Jordaan, Harlemmerstraat, and Utrechtsebuurt areas. Take an hour or two to explore by foot and you'll be excited by your discoveries. And if you have enough time during your stay, shop at one of the outdoor markets for a "total immersion" experience and a sense of how old this city is. At the Albert Cuypmarkt, while bombarded by vendors hawking their wares, the multilingual hubbub and ethnic diversity of the crowd, and the exciting selection of goods, keep in mind that the scene before you is pretty much unchanged from centuries ago. Sooner or later, everybody ends up at the year-round outdoor flea market at Waterlooplein, a holdover from the pushcart days in the Jewish Quarter.

Shopping hours in The Netherlands are regulated by law, with one night a week reserved for late shopping. In Amsterdam, department stores and many other shops are closed Monday morning, and stay open Thursday evening, which is famously known as *koopavonden* ("buying evenings"). Increasingly, following an easing of legislation governing shopping hours, you'll find main branches of major stores in the center of the city open on Sunday afternoon, but note that most stores are shuttered on Sunday. Purchases of €136 or more qualify for a tax refund; refer to our section on the V.A.T. (Value-Added Tax).

If, in the end and nearing your departure time, you haven't been able to find your special gift for your favorite auntie back home, why not traipse over to tulip territory in the Bloemenmarkt, the famed floating flower market, on the Singel. Here you'll find hundreds of varieties of tulip bulbs on sale (ask for bulbs with certificates for export; these are guaranteed healthy and are permitted into the United States). Whether you opt for Coulteren (single-color) or Marquetrian (multicolor) blooms, you'll find you've purchased a piece of Dutch history, for these are the descendants of the Rosen, Violetten, Bizarden, and other species of tulip that helped created Holland's Great Tulip Mania of the 1630s. Back then, *burgemeesters*, bankers, and town fathers bested each other to buy the rarest flowers, paying thousands of dollars for a single black tulip. Happily, today's prices are remarkably fair, even for a collection of a hundred colorful bulbs. Go to it, and how we envy you!

Shopping Districts & Streets

If you are literally out to shop-till-you-drop, Amsterdam will oblige. A "grand tour" route for all the main shopping areas threads itself through the city, running from Dam Square all the way down to De Pijp. But unless their feet are bionic, we suggest that discerning shoppers break the following pilgrimage—running from north to south, with several detours east and west—into several sections. If not, shopaholics will return to their hotel rooms weary and wiped out, and their bathroom scales will show they've become three pounds lighter.

The heart of the city center, or Centrum, **Dam Square** is home to two of Amsterdam's main department stores, the C & A and De Bijenkorf. Beyond the west side of the square sits one of Amsterdam's shopping spectaculars, the **Magna Plaza** (✉ Nieuwezijds Voorburgwal 182, Nieuwe Zijde ⊕ www.magnaplaza.nl). Built inside the city's 19th-century post office—designed by Cornelis Hendrik Peters in "post-office Gothic" (sort of like London's House of Parliament)—this gigantic structure looks like a fairy-tale frontispiece. Set behind the Royal Palace, this is now a top place for A-to-Z shopping in a wide variety of distinctive stores, including Villeroy & Boch; Sissy Boy Home and Fashion Decoration; Tolhuysen (soooo cute "Dutch Kitsch," including sailboat-wooden clogs, pottery cows, and porcelain windmills); Ordning & Reda (Swedish paper merchants); fashion boutiques like Björn Borg, Velvet, and Replay; fabulous wooden toys at Pinokkio and kiddie couture at Bam Bam Kinderwinkel. The central Romanesque-columned, three-story atrium is a knockout.

If department stores aren't your speed, head west from the Dam to the heart of the Grachtengordel canal section and explore the **Negen Straatjes** ("The Nine Streets"), nine charming, tiny streets that radiate from behind the Royal Palace. Here, in a sector bordered by Raadhuisstraat and Leidsestraat, specialty and fashion shops are delightfully one-of-a-kind. Heading even farther to the west you enter the chic and funky sector of the **Jordaan**, where generation after generation of experimental designers have set up shop to show their imaginative creations. The small streets radiating from the Elandsgracht and the Rozengracht contain many artistic boutiques selling handmade clothing, collectibles, and quirky gifts. Antiquarian bric-a-brac shops are also in this part of town.

Returning to the Centrum, two popular streets offer something for nearly all tastes and wallets. Stretching to the north from Dam Square and toward Centraal Station is **Nieuwendijk**, a busy pedestrian mall that is good for bargain hunters. To the south of the Dam runs **Kalverstraat**, the city's main pedestrians-only shopping street, where much of Amsterdam does its day-to-day shopping. Running south to the Muntplein, this street is somewhat down-market but, remember, street-creds are important in this city. Here, too, you'll find the imposing **Kalvertoren shopping mall** (⊠ Kalverstraat, near Munt, Nieuwe Zijde), which is a covered shopping mall with a rooftop restaurant with magnificent views of the city. Running parallel to Kalverstraat is the **Rokin**, a main tram route lined with shops offering high-priced trendy fashion, jewelry, accessories, antiques, and even an old master painting or two. Near the bottom of Kalverstraat's big "C," **Leidsestraat** cuts south to the elegant Museum Quarter. Before you hit Leidsestraat, however, the street is first called Heiligeweg, then Koningsplein. This entire drag offers a range and variety of shopping similar to Kalverstraat's but grows increasingly upscale; pizza parlors are now replaced with gracious cafés, head shops give way to diamond centers. Near here—right off Leidseplein, following the Stadhouderskade—**Max Euweplein** is a small plaza-style shopping mall surrounding a summer café, adjacent to the Amsterdam Casino.

From the Leidsestraat turn east and walk one long canal block to find the **Spiegelkwartier** (Spiegel Quarter), one of Europe's most fabled agglomerations of antiques shops. Antiques always have been a staple item of shopping in Amsterdam, and the array of goods available at any time is broad. There are more than 150 antiques shops scattered throughout the central canal area. The greatest concentration of those offering fine antiques and specialty items, however, is along Nieuwe Spiegelstraat and its continuation, Spiegelgracht. They constitute the main thoroughfare of the Spiegelkwartier, with shops on both sides of the street and canal for five blocks, from the Golden Bend of the Herengracht nearly to the Rijksmuseum. The array of treasures is amazing, from William and Mary armoires to the tiny *spiegels* (mirrors) that gave the quarter its name and were often used, perched from second-story windows, to espy arriving guests. They are still used by a great many homes today!

For possible antiques of the 22nd century, continue east of the Spiegelkwartier several blocks to find **Utrechtsestraat**, which offers a variety of opportunities for the up-to-date home shopper, with stores specializing in kitchen, interior, and design objects. Now head south across the Singel canal to the Museum Quarter, where, a few blocks east of the Rijksmuseum, you'll find the city's posh and prestigious **P. C. Hooftstraat**, generally known as the P. C. Home to chic designer boutiques, this is where diplomats and politicians buy their glad rags. Several blocks to the east, just beyond the Concertgebouw is **Van Baerlestraat**, lined with bookstores specializing in art, music, and language and clothing shops that are smart—but not quite smart enough to have made it to the adjoining P. C. Hooftstraat. To get back to Amsterdam's more democratic roots, continue south to the **De Pijp** neighborhood and exult in its famous Albert Cuypmarkt, a popular-priced playground of stalls that remains a pearl among pearls.

Remember if you want to add the very latest stores to the lists below, check out the suggestions in the Holland's high-style monthly glossies, such as *Dutch, Residence, Elegance, Avenue, BLVD* and the Dutch-language *Elle*.

Department Stores

Perched on the ever-busy Damrak, across the road from the Beurs van Berlage, this representative of the European chain department store **C & A** (⊠ Beurspassage 2 or Damrak 79 (two entrances), Nieuwe Zijde ☎ 0800/022–6768) is a long-time fixture on Amsterdam's shopping landscape. The budget-minded come here for clothing and accessories, while the basement caters to Generation Y and teenagers and their mothers dispute fashion tastes amid disco lighting and music. On the ground floor, there are always sales racks and those with the patience to paw through them may be rewarded with amply discounted goods. Far from the lofty heights of Harrods, akin to Bloomingdales, if not as stylish as Paris's Galleries Lafayette, **De Bijenkorf** (⊠ Dam 1, Nieuwe Zijde ☎ 020/621–8080) is the city's best-known department store and the stomping ground of its monied middle classes. It has come far from its save-a-penny-style days and now stocks top international designer lines in interior decoration and clothing, gourmet goodies, the usual repertoire of suitcases, shoes, and appliances, and hipster choices like zebra-stripe pillows or togs by Bang on the Door. The store café has gone so upscale that even socialites lunch here, while makeup makeovers on the ground floor—involving lots of fanfare, such as appearances by pop singers and even male models in drag—offer surprise "theater" to tourists. You might want to pop into the many branches of **Hema** (⊠ Nieuwendijk 174–176, Nieuwe Zijde ☎ 020/ 623–4176) that dot this town; it not only provides all your basic needs but has some surprisingly hip designer items, and for the friendliest of prices. Cosmetics, vitamins, undergarments, and power tools are some of the best bargains to be found here. Hema is practically a national institution, and can be relied on for quality at a low price. With its Paris-style skylights, chandeliers, silently gliding assistants, and coat of arms, the **Maison de Bonneterie** (⊠ Rokin 140–142, Nieuwe Zijde ☎ 020/531–3400) is Amsterdam's most gracious department store. It has basics such as white goods and appliances, but it is most loved for its array of women's fashions, ranging from supermodel frocks to the most proper basics. Browse on the ground floor, and you're likely to come upon a great buy. They regularly have limited supplies of designer lamps, bedding, or other home objects on special offer. Landmarked by its cupola, the historic and stately **Metz & Company** (⊠ Keizersgracht 455, Eastern Canal Ring ☎ 020/624–8810) has presided over the Grachtengordel since 1908 (but first set up shop elsewhere back in 1740!). Now an outpost of London's famous Liberty store, it carries a range of breathtakingly expensive designer articles from all over the world. Unique leather handbags in bright colors may lure you into the shop—but after purchasing one, will you still have any cash left to keep in it? At the top-floor café you can get the best bird's-eye view of the city. **Peek & Cloppenburg** (⊠ Dam 20, Nieuwe Zijde ☎ 020/622–8837) specializes in durable, middle-of-the-road clothing. They are adding more European lines, with attractive Italian and French knitwear and casuals. **Vroom & Dreesmann** (✉ Kalverstraat 203, Nieuwe Zijde ☎ 020/622–0171), an upmarket version of Woolworth's, sells clothing, and office and household items. You'll find a large stationery section and a fine array of computer software.

Markets

Whether hunting for treasures or trash (a busted Louis XVI ear trumpet has been spotted), you could get lucky at one of Amsterdam's flea markets. Even if you're not looking for anything in particular, you can unearth terrific finds, often at rock-bottom prices. Few markets compare with Amsterdam's **Waterlooplein** flea market, which surrounds the perimeter of the Stopera (Muziektheater/Town Hall complex) building. It is a descendant of the haphazard pushcart trade that gave this part of the city its distinct and lively character in the early part of the century. It can be fun to visit, and if you think your own attic is a mess, you'll be gratified to see the piles of similar stuff dumped here. It's amusing to see the old telephones, typewriters, and other arcana all haphazardly displayed but altogether amazing to see shoppers scrambling and vying with each other to buy it. Professional dealers set up here also, selling secondhand clothing, hats, and purses, often from the past 40 years. New fashions are mostly for the rock music set. The flea market is open Monday–Saturday 9:30–5. The **Bloemenmarkt**, (along the Singel canal, between Koningsplein and Muntplein) is another of Amsterdam's must-see markets, where flowers and plants are sold from permanently moored barges. The market is open Monday–Sunday 8:30–6.

On Saturday 9–4, the **Noordermarkt** (which winds around Noorderkerk and along Lindengracht) hosts a fabric market; on Monday mornings, a flea market evocative of the old world takes over. It's a really sprawling affair, mostly full of used clothing, books, and toys, but you can also find antique silverware and pottery as well as wartime and advertising memorabilia. Collectors browse here for old pearl buttons and sewing notions, dolls, used sewing machines, and books. **Nieuwmarkt** (at northern end of Kloverniersburgwal) hosts an organic farmers' market, with specialist stalls selling essential oils and other New Age fare alongside the oats, legumes, and vegetables. **Sunday art markets** are held in good weather from April to October in the Rembrandtplein area on Thorbeckeplein (10:30–6), and from April–November at in the Dam area at Spui square (10–6), which also hosts a *boeken market* on Friday (10–6) that is a used and antiquarian book–browsing paradise. The **Postzegelmarkt** stamp market is held twice a week (Wednesday and Saturday, 1–4) by the Spui on Nieuwezijds Voorburgwal. A favorite with locals is the ★ **Albert Cuypmarkt,** on Albert Cuypstraat between Ferdinand Bolstraat and Van Woustraat, in the heart of the De Pijp district, and considered the best open-air street market in Amsterdam. It's open Monday–Saturday 9–5. Among the colorful and noisy crowd, vendors sell food, clothing, fabrics, houseplants, and household goods from all over the world. Just about every ethnic culture is represented here (vendors, goods, and buyers), and if you take time out for people-watching, you'll hear a musical melange of spoken languages. Be sure to try some of the exotic street food, or just order the Dutchman's favorite fast food—*frites met mayonnaise* (fries with mayonnaise) served piping hot in a paper cone. Simply delicious. Look for Belgian frites, as these are the tastiest.

Fabric lovers will think they've gone to heaven when they visit the Monday **Lapjesmarkt.** Go early in the morning via the No. 3 or 10 tram to the stop for the Marnixbad. Follow the crowd—most people on the tram will be headed for the market. All along the Westerstraat, you'll find stalls with every possible kind of fabric—beautiful rainbow-colored Asian silks embedded with mirrors and embroidery, batiks from Indonesia, Suriname, and Africa, fabulous faux furs, lace curtains, velvet drapery materials, calicos, and vinyl coverings, all being admired and stroked by eager shoppers. Couturiers rub elbows with housewives, vendors measure out meters, and the crowds keep getting denser. The fabric market continues down the Westerstraat and then merges with a fruit, vegetable, and clothing market; then, at the end of the street, near the Noorderkerk (Northern Church), there is the large Noordermarkt flea market. The Lapjesmarket closes at noon.

Specialty Stores

Antiques & Golden Age Art

A William and Mary–era harpsicord? One of the printed maps that figured prominently in Vermeer's *Lutenist*? An 18th-century bed-curtain tie-up? Or a pewter nautilus cup redolent of a Golden Age still-life? All these and more may be available in Amsterdam's famous array of antiques stores, the **Spiegelkwartier**, or Spiegel Quarter, centered around Nieuwe Spiegelstraat and its continuation, Spiegelgracht. But this section—with shops on both sides of the street and canal for five blocks, from the Golden Bend of the Herengracht nearly to the Rijksmuseum—often requires a House of Orange budget. For more gently priced antiques and curios, visitors to Amsterdam might well opt instead to tiptoe past the 18th-century tulipwood armoires and explore the **Jordaan**, an increasingly popular area for adventurous collectors. In stark contrast to the elegant stores in the Spiegel Quarter with their beautiful displays, the tiny, unprepossessing shops dotted along the Elandsgracht and connecting streets, such as the 1e Looiersdwarststraat, offer equally wonderful treasures, but you need to hunt for them. Those who take the time to carefully examine the backroom shelves, nooks, and crannies of a small shop may be rewarded with a big find. Prices are also more in keeping with the "downtown" neighborhood. Indeed, this is one of the best-kept secrets of New York antiques shop dealers, who often scour the Jordaan for their imported wares. You can also enjoy happy hunting in the shops on Rozengracht and Prinsengracht, near the Westerkerk, which offer country Dutch furniture and household items; you'll also find antiques and curio shops along the side streets in that part of the city. Many of the antiques shops in the Spiegelkwartier and the Jordaan keep irregular hours and some are open by appointment, so it's best to call first.

For a broad range of vintage and antique furniture, curios, jewelry, clothing, and household items, try **Kunst- & Antiekcentrum De Looier** (✉ Elandsgracht 109, Jordaan ☎ 020/624–9038), a cooperative housing more than 80 dealers, making it the largest covered art and antiques market in The Netherlands. You wouldn't be the first to get a great buy on an antique doll, a first-edition book, military memorabilia, or even a jeweled trinket. The best days to go are Wednesday, Saturday, or Sunday, when all the vendors, including the *tafeltjesmarkt* (one-day table rentals), are present. Your fellow browsers may even be dealers back home—right after a book on *Delftsblauw* (Delft Blue pottery) collectibles was published some years ago, a virtual army of dealers from the United States descended on De Looier market and snapped up just about every piece of Delft (if foolishly ignoring the large assortment of equally interesting and collectible Makkumware). Many antiques dealers buy from the fabled auctions held at the Amsterdam branch of **Sotheby's** (✉ De Boelelaan 30, Buitenveldert ☎ 020/550–2200 ⊕ www.sothebys.com), so why not beat them to the bid? The internationally known auction house

FodorsChoice
★

Christie's Amsterdam (✉ Cornelis Schuytstraat 57, Amsterdam Zuid ☎ 020/575–5255 ⊕ www.christies.com) hosts sales of works of art, furniture, wines, jewelry, and porcelain.

The dazzling, enormous, skylighted quarters of **Anouk Beerents** (✉ Prinsengracht 467, Jordaan ☎ 020/622–8598) may cause you to immediately think of the Hall of Mirrors at the Palace of Versailles since several hundred 19th- and 20th-century antique mirrors, replete with ornate gold or silver gilded frames hang upon her walls. You wouldn't be wrong—the collection actually contains original mirrors from the palace. Ms. Beerents buys and restores museum-quality mirrors, mainly from France and Italy. A visit is possible only by appointment. The space is so large that customers may drive their cars inside to park. Shipping can be arranged to other countries, and a number of mirrors have found their way to Ralph Lauren shops in America. You'll find an unusual collection of antique money banks at **Bruno de Vries** (✉ Elandsgracht 67, Jordaan ☎ 020/620–2437), along with Art Deco and Jugendstil lamps and items from the Amsterdam School. There's a glittering array of beautiful antique crystal chandeliers at **D. I. Haaksman** (✉ Elandsgracht 55, Jordaan ☎ 020/625–4116). You'll find just the size you're looking for in 18th- and 19th-century chandeliers from leading names such as Bagues Crystal en Baccarat. **Galerie Frans Leidelmeyer** (✉ Nieuwe Spiegelstraat 58, Spiegelkwartier ☎ 020/625–4627) is a good source of top-quality Dutch Art Deco and Jugendstil artifacts, with furniture by H. P. Berlage, Michel de Clerk and Piet Kramer. For antique European pewter from the 15th to 19th centuries, the authority is **Jan Beekhuizen** (✉ Nieuwe Spiegelstraat 49, Spiegelkwartier ☎ 020/626–3912). Mr. Beekhuizen also carries antique furniture, antique Delft Blue tiles and other collectible objects. **Conny Mol** (✉ Elandsgracht 65, Jordaan ☎ 020/623–2536) specializes in furniture and decorative items from 1880 to 1930, including Art Deco and Jugendstil. **Lyra Antiek** (✉ Elandsgracht 43, Jordaan ☎ 020/420–4970) carries Louis XVI, Empire, and Biedermeier furniture.

As you explore the fascinating maze of small rooms at **Odds & Sods** (✉ 1e Looiersdwarsstraat 11, Jordaan ☎ 020/616–8440), you'll find delightful postwar (1950s–'70s) glass, ceramics, plastics, metalware, and furniture along with Art Deco, Jugendstil, and Amsterdam School designs. Better yet, many affordable small items will fit in a suitcase. The shop is as charming as its owner, who will proudly show you his shop's garden with its artist-made waterfall. Perhaps the biggest treasure in this shop is an exclusive collection of period textiles and wallpapers from 1870 to 1930. They also carry American Archive editions from Archibald Knox, former designer for Liberty of London. In an enormous shop that spans 1,800 square feet, **Prinsheerlijk Antiek** (✉ Prinsengracht 579, Eastern Canal Ring ☎ 020/638–6623) sells a princely assortment of furniture, bric-a-brac, and chandeliers dating from the early 18th century, as well as unique clock cases, Swedish-style birchwood furniture, and Dutch hand-painted folk pieces. Many items come from royal families and palaces, such as the spectacular sofa with gryphon's arms that originally graced a Swedish castle, a chandelier from the Dutch royal palace of Noordeinde, and even a "commode" from an Austrian prince. In the shop's renowned workplace, they restore and upholster antique furniture.

Museum curators do their shopping at **Salomon Stodel** (✉ Rokin 70, Nieuwe Zijde ☎ 020/623–1692). It's not unusual to find people admiring the shop windows at **Steensma & Van Der Plas** (✉ Prinsengracht 272, Jordaan ☎ 020/672–2197), where fine wooden cabinets with a myriad of drawers are often displayed. The shop is known for functional antique furniture (mainly from England) and pub clocks. You'll also find old leather Chesterfields, club chairs, and imposing oak or mahogany desks. **Willem Vredevoogd** (✉ P. C. Hooftstraat 72, Museum District ☎ 020/673–6804) sells antique jewelry, specializing in top names such as Lalique, Cartier, and Boucheron, and is open only on Mondays from 1 to 6. When you squeeze past the marvelous wooden wardrobes that fill **Wildschut Antiquiteiten** (✉ 1e Looiersdwarsstraat 8B, Jordaan ☎ 020/320–8119), chances are you'll encounter the owner at the back, restoring his latest acquisition. The chests and armoires, made of fine woods such as mahogany, come mainly from northern France and are a tribute to European craftsmanship. These have been restored with loving care, and the shop's owner will fit them with shelves or drawers to your wishes. Many of his U.S. customers have their large furniture shipped home, which Mr. Wildschut says is surprisingly inexpensive (he offers advice about it). The shop also sells cabin trunks from the early 1900s and antique travel cases fitted with original drinking glasses or other small personal items.

Art: Modern to Contemporary

Many of the galleries that deal in modern and contemporary art are centered on the **Keizersgracht** and **Spiegelkwartier,** and others are found around the Western Canal Ring and De Jordaan. Artists have traditionally gravitated to low-rent areas. The **De Baarsjes** neighborhood in the western part of the city is increasingly attracting small galleries that showcase exciting works of art. With a shabbiness reminiscent of the early days of New York's Soho, it is worth a detour for adventurous art-lovers. *Day by Day in Amsterdam,* published by the tourist office, is a reasonable source of information on current exhibitions; another is the Dutch-language publication *Alert,* which has the most comprehensive listings available. Opening times at galleries vary greatly. Many are closed between exhibitions, so it is recommended that you check out the magazine listings or call first for information.

For modern art, head for **Collection d'Art** (✉ Keizersgracht 516, Eastern Canal Ring ☎ 020/622–1511), where you'll find paintings, gouaches, and ceramics by Armando, Baselitz, Benner, Brands, Schoonhoven, and others. **De Beeldenwinkel** (✉ Berenstraat 29, Negen Straatjes ☎ 020/676–4903) shines its spotlight on sculpture. Whether you're looking for a serious art piece, a funny ornament, or an item that blends with your home décor, the pieces on view here are always interesting. The shop is filled with visual art from metal, ceramic, and glass, with something to please every taste and budget. A top contender in the Spiegel is **Elisabeth Den Bieman de Haas** (✉ Nieuwe Spiegelstraat 44, Spiegelkwartier ☎ 020/626–1012), which showcases art from the international Cobra collection and specializes in Corneille's early works. **Eurasia Antiques** (✉ Nieuwe Spiegelstraat 40, Spiegelkwartier ☎ 020/626–1594) is a treasure trove of paintings, engravings, and Asian art. **Galerie De Stoker** (✉ Witte de Withstraat 124, De Baarsjes ☎ 020/612–3293) mainly features sculptures in papier-mâché and stone and is noted for its innovative ceramic fountains (the atelier behind the gallery is open to visitors). At **Galerie Ei** (✉ Admiraal de Ruijterweg 154, De Baarsjes ☎ 020/616–3961), artist Judith Zwaan displays her whimsical, colorful paintings and papier-mâché sculptures, influenced by Niki de Saint-Phalle and the Cobra group, as well as the art and culture of West Africa. Other exciting new artists regularly exhibit at this small gallery. **Galerie Espace** (✉ Keizersgracht 548, Eastern Canal Ring ☎ 020/624–0802) holds noteworthy exhibitions by contemporary painters and sculptors, including Pierre Alechinsky and Reinier Lucassen. Since 1945, **Kunsthandel M. L. De Boer** (✉ Keizersgracht 542, Eastern Canal Ring ☎ 020/623–4060) has been renowned for contemporary art from Dutch, French, and Belgian figurative and abstract artists as well as works by Dutch and French masters from the 19th century and early part of the 20th century. Since the death of Mr. De Boer, his son keeps the gallery open only for exhibitions of modern art or works from the gallery's own collection. In the Spiegel Quarter, one of the top galleries is **Hoopman** (⊠ Spiegelgracht 14–16, Spiegelkwartier ☎ 020/623–6538) with artworks by Jits Bakker, Lies Lobatto, Bernard de Wolff, and Willy Belinfante.

Books

Allert de Lange (⊠ Damrak 60–62, Nieuwe Zijde ☎ 020/624–6744) has a good selection of fiction and books on travel and history, but the main emphasis is on textbooks and educational reading matter. True to its name, the **American Book Center** (⊠ Kalverstraat 185, Nieuwe Zijde ☎ 020/625–5537) is strongly oriented toward American tastes and expectations. As reputedly the largest English-language book emporium on the Continent, the selection is vast, but the prices are usually higher than you would pay on the other side of the ocean. **Antiquariaat Kok** (⊠ Oude Hoogstraat 14-18, Oude Zijde ☎ 020/623–1191) is an antiquarian heaven, with oodles of treasures on Amsterdam history. Another floor in the store holds one of Amsterdam's largest selections of second-hand books (the best books are always out of print, right?). **Athenaeum Nieuwscentrum** (⊠ Spui 14–16, Nieuwe Zijde ☎ 624–2972) has the city's best selection of international magazines and newspapers; its sister bookstore next door offers the latest and greatest in international literature. **Architectura en Natura** (⊠ Leliegracht 22, Jordaan ☎ 020/623–6186) stocks beautiful "coffee-table" art and photography books covering architecture, nature, landscape design, and gardening. Rarely does any one leave the shop empty-handed. The browseworthy **Book Exchange** (⊠ Kloveniersburgwal 58, Oude Zijde ☎ 020/626–6266) sells used English-language books on all subjects; you'll find many second-hand paperbacks.

Possibly the largest bookstore in Amsterdam, **De Slegte** (⊠ Kalverstraat 48–52, Nieuwe Zijde ☎ 020/662–4266) is a true haven for book hunters. Every floor stocks tomes in various languages and in every subject (fiction and nonfiction) that you could want. They're particularly known for their large nonfiction section of popular titles at bargain prices, and upstairs floors have a humongous antiquarian book section. Book-lovers could spend hours here. **The English Bookshop** (⊠ Lauriergracht 71, Jordaan ☎ 020/626–4230) serves you tea in cozy confines, while recommending reading matter based on your personal tastes. Armchair and other travelers visit **Evenaar Literaire Reisboekhandel** (⊠ Singel 348, Nieuwe Zijds ☎ 020/624–6289) for books covering travel, anthropology, and literary essays. Anything you need to know about foreign cultures you'll discover here. Even if you weren't planning on buying a travel book, the window displays are so fascinating you will probably be drawn into the shop to make a purchase.

Oudemanhuis Book Market (⊠ Oudemanhuispoort, Oude Zijde) is a tiny, venerable covered book market in the heart of the University of Amsterdam and has been selling used and antiquarian books, prints, and sheet music for more than a century. Tempting window displays draw up into **Premsela** (⊠ Van Baerlestraat 78, Museum District ☎ 020/662–4266), which specializes in art books and stocks many luscious, tempting tomes. **Scheltema** (⊠ Koningsplein 20, Eastern Canal Ring ☎ 020/523–1411) has six floors of books on every imaginable subject with plenty of room for marked-down remainders. It's one of Amsterdam's busiest and best-stocked international bookstores. There is a small café on the first floor. **Waterstone's** (⊠ Kalverstraat 152, Nieuwe Zijde ☎ 020/638–3821) has four floors of English-language books, from children's stories to computer manuals. There's a very large selection of U.K. magazines. For information on the Spui's Friday book market, *see* Markets.

Ceramics & Crystal

You'll find a unique, comprehensive selection of glassware at **Breekbaar** (⊠ Weteringschans 209, Spiegelkwartier ☎ 020/626–1260). **De Jong** (⊠ P. C. Hooftstraat 69, Museum District ☎ 020/672–7473) sells modern art glass from Dutch and Scandinavian designers, as well as collections from Daum, Lalique, Barovier, and Seguso. For superb porcelain and tiles from before 1800, visit **Frides Lamëris** (⊠ Nieuwe Spiegelstraat 55, Spiegelkwartier ☎ 020/626–4066). **De Glaswerkplaats** (⊠ Berenstraat 41, Western Canal Ring ☎ 020/420–2120) is a studio located in the Negen Straatjes area where you can order custom-made designs in art glass, fused glass, or stained glass. Fancy a gift fit for a king? Well-oiled shoppers and devout collectors know there is only one address in Amsterdam that can please. **Hogendoorn & Kaufman** (⊠ Rokin 124, Nieuwe Zijde ☎ 020/638–2736) sells the créme de la crème, with the best designs from Baccarat, Lalique, Daum, and Swarovski in crystal, Royal Delft, Makkum, Lladró, Herend and Royal Copenhagen in porcelain, and special designs from Fabergé, Meissen, Mats Jonasson, and others (and with free worldwide shipping too). You're on equal footing with the Russian Tsar when you consider a fabulous cobalt blue and gold swan egg from Fabergé, while others will covet the Lalique bowl supported by two divinely crafted jugglers or the limited edition Lalique Deux Coeurs perfume flacon. Some items are much more affordable, including the Royal Delft dish with Dik Bruna's Miffy bunny, personalized with your child's name for under € 100. **Ingeborg Ravenstijn** (⊠ Nieuwe Spiegelstraat 57, Spiegelkwartier ☎ 020/625–7720) has a full line of fine glass, silver and silver plate, Majolica, and Continental decorative items. In the glittering interior of **Swarovski** (⊠ Heiligeweg 14, Nieuwe Zijde ☎ 020/618–4108), crystal jewelry, decorative items, and home accessories are for sale. At **'t Winkeltje** (⊠ Prinsengracht 228, Jordaan ☎ 020/625–1352), you'll find a charming jumble of hotel porcelain, glass, and other household collectibles.

Children

You may be hypnotized by the magenta-mustached shop owner Couzijn Simon sports, but it will be his toy treasures here that will make your FodorsChoice ★ child as pop-eyed as some of the vintage dolls found at **Couzijn Simon** (⊠ Prinsengracht 578, Eastern Canal Ring ☎ 020/624–7691). The shop is crammed with wonders like an 18th-century rocking horse as finely carved as an 18th-century sculpture; a four-foot-long wooden ice skate (a former store sign); a one-inch doll with hinged limbs; vintage trains and collector teddy bears; and porcelain dolls dressed for a costume ball. Some of the toys here even date back to the mid-18th century, which was when this shop first opened as a pharmacy. In the back is a small garden and a cottage, now the atelier of Dutch painter Anton Hoeboeur, whose works are for sale. The delightful **De Beestenwinkel** (⊠ Staalstraat 11, Oude Zijde ☎ 020/623–1805) has nothing but animal toys in every price range. Specializing in mobiles from around the world, **Gone with the Wind** (⊠ Vijzelstraat 22, Nieuwe Zijde ☎ 020/423–0230) also sells unusual handcrafted wooden flowers and toys and spring-operated jumping toys.

Designer togs, shoes, and accessories for babies, boys, and girls can be found at **Azzurro Kids** (⊠ P. C. Hooftstraat 122, Museum District ☎ 020/673–0457), which sells Armani Jr., Braez, Dolce & Gabbana, and other fashion notables. The **Bam Bam Kinderwinkel** (⊠ Nieuwezijds Voorburgwal 182, Nieuwe Zijde ☎ 020/624–5215) is one of Holland's most exclusive children's shops. Located in the Magna Plaza shopping center near the Dam, Bam Bam carries children's clothing, toys, and furniture, all with the shop's distinctive look.

Children's clothing has never been the same since Willem "Olli" Olsthoorn and his wife, Marieke Olsthoorn, launched Oilily in Alkmaar in 1963. They burst on the fashion scene with colorful, funky, and wildly chic clothing and accessories. They are most famous for their dazzling, nearly psychedelic, colors and patterns that evoke kaleidoscope visions and glass millefleurs. Now a global name, the only shop in the world that showcases the entire collection is **Exclusive Oilily Store** (⊠ P. C. Hooftstraat 131–133, Museum District ☎ 020/672–3361), set on Amsterdam's most renowned shopping street. This emporium caters to women and children. Here, you'll find babies' toes are kept toasty in flowered "minimukluk" winter booties, their heads kept free from drafts in snug caps with bunny ears. Bigger boys and girls can wear warm fleece coats which, with a few buttons and snaps, resemble penguins (complete with faces and feet). Mothers can color-coordinate their wardrobes to match those of their kids, or mix and match their own distinctive, fun-fashion statements. The toys are equally funny and well made, such as Heddles, a cute plush horse who fits into a red traveling case and can be dressed in his own little overalls.

*Fodor's*Choice
★

You won't find garish, breakable plastic toys at **Kleine Nicolaas** (⊠ Cornelis Schuytstraat 19, Amsterdam Zuid ☎ 020/676–9661). The shop specializes in educational and fine wooden toys, and the owner, a former Montessori kindergarten teacher, has curated a wonderful assortment, including Käthe Kruse and Carolle dolls, soft toys from Steiff, Kösen, and Sigikid, wooden toys from Brio and Selecta, and hard-to-find editions of Ty Beanie Babies. They have much more, and you'll find unique European stocking stuffers for all the kids (grownups, too) back home. Toys may be played with in the shop, which has a special bathroom just for children. Your child will feel like a princeling of the House of Orange if he's lucky enough to have a collection of the beautifully carved old-fashioned wooden toys on offer at **Pinokkio** (⊠ Nieuwezijds Voorburgwal 182, Nieuwe Zijde ☎ 020/622–8914). Set in the Magna Plaza shopping center, this place is stuffed with Pinocchio figures, step-gabled dollhouses, and other dazzlers. Talk about a perfect gift for that toddler back home: a dollhouse version of a gabled canal house, four "stories" tall. This is just one of the adorable toys available at **De Speelmuis** (⊠ Elandsgracht 58, Jordaan ☎ 020/638–5342 ⊕ www.speelmuis.nl), including kiddie-carts in the shape of jumbo jets and fire engines. Knights and castles are currently all the rage in Europe, and here you'll find collectible "medieval" figures from Schleigh, Papo, and Plastoy as well as a large selection of castles. The store artisans make unique Amsterdam dollhouses which you can fill with locally handcrafted decor items. Children particularly love the wooden toys here, which include garages, warehouses, and unusual hobby-horses in a host of other forms such as bears, ducks, and even motorcycles. Your toddler in Armani, Versace, and Da-Da? These fashion-conscience lines are the speciality of **'t Schooltje** (⊠ Overtoom 87, Museum District ☎ 020/683–0444), while many other top brands in clothing and shoes are also on offer for infants to 16-year-olds.

★

Chocolate

Chocoholics, take note. **Arti Choc** (⊠ Koninginneweg 141, Amsterdam Zuid ☎ 020/470–9805) not only sells handmade bonbons, but will also custom design just about anything you could imagine—made from chocolate. **Australian Homemade Amsterdam** (⊠ Singel 437, Nieuwe Zijde ☎ 020/428–7533) uses natural ingredients to make chocolate and ice cream. Amsterdam's best handmade chocolates come from **Puccini Bom-**

★

boni (⊠ Singel 184, Nieuwe Zijde ☎ 020/427–8341 ⊠ Staalstraat 17, Eastern Canal Ring ☎ 020/626–5474), where exotic combinations of chocolate and herbs (such as thyme and pepper) and spices are a specialty. The variety isn't enormous, but there are enough knockouts, including chocolates filled with calvados, Cointreau, rhubarb, and tamarind. The shops are modern and no great shakes, decor-wise. At the Staalstrat store, enjoy cakes and coffees in their small café while you watch the confiseurs create their chocolate by hand.

Coffee, Tea & Spices

Since 1880, **Geels & Co.** (⊠ Warmoesstraat 67 Nieuwe Zijde ☎ 020/624–0683) has sold tea and coffee and brewing utensils. This is a great place to find unique gifts, such as replica antique spice necklaces and traditional Dutch candy (not easy to find elsewhere). Don't miss the tiny museum upstairs with its display of antique coffee paraphernalia from around the world. Wall to wall with teak-wood canisters and jars bearing Latin inscriptions, fragant with the perfume of seeds, flowers, and medicinal potions, **Jacob Hooy & Co.** (⊠ Kloveniersburgwal 12, Oude Zijde ☎ 020/624–3041) has been operating here beside the Nieuwmarkt since 1846. Gold-lettered wooden drawers, barrels, and bins contain not just spices and herbs but also a daunting array of *dropjes* (hard candies and medicinal drops) and teas.

Diamonds & Jewelry

Diamonds are hardly a bargain. But compared to other cities, and thanks to Amsterdam's centuries-old ties to South Africa, they almost fall into that category here. The city's famous factories even allow one-stop shopping. The **Amsterdam Diamond Center** (⊠ Rokin 1–5, Nieuwe Zijde ☎ 020/624–5787) houses several diamond sellers. Set near the Rijksmuseum, **Coster Diamonds** (⊠ Paulus Potterstraat 2–4, Museum District ☎ 020/676–2222 ⊕ www.costerdiamonds.com) not only sells jewelry and loose diamonds but gives free demonstrations of diamond cutting so you can learn all about the "four Cs"—carat, color, clarity, and cut. You can see a replica of the most famous diamond cut in the factory—the Koh-I-Noor, one of the prize gems of the British crown jewels. After your tour, enjoy the petit café here. **Van Moppes Diamonds** (⊠ Albert Cuypstraat 2–6, De Pijp ☎ 020/676–1242 ⊕ www.moppesdiamonds.com) has an extensive diamond showroom and offers glimpses into the processes of diamond cutting and polishing.

One of the international leaders in contemporary jewelry design is **Hans Appenzeller** (⊠ Grimburgwal 1, Nieuwe Zijde ☎ 020/626–8218). Set in the Negen Straatjes shopping area, **BLGK** (⊠ Hartenstraat 28, Western Canal Ring ☎ 020/624–8154) specializes in Byzantine-inspired silver and gold jewelry. **Bonebakker** (⊠ Rokin 88/90, Nieuwe Zijde ☎ 020/623–2294) is one of the city's oldest and finest jewelers and carries an exceptionally wide range of fine watches and silverware. They've been in business since 1792, and Adrian Bonebakker, the founder, was commissioned by King Willem II to design and make the royal crown for the House of Orange. You'll find watches by Patek Philippe, Cartier, Jaeger-leCoultre, Gucci, and Panerai and beautiful silver and gold tableware. Some of the silver designs they produced in the 1920s have been exhibited in Dutch museums, such as the Willet-Holthuysen. The firm has a custom design service which is often patronized by businesses for special employee gifts. **Galerie RA** (⊠ Vijzelstraat 80, Nieuwe Zijde ☎ 020/626–5100) boasts wearable art by Dutch and international jewelry designers. **Grimm Sieraden** (⊠ Grimburgwal 9, Nieuwe Zijde ☎ 020/622–0501) is savvy about discovering the latest cutting-edge (but wearable) jewelry produced by young designers. **Premsela & Hamburger** (⊠ Rokin 120, Nieuwe Zijde

Fodor'sChoice ★

★

☎ 020/624–9688) has sold fine antique silver and jewelry since 1823; it is open most Sundays. The century-old **Schaap and Citroen** (✉ Heiligeweg 36, Nieuwe Zijde ☎ 020/626–6691) is so knowledgeable about jewelry that they even teach students at the butlers' academy how to clean and care for priceless baubles. They carry top brands like Rolex, but you can also find affordable watches and jewelry here.

Gifts & Souvenirs

A Space Oddity (✉ Prinsengracht 204, Jordaan ☎ 020/427–4036) combs the world for robots, toys, and memorabilia from TV and film classics. The interior of **Baobab 1** (✉ Elandsgracht 128, Jordaan ☎ 020/626–8398) is like something out of Ali Baba's cave of treasures or 1001 Nights. You'll find a rich trove of jewelry, statuary, and all kinds of objects from such locales as India and the Middle East. **Baobab 2** (✉ Elandsgracht 34, Jordaan ☎ 020/626–8398) handles the overflow of exotic home furnishings from its brother store. Located in the Negen Straatjes area, **Brilmuseum–Brillenwinkel** (✉ Gasthuismolensteeg 7, Western Canal Ring ☎ 020/421–2414) displays a collection of eyeglasses from antique to contemporary in a shop that evokes the atmosphere of the 17th century (the upstairs galleries actually have museum status); it's open Wednesday–Saturday. Cat-lovers return again and again to **Cats & Things** (✉ Hazenstraat 26, Jordaan ☎ 020/428–3028), where cat-related gifts and utilitarian items for cats are sold. The shop's owner, who is also a cat breeder, is very knowledgeable about felines. Of course, two real *katjes* are on hand to greet customers. At **De Condomerie** (✉ Warmoesstraat 141, Oude Zijde ☎ 020/627–4174) the discreet, well-informed staff promotes healthful sexual practice in this shop, which specializes in condoms.

You can't visit Holland and not buy a pair of *klompen,* can you? Perhaps not what you'd don for clubbing, but wooden shoes are still worn by farmers, fishers, and country folk and are the best footwear for wet and muddy surfaces. They're traditionally worn over a thick pair of *geitenwollen sokken* (goat's wool socks). Located in a former metro station, **De Klompenboer** (✉ Sint Anthoniesbreestraat 51, Nieuwmarkt ☎ 020/623–0632) sells toys upstairs and klompen downstairs. They no longer make the shoes they sell, but they still handpaint or woodburn designs on them and will also do custom orders. They have wooden shoes in the classic bright yellow/orange color, but also in red, blue, and natural wood in sizes to fit feet from two-year-olds to Darling Clementine. Novelty wooden shoe banks and brush holders are also sold, or you can go native and nail your clogs to a wall and fill them with plants. Although souvenir shops are to be found on every other street corner, **Holland Souvenirs Shopping** (✉ Nieuwendijk 226, Dam ☎ 020/624–7252) is distinguished by selling a better class of souvenirs, such as Royal Delft, cuckoo clocks, and automated miniature windmills. Sure, you may find a number of these items elsewhere, but they'll be in cheesy surroundings sometimes just down the aisle from risqué gift items and even drug paraphernalia. You could bring your grandmother to this shop. Holland's leading fashion and theatrical costume designers frequent **Kerkhof** (✉ Wolvenstraat 9, Jordaan ☎ 020/623–4084), where unusual ribbons, ornaments, lace edgings, and other fashion trimmings are available for retail customers. Small, quirky gifts can be found in the Negen Straatjes area at **Nieuws** (✉ Prinsengracht 297, Western Canal Ring ☎ 020/627–9540). The shop stocks gag gifts as well as kitsch and novelty items. What better place to buy ice skates than in Holland? Hans Brinker would have loved modern skating emporium **Skatezone** (✉ Ceintuurbaan 57–59, De Pijp ☎ 020/662–2822) which stocks well over 150 models of ice skates and also carries every other kind of skate. For beginners, figure skaters, racers, or those looking for ice hockey skates (and equipment), the shop carries top brands such as Viking, Raps, Bauer, CCM, Zandstra, Graf, A merk, and a host of others. There is a large variety of *noren*, the most popular style of skates for adults, but they also have traditional Dutch wooden training skates for children. These have double blades so kids can keep their balance. If you're concerned about your dental health, head to the Negen Straatjes and **De Witte Tanden Winkel** (⊠ Runstraat 5, Western Canal Ring ☎ 020/623–3443), which offers everything you could need—and more. Anyone for champagne-flavored toothpaste?

Grooming

The young and daring frequent **Hairpolice** (⊠ Geelvincksteeg 10 Eastern Canal Ring ☎ 020/420–5841) for wild hairstyles and colorful extensions (they also do regular haircuts). In addition to the usual business hours, they are open evenings and Sundays. As you can tell from the name, **Kinki Kappers** (⊠ Overtoom 245 Museum District ☎ 020/689–4553) attracts the adventurous with their way-out interior and matching staff. You can watch yourself on TV while your hair is innovatively colored—expect your hairdresser to be adorned with tattoos, piercings, and a memorable coif. Only the top brands of cosmetics and perfumes are sold at **Ici Paris XL** (⊠ P. C. Hooftstraat 132–134, Museum District ☎ 020/675–8032). The staff is as polished and sophisticated as the shop—the salesladies look like they've just been worked on by leading make-up artists. **Ariane Inden** (⊠ Leidsestraat 40, Eastern Canal Ring ☎ 020/420–2332) has a full line of Dutch cosmetics and does makeovers. The upstairs beauty salon offers a range of skin treatments. Enticing scents lure you into **Lush** (⊠ Leidsestraat 14, Eastern Canal Ring ☎ 020/423–4315), whose handmade soaps and cosmetics smell good enough to eat. A Europe-wide chain, their "bath bombs" are prized by movie stars and celebs the world over. Travelers, note: the lemon soap with pumice is great for scrubbing tired, callused feet. The ultramodern surroundings at **Rob Peetoom** (⊠ Elandsgracht 68 Jordaan ☎ 020/528–5722) are popular with stylish women and men for treatment by hair and makeup specialists. Set in the Negen Straatjes area, **Skins** (⊠ Runstraat 9, Western Canal Ring ☎ 020/528–6922) carries an extensive selection of exclusive brands of cosmetics and hair-care products, including Laura Mercier, Philosophy, and Wu. Hairdressers (for men and women) and makeup artists tend to your looks.

Housewares

Bebob Design Interior (⊠ Prinsengracht 764, Eastern Canal Ring ☎ 020/624–5763) supplies collectors and galleries with hard-to-find historic designs of chairs, sofas, tables, office chairs, and lighting fixtures from top lines. **Capsicum** (⊠ Oude Hoogstraat 1, Oude Zijds ☎ 020/623–1016) makes fabricholics drool over gorgeous weaves, prints and colors; this is not your run-of-the-mill fabric store.Since opening this Dutch flagship shop in May of 2003, the Greek chain **Coco-Mat** (⊠ Overtoom 89, Museum District ☎ 020/489–2927) has been crowded with customers seven days a week, here trolling for deliciously comfortable orthopedic beds, ergonomic sofas, and tables, curtains, lush towels, and bedding hard to resist. Glass floor panels reveal the downstairs area, which is devoted to children's furnishings and a range of endearingly comical soft toys. The service is unique for Holland, as the staff welcomes you with Greek hospitality, replete with gifts of olive oil, wine, and nut-filled figs; they'll even press a glass of fresh fruit juice which you can enjoy in the peaceful garden. At **Dreamz** (⊠Willemsparkweg 8, Museum District ☎020/470–4718) everything is handmade by European designers exclusive to the store. Browse and you'll discover art glass objects from Prague, elaborate Parisian chairs that resemble thrones, and a stunning chrome wine rack.

De Kasstoor (⊠ Rosengracht 202-210, Jordaan ☎ 020/521–8112) is an interior design department store offering three floors of 20th- and 21st-century design for every room in the home. Fine cookware can be found at **De Pittenkoning** (⊠ 1e van der Helststraat 35, De Pijp ☎ 020/671–6308). **Droog Design** (⊠ Rusland 3, Nieuwmarkt ☎ 020/626–9809) is rapidly gaining an international reputation for ground-breaking industrial and interior designs. Droog started out as a Dutch design collective, but now cutting-edge designers from all over the globe participate in their exhibitions. Their designs are among the most influential in contemporary design. Situated in a canal house, **The Frozen Fountain** (⊠ Prinsengracht 629–645, Eastern Canal Ring ☎ 020/622–9375) carries innovative contemporary/futuristic furniture and home accessories from top Dutch designers, such as a pieced wooden *kast* (closet) by Piet Hein EEk, but you'll also find artistic perfume dispensers, jewelry, and carpets. The store mixes minimalism with chandeliers and rococo seats. Part of the store is a museum shop for the Textile Museum, where original European fabrics are on offer. Frozen Fountain's exhibition space showcases the hottest young design talents—names making the headlines are Hutton, Arad, Newsom, Starck, Wanders, and Jongerius.

Even the Dutch equivalent of Woolworth's, **Hema** (⊠ Nieuwendijk 174-176, Nieuwe Zijds ☎ 020/623–4176), has high-style household items at reasonable prices. You'll find yourself in a rainbow world at **& Klevering Zuid** (⊠ Jacob Obrechtstraat 19a, Amsterdam Zuid ☎ 020/670–3623), thanks to its wide range of tints in porcelain and glass tableware, colorful household accessories, and bright table linens. Top European design brands are all here, including stainless steel cookware from Hackmann, Peugeot pepper mills, lush towels and bathrobes from Van Dijck Sanger, and artistic storage boxes from Galerie Sentou. For an unusual gift, consider their "ironing perfume" from France. World-renowned for his hand-patinated leather chairs, **Nico van Ooorschot** (⊠ Bosboom Toussaintstraat 20, Oud West ☎ 020/612–5961) has even sold chairs to Barbra Streisand. The coloring process is a family secret. The entire harbor district was given a shot in the arm with the five-story showcase for home design, **Pakhuis** (⊠ Oostelijke Handelskade 15-17, Eastern Docklands ☎ 020/421–1033). An 1883 warehouse renovated to house more than 30 design boutiques under one roof, it was modernized by the Dutch architectural firm of Meyer and Van Schooten, who added Minimalist glass and stainless steel to the historic ambience. Don't be surprised to find the editors of top home design magazines browsing here for inspiration, as this is a showcase for the hottest new trends. You can see the newest international collections, fresh from the big trade expositions. Catch your breath and enjoy a meal in the Pakhuis café, then turn breathless again at the fantastic view of the IJ through the glass-walled lounge. If you weren't born with a silver spoon in your mouth, you can purchase one from **Robbe & Berking** (⊠ P. C. Hooftstraat 130, Museum District ☎ 020/471–1600). This German firm has been in business for 130 years, with five generations of the same family recognized throughout the world as top silversmiths. Superb craftsmanship and design are apparent not only in their cutlery, but also in the elegant tea and coffee services. Don't neglect their other offerings, such as the beautiful crystal caviar dish with a silver handle that is shaped like a sturgeon.

Men's Clothing
The **English Hatter** (⊠ Heiligeweg 40, Nieuwe Zijds ☎ 020/623–4781) has tweed jackets, deerstalkers, and many other trappings of the English country gentleman. The cozy shop barely has room in which to turn around, but they've managed to keep a large inventory and do a bustling business. Women can also buy hats here. **Gaudi** (⊠ P. C. Hooftstraat 116,

Museum District ☎ 020/679–9319) is a mecca for the trendy and label conscious. **H & M** (✉ Kalverstraat 125-9, Nieuwe Zijde ☎ 020/624–0624) offers remarkably cheap classic and trendy threads. If you've got a small clothing budget, this store will "suit" you. Other good buys here are blazers and casual wear. For European menswear, **Hugo Boss** has four lines available in Amsterdam. The sportswear line is available at **Boss Sport** (✉ P. C. Hooftstraat 112, Museum District ☎ 020/379–5050) Hugo Boss's high-end and trendy design lines for men are available at **Hugo** (✉ P. C. Hooftstraat 140, Museum District ☎ 020/470–2297). **McGregor and Clan Shop** (✉ P. C. Hooftstraat 113, Museum District ☎ 020/662–7425) has a distinctly Scottish air, with chunky knitwear and the odd flash of tartan. **Mulberry Company** (✉ P. C. Hooftstraat 46, Museum District ☎ 020/673–8086) sells stylish fashions from England.

Wives accompany their husbands so they can ogle the staff at **Oger** (✉ P. C. Hooftstraat 75–81, Museum District ☎ 020/676–8695), where the shop clerks look like handsome male runway models and are elegantly attired. You may not match them for looks, but you'll be just as stylish when you leave. **Paul & Shark** (✉ Van Baerlestraat 38, Museum District ☎ 020/675–0818) carries maritime wear for yachting enthusiasts. They also have apparel for women and children. **Possen.com** (✉ Van Baerlestraat 38, Museum District ☎ 020/471–2050) uses 3-D body scanning to custom-tailor clothing. You're assured of a perfect fit, and the quality clothing makes this the closest thing to having your own personal designer. Hip and casual threads are found at the three locations of **Sissy-Boy** (✉ Van Baerlestraat 12, Museum District ☎ 020/672–0247 ✉ Kalverstraat 199, Nieuwe Zijde ☎ 020/638–9305 ✉ Leidsestraat 15, Eastern Canal Ring ☎ 020/623–8949). **Society Shop** (✉ Van Baerlestraat 20–22, Museum District ☎ 020/664–9281) stocks the classics that Dutch politicians and businessmen like.

Music

Near the Concertgebouw, **Broekmans & Van Poppel** (✉ Van Baerlestraat 92–94, Museum District ☎ 020/675–1653) specializes in recordings, sheet music, and accessories for classical and antiquarian music. There's an antiques-store atmosphere at **Datzzit Verzamel—Muziek en Filmwinkel** (✉ Prinsengracht 306, Eastern Canal Ring ☎ 020/622–1195). The merchandise includes music on 78s, vinyl, and CD as well as film memorabilia. Hip-hop enthusiasts shop at **Fat Beats Amsterdam** (✉ Singel 10, Nieuwe Zijde ☎ 020/423–0886).

Concerto (✉ Utrechtsestraat 54–60, Eastern Canal Ring ☎ 020/626–6577) is filled with new and used records and CDs covering all imaginable genres. If you're looking for a particular recording, this should be your first stop. **Get Records** (✉ Utrechtsestraat 105, Eastern Canal Ring ☎ 020/622–3441) is the best place to go for alternative, roots, and world music. The well-informed staff at **Kuijper Klassiek** (✉ Ferdinand Bolstraat 6, De Pijp ☎ 020/679–4634) offers hard-to-find recordings. **Sounds of the Fifties** (✉ Prinsengracht 669, Eastern Canal Ring ☎ 020/623–9745) offers vintage recordings, nostalgia, and the owner's vast knowledge, kept on the tip of his tongue. The vast **South Miami Plaza** (✉ Albert Cuypstraat 116, De Pijp ☎ 020/662–2817) has just about every music category, including the Dutch answer to country music, *smartlap*; listening booths are available, too.

Shoes

Located in the Negen Straatjes area, **Antonia Shoes** (✉ Gasthuismolensteeg 18–20, Western Canal Ring ☎ 020/320–9433) offers two stores of hip footwear from top European designers for men and women. Extreme, classic, high heels, flat shoes—if it's available in footwear, they carry it, with handbags to match. There are styles for men, too. **Antonia Shoes** (✉ Gasthuismolensteeg 16, Western Canal Ring ☎ 020/627–2433) sells slippers only. **Bally Shoes** (✉ Leidsestraat 8–10, Eastern Canal Ring ☎020/622–2888) is a byword for good taste (and high prices) in women's shoes. **Dr. Adams** (✉ P. C. Hooftstraat 90, Museum District ☎ 020/662–3835 ✉ Leidsestraat 25, Eastern Canal Ring ☎ 020/626–4460) sells chunkier, more adventurous styles of shoes for men and women. **Jan Jansen** (✉ Rokin 42, Nieuwe Zijde ☎ 020/625–1350) has the crème de la crème of shoes, with gorgeous color combinations and stunning designs. Famed Jansen is an artist/craftsman who designs and makes his special shoes in very small series, but he also has a manufactured line, Jan Jansen Sense, that is carried in shops worldwide. He's won numerous design awards and his shoes are in many museum collections. The

FodorśChoice ★ futuristic interior of **Shoebaloo** (✉ P. C. Hooftstraat 80, Museum District ☎ 020/671–2210) is like being in a disco on a spaceship, and the shoe styles are just as wild, some in neon colors to match the weird lighting in the shop. Just entering the store is an experience you won't soon forget, and you may leave with Day-glo tiger-striped stilettos. They have other shops around the city. **Smit Bally** (✉ Leidsestraat 41, Eastern Canal Ring ☎ 020/624–8862) sells classically smart shoes for men.

Women's Clothing

In the **Jordaan** neighborhood, generation after generation of experimental designers has set up shop to show its imaginative creations. (Antiques-and used-clothing shops are also in this part of town.) Designer shops

FodorśChoice ★ stand shoulder to shoulder on **P. C. Hooftstraat,** in the city's Museum Quarter. The chandeliers and marble floors of the elegant interior of **AM** (✉ P. C. Hooftstraat 97, Museum District ☎ 020/662–3588) are a suitable setting for attire by Valentino, Celine, Givenchy, and Missoni. **Boetiek Pauw** (✉ Van Baerlestraat 66 and 72, Museum District ☎ 020/662–6253), which also operates men's and children's shops, is part of a chain that stands out for the quality of both design and craftsmanship of its clothing. Best termed stylishly casual, their clothes look good anywhere, at the office or on a day out. You're unlikely to find bright colors; the Dutch prefer played-down neutral tones. "Futuristic" fashions (dated as this concept may be) and club wear are sold at **Cyberdog** (✉ Spuistraat 250, Nieuwe Zijde ☎ 020/330–63885)—if you're out to wear clothes that glow in the dark or react to sound, this is your place. **Benetton** (✉ P. C. Hooftstraat 72, Museum District ☎ 020/679–5706) is the Amsterdam outpost of the ubiquitous Italian chain known for its suave designs and colorful cottons. **Bodysox** (✉ Leidsestraat 35, Eastern Canal Ring ☎ 020/422–3544) sells conservative, feminine, and wacky socks, stockings, and tights (as well as some lingerie). The international fashion house **Esprit** (✉ Spui 1c, Nieuwe Zijde ☎ 020/626–3624) has a large branch in central Amsterdam. Browse several floors of clothing, all bearing their signature look. The downstairs café is infamous for slow service, but if you're not in a hurry and all shopped out, it's a good place to take a break.

The Dutch minichain **Cora Kemperman** (✉ Leidsestraat 72, Eastern Canal Ring ☎ 020/625–1284) offers architecturally designed clothes that are ageless and elegant. Designer fashions from Jean Paul Gaultier and Yves Saint Laurent are sold at **Leeser** (✉ P. C. Hooftstraat 117, Museum District ☎ 020/679–5020). Those who really want to make an individual fashion statement pay a visit to **Marlijn** (✉ Govert Flinckstraat 394 hs, De Pijp ☎ 020/671–4742). Move over, Jean-Paul Gaultier—here's a Dutch rival that Madonna hasn't discovered yet, although she's designed for numerous celebrities. If you want to stop traffic or turn heads, Marlijn will design a unique, flamboyant garment for you. Fancy a transparent plastic suit, a dress made of yards of iridescent silk, pleated and slashed, or just something beautiful and outrageous? Anything's possible here, including bridal apparel for both sexes. The Dutch outpost of **Max Mara** (⊠ P. C. Hooftstraat 110, Museum District ☎ 020/671–7742), although known in Paris and Milan for luxe clothing, here caters to the local taste. You'll find some well-tailored business attire and good sweaters, but the majority of clothes on offer, while quality garments, are casual and sporty, such as jeans and the baggy look. The chic Negen Straatjes boutique, **Van Ravenstein** (⊠ Keizersgracht 359, Eastern Canal Ring ☎ 020/639–0067), is the only retail outlet in Holland for Viktor & Rolf ready-to-wear. But don't expect A-bomb fashion—that's seldom seen outside museums and off the catwalk. The design duo also produces smart, beautifully cut clothing that can be worn anywhere, sometimes with three different collars. The shop also carries top Belgian designers such as Martin Margiela and Dries van Noten. **Revolution** (⊠ Utrechtsestraat 88, Eastern Canal Ring ☎ 020/623–3968) is a boutique offering fashions that are both fun and stylish for businesswomen who don't wish to appear too formal. For a funky look go to **Sjerpetine** (⊠ 1e van der Helststraat 33, De Pijp ☎ 020/664–1362). The shop is aesthetically organized in a rainbow of colors and patterns. **Edgar Vos** (⊠ P. C. Hooftstraat 136, Museum District ☎ 020/671–2748) is a Dutch designer who caters to women desiring sophisticated, classic, feminine, but never frilly, garments. Hand-beaded and hand-embroidered details on fine silk, wool, and linen make his clothes especially attractive and spotlight the influence of his apprenticeship to Dior and Balmain.

SIDE TRIPS FROM AMSTERDAM

7

FODOR'S CHOICE

Alkmaar, *a town of medieval courtyards and gables*

Bollenstreek Route, *for its checkerboards of tulip fields*

Delft, *to step back 350 years in time to the days of Vermeer*

Edam, *a historic city famed for its cheese market*

Haarlem, *home to the merrymaking portraits of Frans Hals*

Leiden, *a place where windmills still rise over the cityscape*

Marken, *the houses here are as tidy as ship cabins*

Zaandam, *for the village museum at Zaanse Schans*

HIGHLY RECOMMENDED

FOLKLORE Broek-in-Waterland, *fishermens' houses galore*

Enkhuizen, *for its open-air Zuiderzeemuseum*

Volendam, *where winged lace caps are still worn*

MUSEUMS Lambert van Meerten Museum, *Delft*

Molenmuseum de Valk, *Leiden*

Teylers Museum, *Haarlem*

Many other great sights enliven this region. For other favorites, look for the black stars as you read this chapter.

Revised and
updated by
Jonette
Stabbert

How could you visit Holland and not tiptoe through the tulip fields? Or, for that matter, follow in the footsteps of Vermeer in Delft or take in some of the famous folkloric "costume towns"? Indeed, the country is so manageably small, many travelers use its size as a rationale to "do" many of its towns and cities on day trips. Availing themselves of Holland's terrific trains, they find it entirely possible to base themselves in Amsterdam and head out by day to heritage-rich Leiden, Delft, and Haarlem. In a certain sense, every corner of the country could be considered for an outing, but you need to draw the line. For when it comes to historic towns such as The Hague, giant metropolises such as Rotterdam, or more distant destinations such as Maastricht, Limburg, Noord-Brabant, and Groningen, it is better to plan accordingly and consult our sister book, *Fodor's Holland.*

Happily, the regions north and south of Amsterdam are packed with touristic plenty in themselves. Here, in the provinces of Noord (North) Holland and Zuid (South) Holland, you can feast the eye on field after field of flowers, soothe the spirit with solitary walks through the Zaanse Schans—a jewel of windmill-studded countryside—or the Noord-Holland Noordwijk dune reserve, and enjoy time-machine getaways such as Hoorn and Zuiderzee. Though you would miss much of interest if you left Holland after visiting no more than these corners of the country, few other regions so well merit day trips. For this is The Netherlands in a nutshell. The flat horizon broken by distant spires, the scudding clouds chasing their reflections along the motionless surface of a canal, the fresh-scrubbed farmhouses, and the magisterial art cities all remind us of the eternal struggle between land and sea, between man and nature.

Numbers in the margin correspond to points of interest on the Haarlem, Leiden, and Side Trips from Amsterdam maps.

THE BULB FIELDS

Even if you are in Amsterdam for just a couple of days, it is easy to sample one of the best-known aspects of quintessential Holland, the bulb fields. Located in an area around the town of Lisse—address to the famous Keukenhof Gardens—this flower-growing area to the west of Amsterdam is a modern-day powerhouse of Dutch production techniques, resulting in a blizzard of Dutch flowers falling on every corner of the earth at any time of the year. In spring, the bulb fields blaze with color: great squares and oblongs of red, yellow, and white look like giant Mondriaan paintings laid out on the ground (you're intrigued from the moment you see them from your airplane window). It is a spectacular sight, whether you travel through the fields by bike or bus, or pass by in the train on your way to Leiden. Such great progress has been made in producing new varieties of the main bulb plants that the calendar is no longer quite the tyrant it used to be. In the days gone by, it was usually the first week of May that brought optimum tulip viewing. If spring came early, however, the peak of the tulips, hyacinths, and narcissi (many other blooms than tulips are cultivated in this region) could be as early as the middle of April, with nothing but heaps of discarded blooms left in the fields two weeks later. Everything then depended on the weather during the final critical 10 days after the buds were fully formed. Now with much hardier strains developed, it is no longer such a timely concern. Still, there is a general progression in this part of Holland from crocus from the middle of March, daffodils and narcissi from the end of March to the middle of April, early tulips and hyacinths from the second week of April to the end of the month, and late tulips immediately afterward.

An early or late spring can move these approximate dates forward or backward by as much as two weeks. It's good news, then, that most people visit the bulb fields using Amsterdam as their excursion base, so if the blooms don't cooperate they can also check out some of the great 17th-century Dutch floral still-life paintings in the Rijksmuseum.

Those paintings, in fact, should be discovered in any event, since they are telling evidence of "tulipmania," the astounding frenzy that broke out in 1630s Holland for the buying and cultivating of the tulip, recently imported from Turkey, which became a sort of 17th-century futures market. The rarest bulbs became more expensive than houses, only to have the whole market crash in due course, taking many fortunes with it. The first tulip bulbs were brought to Holland from Turkey in 1559. The name "tulip" was taken from *tulband,* the Dutch word for turban, because of the blossom's appearance. In 1625 an offer of Fl 3,000 for two bulbs was turned down, but the speculation in bulbs became a mania during the years 1634–37, as irrational and popular as stock market speculation in the late 1920s, when fortunes were made—and lost—in a single day. One Semper Augustus bloom clocked in at today's equivalent of €4,000—little wonder the great artist of the time, Sir Peter Paul Rubens, was heard to lament he could only afford to buy one tulip for his wife's birthday. Today, scientists diagnose the rarest tulips illustrated in that era's books as suffering from viruses that caused abnormal (and beautiful) coloring or shape. The most famous abberration is the "black" tulip, which is really darkest purple. This flower was immortalized in Alexandre Dumas's novel *The Black Tulip,* which tells the saga of the development of this strain in the 17th century.

The bulb fields extend from just north of Leiden to the southern limits of Haarlem, but the greatest concentration is limited to the district that begins at Sassenheim and ends between Hillegom and Bennebroek. In a neat checkerboard pattern of brilliant color, the fields stretch out as far as the eye can see on either side of the road that joins these towns. You must prepare yourself for a surprise—the landscape looks exactly like the color postcards you have seen. The bluest of skies combines with the brilliantly colored living flower quilt to create a dazzling Technicolor world; colors appear clearer and brighter than you've ever experienced them. The apparent artificiality of the sharply defined rectangular fields is not a concession to taste. It is part of the businesslike efficiency of an industry that has made tulip bulbs one of Holland's leading export commodities. It must be remembered that here the bulb, not the flower, is the most important part of the plant. When the flowers are ripe, so to speak, they are cut off, leaving only the green stalks. The children play with the discarded blooms, threading them into garlands that they sell to passing motorists or making floral mosaics with them. If you're really serious about your tulips, attend the annual **Bulb District Flower Parade**, held on the last Saturday in April, a 20-mile route that extends from Haarlem to Noordwijk, a colorful processional filled with floats and marching bands.

FodorsChoice
★

Lisse is one of the hubs for the famed **Bollenstreek Route** (Bulb District Route), but more popularly known as the Bloemen Route (Flower Route). Daytrippers from Amsterdam head here by taking the A4 southbound toward Leiden, then the N207 turning for Lisse if venturing here by car. You can also get to Lisse by train from Amsterdam. Other modes of transport are to rent bikes from the train station in Haarlem, or, more comfortably, take bus nos. 50 or 51 at the rail stations in either Haarlem or Leiden to disembark near a Van Gogh field you want to explore—Hillegom is a top village stop hereabouts. When the bulbs are at their best, they are often "beheaded" (in insure future growth) by armies of wood-shoed garden-ers, who remind us that these bulb fields are private property (so be cir-cumspect about heading down any field lanes). Tour companies and the local VVVs (Tourist Information Offices) also organize walking and bi-cycle tours, often including a visit to Keukenhof. When you take a walk-ing or bicycle tour, or independently travel one of these ways following a map route, you get to experience the subtle scents in the fields. You'll find road-side flower stalls selling flowers, bulbs, and garlands.

The Bollenstreek was designed as a special itinerary through the heart of the flower-growing region and laid out by the Dutch auto club, ANWB. The route is marked with small blue-and-white signs that read BOLLENSTREEK. It begins in **Oegstgeest,** near Leiden, and circles through **Rijnsburg** (site of one of Holland's three major flower auction houses), where there is a colorful Flower Parade in August. The route extends to the dunes north of **Noordwijk,** a vast, sandy nature reserve almost as big as the bulb district itself. Small canals and pools of water are dot-ted about in between the dunes, providing a haven for bird life. This is also a popular seaside resort, drawing Dutch, English, and German va-cationers who rent rooms from locals. You might want to make a small stop along the way to see the historic white church in **Noordwijkerhout;** although much of the church has been restored, part of it was a ship that dates from the year 1000. In addition to Noordwijk, the Bulb Route passes through the beach community of **Katwijk** and through **Sassenheim,** where there is an imposing 13th-century ruined castle.

Lisse, the middlemost of the main bulb towns, is noted for its Keuken-hof Gardens, but drivers should keep straight ahead to Sassenheim, turn-ing right (west) into the bulb fields at the north edge of town. At Loosterweg we head north again, following the zigs and zags of this coun-try lane as it passes through the very hearts of the fields so overburdened with color. Presently we are back at Lisse again, and follow the signs for Keukenhof.

Lisse

❶ *27 km (17 mi) southwest of Amsterdam.*

Heart of Tulip Country, the town of Lisse is home to the famous 17-acre Keukenhof park and greenhouse complex, which draws the crowds especially during the spring, from the end of March to the end of May. Founded in 1950 by Tom van Waveren and other leading bulb grow-ers, the Keukenhof is one of the largest open-air flower exhibitions in the world. As many as 7 million tulip bulbs bloom every spring, either in hothouses (where they may reach a height of nearly 3 feet) or in flower beds along the sides of a charming lake. In the last weeks of April you can catch tulips, daffodils, hyacinths, and narcissi all flowering simul-taneously. In addition there are 50,000 square feet of more exotic blooms under glass. Keukenhof is the creation of the leading Dutch bulb-growing exporters, who use it as a showcase for their latest hybrids. Un-fortunately, this means that commercial, not creative, forces are at play here. There are many open gardens adorned with colorful flowers (even "black" tulips) and gaudy frilled varieties. Also in evidence is a depressing lack of style. Garden after flat garden has bright floral mosaics, mean-dering streams, placid pools, too many paved paths, and hordes of peo-ple. Any sense of history—Keukenhof's roots extend way back to the 15th century, when it was the herb farm (Keukenhof means "kitchen courtyard") of one of Holland's richest ladies, the Countess Jacoba van Beieren—has been obliterated. Tulip time is famous here, but there are special shows on view every season of the year. For information about

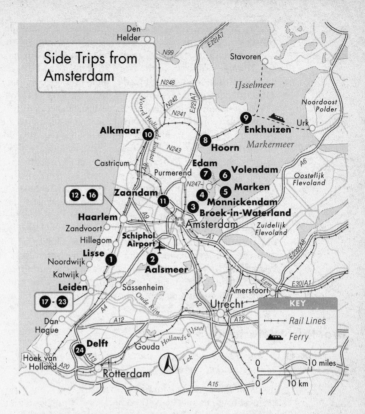

Side Trips from Amsterdam

KEY
⊢—⊣ Rail Lines
⛴ Ferry

0   10 miles
0   10 km

rail access to this destination in the town of Lisse, log on to ⊕ www.
ns.nl or call the main **rail info number** (☎ 0900/9292). ✉ *N207, Lisse*
☎ *0252/465–555* ⊕ *www.keukenhof.nl* ✉ *€7.95* ⊙ *Late Mar.–May,
daily 8–7:30, early Aug.–mid-Sept., daily 9–6.*

Aalsmeer

❷ *20 km (12 mi) east of Keukenhof.*

At Aalsmeer, about 19 km (12 mi) southwest of Amsterdam near
Schiphol Airport, the **Bloemenveiling Aalsmeer** (Aalsmeer Flower Auction) is held five days a week from the predawn hours until midmorning. The largest flower auction in the world, it has three auction halls
operating continuously in a building the size of several football fields.
You walk on a catwalk above the rolling four-tier carts that wait to move
on tracks past the auctioneers. The buying system is what is called a Dutch
auction—the price goes down, not up, on a large "clock" on the wall.
The buyers sit lecture-style with buzzers on their desks; the first to register a bid gets the bunch. Note that you can reach the auction hall by
taking NZH Bus 172 from the stop opposite the American Hotel near
Amsterdam's Leidseplein. ✉ *Legmeerdijk 313, Aalsmeer* ☎ *0297/392–
185* ⊕ *www.aalsmeer.com* ✉ *€4* ⊙ *Weekdays 7:30–11* AM.

FOLKLORIC HOLLAND

If you want your postcards to come to life, head here. In the famous
"folkloric" towns of Zuiderzee, Volendam, and Marken, boys can still
be seen wearing Hans Brinker costumes, sleepy little fishing ports are
lost in time, with wooden fishermen's cottages and tow-headed children

at play, and canal vistas recall ink sketches by Rembrandt. This region is found in the province of Noord-Holland (whose southernmost sector includes Amsterdam). Just across the amazing Noordzee Kanaal (North Sea Canal)—first built in the late 19th century to be one of Holland's most important commercial trade "highways"—running from behind Amsterdam's Centraal Station to as far as the Kop van Holland (the Top of Holland) and the island of Texel, this part of the country offers a taste of unspoiled rural life. Characterful towns, once home to the Dutch fishing fleets and the adventurous captains of the Dutch Golden Age who traveled to the East and West Indies and beyond, are now obsolete because of the Afsluitdijk (Enclosing Dike) at the north end of the former Zuider Zee. They have been resurrected, however, thanks to tourism. The Afsluitdijk was an extraordinary piece of civil engineering completed in 1932 to protect the low-lying land from the ravages of the open seas. It created a massive freshwater lake, called the Ijsselmeer lined with ports and harbors for leisure craft that ply the protected waters. This particular region around the Zaan River and the Ijsselmeer "sea" is called Zaanstreek and Waterland (despite there being water everywhere in The Netherlands). Thanks to its idyllic, watery surroundings, it is a great area for fishing, swimming, and sailing. A fun (even convenient) way to travel hereabouts is by water (*see* Guided Tours *in* Side Trips A to Z), making stops along the way.

Broek-in-Waterland

★ ❸ *14 km (9 mi) northeast of Amsterdam. Follow route N247 and take exit S116 from the ringroad.*

Broek-in-Waterland maintains its centuries-old reputation of being the cleanest town in all The Netherlands; everything is so immaculate that visitors are tempted to walk barefoot on the roads. It's hard to imagine, but the picture-perfect 17th- and 18th-century wooden houses are said to be even tidier inside. Note the color differences: gray houses belonged to "commoners," whereas the wealthy class distinguished theirs with a purplish tint. As you tour the houses, note their famous **De Kralentuinen,** or Bead Gardens, which actually incorporate antique blue glass beads to stud their mosaic designs comprising hedges clipped in Baroque patterns. Hundreds of years ago, Dutch sea merchants used these beads to trade with primitive cultures for spices and other goods. The beads that were left over and brought back to Holland were used to decorate such gardens, lending a foreign flavor to the area.

One of the best ways to view the region is via water; you can rent a kayak or canoe and travel over the **Havenrak,** the large lake that is also popular with ice-skaters in the wintertime. For a perfect day out, take along a picnic—there are many suitable places to stop and enjoy the scenic surroundings.

Monnickendam

❹ *4.7 km (3 mi) north from Broek-in-Waterland, 16 km (10 mi) northeast of Amsterdam. Take Route N247.*

Hardly is the salty odor of curing cheese from nearby towns out of the air than the towers of Monnikendam's Grote Kerk (Great Church) and Speeltoren signal our next stop. Every quarter hour, people hasten to the latter, which is the tower of the 18th-century town hall. Instead of bells, a carillon chimes while knights perform a solemn march. Unless they are stuck again. The oldest working carillon (16th century) in the world, this is the centerpiece of the **Museum De Speeltoren,** and its bells still chime musically every 15 minutes. The 5-ton clock was too heavy for the Germans to remove during the World War II occupation, so it was spared being melted down for munitions. Inside, a museum has a permanent exhibit about local historical architecture and findings from architectural "digs." ⊠ *Noordeinde 4* ☎ *0299/ 652–203* ⊙ *Easter–June 1, Sat. 11–5, Sun. 1–5; June 2–second Sun. in Sept., Tues.–Sat. 11–5, Sun. 1–5.*

Take a moment to stroll down an avenue of dainty gabled houses to the harbor, which is brimming with history. The entire historic center of the Monnickendam is well preserved, with many listed monuments; repairs and new constructions are required to be carried out in the same style. You are surrounded by the past, with some buildings dating from the 14th century. Monk's Dam was named in 1273 in reference to a medieval monastery that had stood on the site. By the 17th century, the harbor at the edge of the Zuiderzee had great importance; now it is possibly the largest yacht harbor in Europe, yet it still has the feeling of olden times. Virtually every monument has an interesting history, including one house that was a hiding place for Jews during World War II. To enjoy the stories behind every structure, join a **walking tour** (some are free); inquire at the local VVV (Tourist Information Office) or at the Speeltoren.

Where to Eat

$$$ ✕ **De Waegh.** Situated in the former *Waeghgebouw*—a 1688 weigh house—this lovely restaurant still has the structure's original scales as part of its decor. Immerse yourself in the past with a view of the harbor, locks, and old inner city while you dine on fine French cuisine for lunch or enjoy dinner by candlelight. The large menu offers so many delicious possibilities you'll be spoiled for choice. Tip-tops include thick Breton fish soup or tender lamb with apples and a sauce from calvados and thyme. ⊠ *Middendam 5-7* ☎ *0299/651–241* ▭ *MC, V* ⊙ *Closed Tues.*

Marken

❺ *8.9 km (6 mi) east of Monnickendam, 16 km (10 mi) northeast of Amsterdam. Take Route N518.*

Quaint Marken has its one-up on other folkloric destinations: this little fishing village is on its own island (or was—a causeway built in 1957 connects it to the mainland). The contrast between Protestant Marken and Catholic Volendam is greater than the distance separating them. Despite the comment of one expert that "the baggy knee breeches of the Markenaars give them the look of boatmen from Greece," the effect is more Asian than Mediterranean. The women's flowered chintzes, inspired by the Dutch East Indies, are one reason for the impression. The children, dressed alike in skirts up to the age of six, are another puzzle, and you find yourself unconsciously trying to separate brothers from sisters by some other means. The answer: boys have blue skirts. You'll often see wooden shoes bearing beautiful hand-painted flowers, with the wearer's name in calligraphy; note the intricately carved designs on the bridal klompen. Bring your camera—the locals are happy that tourism has replaced fishing here.

But the water is never far away. Many of the small, dark, gabled wooden homes are built on wooden piles, dating from when the Zuiderzee used to flood the island. House interiors here are as compact and tidy as the cabin of a ship; similarly, a herring boat and barque in full sail hang from the ceiling of the town church. The local VVV (Tourist Information Office) organizes a boat tour, **Marken Express,** between Volendam and Marken, with a guided walk and meals.

The **Marker Museum** consists of four small fishermen's cottages that were used as fish smokehouses and gives you an idea of present and past life in Marken. ✉ *Kerkbuurt 44–47* ☎ *0299/601–904* 🏷 *€2* ⏱ *Jan.–Sept., Nov., and Dec., Mon.–Sat. 10–5, Sun. noon–4; Oct., Mon.–Sat. 10–5, Sun. 11–4.*

Volendam

★ ❻ *6.7 km (4 mi) northwest of Marken, 18 km (11.5 mi) northeast of Amsterdam. Take Routes N247–N517.*

Assuming that other visitors don't block your view, you can stare to your heart's content at the residents of Volendam still wearing traditional costumes immortalized in Dutch dolls the world over. Yes, indeed, they dress this way for real (even cosmopolitan Amsterdammers stop in their tracks when someone from Volendam or Marken visits the city in full gear.) The men wear dark baggy pantaloons fastened with silver guilders instead of buttons, striped vests, and dark jackets with caps. Women wear long dark skirts covered with striped aprons and blouses with elaborately hand-embroidered floral panels. Their coral necklaces and famous winged lace caps complete the picture. Of course, everyone wears *klompen* (wooden shoes). You'll have the most fun in Volendam if you have your photo taken in traditional costume (a real hoot for the folks back home), enjoy a stroll on the dike (or maybe even a swim on one side of it), and explore the narrow streets with their small nostalgic fishermen's cottages. Don't let the many tacky touristy businesses—a room wallpapered with cigar bands?—throughout the main area selling souvenirs put you off; once you head off the beaten track and see the way the native Volendammers live, you'll get to see the "real" unspoiled Volendam. Be sure to sample the region's renowned smoked eels; they're truly delicious.

Learn about Volendam's history at the **Volendams Museum,** which has rooms filled with mannequins adorned with folkloric costumes. ✉ *Zeestraat 41 Volendam* ☎ *0299/369–258* ⊕ *www.volendams-museum.com* 🏷 *€1.75* ⏱ *Mar.–Dec. Daily 10–5.*

Visit a working cheese farm at **Kaasboerderij Alida Hoeve,** where you'll learn how cheese is made and can also purchase various cheeses. ✉ *Zeddeweg 1 41 Volendam* ☎ *0299/365–830* 🏷 *Free* ⏱ *Mon.–Sun. 8:30–6.*

Edam

❼ *9 km (11 mi) northeast of Volendam, 22 km (14 mi) northeast of Amsterdam.*

Fodor'sChoice
★

Say "cheese" and you might think of those lovely red wax–covered balls that get their name from the historic city of Edam, first established in the 12th century. Walking around this city, however, you'll find the famed cheese encased in yellow (the red is for export only). "Aye-dam" provides a great sense of the past, as most of its bridges, gables, squares, and monuments date from the 17th century. The weekly cheese market is held Wednesday mornings in July and August. During the colorful activities, pairs of cheese bearers, outfitted in white with matching straw hats, carry cheese-laden wooden stretchers to the **Kaaswaag** (Weigh House), which dates from 1778. You can taste and buy cheese inside. Elsewhere note the 18th-century Town Hall, with a beautiful historic civic room, and the town's 15th-century church.

The **Edams Museum** is well worth a visit, as this former merchant's house has barely changed from 1640. The kitchen, living, and sleeping quarters have been furnished and decorated with authentic furniture, utensils, costumes, and paintings to give you a realistic impression of what life was like back in the 17th century. Three portraits from Edam are on view and may make you look more closely at the locals. One is a portrait of Trijntje Kester, who was 13 feet tall at age 13 (so they say), another of Pieter Kirksz, whose red beard was so long it would get wet when he leaned over the town bridge (thereby telling all that the tide was in); and the innkeeper Jan, whose vast girth would doubtless have sent him into bankruptcy if it hadn't sent him to the grave first. Most noteworthy is the "floating cellar," which is watertight and literally floats on the subsoil water, rising and falling according to the water table. The museum and its annex (dating from 1737) hold exhibitions relevant to the city, such as a history of cheese making in Edam or antique pottery from the area. ⊠ *Damplein 8* ☎ *0299/372–644* ⊕ *www.zaanseschans.nl* 🎫 *€2* ⊙ *Week before Easter–late Oct., Tues.–Sat. 10–4:30, Sun. 1–4:30.*

Hoorn

8 *20 km (13 mi) northeast of Edam, 43 km (27 mi) northeast of Amsterdam. Take Routes N247–A7 (E22).*

Hoorn's development was abruptly arrested in the 17th century when England, not limited to flat-bottom boats that could clear the sandbanks of the Zuider Zee, eclipsed Holland in the carrying trade. In a sense the city went to sleep, thus enabling the visitor to step 300 years back in time to an era when Hoorn sent her ships around the world. As the former capital of West-Friesland, Hoorn was an important center for the fleets of the VOC (Dutch East India Company) during the 17th century. William Cornelis Schouten, one of the town's sons, was the first sailor to round the southern cape of America (in 1616), and christened it Cape Hoorn (Cape Horn). Jan Pieterszoon Coen, whose statue lords over the **Rode Steen square,** founded the city of Batavia in Java, the present-day Jakarta, and governed it from 1617 until his death in 1629. Hoorn's decline was precipitated by the growing naval power of the British during the 18th century and the opening of Noord-Holland's canal linking Amsterdam directly to the North Sea.

Although a city with nearly 20,000 residents, Hoorn has many historic nooks and crannies, time-burnished side streets, and a fetching harbor landmarked by the 1532 **Hoofdtoren tower,** now home to a handy restaurant.

The **Westfries Museum** (West Frisian Museum) is housed in the provincial government building dating from 1632, where the delegates from the seven cities of West-Friesland used to meet. The cities are represented by the coats of arms decorating the stunning facade, a testimony to the province's former grandeur. The council chambers are hung with portraits of the region's grandees, and the exhibitions explain the town's maritime history and the exotic finds of its adventurous sailors. ⊠ *Rode Steen 1* ☎ *0229/280–028* ⊕ *www.westfriesmuseum.nl* 🎫 *€2. 50* ⊙ *Weekdays 11–5, Sat. and Sun. 2–5.*

Where to Eat

$–$$ ✕ **De Waag.** A monumental building dating from 1609, with wooden beams and the antique weighing equipment still intact, the "Weigh House" was designed by Hendrick de Keyser. There are soups, salads, and well-filled sandwiches during the day, and at dinnertime you can choose from fish specialties or French cuisine. The terrace affords a stunning view of the towering ornamental facade of the Westfries Museum across the square. *(The Weigh House)* ⊠ *Rode Steen 8* ☎ *0229/215–195* ▤ *AE, M, V* ⊙ *Closed Tues. from Sept. to Apr.*

Enkhuizen

❾ *20 km (13 mi) northeast of Hoorn, 60 km (37 mi) northeast of Amsterdam. Take Routes N506 or N302.*

★ ☾ Near the former harbor town of Enkhuizen, about 19 km (12 mi) east of Hoorn, is perhaps the most famous of the "costume villages," the **Zuiderzeemuseum.** It is one of The Netherlands' most complete outdoor museums, with streets, neighborhoods, and harbors created with historic buildings. There are 130 houses, shops, and workshops where the old crafts are still practiced. To reach the museum you have to take a boat from the main entrance, a romantic way to take a step back in time. Assorted historical treasures here include a 19th-century apothecary, cottages moved from the isle of Urk and the village of Zoutkamp, sail-making and herring shops, picturesque lime kilns from Noord-Holland, and a children's island that takes youngsters back to life in the former fishing village of Marken during the 1930s. The indoor Marine Hall museum houses permanent exhibitions depicting the rich history of the Zuiderzee (now the Ijsselmeer) and inhabitants of the area, including traditional costumes and a history of the battle to reclaim the land from the encroachments of the sea. ✉ *Wierdijk 12–22, Enkhuizen* ☎ *0228/351-111* 🖾 *€9.50; indoor museum only, €5* ⏱ *Indoor museum daily 10–5; outdoor museum Apr.–Oct., daily 10–5.*

Alkmaar

❿ *45 km (13 mi) southwest of Enkhuizen, 40 km (25 mi) northwest of Amsterdam. Take Routes N302–A7/E22–N243–N242.*

Fodor'sChoice
★

As one of the "cheese towns," Alkmaar may be most noted for its traditional cheese market, but it is also worth visiting for its several hundred historical monuments, many windmills, and beautiful medieval courtyards—a concentration of all things Holland. On June 11, 2004, the city will have been on the map for 750 years, but birthday celebrations in the form of special events will go on throughout the year. Town spot- and floodlights will illuminate monuments, gables, and bridges. The town is littered with monuments: the St. Lawrence Church—with its great centuries-old organ and tomb of Count Floris V; the Town Hall, a beautiful Gothic building from 1520; the Remonstraat Church; and the House of the Cannonball (bearing a vestige of Spanish invaders).

But the glory of Alkmaar is the **Waaggebouw,** or Weigh House, a 15th-century chapel with a tower added in 1597. As you stand below its ornate step gables, your eye is drawn upward by a labyrinth of receding planes that culminate in the weather vane. If the hour is about to strike, pause to enjoy the chimes and watch the moving figures of mounted knights and trumpeters (the noon hour gets the biggest show). Then climb the tower for a view of the town: canals cross this way and that, and the former ramparts are outlined by gardens often ablaze with flowers. In the distance, windmills turn in the face of a breeze perfumed with the faint scent of the salt sea.

If it is a Friday morning, it won't be easy to tear yourself from the spectacle taking place at your feet. The cheeses arrive at the market by barge (the factory may be as little as half a mile away) and are unloaded by means of a juggling act that would do credit to any circus as the balls are pitched from the barge to barrows that look like stretchers. At this point pairs of colorfully attired men from the Porters' Guild (in existence for 400 years) carry the cheeses away, no mean feat, as the average weight is about 350 pounds per barrow. A "father" directs the activities of the 28 porters, who are divided into four groups, or *veems*, dressed alike in white shirts and trousers but distinguished by blue, red, green, or yellow straw hats. The actual selling of the cheeses takes place in a ring and is consummated by a handclasp that is as binding as a signed contract. The cheese market takes place from the first week in April to the first week in September on Friday mornings from 10 to 12:30. After the sale—the auction is done through traditional hand-clapping signals—the official weighing of the cheese is done at the Weigh House. All in all, it may be easier to buy your cheese at a supermarket, but it's nice to remember a world that has a place for pageantry.

The local VVV (Tourist Information Office) organizes a walking tour of noteworthy sites. The 1½-hour tour costs €3.50. It starts at 12:30, except in September, when it starts at 11. Tickets can be purchased at the Alkmaar VVV office. If planning to explore on your own, pick up a map from the VVV.

The **Stedelijk Museum Alkmaar** focuses on the history of the region from Alkmaar's "Golden Age"—the 16th and 17th centuries—to the present day. There is an intriguing display of city life shown in detailed miniature dioramas. Paintings depict the Spanish siege of the city, portraits capture noblemen and militia leaders, and other historic artifacts make this a good starting point before exploring Alkmaar itself. ⊠ *Canadaplein 1* ☏ *072/511–0737* ✎ *€3.40* ☉ *Tues.–Fri. 10–5, Sat. and Sun. 1–5.*

While attending the cheese market, you'll see the cheese being weighed at the Waaggebouw, which is also where the **Dutch Cheese Museum** is located. Cheese has been produced in Noord-Holland for nearly 2,500 years, so it's no wonder Dutch cheese is so good. You'll learn about past and present-day cheese making (farm versus factory). Twenty-four 16th-century panels, painted by women, depict regional costumes from all over Noord-Holland, with some full-size replica outfits on display. ⊠ *Waagplein 2* ☏ *072/511–42 84* ✎ *€2.50* ☉ *Apr.–end of Oct., Mon.–Thurs., Sat. 10–4, Fri. 9–4.*

Zaandam

⓫ *31 km (19 mi) southeast of Alkmaar, 16 km (10 mi) northwest of Amsterdam. Take Route N203 via Zaanse Schans (Zaandijk).*

Fodor'sChoice
★

During the 17th century Holland was renowned as the leading shipbuilding nation of the world, with Zaandam as its center. One of the many people who came here to learn the craft of shipbuilding was Peter the Great of Russia (whose statue now adorns the Damplein, the town marketplace). Today, modern shipyards stud the area—once immortalized in several canvases by Claude Monet—but set within the Zaanstreek region is a jewel: the **Zaanse Schans**, a living open-air museum. Time appears to stand still, and you can easily immerse yourself in the 17th and 18th century. The village, built along the Zaan River, is filled with a great many working windmills and original Zaanse-style green wooden houses. Many have been restored as private homes, but a whole cluster are open to the public, and traditional crafts and businesses are still kept alive. You can see warehouses from the Dutch East India Trading Company and visit the workshop of a clog maker, the shops of a traditional cheese maker, a bakery museum, and the working windmills themselves. Each of these "mini museums" has its own low admission price. The Zaanse Schans presents a terrific skyline when viewed from the water, so avail yourself of the local VVV (Tourist Information Office) canal cruises. A mile or so north of Zaandam you come to Koog aan de Zaan, notable chiefly for the old (1751) **Het Pink windmill**, now a museum devoted to the history and construction of mills. ⊠ *Kraaienest, Zaandam* ☎ *075/ 616–8218* ⊕ *www.zaanseschans.nl* ⊠ *Free* ⊙ *Daily 8–4.*

THE FAR HORIZONS: HALS'S HAARLEM TO VERMEER'S DELFT

A route south of Amsterdam, running near the coast, takes you through the heart of metropolitan Holland, starting with Haarlem and ending at Delft. Here, great city centers still bear witness to the Golden Age of the 17th century: Haarlem, the only competition to Amsterdam as an art center, thanks to the glories of Sint Bavo's and the celebrated portrait skills of local Frans Hals; Leiden, where a child was baptized and left town two decades later to find fame and riches as Rembrandt van Rijn; and Delft, whose frozen-in-amber scene seems not so distantly removed from that painted in Vermeer's legendary *View of Delft*. Once past the bright lights of these town centers, you'll find that the land stretches flat as far as the eye can see, though the coast west of Haarlem and Leiden undulates with long expanses of dunes, many of which are nature reserves. In spring, the farmland between these two towns is bright with tulips and other blooms. Venture down some unmarked roads and you can still find a storybook Holland of green meadows, hayracks, brimming canals, and—dare we say—a rosy-cheeked child or two. Cows graze in the fields nearly all year round, and only the distant spires destroy the illusion of a flat infinity leading endlessly onward.

Haarlem

Fodor'sChoice
★

20 km (13 mi) west of Amsterdam.

It is just a short hop from the ocean of annual color that is Holland's Bulb Route to this haven of perennial color. For Haarlem's historic center is beautiful, dotted with charming *hofjes* (courtyards), and has a lively population—often the spillover of students who can't find lodgings in Amsterdam or Leiden. The city is also home to fine museums stuffed with art by masters of the Haarlem School, such as the renowned Teyler Museum, and the town center is adorned with the imposing Grote Kerk, often painted by the masters of the Golden Age. All in all, if on occasion eclipsed by Amsterdam, Haarlem is an independent little city in its own right. Plenty of top-quality restaurants and shops cater to well-heeled locals, and people tend to be more friendly than in the downtown districts of Amsterdam. Lying between Amsterdam and the coastal resort of Zandvoort, Haarlem is very close to the dunes and the sea and therefore attracts hordes of beach-going Amsterdammers and Germans every summer.

If you arrive by train (it's just a 15-minute trip from the capital), take a long look around before you leave the railway station—a fabulous Art Nouveau building dating from 1908. Head down Jans Weg (to the left of the station as you exit) for several blocks, over the Nieuwe Gracht canal, and into the city center, where, farther along on Jans Straat you

12 hit Haarlem's pulsing heart, the famous **Grote Markt**. Around this great market square the whole of Dutch architecture can be traced in a chain of majestic buildings ranging through the 15th, 16th, 17th, 18th, and 19th centuries. With a smile and a little bravado, you can enter nearly all of them for a quick look. But all eyes are first drawn to the imposing mass of Sint Bavo's.

13 The Late Gothic Sint Bavo's church, more commonly called the **Grote Kerk**, or Great Church, dominates the square and was built in the 14th

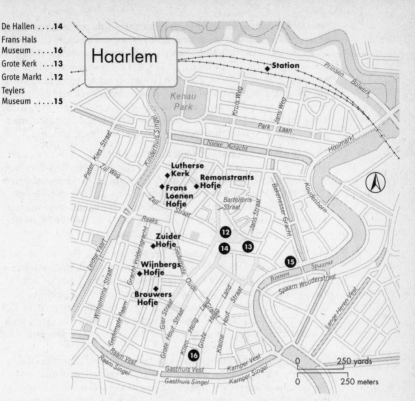

Haarlem

century, but severe fire damage in 1328 led to a further 150 years of rebuilding and expansion. St. Bavo was the patron saint of the community. This is the burial place of the famed 17th-century portraitist Frans
Hals—a lamp marks his tombstone behind the brass choir screen. Here,
too, is buried Laurens Coster, who in 1423 invented printing—sorry,
Gutenberg—seemingly when the love-struck Coster was inspired when
carved-bark letters fell into the sand below a tree he was etching with
a valentine (a statue of Coster adorns the square outside). The imposing wooden vault shelters two whimsical historic sights. In the north
transept, the Dog Whippers' chapel pays tribute to men who ejected
snarling dogs from the sacred premises; a carved capital on the left-hand
arch depicts a man whipping a dog. The church is the home of the Müller
organ, on which both Handel and Mozart played (Mozart at age 10).
Between May and October the official town organists of Haarlem give
free weekly or twice-weekly concerts. You may be lucky enough to hear
orchestras rehearsing for concerts as you tiptoe through. One thing is
clear: there are few places where a Bach prelude or fugue sounds as magisterial. ⊠ *Grote Markt* ☎ *023/553–2040* 📷 *€1.50* ☉ *Apr.–Aug.,
Mon.–Sat. 10–4; Sept.–Mar., Mon.–Sat. 10–3:30.*

❶ Overlooking the Grote Markt is the **De Hallen,** or The Halls museum
complex, whose two buildings—the Vleeshal and the Verweyhal House—
contain a variety of artworks, ranging from temporary special exhibitions to a permanent collection of modern art by artists from Haarlem
and surrounding areas. A branch of the town's Frans Hals Museum, De
Hallen has an extensive collection, with the works of Dutch Impressionists
and Expressionists, including sculpture, textiles, and ceramics, as well
as paintings and graphics. The **Vleeshal** (Meat Market) building is one
of the most interesting cultural legacies of the Dutch Renaissance. Ex-

ternally it is unique, for nowhere in the country is there such a fine sweep
of stepped gables that invite you, had you a giant's stride, to clamber
up to the pinnacle that almost seems to pierce the scudding clouds. It
was built in 1602–03 by Lieven de Key, Haarlem's master builder. The
ox heads that look down from the facade are reminders of the building's original function: it was the only place in Haarlem where meat could
be sold, and the building was used for that sole purpose until 1840. Today
it is used for exhibitions—generally of works of modern and contemporary painting, glass, furniture, clocks, and sculpture.

The **Verweyhal Gallery of Modern Art** was built in 1879 as a gentlemen's club, originally named *Trou moet Blijcken* ("Loyalty Needs to
Be Proven"). The building now bears the name of the deceased native
Haarlem artist Kees Verwey. The Verweyhal is used as an exhibition space
for selections of the work from the Frans Hals Museum's enormous collection of modern and contemporary art. ⊠ *Grote Markt 16* ☎ *023/
511–5778* ▣ *€5.40* ☉ *Tues.–Sat. 11–5, Sun. noon–5.*

★ ⑮ The beloved and world-famous **Teylers Museum** is the best sort of small
museum, based on the taste of an eccentric private collector, in this case
the 18th-century merchant Pieter Teyler van der Hulst. Founded in 1784,
it's the country's oldest museum and has a mixture of exhibits, with
fossils and minerals sitting alongside antique scientific instruments. The
museum itself is a grand old building with mosaic floors; its major artistic attraction is the legendary collection of drawings and prints by
19th-century masters Michelangelo, Rembrandt, Raphael, and others,
based on a collection that once belonged to Queen Christina of Sweden. Unfortunately, only a few of the drawings are on display at any
one time because of their fragility. Some of the collection is housed in
beautiful wooden display cases in the original 18th-century museum
building, and the drawing collection is in a discreetly extended modern wing. ⊠ *Spaarne 16* ☎ *023/531–9010* ▣ *€4.50* ☉ *Tues.–Sat. 10–5,
Sun. noon–5.*

★ ⑯ The **Frans Hals Museum,** set near the river Spaarne, is named after the
celebrated man himself and holds a collection of amazingly virile and
lively group portraits by the Golden Age painter; these portraits depict
the merrymaking civic guards and congregating regents for which Hals
became world famous. The museum is in one of the town's smarter hofjes, in an entire block of almshouses grouped around an attractive garden courtyard, a setting that in itself is a gem of artistry. In the 17th
century this was an old men's home, an *Oudemannerhuis.* The cottages
now form a sequence of galleries for paintings, period furniture, antique
silver, and ceramics. The 17th-century collection of paintings that is the
focal point of this museum includes the works of Frans Hals and other
masters of the Haarlem School.

You might find yourself overwhelmed by the visual banquet of Hals paintings, but take time to look in all the rooms branching off the main route,
festooned with works by other masters. Many of the works on display
represent Frans Hals at his jovial best—for instance, the *Banquet of the
Officers of the Civic Guard of St. Adrian* (1623) or the *Banquet of the
Officers of the St. George Militia* (1616), where the artist cunningly allows for the niceties of rank (compositionally, captains are more prominent than sergeants, who are more central than ensigns, and so on
down the line) as well as emotional interaction, for Hals was the first
to have people gaze and laugh at each other in these grand *schutter* (officer) group portraits. In many instances, Hals leaves "Class Portrait"
decorum well behind: in a group scene of the *Regentesses of the Old
Men's Home* (1664) he appears to have taken revenge on their strict gov-

ernance, immortalizing the women as a dour and frightening group. Nineteenth-century academicians later criticized Hals for his imprecise handling of details, but remember that Hals was 80 when completing this portrait, and it was his *mouvementé,* nearly proto–Jackson Pollock way with the brush that made him the darling of 20th-century artists and art historians.

As respite from nearly 250 canvases, step into the museum's courtyard—small, lovely, planted with formal-garden baby hedges, of which you hardly get a glimpse as you work your way through the galleries (since most of the blinds are shut against the sunlight to protect the paintings). In one such room, with curtains drawn for extra protection, is **Sara Rothè's Dolls' House**; nearby is an exquisitely crafted miniature version of a merchant's canal house. On leaving, *View of Haarlem* (1655) by Nicolaes Hals, Frans's son (1655), bids you good-bye. ⊠ *Groot Heiligland 62* ☎ *023/511–5775* ✉ *€5.40* ☾ *Tues.–Sat. 11–5, Sun. 1–5.*

In the lower, southwestern sector of the city, you'll find many of the quaint and historic hofjes that make Haarlem such a pleasant place. In and around Voldersgracht, Gasthuisstraat, Zuiderstraat, and Lange Annastraat, look for the Zuider Hofje, the Hofje van Loo, the Winjbergs Hofje, and the Brouwershofje. Closer to the Grote Markt are the Remonstrants Hofje, the Luthershofje, and the Frans Loenen Hofje.

Where to Eat

¢–$ ╳ **Pieck.** One of Haarlem's best *eetlokaals,* this attracts locals with its long bar, cozy tables, and lovely sun trap of a garden. The menu offers standards but with a twist: try the "Popeye Blues Salad"—a wild spinach, blue cheese, and bacon number, with creamy mustard dressing for a lighter option—or, for dinner, a butterfish fillet with okra and sugar snaps in a Tuscan dressing. ⊠ *Warmoestraat 18* ☎ *023/532–6144* ⊟ *No credit cards* ☾ *Closed Sun. No dinner Mon.*

Leiden

FodorsChoice ★   *45 km (28 mi) south of Amsterdam.*

The town from which the Pilgrims set out on their journey to America (stopping first in England, however), Leiden owes its first importance to its watery geography—it stands at the junction of two branches of the Rhine—the "Old" and the "New." Birthplace of Rembrandt and site of the nation's oldest and most prestigious university, Leiden has played an important part in Dutch history. A place where windmills still rise over the cityscape, Leiden offers the charm of Amsterdam with little of the sleaze. Despite its wealth and historical air, Leiden, it is often said, could not be pompous if it tried.

Cobbled streets, gabled houses, narrow canals overhung with lime trees, and antiques shops give the historic center a tangible feeling of history, and Leiden's university's academic buildings, the historic Waag (Weigh House) and the Burcht fortress, the stately mansions lining the Rapenburg—the most elegant canal in the town—and no fewer than 35 hofjes make it a rewarding place for a stroll. As you walk about, keep a watch for verses painted on lofty gables, a project started some 10 years ago. Don't keep an eye out for any Rembrandt sightings: although he lived here for 20 years, Rembrandt left almost no trace of his life here—his birthplace was knocked down years ago (marked only by a plaque on a very modern wall), and his actual birth date (1606 or 1607) is disputed. A Rembrandt "walk" is marked by the absence of any real site, although you can see where his sister Trintje lived and where his brother Adriaen worked as a cobbler. Museum-lovers will have to be selective. Don't expect the Rijksmuseum: windmill history, Japanese artifacts, and Egyptian antiquities are some of the specialties on tap here. The historic center is marked by the Burcht, an 11th-century mound of earth with a fortification on top to control the confluence of the Old and New Rhine ("De Rijn," whence Rembrandt took his last name), which almost encircle it.

★ ⑰ **Molenmuseum de Valk** (Windmill Museum of the Falcon). Set not far from the main train station, this enchanting windmill-turned-museum began grinding grain in 1743 and is occasionally pressed back into service to produce whole-wheat flour (which you can purchase at the shop here). Perfectly preserved living quarters on the ground floor greet you as you clamber past massive millstones and head up seven stories to the top of the mill—stop on the way up to step out onto the "reefing stage," the platform than runs around the outside for a view of the city, where the gleaming canals remind us that they were once "paved with gold" (as thoroughfares used to ship the grain made at this windmill, and many others, to surrounding towns). Most afternoons from April to the end of September the sails of the windmill are put into operation—get your camcorders ready. ⊠ *2e Binnenvestgracht 1* ☎ *071/516–5353* ⌸ *€3.25* ⊙ *Tues.–Sat. 10–5, Sun. 1–5.*

★ ⑱ **Stedelijk Museum De Lakenhal** (Lakenhal Museum). Built in 1639 for the city's cloth merchants, this grand structure is adorned with decorations alluding to the manufacture of textiles. Leiden enjoyed a Golden Age of the late 16th and 17th centuries in both textiles and art. It was during this period that the city's artist community was most prolific, spawning three great painters of the time: Rembrandt, Jan van Goyen, and Jan Steen. Although few works by these three artists remain in the city, this collection does have an early Rembrandt, though its rawness comes as quite a surprise to loyal followers. The museum is repository for an impressive collection of paintings, furniture, and silver and pewter pieces, set in the sumptuous surrounds of a 17th-century Cloth Hall, a witness to Leiden's great importance in the wool trade. This is the building where the cloth was inspected and traded, and reconstructed guild rooms, replete with authentic antiques, show where the Guild Governors met. Galleries are hung with paintings by Gerrit Dou, Jan Steen, and Salomon van Ruysdael, as well as a grand collection of the works of Lucas van Leyden (another local boy who made good), including his triptych, the *Last Judgment.* ⊠ *Oude Singel 28–32* ☎ *071/516–5360* ⌸ *€3.60* ⊙ *Tues.–Fri. 10–5, weekends noon–5.*

⑲ **Rijksmuseum van Oudheden** (National Museum of Antiquities). Perhaps Leiden's most notable museum, this building houses the largest archaeological collection in Holland. Collections include pieces from ancient Egypt, the classical world, the Near East, and the Roman Netherlands. As you tour the galleries, you may encounter a "guide from antiquity" who will charmingly provide a "personal" perspective on the objects, which are further placed in context through elaborate scenery, scale models, film footage, and 3-D reconstructions. ⊠ *Rapenburg 28* ☎ *071/516–3163* ⌸ *€6; additional charge for temporary exhibitions* ⊙ *Tues.–Fri. 10–5, weekends noon–5.*

⑳ **Pieterskerk** (St. Peter's Church). Within a stone's throw of the University of Leiden, this noted church is often surrounded by students sunning themselves in the church square. The oldest church in the city, dating from 1428, it is rarely used as a place of worship, as its upkeep became overwhelming in the 1970s. Happily, though, it hasn't been abandoned but has diversified into hosting an extraordinary range of events from fashion shows (with a long catwalk stretching the magnificent length

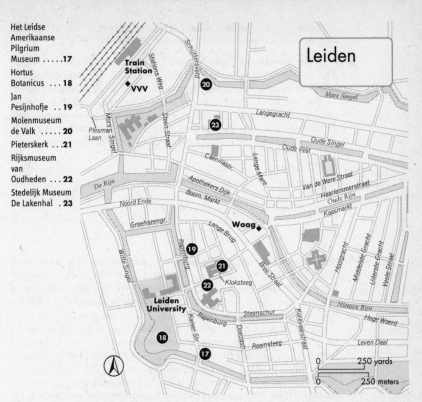

of the nave) to student examinations to post-examination graduation balls. But history can be found here—in that corner and in this. The grave of the painter Jan Steen lies on one wall, and somewhere in an unmarked burial chamber Rembrandt's parents sleep on. More important to Americans (who gather here every Thanksgiving Day for a special service), there is a corner devoted to the Pilgrim Fathers—Puritan refugees from English religious persecution—who often worshiped here. They had petitioned the city fathers in 1609 to relocate here from Amsterdam, which they found "torn by the spirit of controversy." Plaques inside and out pay tribute to the Reverend John Robinson, who was spiritual leader to this community of Puritans; his grave is here, as he grew ill before the Pilgrims set out on their momentous journey to the New World. A stroll from the church down Herensteeg can bring you to a house (marked by a plaque) where William Brewster and his Pilgrim Press published the theological writings that clashed so strongly with the dogmas of the Church of England. ✉ *Pieterskerkhof* ☎ *071/512–4319* 🎟 *Free* ⊙ *Daily 1:30–4.*

㉑ Jan Pesijnhofje. This is just one of a number of Leiden's pretty hofjes. Centered on a tranquil garden and founded in the 17th century by a distant ancestor of President Franklin Delano Roosevelt, it marks the site where the Reverend John Robinson, spiritual head of the Pilgrims, lived and died (1625). Robinson had settled in Leiden a decade before his flock arrived on their *Mayflower* and, unfortunately, fell ill before they departed for the wilder shores of America. Other Pilgrim sites nearby are the Pieterskerk and a plaque marking the Pilgrim Press on William Brewster Alley. Many of the city's hofjes are still used as residential accommodation for the elderly, so if you see a sign that says VERBODEN, respect their privacy. Other almshouses can be found at **Coninckshofje**

(✉ Oude Vest 15), **St. Stevenshof** (✉ Haarlemmerstraat 48–50), and the Groeneveldstichting (✉ Oude Vest 41). ✉ *Pieterskerkhof 21.*

㉒ Het Leidse Amerikaanse Pilgrim Museum (Leiden American Pilgrim Museum). This documentation center occupies a small 14th-century house furnished to illustrate what the Pilgrims' daily life was like before they left for the New World. Brief texts and 17th-century engravings tell the story of their extraordinary odyssey. You can get complete information here about the Pilgrim sites throughout the city, notably those at the Pieterskerk. ✉ *Beschuitsteeg 9* ☎ *071/512–2413* 🎫 *€2* ☉ *Wed.–Sat. 1–5.*

need a break?   **De Waterlijn** (✉ Prinsessekade ☎ 071/512–1279) occupies one of the most attractive spots in town. Just past the end of the Rapenburg canal (which is itself lined with gracious buildings), this strikingly modern, glass-walled café on a moored boat offers views of old boats, gabled houses, and a windmill. The Dutch apple tart will please most.

★ **㉓ Hortus Botanicus** (Botanical Garden). Following the wide Rapenburg canal from the center of town, you reach Leiden University's renowned botanical garden, a leading shrine for tulip-lovers the world over. Planted in 1594, the garden was meant to be a *hortus academicus* (garden for study purposes) and was originally laid out by the greatest botanist of the age, Carolus Clusius, who had bounced around Europe surveying flowers and writing important studies for various societies and princely patrons until an offer from the fledgling University of Leiden brought him north to Holland. It is commonly reported that this garden was the first place that tulip bulbs were planted in Holland, but this is far from the case. Dutch merchants with connections to Istanbul had decades before received bulbs as gifts, and before long they, and scholars such as Clusius, were busy dispatching seeds to all corners of the land.

But it was here in Leiden that Clusius put the cap on a study of tulips, divining their schools and species, making distinctions between free-growing ones and hybrid cultivars, and bedding out his garden with wonderful displays of Couleren (single-color) and Marquetrian (multicolor) tulips. This started the enormous vogue for Rosen, Violetten, Bizarden, and numerous other species of tulip that came to rage in Holland in the following decades, leading to the Great Tulip Mania of the 1630s. Today, in addition to seeing the tulip beds of the original design, you can find Clusius's garden laid out with extensive rose gardens, shrubs, and towering trees, as well as an orangery, a Japanese garden, and several hothouses of orchids and other rarities. ✉ *Rapenburg 73* ☎ *071/527–7249* 🎫 *€4.60* ☉ *Mon.–Sun. 10–6 except Sat. Mar.–Nov.*

Where to Eat

$ ✕ **Oudt Leyden.** This restaurant is a traditional Dutch pancake house with red-check tablecloths and a relaxed mood. Besides pancakes, you can order *poffertjes,* small, thick, puffed-up pancakes the size of a silver dollar. They're covered with powdered sugar and served with *stroop,* a kind of molasses, and are a favorite with children. ✉ *Steenstraat 51–53* ☎ *071/513–3144* ▭ *No credit cards* ☉ *Closed Sun.*

Delft

㉔ *71 km (45 mi) southwest of Amsterdam.*

Fodor'sChoice ★   With time-burnished canals and streets, Delft possesses a peaceful calm that recalls the quieter pace of the Golden Age of the 17th century. Back then the town counted among its citizens the artist Johannes Vermeer, who decided one spring day to paint the city gates and landscape across the Kolk harbor from a house's window on the Schieweg (now the Hooikade). The result was the 1660 *View of Delft* (now the star of the Mauritshuis Museum in The Hague), famously called by Marcel Proust "the most beautiful painting in the world." Spending a few hours in certain parts of Delft, in fact, puts you in the company of Vermeer. Imagine a tiny Amsterdam, canals reduced to dollhouse proportions, narrower bridges, merchants' houses less grand, and you have the essence of Old Delft. But although the city has one foot firmly planted in the past, another is firmly planted in the present: Delft teems with hip cafés, jazz festivals, and revelers spilling out of bars—all, in fact, when most regional Dutch towns are still in hibernation.

For many travelers, few spots in Holland are as intimate and attractive as this town, whose famous blue-and-white earthenware has gone around the world. Compact and easy to traverse, despite its web of canals, Delft is best explored on foot, although water taxis are available in the summer to give you an armchair ride through the heart of town. Many streets in the historic center—called Oude Delft—are lined with medieval Gothic and Renaissance houses, and tree-shadowed canals still reflect the same blue sky from which the pottery and tile makers of 350 years ago snatched their matchless color. And at many corners you see a small humpback bridge or facade that looks as lovely as Delftware itself.

But Delft has more than painterly charm, for it nearly rivals Leiden for historical import. Great men lived and died here. By the end of the 16th century Prince William of Orange (known as William the Silent) settled in Delft to wage his war against Spanish rule. He never left: in his mansion the founder of the nation was assassinated in 1584 by a spy of the Spanish duke of Alva and buried with great pomp in the Nieuwe Kerk (New Church). Here, too, is buried Grotius, the great humanist and father of international law. Delft was also home to Anthonie van Leeuwenhoek, who mastered the fledging invention of the microscope and was born the same year as Vermeer, 1632. Vermeer, many people will be interested to know, was just one of many artists who set up shop in Delft; Delft could support many artists since it had grown fat with the trade in butter, cloth, beer, and, in the 17th century, pottery.

As the headquarters of the Dutch East India Company (whose power can only be compared to Microsoft's today), Delft was a very rich town. The porcelains brought back by its traders from the Far East proved irresistible, and in 1645, De Proceleyn Fles started making and exporting the blue-and-white earthenware that was to make the town famous. Civil war in China had dried up the source for porcelains, and Delft potters leapt in and created the blue faience that soon became known as Delft Blue. This technological expertise had a result in the founding of the Technical University of Delft in 1842; today, its 13,000 students give a youthful spin to this historic city. Everything you might want to see in this compact city is in the old center, where the best views are also to be found.

Following Oude Delft canal brings you to the very heart of historic Delft, where you'll find the grouping of the Oude Kerk, the Prinsenhof Museum, and the Museum Lambert van Meerten. The Gothic **Oude Kerk** (Old Church), with its tower 6 feet off kilter, is the last resting place of Vermeer. The tower manages to lean in all directions at once, but then, this is the oldest church in Delft, having been founded in 1200. Building went on until the 15th century, which accounts for the combination of architectural styles, and much of its austere interior dates from the latter part of the works. The tower, dating back to 1350, started leaning in the Middle Ages, and today the tilt to the east is somewhat stabilized by the 3-foot tilt to the north. The tower, whose tilt prevents ascension by visitors, holds the largest carillon bell in The Netherlands; weighing nearly 20,000 pounds, it now is used only on state occasions. At the recent opening after several years of renovations, Queen Beatrix officially marked the occasion. ⊠ *Heilige Geestkerkhof* 🕾 *015/212–3015* 🎫 *Combined ticket to Oude Kerk and Nieuwe Kerk €2.25* ☉ *Apr.–Nov., Mon.–Sat. 10–5.*

A former dignitary-hosting convent of St. Agatha, **Het Prinsenhof** is celebrated as the residence of Prince William the Silent, beloved as *Het Vader de het Vaderland* (Father of the Country) for his role in the Spanish Revolt and a hero whose tragic end here gave this structure the sobriquet "cradle of Dutch liberty." The complex of buildings was taken over by the government of the new Dutch Republic in 1572 and given to William of Orange for his use as a residence. On July 10, 1583, fevered by monies offered by Philip II of Spain, Bathasar Gerard, a Catholic fanatic, gained admittance to the mansion and succeeded in shooting the prince on the staircase hall, since known as Moordhal (Murder Hall). The fatal bullet holes—the *teychenen derkoogelen*—are still visible (protected by glass) in the stairwell. Today, the imposing structure is a museum, with a 15th-century chapel, a quaint courtyard, and a bevy of elegantly furnished 17th-century rooms filled with antique pottery, silver, tapestries, and House of Orange portraits, along with exhibits on Dutch history. ⊠ *Sint Agathaplein 1* 🕾 *015/260–2358* 🎫 *€5, combined ticket with Meerten and Nusantara museums €6* ☉ *Tues.–Sat. 10–5, Sun. 1–5.*

Between the Prinsenhof and the Nusantara Museum is the Agathaplein, a Late Gothic leafy courtyard, built around 1400, which has huge chestnut trees shading an adjacent green, and a somewhat cultivated square, the **Prinsentuin** (Prince's Garden), which, if it's not too busy, is a calming place for a five-minute respite from the city streets.

★ Within the shadow of the Oude Kerk is the **Lambert van Meerten Museum,** a Renaissance-era, canal-side mansion whose gloriously paneled rooms provide a noble setting for antique tiles, tin-glazed earthenware, paintings, and an extensive collection of ebony-veneered furniture. Although many of the works on display are not the original patrician owner's (who lost a fortune when his distillery burned down and he had to auction off everything), the house and some of his collection was bought back by van Meerten's friends. Note especially the great collection of tiles, whose subjects range from foodstuffs to warships. The gardens here are alluring, with a spherical sundial, two busts, and a stone gateway leading the eye through to the tangled woods beyond. ⊠ *Oude Delft 199* 🕾 *015/260–2358* 🎫 *€5, combined ticket with Nusantara Museum €6* ☉ *Tues.–Sat. 10–5, Sun. 1–5.*

From the Oude Kerk area, head south several blocks to find the **Markt** square, bracketed by two town landmarks, the Stadhuis (Town Hall) and the Nieuwe Kerk. Here, too, are cafés, restaurants, and souvenir shops (most selling imitation Delftware) and, on Thursdays, a busy general market. On the Markt you can find the site of Johannes Vermeer's house at No. 52, where the 17th-century painter spent much of his youth. Not far away is a statue of Grotius, or Hugo de Groot, born in Delft in 1583, who was one of Holland's most famous humanists and lawyers.

Presiding over the Markt is the Late Gothic **Nieuwe Kerk** (New Church), built between 1483 and 1510. More than a century's worth of further Dutch craftsmanship went into its erection, as though its founders knew it would one day be the last resting place of the builder of Holland into a nation, William the Silent, and his descendants of the House of Orange.

VERMEER: SPHINX OF DELFT

S ONE OF THE MOST ADORED ARTISTS IN THE WORLD, *Johannes Vermeer (1632–75) has recently been the subject of a best-selling novel and new film (Tracy Chevalier's Girl with a Pearl Earring), blockbuster museum exhibitions, and new theater pieces (Peter Greenaway's Writing to Vermeer). He enjoys cultlike popularity, yet his reputation rests on just 35 pictures. Of course, those paintings—ordinary domestic scenes depicting figures caught in an amber light and in fleeting gestures that nearly anticipate cinema—are among the most extraordinary ever created. But Vermeer's glory is of a relatively recent vintage. He died at age 42, worn out by economic woes: at his death, a change in taste for a style of flamboyant art saw his name fall into total obscurity. Only in the mid-19th century did critics rightfully reattribute to him his masterpieces. Yet ever since Proust proclaimed his View of Delft (Mauritshuis Museum, The Hague) "the most beautiful painting in the world," audiences worldwide have been enraptured by Vermeer's spellbinding work.*

Like most artists, Vermeer courted fame, as his legendary Artist in His Studio (Kunsthistoriches Museum, Vienna) reveals. This imposing work (which long hung in his atelier to impress prospective patrons) shows Vermeer sitting at his easel painting a model garbed as Clio, the Muse of History. Her crown of laurels and trumpet, art historians have recently announced, prove that she is, instead, a symbol for fickle Fame. The expected Vermeerian icons—swagged tapestry, gleaming brass chandelier, map of Holland on the wall—are in place, but all eyes first fall on the figure of the artist, whom we see from behind. "This artist who keeps his back to us," as Proust put it, doesn't reveal his face, or little else. Indeed, the more books that are devoted to Vermeer, the less we seem to know of him.

How did he paint scenes of such an incomparable quietude, yet live in a house filled with his 11 children? Why are his early works influenced by Caravaggio, but there is no proof he ever visited Italy? His family was Calvinist, but did he convert when he married a Catholic wife? Did he use a camera obscura box to capture his amazing light effects? In an age fraught with drama—Holland was at war with France—why did he bar the outside world from his paintings? Such questions are difficult to answer, for between baptism and betrothal (a span of 20 years), the archives are totally mute about Vermeer. But we do know his grandfather was arrested for counterfeiting money and his father ran the heavily mortgaged inn known as the Mechelen, set on the Voldersgracht just a few paces from Delft's Nieuwe Kerk; his father also sidelined as an art dealer (he needed something to hang on those tavern walls) as did Johannes himself. Vermeer's rich mother-in-law didn't want him to marry her daughter, but the artist won her over; he married Catharina Bolnes and enrolled as the youngest syndic of the Guild of St. Luke—Delft's thriving confraternity of painters—in 1654.

In the end, the only "reality" that matters is the one that Vermeer claustrophobically caught within the four walls of his house—but that unique universe is enough. His ability to transform oil paint into a world is so credible that we even gain an impression of the warmth or chill of the room. His light captures the most transient of effects—you almost find yourself looking around to see where the sunlight has fallen, half expecting it to be dappling your own face. And then there is the telling way Vermeer captures an entire story in a single moment, as in the Glass of Wine (Staatliche Museum, Berlin). A man stands over a woman as she drains her glass, his hand firmly clasping the silver-lipped jug as though intending to refill it—laying the question of his intentions (is he planning to get her tipsy?) open to interpretation. Here, as always, Vermeer keeps us guessing.

In 1872 noted architect P. J. H. Cuypers raised the tower to its current height. No fewer than 22 columns surround the ornate black marble and alabaster tomb of William of Orange, designed by Hendrick de Keyser and son. Figures of Justice, Liberty, and Valor surround a carving of the prince, at whose feet is shown his small dog, which starved to death after refusing to eat following his owner's death. Below is the Royal Crypt, where 41 members of the House of Orange–Nassau are buried. Throughout the church are paintings, stained-glass windows, and memorabilia associated with the Dutch royal family. In summer it is possible to climb the church tower for a view that stretches as far as The Hague and Scheveningen. ⊠ *Markt 2* ☎ *015/212–3025* ✉ *Combined ticket for Oude Kerk and Nieuwe Kerk €2, tower €1.60* ☉ *Apr.–Oct., Mon.–Sat. 9–6; Nov.–Mar., Mon.–Sat. 11–4.*

At the eastern end of the Markt, you can take Oosteinde south to the twin turrets of the fairy-tale **Oostpoort** (East Gate), the only remaining city gate, dating back to 1400, with the spires added in 1514. Parts of it are a private residence, but you can still walk over the drawbridge. Although it is a short walk out of the center, the effort of getting there is more than rewarded with the view.

From Oostpoort, head east back toward the train station, taking Zuiderstraat or hewing instead to the canal bank over to the Zuidwal avenue, which leads to the site of Rotterdamse Poort. Here, at the south end of Oude Delft canal, cross the busy road to overlook the harbor; here is **"Vermeer's View,"** for it was on the far side of this big canal that Vermeer stood when painting his famous cityscape. For a profile of the artist, *see* the Close-Up box "Vermeer: Sphinx of Delft."

If you want to purchase Delftware, head south of the city center to **De Porceleyn Fles.** This factory first opened its doors in 1653 and is the only extant pottery works; tours are given through the facility, but you can also potter around by yourself. This is the real McCoy, and there are numerous examples of the town's fabled blue-and-white porcelain ware to tempt all shoppers. ⊠ *Rotterdamseweg 196* ☎ *015/251–2030* ⊕ *www.royaldelft.com* ✉ *€3.50* ☉ *Mon.–Sat. 9–5, Mar.–Oct. also Sun. 9–5.*

In addition to De Porceleyn Fles, visitors can also tour **De Delftse Pauw,** pottery works to watch painting demonstrations. ⊠ *Delftweg 133* ☎ *015/212–4920* ✉ *Free* ☉ *Apr.–Oct., daily 9–4:30; Nov.–Mar., weekdays 9–4:30, weekends 11–1.*

Where to Eat

$ ✕ **De Nonnerie.** In the arched cellar of the famous Prinsenhof Museum, this luncheon-only tearoom has a sedate, elegant atmosphere. If you can, get a table in the grassy courtyard under an umbrella, and—since you're within the House of Orange—order an Oranjeboom beer to wash down the fine *Delftsche Meesters plaet* (three small sandwiches of paté, salmon, and Dutch cheese) served here. Entry is via the archway from Oude Delft into the Prinsenhof Museum, down a signposted path beside the gardens. ⊠ *St. Agathaplein* ☎ *015/212–1860* ▤ *No credit cards* ☉ *Closed Sun.*

Side Trips A to Z

To research prices, get advice from other travelers, and book travel arrangements, visit www.fodors.com.

ARRIVING & DEPARTING

By Bus: Many of the larger destinations in this chapter are reached easily (and quickly) by train, but several of the smaller "folkloric" villages, such as **Volendam** and **Monnickendam,** have only bus service connecting to Amsterdam. The **Zuiderzeemuseum** can be reached using a bus from Hoorn. To reach **Marken,** catch a bus from Monnickendam. There are no trains to **Edam,** so use a bus from Amsterdam's Centraal Station.

By Car: To **Keukenhof:** From Amsterdam, take the A4 toward Schiphollen Haag, then take Turnoff 4. Continue on the N207 to Lisse. Signs will direct you further. To reach the **Zaanse Schans,** you need to navigate the most confusing part of the country's road system, Amsterdam's A10 ring road, from which you take the exit for A8 toward Zaandam. Take the Zaandam exit, and then follow local signs. **Hoorn** is north of Amsterdam just off E22/A7. To reach **Enkhuizen,** take the Hoorn exit from E22/A7 and continue eastward on N302. N5/A5 goes to **Haarlem** from Amsterdam (from there N208 leads through the bulb district to **Leiden**); to reach Leiden and **Delft** directly from Amsterdam, take E19 via Amsterdam Schiphol Airport. To reach the **Bulb Fields area,** drive south from Amsterdam on A4 (E19) to the Nieuw-Vennep junction, then turn northeast on N207. You can also reach them directly from Haarlem by heading south on N208 and driving through the tulip towns of Lisse and Sasssenheim. To reach **Alkmaar** from Amsterdam, take the A8 and A9 north. To get to **Enkhuizen** and its famous Zuiderzeemuseum, follow the A7 via Purmerend and Hoorn, then take the N 302 in the direction of Enkhuizen. ANWB signs direct you to the museum.

By Train: To get to **Keukenhof,** take the train to Leiden Centraal Station and from there take Bus No. 54 (a.k.a. "Keukenhof Express"). For bus departure times, call 0900/9292. **Koog-Zaandijk** is the station nearest to Zaanse Schans, on the local line from Amsterdam to Alkmaar. The village can be reached on foot in a few minutes. **Local trains** operate once an hour direct from Amsterdam to Alkmaar, Hoorn, Zandvoort, and Enkhuizen, and more often to Delft, Haarlem, and Leiden.

Call for **national train information** (☎ 0900/9292).

By Steam train and ferry: The NS (Dutch Railways) offer a special travel arrangement in which you can visit several folkloric towns: take a train from Amsterdam to Enkhuizen, then travel by museum ferry boat over the IJsselmeer to Medemblik, then ride a museum steam train to Hoorn and return to Amsterdam by train. Call for **national train information** (☎ 0900/9292).

BOAT RENTALS

When exploring folkloric Holland, go native and rent a canoe or a kayak from **De Paashaas**; take along a picnic basket for a great day out. (✉ Molengouw 40, Broek-in-Waterland ☎ 020/403–1492).

CONTACTS & RESOURCES

Guided Tours: Contact the local or regional VVV tourist offices for information about guided group tours and qualified guides.

A special bicycle **Tulip Tour** of the bulb fields can be booked through the Amsterdam VVV tourist office or through the organizer's Web site (⊕ www.letsgo-amsterdam.com).

When it comes to Zaanstreek and Waterland, a convenient way to travel is by water, making stops along the way. Here's your chance to "walk on water." **Wetlands Safari** organizes a five-hour guided canoe tour (€30) of many of the villages, with stops for a picnic and a walk through reed lands and moors. Be sure to wear rain boots or old footwear. (☎ 020/686-3445 ⊕ www.wetlandssafari.nl).

Sail Track gives you the opportunity to explore the Waterland region on a traditional sailing ship for one day or longer, and you may assist the crew if you wish. Trips take place during July and August and cost €35–€49. Departures are from Amsterdam or Waterland towns, depending on the trip selected. You can choose from a variety of sailing vessels, including a clipper ship. (✉ Stationsplein 3, 1601 EN Enkhuizen ☎ 0228/350–026 ⊕ www.sailtrack.nl).

VISITOR INFORMATION
VVV Delft (✉ Hippolytusbuurt 4, 2611 HN ☎ 0900/515–1555). **VVV Haarlem** (✉ Stationsplein 1, 2011 LR ☎ 0900/616–1600). **VVV Leiden** (✉ Stationsplein 2D, 2312 AV ☎ 0900/222–2333). **VVV Lisse** (✉ Grachtweg 53, 2161 HM ☎ 0252/414262). **VVV Noord-Holland** (✉ Oranjekade 41, 2011 VD, Haarlem ☎ 023/531–9413). **VVV West-Friesland** (✉ Veemarkt 4, 1621 JC, Hoorn ☎ 0900/403–1055 🖷 0229/215–023). **VVV Zaanstreek/Waterland** (✉ Gedempte Gracht 76, 1506 CJ, Zaandam ☎ 075/616–2221 🖷 075/670–5381).

UNDERSTANDING AMSTERDAM

GOING DUTCH

F YOU COME TO HOLLAND EXPECTING to find all its residents shod in wooden shoes, you're years too late; if you're looking for windmills at every turn, you're looking in the wrong place. Although the wings of windmills do still turn on government subsidy and the wooden shoe recently has been recognized by the European Union (EU) as acceptable safety footwear, the bucolic images that brought tourism here in the decades after World War II have little to do with The Netherlands of the 21st century. *Ja,* this may be a country where you can find the old world in spades, but this is very, very far from a senile land. Walk through the Red Light District of Amsterdam—gorgeously adorned with some of the most historic structures in town—and be startled by scarlet women sitting immobile behind scarlet-neon framed windows, their pose suggesting that of Whistler's Mother (the resemblance ends there, however). Or marvel at today's Vermeers and Mondriaans now globally championed as being on the very cutting edge of both Web design and urban planning. Holland is bustling, busy, and clangorous, filled with noise and hullabaloo, festivals and floodlights.

But for visitors, it is also a land where you can happily and effortlessly trade in sophisticated modernity for medieval mellowness or the featherbed finesse of the 17th-century Golden Age. A walk down a time-stained alley in Amsterdam or a horseback ride up a dune path along the North Sea often lets you lose five or six centuries in six or seven minutes. And rest assured: there also remains a wealth of villages that have changed little since the time of Hobbema, interiors seemingly plucked from the paintings of Terborch and Rembrandt, and landscapes that suggest the work of Van Ruysdael and—on particularly windy days—even Van Gogh. Holland, in fact, is one big throbbing canvas.

The Netherlands has always had great press agents in its Golden Age painters, who portrayed a shimmering and geometric landscape of fields and orchards sporadically dotted with stretches of color-coded tulips, windmills keeping the sea at bay, cozy villages burnished with age and history, and bustling cities bursting with culture and merchant spirit—all forming a grand tapestry by the lacework of canals. The local saying "God made the world but the Dutch made The Netherlands" would sound cocky if it were not true. But one can certainly call the Dutch stubborn: half of this New Jersey–size democratic monarchy's 15,450 square mi has been reclaimed from the sea, and to this day, it remains a full-time job of many to stop this land from slipping back whence it came. As the primary element, water does much to define this country's landscape, history, people, and politics, and the predominance of water and the relative lack of terra firma have also helped create the image of the Dutch for visitors of days long past: Sir F. B. Head called the Hollanders a "heavy, barge-built, web-footed race," and that 18th-century English snob William Beckford said, "A certain oysterishness of eye, and flabbiness of complexion, are almost proofs sufficient of their aquatic descent." Although these observers were obviously victims of propagandists of the various Dutch-Anglo Wars, it cannot be denied that the nation's long-ingrained respect for how water derives its power through its flexibility accounts for the Dutch being more renowned for their pragmatism than their stubbornness. And perhaps it was as compensation that the Dutch developed a humor best described as "earthy."

But a certain visionary pragmatism has seen Holland evolve beyond the bucolic images with which it's long been associated to embrace the future and its accompanying flurry of—mostly happy—contradictions. Certainly its greatest enigma is the fact that although it is one of Europe's smallest countries, the modern and sophisticated Netherlands has an economic strength and cultural wealth that far surpass its size and population. It may be small enough to drive through in a few hours, but with more art treasures per square mile than any other country on earth and with an international clout that has led it to become one of the largest investors in the U.S. economy, you will need more than a few weeks to unlock all its secrets.

Besides striving to make things as *gezellig*—an endemic word that describes a feeling of comfort and coziness in a social situation—as possible, you should also come equipped with the maximum respect for the concept of the *individual*. After all it was the painters of the Low Countries who realized that the 17th-century variations of our present-day Mr. Smiths, Mr. Browns, and Mr. Johnsons were just as worthy subjects for the artist's brush as were the St. Marks, St. Matthews, St. Jeromes, St. Sebastians, and the rest. It was these painters who dared to paint simple subjects for the little, though usually extremely well off, patrons. It was the painters of the Dutch School who first came to the conclusion that the minimum acceptable size for a picture was not 30 by 25 feet. Frescoes and paintings executed to the order of the church and intended to be displayed in cathedrals must be large; but it took the Dutch masters to realize that the private dwellings of the well-to-do bourgeoisie were also suitable places for their works.

And it was the Dutch who first thought of building houses—that is to say, dwellings where these pictures might suitably be hung. Until then, "architecture" meant the building of churches, cathedrals, royal and ducal palaces, or huge municipal buildings. It was the Dutch who were not ashamed to start building pretty, charming, and often beautiful houses—just for ordinary people to live in. That a private house might be or should be tasteful and lovely was practically a revolutionary idea in the 17th century, and it is the upper-middle-class burghers and merchants of Holland to whom we owe so much of our present-day delight in our domestic surroundings. The Dutch were the first people to enshrine the concepts of coziness, intimacy, and privacy in everyday life.

Their pride in home and hearth is one reason why nearly every square inch of the country looks as though it were scrubbed with Dutch cleanser. If the state of a Dutch cottage or apartment is today best explained as a coping mechanism of living in a densely populated land that now numbers more than 16 million souls, that is because, in spite of constant elbow-rubbing in this crowded country, Hollanders retain a strong sense of personal privacy. They also respect your privacy—on first meeting, the Amsterdammer can occasionally be reserved to the point of seeming brusque, but this is not because he is cold or hostile; rather, he regards over-friendliness as an imposition on you. Still, in Holland folks are comfortable with living without curtains and having their lives and possessions open to viewing by passersby. When summer comes, many pack their curtainless trailers and head south, only to cluster together again in crowded trailer parks. Although these actions may help you understand why The Netherlands was the birthplace of TV's *Big Brother* concept—a show that bloomed with the turn-of-the-21st-century's infatuation with "reality TV"—do not conclude that the Dutch are an exhibitionist people. They are merely the "live and let live" philosophy personified.

Centuries of international trade and the welcoming of endless streams of immigrants have also played their role in creating a form of conflict resolution that requires long meetings that strive to make everyone happy; the Dutch have long loved to organize themselves and form societies (as witnessed by the famous group portraits of the 17th century, such as Rembrandt's *Syndics of the Cloth Guild*) for every conceivable purpose. On the opposite side of the coin, the country's brand of liberalism ironically runs on encyclopedias filled with laws, both strict and elastic but always based on libraries full of reports and studies, that seek to give the greatest possible freedoms to the individual. It is, therefore, understandable why The Netherlands is a tangle of inner conflicts—Catholic versus Protestant (it leans 60–40 toward the latter, that 60% still functioning as one of Europe's Reformation strongholds); puritanical versus prurient (you can't buy liquor on Sunday in some areas, and in others prostitutes sit, whalebone-stayed, in display windows).

It is, in fact, a luxury that The Netherlands can afford to take the time and effort to experiment with alternative—and, dare one say, more pragmatic—ways of dealing with the realities of sex and drugs. Its economic power, rooted in the 17th century when it was *the* great colonial power, also accounts for its cultural wealth. In days of seafaring yore, money raised through its colonial outposts overseas was used to buy or commission portraits and paintings by young artists such as Rembrandt, Hals, Vermeer, and Van Ruysdael. But it was not only the arts that were encouraged: The Netherlands was home to the philosophers Descartes, Spinoza, and Comenius; the jurist Grotius; the naturalist Van Leeuwenhoek, inventor of the microscope; and other prominent people of science and letters, who flourished in the country's enlightened tolerance. This tradition continues today with The Netherlands still subsidizing its artists and performers and supporting an educational system in which creativity in every field is respected, revered, and given room to express itself.

Contemporary Dutch design and architecture, in particular, are enjoying a new golden age of sorts. In a tiny land where space has always been maximized and where much is essentially artificial, these arts have long been dealing with issues that the rest of the rapidly shrinking world is only now beginning to recognize. The influence of such homegrown luminaries as Rem Koolhaas, whose architecture springs from a reaction to realities instead of historical legacies, and Viktor & Rolf, whose fashions showcase the country's more flamboyant side, have filtered across the globe. So please enjoy Amsterdam's historical legacy but also keep yourself open to the new. You will then have a well-rounded trip indeed. Now if only the Dutch could do something about their impeccable English—you are abroad, after all . . . .

— Steve Korver

THE MAKING
OF AMSTERDAM

POET H. MARSMAN WRITES IN "Herinnering aan Holland" ("Thinking of Holland") of wide rivers in a flat lowland: "the voice of water and its endless disasters / is feared and heard" (translation by Olivia Mollet). As the poem painfully but accurately illustrates, most of The Netherlands' territory is swampy marshland. The Dutch have been conquering water as far back as Roman times, when the Belgae, the Batavi, and the Frisian tribes occupied the area now known as The Netherlands. Whereas the first two tribes were eventually incorporated into the greater Roman Empire, the northernmost Frisians held on to their independence, and as a result, the Rhine served as the Empire's northernmost border. To this day, the Frisians are known for speaking their own language and asserting their fierce individuality within the unified country. As the people tamed more and more of the water and dammed parts of the river IJ, more land became habitable, and soon the area around what is now known as Amsterdam began to attract fishermen for its easy access to lucrative fishing waters, both in the IJ and the Zuiderzee. In 1240, the river Amstel was dammed to control the flow of water and "Aemstelledamme," or what is now known as Amsterdam, was born. Two sluices at the edge of the city still control the water level today. The city's official birthday, however, is October 27, 1275, when Count Floris V granted the people of Amsterdam toll privileges on travel and trade, thus allowing them to sail through the many locks and bridges of Holland without paying. Soon after, Amsterdam received full city stature with the right to self-govern and tax its inhabitants.

The City Grows

Thanks to trade, the city grew rapidly. In 1323 Amsterdam was granted the sole right to import beer from Hamburg, which was then the largest brewing town in Europe. Because the water was so infected and germ-ridden, most people drank beer, and thus merchants began to get rich. Another invention that helped advance trade was the ability to preserve herring more efficiently, which allowed merchant ships to stay at sea for longer periods of time. When the herring then decided to move their spawning ground south, from the Baltic to the North Sea, it seemed that the roads—or the seas—were paved with gold. At the time, maritime trade in the North and Baltic seas was dominated by the Hanseatic League. Instead of joining the league, the Dutch merchants had no qualms about breaking in on the league's trade routes as well as developing new ones of their own, and soon Amsterdam was considered fierce competition.

During medieval times, Amsterdam had remained relatively small, with dwellings mostly along the Amstel. In 1300, Amsterdam had only one church, the Oude Kerk, and two streets, the contemporary Warmoesstraat and Nieuwendijk, but it was growing. In 1452, however, a great fire razed the city and most of its wooden buildings. It was soon rebuilt with stricter regulations, and the use of mortar and brick was adopted as a safeguard. New churches as well as monasteries, chapels, and inns were added to handle the influx of pilgrims who had begun to flock to the scene of the Miracle of the Host. Legend has it that on the Tuesday before Palm Sunday in 1345, a dying man vomited up the eucharistic bread after his last communion. The vomit was quickly cast into the fire, but the host refused to burn and was later imbued with healing powers. A shrine was built to commemorate this miracle, and the host became an object of worship to many. Today it is still honored during the Stille Ommegang (Silent Procession), which takes place every year on the Saturday night after March 10. When the host allegedly cured ailing Maximilian I, emperor of Austria, he returned the favor by granting to the city the use of his royal insignia in its coat of arms. By the mid-15th century, Amsterdam had become one of the strongest trade forces around.

The Reformation

In the 16th century, separation of church and state was virtually nonexistent. Europe was firmly in the grip of the Roman Catholic Church. In 1517, when Martin Luther nailed his "95 Theses"—condemning superstition and indulgent practices within the church—to the door of a Catholic chapel in Wittenberg, Germany, Protestantism and its ideas for the reformation of the Roman Church spread through Europe. The church responded fiercely, and the infamous Inquisition took its toll throughout Europe, killing those—such as Lutherans, Jews, and intellectuals—considered heretics.

During this time of religious fervor and upheaval, Amsterdam stayed characteristically tolerant, holding its trade interests at heart. The religious struggles quickly pervaded life even here, however, and although Calvin's austere doctrines appealed to the newer wealthy merchants, Catholicism maintained its firm roots within the aristocracy and landowning classes. The Netherlands was then ruled by the fanatically Catholic Spanish King Philip II, who was known as a cruel despot. Even the Dutch Catholics could not condone the monarch's zeal, and Calvinism became integral to the natives' struggle for independence.

Intent on defeating the Reformation throughout his entire empire, Philip II introduced the Inquisition to The Netherlands in the summer of 1556, despite a counterpetition signed by an interreligious alliance of the key nobles of the city. This act marked the beginning of the long Dutch war of independence against Spain. Fanatical Calvinists organized themselves in bands of brigands nicknamed *geuzen* (beggars) and began terrorizing the land, killing priests and nuns and destroying religious artifacts in churches. In 1578, the *watergeuzen*, similar bands operating on the canals and led by Willem the Silent (he earned his name when he refused to engage in religious discussions), of the House of Orange, captured Amsterdam after a long siege and signaled the so-called Alteration. With the final backing of Amsterdam, the seven northern provinces signed the Union of Utrecht and became the Seven United Provinces, thus rejecting Spanish rule. The Dutch Republic, also referred to as Holland (the dominant province within the republic), held as its core the freedom of religious beliefs, the 16th-century equivalent of a "don't ask, don't tell" policy, where one was allowed to *be* a Catholic but not to worship openly. Again, Amsterdam looked the other way when clandestine churches began opening their doors.

The Golden Age

Amsterdam was now about to enter the 17th century, its most prosperous era. When trade rival Antwerp was recaptured by the Spanish (1589), many Protestants and Jews fled north to this historically tolerant city. They brought along information about trade routes, introduced the new diamond industry, and made Amsterdam a tobacco center. The city continued to grow and assert its place in the world economy. By 1650, the population had shot past 200,000. Fortunately, city planners had begun building the city's canal system as early as 1613, and by 1662 the familiar half-moon shape was completed. The arts flourished as a result of the intellectual influx to the city and the newly rich commissioned portraits from Rembrandt and Hals for their beautiful houses along the recently dug canals.

Meanwhile, by 1600, Amsterdam dominated the maritime trade. The Verenigde Oostindische Compagnie (VOC, or United East India Company) was founded in 1602 and held a trade monopoly from the Cape of Good Hope to Cape Horn. The Dutch ran plantations and established posts in America—New Amsterdam being the most famous example—and Africa. The Dutch were traders first, however, and since they did not have the population to sustain most of their colonies, they were not able to adopt the long-term colonizing strategies employed by most other European countries. At the beginning of the 18th century, the ports of London and Hamburg became powerful rivals, and although Amsterdam remained the wealthiest city in Europe, it lost some of its enthusiasm to conquer the world.

The Decline

In 1648, the war with Spain officially ended. After a period of independence with the Republic, Napoléon and his revolutionary French troops invaded Amsterdam in 1794, putting an end to their hard-fought freedom. In 1806, he appointed his brother, Louis Napoléon, as king of The Netherlands. The king Louis set up palace in the old Stadhuis (Town Hall), but reigned without insight. The French rule was short-lived, and after

Napoléon's defeat at Leipzig in 1813, the French departed peacefully. The Dutch proclaimed themselves a constitutional monarchy under the House of Orange with William I (Willem Frederik to the Dutch, son of William V)—they reset the counter and started numbering their kings afresh.

The first half of the 19th century proved calm except for Belgium's declaration of independence in 1830 and its secession from the Low Countries. Amsterdam woke from its torpor as the railway system began to develop and the country took to equipping itself for modern trade. The building of the Suez Canal in 1869, which facilitated travel to Asia, allowed the city to take an active part in the industrial revolution. Amsterdam's port expanded, and in 1889 the building of the city's Centraal Station, the main railway station, cut off Amsterdam's open waterfront. The population grew tremendously between 1850 and 1900, and a sudden housing problem ensued. Life in the city became harsh as the city began to outgrow itself.

The Depression & World War II

Amsterdam remained neutral during World War I, and the city flourished once again in the 1920s. The Wall Street crash of 1929 rang in the beginning of the depression, and the densely populated Netherlands was hit hard. Unemployment reached a previously unseen high of 25% and, ironically in retrospect, many poor families fled to Germany, where more jobs were available. The Netherlands was unable to remain neutral during World War II, and in May 1940 German troops marched through the streets of Amsterdam. After 400 years, the country found itself in the midst of a war again. Queen Wilhelmina and her parliament fled to England, and five hard years followed. After the severe winter of 1944–45, later dubbed the Hunger Winter, Amsterdam was finally liberated by the success of the Allies.

Post-World War II

The war had certainly taken its toll on The Netherlands. Only 1 in 16 of its Jews had survived, and many Dutch soldiers were killed at the Eastern front. The country found itself licking its wounds. With the help of the Marshall Plan, the economy was jump-started and the country began its recovery. In 1948, Juliana was crowned queen and citizens celebrated for the first time since the liberation. In the 1960s, Amsterdam became a center of radical politics, and a blossoming youth culture invaded the streets. The Provos, a small radical group, began staging actions throughout the city and, although they disbanded in 1967, their ideas were taken over by the Kabouters (or Green Gnomes), who successfully won several seats in the municipal council. Although Amsterdam long remained famous for its political and social activity, free love, and drug culture, these traits were tempered. The '70s and '80s were turbulent, with various protests such as those against the underground metro, squatters' movements, and the first influx of non-European immigrants. The growing economy of the '90s brought a new kind of prosperity to the city, and like many other Western cities, Amsterdam experienced an urban renewal. Even though Amsterdam has been hailed as the new financial center of Europe, it has retained its characteristically independent and spirited edge.

FURTHER READING

For a magical peek into Golden Age Holland, read the best-selling novel by Tracy Chevalier, *Girl with a Pearl Earring*, which evocatively paints a picture of the Delft household and its emotional undoing of the great 17th-century painter Johannes Vermeer. The film version, directed by Peter Webber and starring Colin Firth as Vermeer and Scarlett Johansson as the maid Griet, who became the subject (so Chevalier feels) of one of the greatest portraits every painted, premiered in late 2003. Numerous art-history books are devoted to Vermeer, and you'll find many of them discussed in Anthony Bailey's enjoyable biography, *Vermeer: A View of Delft*. For a view into Golden Age Amsterdam, check out David Liss's novel, *The Coffee Trader*, which is set in the city's Jewish community of the 17th century and deals with the attempts of its merchants to market the then-new coffee bean in Europe. Colin White's *The Undutchables* is more than an observation of The Netherlands, its culture, and its inhabitants—it is everything you ever wanted to learn about the Dutch and that they'd rather you never found out. Jacob Vossestein takes you under the surface in getting to grips with Netherlanders in his *Dealing with the Dutch*. *The Low Skies* offers good background reading from Han van der Horst. From beloved U.S. author John Irving, *The Widow for One Year* is set partly in Amsterdam's Red Light District. Booker Prize winner Ian McEwan's *Amsterdam,* a craftily engineered thriller, is also set in the first city to decriminalize euthanasia (a very salient point). To get an idea of the current literary scene, *The Dedalus Book of Dutch Fantasy* is an anthology of short stories from modern Dutch writers. Cees Nooteboom has written several books worth looking out for, *Rituals* and *In the Dutch Mountains* especially, but his *The Following Story* is a provoking exploration of the differences between platonic and physical love. Renowned Dutch journalist Renate Rubinstein's moving diary *Take It or Leave It* deals with her fight against multiple sclerosis.

Another diary, this one set in war-ravaged Amsterdam, is Anne Frank's famous *Diary,* which has been translated into 55 languages; read it in conjunction with *Anne Frank Remembered,* a collection of essays retelling the story of the woman who helped the Frank family during the war. In *Bitter Herbs,* Marga Minco traces the tragedy of the breakup of a Jewish family during and after World War II. To put a historical spin on your visit, try Multatuli's classic, *Max Havelaar (or the Coffee Auctions of the Dutch Trading Company),* which relates the story of a colonial officer and his clash with a corrupt government; this novel did much to uncover the evils of Dutch colonialism. The celebrated Scot Irvine Welsh set one of his short stories in Amsterdam's dodgy narcotics underworld in *The Acid House.* Tim Krabbé's *The Vanishing,* relating one man's search for his vanished lover, was made into a nightmarish, unforgettable feature film.

Super-Dutch is the unforgettable name for a new tome devoted to that hotter-than-hot subject, contemporary architecture in The Netherlands. Published by the Princeton Architectural Press—and as graphically striking as the subject it covers—the incisive text by Bart Lootsma and dazzling photographs make this the perfect introduction and survey of the subject.

Ideal for taking a highly personalized and lovingly picturesque stroll around the capital, Derek Blyth's *Amsterdam Explored* describes nine walks around the city. A magisterial overview of the city's history is found in Geert Mak's *Amsterdam*. Mike Dash's *Tulipomania* is an unbelievably fascinating account of the great tulip craze of the 17th century. And hand in hand with that volume, take a long and lingering look at Barbara Abbs's *The Garden Lover's Guide to The Netherlands and Belgium.* If you're looking to find the most gorgeous and magisterial gardens, estates, and manors in Holland, this text, fitted out with lovely photos, is certainly a must-read. The philosopher Witold Rybczynski devotes a chapter to the history of Dutch domesticity in his thought-provoking *Home: A History of an Idea.*

If you want to get into the legendary art tradition of Holland, the first place to start is Simon Schama's award-winning 1987 *The Embarrassment of Riches,* a lively social and cultural history of The Netherlands) that deals with the country's infatuation with the visual arts during the 17th century. A dazzling perspective on the Golden Age, it provides the context and the "why" behind such great artists as Rembrandt, Vermeer, and Hals. Schama's biography of sorts, *Rembrandt's Eyes,* is also definitely worth a read. For a comprehensive guide to Dutch painting, see Rudolf H. Fuchs's guide on that very subject, *Dutch Painting.* Another comprehensive guide is Seymour Slive's volume on *Dutch Painting, 1600–1800,* for the Pelican History of Art Series, published by Yale University Press. Any general survey, of which there are many published, will yield unbelievably rich bibliographies, detailing hundred of volumes devoted to Dutch art and artists. Finally, Paul Overy's *De Stijl* unravels the greatest 20th-century Dutch art movement.

DUTCH VOCABULARY

	English	Dutch	Pronunciation
Basics			
	Yes/no	Ja, nee	yah, nay
	Please	Alstublieft	**ahls**-too-bleeft
	Thank you	Dank u	**dahnk** oo
	You're welcome	Niets te danken	neets teh **dahn**-ken
	Excuse me, sorry	Pardon	pahr-**don**
	Good morning	Goede morgen	**hoh**-deh **mor**-ghen
	Good evening	Goede avond	**hoh**-deh **ahv**-unt
	Goodbye	Dag!	dah
Numbers			
	one	een	ehn
	two	twee	tveh
	three	drie	dree
	four	vier	veer
	five	vijf	vehf
	six	zes	zehss
	seven	zeven	**zeh**-vehn
	eight	acht	ahkht
	nine	negen	**neh**-ghen
	ten	tien	teen
Days of the Week			
	Sunday	zondag	**zohn**-dagh
	Monday	maandag	**mahn**-dagh
	Tuesday	dinsdag	**dinns**-dagh
	Wednesday	woensdag	**voons**-dagh
	Thursday	donderdag	**don**-der-dagh
	Friday	vrijdag	**vreh**-dagh
	Saturday	zaterdag	**zah**-ter-dagh
Useful Phrases			
	Do you speak English?	Spreekt U Engels?	sprehkt oo **ehn**-gls
	I don't speak Dutch	Ik spreek geen Nederlands	ihk sprehk **ghen** **Ned**-er-lahnds
	I don't understand	Ik begrijp het niet	ihk be-**ghrehp** het neet
	I don't know	Ik weet niet	ihk **veht** ut neet
	I'm American/English	Ik ben Amerikaans/Engels	ihk ben Am-er-ee-**kahns**/Ehn-gls
	Where is . . .	Waar is . . .	vahr iss

the train station?	het station?	heht stah-**syohn**
the post office?	het postkantoor?	het **pohst**-kahn-tohr
the hospital?	het ziekenhuis?	het **zeek**-uhn-haus
Where are the restrooms?	waar is de WC?	**vahr** iss de **veh**-seh
Left/right	links/rechts	leenks/rehts
How much is this?	Hoeveel kost dit?	hoo-**vehl** kohst deet
It's expensive/ cheap	Het is te duur/ goedkoop	het ees teh **dour**/ **hood**-kohp
I am ill/sick	Ik ben ziek	ihk behn zeek
I want to call a doctor	Ik wil een docter bellen	ihk veel ehn **dohk**-ter **behl**-len
Help!	Help!	help
Stop!	Stoppen!	**stop**-pen

Dining Out

Bill/check	de rekening	de **rehk**-en-eeng
Bread	brood	brohd
Butter	boter	**boh**-ter
Fork	vork	fork
I'd like to order	Ik wil graag bestellen	Ihk veel khrah behs-**tell**-en
Knife	een mes	ehn mehs
Menu	menu/kaart	men-**oo**/kahrt
Napkin	en servet	ehn ser-**veht**
Pepper	peper	**peh**-per
Please give me . . .	mag ik [een] . . .	mahkh ihk [ehn] . . .
Salt	zout	zoot
Spoon	een lepel	ehn **leh**-pehl
Sugar	suiker	**sigh**-kur

INDEX